'Criminals, Idiots, Women, and Minors'

'Criminals, Idiots, Women, and Minors'

Victorian Writing by Women on Women

Second Edition

Edited by

Susan Hamilton

broadview press

National Library of Canada Cataloguing in Publication

'Criminals, idiots, women, and minors': Victorian writing by women on women / edited by Susan Hamilton. — 2nd ed.

Includes bibliographical references.
ISBN 1-55111-608-1 (pbk.)

1. Women – Great Britain – History – 19th century.   2. Feminism – Great Britain – History – 19th century.   3. Women's rights – Great Britain – History – 19th century.
I. Hamilton, Susan, 1960–

HQ1596.C76 2004   305.42'0941   C2004-900697-5

Broadview Press, Ltd. is an independent, international publishing house, incorporated in 1985. Broadview believes in shared ownership, both with its employees and with the general public; since the year 2000 Broadview shares have been traded publicly on the Toronto Venture Exchange under the symbol BDP.

We welcome any comments and suggestions regarding any aspect of our publications— please feel free to contact us at the addresses below, or at broadview@broadviewpress.com / www.broadviewpress.com

North America
Post Office Box 1243, Peterborough, Ontario, Canada K9J 7H5
Tel: (705) 743-8990; Fax: (705) 743-8353;
e-mail: customerservice@broadviewpress.com
3576 California Road, Orchard Park, New York, USA 14127

UK, Ireland, and continental Europe
NBN Plymbridge, Estover Road, Plymouth PL6 7PY UK
Tel: 44 (0) 1752 202301   Fax: 44 (0) 1752 202331
Fax Order Line: 44 (0) 1752 202333
Customer Service: cservs@nbnplymbridge.com   Orders: orders@nbnplymbridge.com

Australia and New Zealand
UNIREPS, University of New South Wales
Sydney, NSW, 2052
Tel: 61 2 9664 0999; Fax: 61 2 9664 5420
email: infopress@unsw.edu.au

Broadview Press Ltd. gratefully acknowledges the financial support of the Government of Canada through the Book Publishing Industry Development Program for our publishing activities.

Typesetting and assembly: True to Type Inc., Mississauga, Canada.

This book is printed on 100% post-consumer recycled, ancient forest friendly paper.

PRINTED IN CANADA

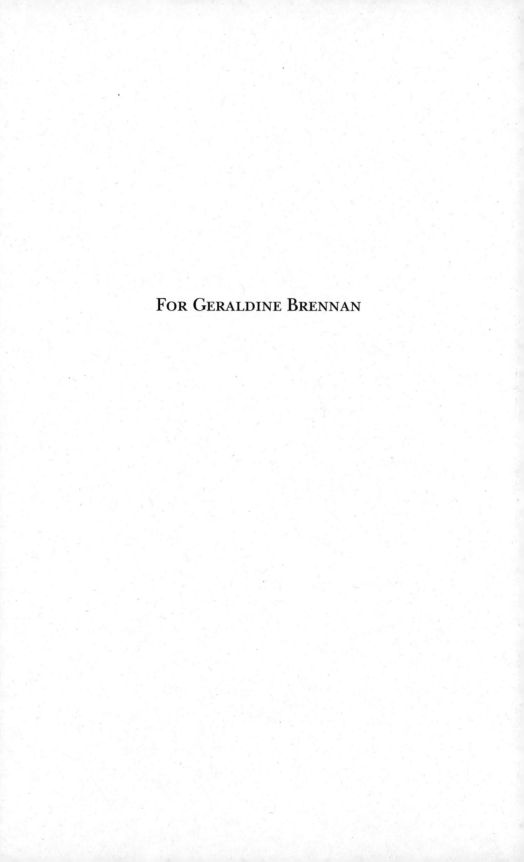

FOR GERALDINE BRENNAN

CONTENTS

ACKNOWLEDGEMENTS ix
INTRODUCTION xi
CHRONOLOGY xxi
A NOTE ON THE TEXT xxvii

ANNA BROWNELL JAMESON (1794-1860) 1
   "The Milliners" 1
   Biographical Note 6

HARRIET MARTINEAU (1802-1876) 9
   "Female Industry" 9
   Biographical Note 47

FRANCES POWER COBBE (1822-1904) 50
   "Celibacy v. Marriage" 50
   "'What Shall We Do with Our Old Maids?'" 59
   "The Education of Women, and How it Would be Affected by University Examinations" 79
   "'Criminals, Idiots, Women, And Minors'" 90
   "Wife-torture in England" 111
   Biographical Note 144

ELIZA LYNN LINTON (1822-1898) 147
   "The Girl of the Period" 147
   "The Modern Revolt" 151
   "The Wild Women: as Politicians" 161
   "The Wild Women: as Social Insurgents" 170
   Biographical Note 179

MARGARET OLIPHANT (1828-1897) 181
   "The Condition of Women" 181
   "The Grievances of Women" 201
   Biographical Note 214

HELEN TAYLOR (1831-1907)   217
   "Women and Criticism"   217
   Biographical Note   224

MILLICENT GARRETT FAWCETT (1847-1929)   225
   "The Emancipation of Women"   225
   Biographical Note   236

MONA CAIRD (1854-1932)   239
   "Marriage"   239
   "A Defence of the So-called 'Wild Women'"   253
   Biographical Note   271

ACKNOWLEDGEMENTS

I am grateful to the Social Sciences and Humanities Research Council of Canada and the University of Alberta for supporting the production of this anthology. I would also like to thank Glenn Burger, JoAnn Wallace and Paul Brennan for their encouragement and advice, and Garrett Epp and Lahoucine Ouzgane for their help with translations.

INTRODUCTION

Feminists did not fare well in the mainstream Victorian press. Routinely ridiculed, frequently attacked, silenced or given only minimal coverage, Victorian feminists did not find it a simple matter to speak out about women's place in Victorian culture in the commercial periodicals, journals, reviews and newspapers that proliferated from the late 1850s on. And they worried about it. The mainstream commercial press was extraordinarily influential in Victorian society, affecting the scope and tenor of public debates on political questions of the period. The absence of feminist voices in what was recognized at the time as one of the key political debates of the century—the debate on "The Woman Question"—could have proven disastrous to the range of social and political claims that Victorian feminists were committed to making for women. The paucity of feminist voices on this question should not, of course, completely surprise us. At a time when women could not vote, could not own property if married, and were denied access to the kinds of education and occupations available to men, the difficulties that Victorian feminists experienced with the commercial press are to be expected. Here is simply one more straightforward denial, one more commonplace restriction experienced by Victorian women to document for the historical record.

To simply document this restriction and move on would be historically inaccurate in at least two ways. On the one hand, Victorian feminists themselves responded to the problem of access by setting up their own reviews, journals and periodicals. As Josephine Butler, leader of the campaign to repeal the Contagious Diseases Acts, said, "The conspiracy of silence of the press has done us this service ... it has forced us to create a literature of our own."[1] Borne of frustration with the lack of feminist voices in the mainstream commercial press, journals like the *English Woman's Journal* (1858), its successor, the *Englishwoman's Review* (1865), the *Woman's Gazette* (1875), *Woman and Work* (1874), and the *Shield* (1870), were established. Certain that participation in the commercial market of the mainstream press would erode political and critical rigour, Victorian feminists created journals that provided the opportunities for uncompromised political debate and undiluted advocacy on behalf of women, which they knew was necessary for the success of their cause.[2] In her rationale for the existence of a separate feminist press, or that which she termed a "special periodical," Bessie Raynor Parkes (co-editor with Matilda Hays of the *English Woman's Journal*) argued that:

there is something in a reiterated effort which far outweighs the effect of the separate thoughts. It is not this or that number of a magazine, this or that article from a given pen, which does the work: it is partly the effect of repetition—line upon line—and partly the knowledge that there is in the world a distinct embodiment of certain principles.... Even if this embodiment be in itself far from mighty, it serves to sustain a great amount of scattered energy, and may be a rallying point of much value to the whole of the field[.][3]

In many ways, the establishment of a separate feminist press points to a new level of organisation in the feminist movement in Britain. The formation of societies dedicated to helping women, such as the Society for the Promotion of the Employment of Women, the Female Emigration Society, the Governesses' Benevolent Institution, coupled with the continuous public discussion of issues concerning women to which this separate press contributed, marks Victorian feminism as "modern."[4]

We need to know about the extensive feminist literature that emerged in this period. We also need to pay close attention to the writing by Victorian women (feminist and non-feminist) on women's issues that managed to find their way into the commercial periodical press.[5] More important, we need to understand and investigate the impact and significance that this writing has on our understanding of Victorian women's place in society by virtue of its distinctive place of publication.[6] Parkes' comments on the value of the "special periodical," gesture towards the relevance of this particular line of enquiry. The mainstream Victorian press as a whole did not readily give column inches to women on *any* political or social questions. Nonetheless, the topic of "Woman"—as worker, spinster, citizen, moral guide, prostitute—glutted the press from about the mid 1860s.[7] "This or that article by a given pen" on the Woman Question might ultimately be ineffectual in contributing to the sense of cohesion and the collective energies Parkes felt the feminist movement needed in order to work effectively. Still, the publication of such an article by a woman in the mainstream press tells us something about the state of Victorian feminism, its growing status, its emerging political and cultural authority, *through* its ability to command a stake in public debates on women's issues, whether as active commentator or as object of commentary.

When occasionally a woman's contribution to "The Woman Question" appears in the mainstream press, we need to ask a series of related questions. Amongst these is the relation of this writing to the separate feminist press. I am not suggesting that all Victorian women's writings be evaluated as acceptably or unacceptably "feminist" by current standards. I am arguing that in a period when feminists and their allies (who were interested in improving women's condition) were increasing in power, organisation, and so visibility, assessments of women's contributions (feminist or not) to the Woman Question debate in the mainstream press, needs to take into account this developing, feminist movement wherever historically appropriate. In particular, the different task of writing in the mainstream press must be recognized. If Bessie Parkes saw feminist periodicals as, in a sense, helping to form a specifically feminist consciousness, a "distinct embodiment of certain principles," writing on the Woman Question in mainstream periodicals performed a different, if related, function for their intended audiences.

Most Victorian periodicals were the products, though not the official organs, of specific political affiliations. They appealed to audiences likely to identify, however broadly or unevenly, with prevailing party spirits and agendas.[8] Significantly, most periodical essayists and reviewers were men. In fact, the periodical press has been seen as central to the consolidation and coming-of-age of a new professional class composed of reviewers, essayists, historians, social critics and others. The reviewer, or man of letters as he is sometimes called, exercised real social and political clout in Victorian England. To write an "able" article in the *Edinburgh Review*, for example, was to lay claim to the original thought, broad learning, and skill at exposition understood to characterize such writings.[9]

Not surprisingly, to write as a woman in such a space was rare indeed. As Carol T. Christ has discovered, the eleven thousand plus writers indexed in the standard reference guide to the periodical press, the *Wellesley Index to Victorian Periodicals*, are overwhelmingly male. A mere thirteen percent are women. Christ tells us further that only eleven women, out of the approximately fifteen hundred women listed in the index, have fifty or more entries to their name, indicating that they might have made a living by writing regularly for the periodical press. Those eleven women are Agnes Mary Clerke, historian of astronomy and miscellaneous writer; Frances Power Cobbe, miscellaneous writer; Marie Louise de la Ramee (Ouida), novelist; Lady Elizabeth Eastlake, art historian; Catherine Gore, novelist; Eliza Lynn Linton, novelist; Hannah Lawrance, novelist and miscellaneous writer; Margaret Oliphant, novelist and historical writer; Violet Paget (Vernon Lee), critic; Lady Anne Isabella-Ritchie, novelist and essayist; and Ellen Wood, novelist.

Though prominent women like Harriet Martineau and George Eliot did write for the leading reviews, clearly few women could claim the social and political authority associated with writing there. Importantly, six of these eleven women—Ouida, Gore, Linton, Oliphant, Ritchie and Wood—were also novelists; and as we might expect, a substantial amount of their work in the periodical press takes the form of literary reviews or literary pieces for reviews. The other five women who wrote frequently for the periodical press were not novelists. They are variously defined in the *Wellesley Index* as art historians (Eastlake), historians of astronomy (Clarke), critics, "authors" and miscellaneous writers. But even among these five, three women (Eastlake, Vernon Lee, and especially Lawrance) wrote fairly frequently on literary topics in the form of fiction and poetry reviews, notices on authors, and discussions of writing. Only two of these women, Clerke and Cobbe, did not write at any length or with any regularity about literary issues. In a period when creative writing—especially novel writing—was seen as an appropriately "feminine" pursuit, the strong concentration on literary matters of the extremely few women contributors to the press is striking and significant. On the whole, it would seem that women wrote regularly for the press when they wrote on those matters deemed sufficiently, and appropriately, women's work. Women's writing in the periodical press, in other words, seems to maintain a fairly rigid gender distinction in what counts as appropriate women's writing in a highly masculinized, and professionalised writing space.[10]

What then does it mean for a woman to write in the mainstream, respectable press on the Woman Question? On the most simple level of course the woman reviewer or essayist makes a specific argument and presents (or synthesizes) any material relevant to her position. But in addition, her writing has specific effects. Whether feminist or not, the woman who participates in the mainstream press debate on women's issues contributes to the legitimizing of women's participation in public discussion of political issues. Clearly, this legitimization proceeds at least partly in a way similar to women's writing on "feminine" issues. To write on the Woman Question is, in some ways, to continue in the tradition of writing on acceptably feminine topics. At the same time, such writing is distinctive, given the straightforward "political" nature of commenting upon women's place in society at this time. Even those women who write expressly to denounce women's participation in public and political debates are *in effect* legitimating the very practice they decry. If the writing is also clearly marked as feminist, its publication in the "respectable" press serves to legitimate a feminist critique of women's position, both locally (the legitimacy of these comments on this particular issue) and more generally (the legitimacy of a feminist position on a range of public issues). Important too, the woman who succeeds in writing for the respectable press builds up a reputation as journalist or essayist, as reviewer or critic, at a time when the press claims a great deal of social and political authority. Interestingly, discussion circulating around the Woman Question seems to have played an important role in establishing the professional identity of that rare creature: the woman periodical writer. The three women who wrote most regularly for the mainstream press—Frances Power Cobbe, Eliza Lynn Linton and Margaret Oliphant—all wrote articles on the Woman Question that were significant in various ways in their day. For a woman to write regularly for the respectable press then does not simply mean that she has overcome a workaday problem with access. She also, *in the very act of writing*, helps to establish the legitimacy and authority of women's participation and perspective on public issues, and helps to produce a public, professional identity for women as social and political critics.

In choosing the material for this anthology I have been guided by two concerns. The first, is to address the current lack of accessible primary material available to anyone interested in the Victorian periodical press and women's involvement therein. Though Victorian periodicals are widely available on microfilm and many academic libraries have rich holdings, the sheer abundance of the material is often bewildering or overwhelming for people taking their first plunge into this kind of Victorian writing. Searching for information specific to Victorian women amongst this wealth of material is like looking for a needle in a haystack. The second concern is how to supplement the growing body of primary source readings in Victorian feminism now available to the student of Victorian culture, by collecting essays on the status, place, and concerns of Victorian women about their role in society, that were published in the mainstream, rather than specialist press, and by including non-feminist Victorian voices in the debate.[11] The discussion in the mainstream press has a distinctive flavour that can only complement our understanding of the full range of Victorian feminisms articulated in the special periodicals. In the end, this anthology has been shaped by the connections between these two concerns. Its focus on women's particular relation to the Victorian periodical press, and the centrality of the Woman Question debate in the mainstream press to all Victorian women, feminist or not, means that all of the writers represented here are middle-class by birth and education. Their writings do not in any way convey the complexity of all women's lives in Victorian England; but they can tell us a great deal about the specific investments that middle- class Victorian women had in the debate on women.

All of the essays reprinted here first appeared in one of the major reviews, journals or periodicals of the time. Within this already selective compass, I have focused on writings by the three women who wrote extensively for the press, and regularly on the Woman Question—Frances Power Cobbe, Margaret Oliphant and Eliza Lynn Linton. The writings of these three women, one a well-known feminist in her day, the other two well-known opponents of the women's movement, offer us a glimpse of that small sphere that was the world of the professional woman periodical writer.

I have also tried to provide a range of material that adequately represents the broad sweep of Victorian feminism, as it was expressed in the mainstream press. This material represents something of the diverse, often contradictory, nature of Victorian feminism. There is no one Victorian feminist line on any issue. In choosing material that reflects this complexity, I hope to shift the reader away from an approach to Victorian feminism that sees it as fairly homogenous and consistent—a suffrage movement focusing specifically on legal reform—to a deeper understanding of that which Victorian feminisms encompass.[12] This anthology does include writing by essayists primarily concerned with legal reform for women, whether of marriage or property law or suffrage qualifications. Frances Power Cobbe's "Criminals, Idiots, Women, and Minors," argues for women's civil rights on the grounds of women's moral and intellectual capabilities. Similarly, Helen Taylor's essay, "Women and Criticism," argues for the application of a "free trade" or non-restrictive model of law to legislation affecting women.

However, the anthology also offers a selection of essays that point to the debate and disagreement among Victorian feminists, about exactly what constituted the "womanliness" of the women on whose behalf they sought reform. Women like Cobbe, for example, argued for an essentialist or biological understanding of sexual difference and the nature of woman, that granted her a distinctive moral status because of her special gifts of compassion and nurturance. It was precisely on the basis of this special moral status that Cobbe argued for the extension of women's work and responsibilities into the public sphere. For Cobbe, women's moral autonomy from men not only authorized, in fact required, the enlargement of women's traditional sphere of activity to include public concerns.

Feminists such as Millicent Fawcett acknowledged the existence of sexual differences between men and women, but thought that those differences had been greatly exaggerated. Unlike Cobbe, Fawcett tended to stress the intellectual and emotional similarities between the sexes, and used those similarities to argue for the extension of women's rights—be they legal, political or social. In other words, the question of sexual difference was something that was in contention amongst Victorian feminists. For Cobbe, sexual difference is a natural biological fact. For Fawcett, it was very much an overplayed biological fact which she sought to downplay.

Sexual difference was of course central to the Woman Question debate, and both feminist and non-feminist writers engaged in discussion as to its nature and significance. Margaret Oliphant believed, like Cobbe, that there existed an essential, biological womanliness, and therefore a womanly identity common to all women, and this belief underpinned her opposition to the Victorian women's movement. Oliphant's anti-feminism does not necessarily mean that, in opposition to Victorian feminists' call for change, she supported the denigration or undervaluation of women. The Oliphant essays are valuable explorations of the nature of womanliness and the place of women in society by a conservative woman who was, nonetheless, striving to carve out an appropriate space for Victorian women's activities. Though she did not agree with Victorian feminists like Cobbe about the extension of women's rights, she nonetheless did not employ, but rather dismissed the stereotypes of womanliness that portrayed women as physiologically unqualified for anything but the most domestic of duties.

Oliphant's very distinct use of the notion of the nurturing, compassionate woman points to the different ways in which ideas shared across a community of women—ideas of sexual difference or women's inherent domesticity, for example—can be used to authorise both a feminist commitment to change and a non-feminist rejection of social change. Eliza Lynn Linton's essays, for example, argue that the idea of biological sex difference requires the absolute separation of men's and women's duties, responsibilities, and rights. It also renders ridiculous the "Girl of the Period," with her painted face and vitiated taste. The essays collected here—"The Girl of the Period," "The Modern Revolt," and her "Wild Women" series—lambaste any and all of the activities of any woman who dares to change the status quo.

In this anthology, I have also tried to give a sampling of the pivotal issues for Victorian feminists. Harriet Martineau's "Female Industry" and Anna Jameson's very early piece of reportage on milliners for the *Athenaeum* deal with the place, status and nature of women's work in Victorian society, an interest shared by many of those women who first articulated a feminist perspective on women's place in Victorian society. Central to these essays, in the form of the census and Blue Book reports, is the extraordinary outpouring of official government information on the condition and activities of the population of Great Britain. Martineau's "Female Industry" documents the great significance that this kind of information provided for Victorian feminists' understanding of what constituted a woman's issue. Government information had revealed an "excess" of women to men in Great Britain. The perceived result of this excess—women's failure to marry—generated concern that current restrictions on women's opportunities for work would create severe distress for women forced to seek employment in overcrowded and ill-paid lines of business, and that such distress would increase as marriage opportunities continued to decline. Essays such as Cobbe's "What Shall We Do with Our Old Maids?"—an incisive retort to W.R. Greg's essay, "Why Women are Redundant," which argues for the enforced emigration of women and, amazingly, middle-class women's imitation of the world of high-class prostitution—attest to the continued concern with questions of employment for women in Victorian feminism.

Another pivotal issue in the Woman Question debate was the nature and the status of the institution of marriage. Though Cobbe's "What Shall We Do with Our Old Maids?" concedes that "for the mass of mankind, marriage is the right condition, the happiest, and the most conducive to virtue," it is also highly critical of the suffering caused to women by the very structure of marriage. It might make sense to a student of contemporary feminism that Cobbe, who grounded her feminism in an essentialised notion of the nurturing woman, was one of the first Victorian women to take interest in what we now term "domestic violence." Her piece, "Wife-torture in England," explored the "kicking districts" of England, and was an important journalistic boost in the campaign for the Matrimonial Causes Act that would grant women separations from their husbands on the grounds of such violence.[13] Elsewhere, in "Celibacy v. Marriage," Cobbe celebrates women's capacities for "true and tender friendships" with each other that make single life as emotionally rewarding (if not more so) as any marriage. Though marriage might be the "right condition" for most women, for Cobbe this does not mean that women must serve men or be unfulfilled. Other women such as Mona Caird, who wrote later in the century, continued this signature concern for women and marriage. Her essay, "Marriage," provides a history of the institution, and calls for freedom in marriage, the economic independence of women, and better education for women as a way out of the "false sentiment and shallow shrewdness" that, in her opinion, characterized late-Victorian marriages. Writers like Eliza Lynn Linton took up the feminist critique of marriage with a vengeance, vilifying the "wild women" as sexual inverts whose ideas on reforming marriage were the philosophical equivalents of bearded chins, bass voices, flat chests and lean hips in women. Linton also directly challenged a central metaphor in Victorian feminists' critiques of marriage: the description of marriage as a form of sexual slavery. Linton pillories "our Wild Women [who] break out as adventurous travellers," arguing that Victorian women's repugnance at the mere sight of the harem, or zenana, is simply the response of those who are "desirous of making all other women as restless and discontented as themselves."

The wildness and turbulence, as well as the humour and irony, of the debate on the Woman Question in the "respectable press" might take some readers by surprise. If this anthology manages to convey even a small sampling of the wit, intelligence and gleeful exuberance of the debaters on both sides of the question, it has accomplished its task.

NOTES

1 Butler, 402.
2 See Nestor and Levine (1990).
3 Bessie Raynor Parkes, "The Uses of a Special Periodical," *Alexandra Magazine* 1 (September 1864): 258. Quoted in Herstein, 26.
4 See Rendall, especially chapter eight.
5 In addition to Levine, Herstein and Nestor on Victorian feminist periodicals, see also Harrison and Lacey (for a collection of writing by women associated with Bodichon).
6 For an excellent study of gender and the Victorian periodical press, see Brake (1994).
7 Levine notes the importance of John Stuart Mill's support for women's suffrage in making feminist issues worth covering in the "serious" press. See Levine (1990) 294.
8 See Brake and Houghton.
9 There is a growing literature on the role of the periodical press in establishing the authority of the professional 'man of letters.' See Christ, Ferris (Introduction) and Newton. For more general discussions of the pro-

fessionalisation of intellectual life in Victorian Britain, see Gross and Heyck.

10 Newton's work on the status of writing about women in the *Edinburgh Review* complements this point.

11 See collections by Candida Lacey, Murray, Bauer and Rat (1979), and Jeffreys.

12 See Levine (1987) and Caine.

13 See Caine, Shanley, and Bauer and Ritt.

WORKS CITED

Bauer, Carol and Lawrence Ritt. "'A Husband is a Beating Animal'—Frances Power Cobbe Confronts the Wife-Abuse Problem in Victorian England." *International Journal of Women Studies* 6 (1983): 99-118.

—. *Free and Ennobled: Source readings in the development of Victorian feminism.* Oxford: Pergamon Press, 1979.

Brake, Laurel. "Theories of Formation: The *Nineteenth Century*," *Victorian Periodicals Review* 25 (Spring 1992): 16-21.

—. *Subjugated Knowledges: gender and journalism in the Nineteenth-century.* London: Macmillan, 1994.

Brown, Lucy. *Victorian News and Newspapers.* Oxford: OUP, 1985.

Butler, Josephine. *Personal Reminiscences of a Great Crusade.* London: H. Marshall and Son, 1896.

Caine, Barbara. *Victorian Feminists.* Oxford: OUP, 1992.

Christ, Carol T. "'The Hero as Man of Letters': Masculinity and Victorian Nonfiction Prose," Ed. Thais Morgan. *Victorian Sages and Cultural Discourse.* 19-31.

Doughan, David and Denise Sanchez. *Feminist Periodicals, 1855-1984: An Annotated Critical Bibliography of British, Irish, Commonwealth and International Titles.* Brighton: Harvester Press, 1987.

Ferris, Ina. *The Achievement of Literary Authority: Gender, History and the Waverley Novels.* Ithaca: Cornell UP, 1991.

Gross, John. *The Rise and Fall of the Man of Letters.* London: Macmillan, 1969.

Harrison, Brian. "Press and pressure group in modern Britain." Ed. Shattook and Wolff. *The Victorian Periodical Press: Samplings and Soundings.* Leicester: Leicester UP, 1982. 261-295.

Herstein, Sheila. "The Langham Place Circle and Feminist Periodicals of the 1860s." *Victorian Periodicals Review* 26 (Spring 1993): 24-27.

Heyck, T.W. *The Transformation of Intellectual Life in Victorian England.* New York: St. Martin's Press, 1982.

Houghton, Walter. "Periodical Literature and the Articulate Classes." Ed. Joanne Shattock and Michael Wolff. *The Victorian Periodical Press: Samplings and Soundings.* Leicester: Leicester UP, 1982. 3-27.

Jeffreys, Sheila, ed. *The Sexuality Debates*. Women's Source Library. New York: Routledge, 1987.

Lacey, Candida Ann. *Barbara Leigh Smith Bodichon and the Langham Place Group*. New York: Routledge & Kegan Paul, 1987.

Levine, Phillipa. *Victorian Feminism, 1850-1900*. London: Hutchinson, 1987.

—. "The Humanising Influences of Five o'clock tea: Victorian Feminist Periodicals." *Victorian Studies* 33 (1990): 293-306.

Morgan, Thais E. *Victorian Sages and Cultural Discourse: renegotiating gender and power*. New Brunswick: Rutgers UP, 1990.

Murray, Janet H. *Strong-Minded Women and Other Lost Voices from Nineteenth-Century England*. London: Pantheon, 1982.

Nestor, Pauline. "A New Departure in Women's Publishing: *The English Woman's Journal* and *The Victoria Magazine*." *Victorian Periodicals Review* 15 (1982): 93-106.

Newton, Judith. "Engendering history for the middle class: sex and political economy in the *Edinburgh Review*." Ed. Linda M. Shires. *Rewriting the Victorians: theory, history and the politics of gender*. New York: Routledge, 1992. 1-17.

Rendall, Jane. *The Origins of Modern Feminism: Women in Britain, France and the United States, 1780-1860*. London: Macmillan, 1985.

Shanley, Mary E. *Feminism, Marriage and the Law in Victorian England*. Princeton: Princeton UP, 1989.

Shattock, Joanne and Michael Wolff, eds. *The Victorian Periodical Press: Samplings and Soundings*. Toronto: U of Toronto P, 1982.

Shires, Linda M. *Rewriting the Victorians: theory, history and the politics of gender*. New York: Routledge, 1992.

CHRONOLOGY

1832 First *Reform Act* extends franchise to adult men meeting property qualifications. The act is the first to expressly restrict the vote to men, legally enshrining past practice.

1834 *New Poor Law* abolishes outdoor relief, installing the workhouse test and the principle of 'less eligibility' under which conditions in the workhouse were to be inferior to the living conditions of the lowest paid worker.

1837 Death of William IV; accession of Queen Victoria.

1839 *Infants Custody Act* permits, but does not require, courts to grant custody of children under the age of seven to the mother, providing she has not been found guilty of adultery.

     First Chartist petition presented to Parliament with 1,280,000 signatures. The Charter called for annual parliaments, universal male suffrage, abolition of property qualification for MPs, the secret ballot, salaries for MPs, and equal electoral districts.

1840 World Anti-Slavery Convention in London. American women delegates are refused seating.

1842 *Mines and Collieries Act* forbids underground work in mines for women, girls, and boys under ten.

     Chartist activity increases.

1843 Governesses' Benevolent Institute established, serving as a registry of employment for governesses and, later, as a source of charity for destitute governesses.

1848 Queen's College for higher education of women opens.

     Final Chartist petition presented to Parliament.

1849 Bedford College for Women opens.

1850 North London Collegiate School for Girls founded by Frances Buss.

1851 Harriet Taylor Mill's, "The Enfranchisement of Women" printed anonymously in *Westminster Review.* The article was reprinted as a pamphlet and distributed by the National Association of Women's Suffrage Societies in 1868.

1853 Cheltenham Ladies College established.

1854   Caroline Norton publishes *English Laws for Women in the Nineteenth-Century* demanding divorce, property and improved child custody rights.

1855   Barbara Leigh Smith (later Bodichon) forms Married Women's Property Committee and publishes *A Brief Summary in Plain Language of the Most Important Laws Concerning Women.*

1856   Petition for Reform of Married Women's Property Law presented to Parliament. Signatories include Elizabeth Barrett Browning, Elizabeth Gaskell, Anna Jameson, Harriet Martineau, Bessie Rayner Parkes and Barbara Leigh Smith (Bodichon).

1857   *Matrimonial Causes Act* makes divorce available for the first time without Act of Parliament and establishes the Divorce Court in London.
         National Association for Promotion of Social Science formed.

1858   The Langham Place circle, a middle-class women's rights group led by Barbara Bodichon, Bessie Rayner Parkes and Emily Davies, publishes the *English Woman's Journal* (1858-1864), the first feminist periodical. The Langham Place circle, active from the mid 1850s through to about 1870, oversaw a range of feminist activities, including a women's employment register and a women's reading room in its London headquarters. Its members launch the Society for the Promotion of the Employment of Women (SPEW) in 1860, the Victoria Press, and the Female Middle-Class Emigration Society. They also form the first major women's suffrage committee, and a range of journals including *Alexandra Magazine* (1864-5), *Victoria Magazine* (1863-1880), and the *Englishwoman's Review* (1866-1910).

1859   After attending a US medical school, Elizabeth Blackwell registers in England as a qualified physician.

1860   Victoria Press founded by Emily Faithfull of the Langham Place Circle.
         Society for the Promotion of the Employment of Women (SPEW) founded.
         Nightingale Training School for Nurses established in London.

1861   Maria Rye of the Langham Place Circle founds the Female Middle-Class Emigration Society.

1863   Cambridge Local Examinations admits girls.

1864   First *Contagious Diseases Act* establishes a registry of 'common prostitutes,' and compels women so defined to undergo internal examinations and, if required, detention in a lock hospital for three months. The Act applies to eleven garrison and port towns in England.
         Octavia Hill begins plans for model lodgings, purchasing three slum houses for the project.

1865   Barbara Bodichon (Langham Place) forms Women's Suffrage Committee.

1866   John Stuart Mill presents Women's Suffrage Petition, signed by 1500 women, to Parliament.
  Second *Contagious Diseases Act* extends the act to more areas and lengthens the lock hospital stay to nine months.
  Emily Davies (Langham Place) publishes *The Higher Education of Women* and founds the London School Mistresses Association.

1867   Second *Reform Act* extends suffrage to all male householders satisfying the residential requirement. Electorate nearly doubles. John Stuart Mill's amendment to substitute 'person' for 'man' is defeated 196 to 73.
  National Society for Women's Suffrage founded.

1868   London University admits women to examinations.
  First public meeting on women's suffrage takes place in Manchester.
  Women's suffrage declared illegal by Court of Common Pleas.
  Married Women's Property Committee established by Elizabeth Wolstenholme Elmy and Ursula Mellor Bright.

1869   Third *Contagious Diseases Act* extended.
  National Association for Repeal of the CD Acts established (does not admit women).
  Ladies National Association for Repeal of the CD Acts formed by Josephine Butler to protest against the institutionalised "instrumental rape" of women. The association is the first independent public agitation on a sexual issue by middle-class women.
  Emily Davies opens a women's residence at Hitchin, Cambridge, the precursor to Girton College.
  J.S Mill publishes *The Subjection of Women.*
  Josephine Butler publishes *Woman's Work and Woman's Culture* with contributions by Frances Power Cobbe, Jessie Boucherett, Sophia Jex Blake, Elizabeth Wolstenholme Elmy and others.
  Women's right to vote in municipal elections restored.

1870   *Married Women's Property Act* grants women the right to wages earned after marriage, certain investments, and legacies under L200.
  Elementary Education (Forster's) Act establishes principle that elementary education should be available to all children. Establishes system of local school boards.
  First London School Board Elections. Women stand as candidates and can vote. Emily Davies takes her seat.
  Women eligible to serve as Poor Law Guardians.

1871   Women's Education Union founded.

Vigilance Association founded for the defense of personal rights and the amendment of laws relating to women.

1872 Slade School of Art opens to women.

Maria Shirreff Grey launches the Girls' Public Day School Company (later Trust).

Infant Life Protection Act regulates baby farming.

1873 *Infant Custody Act* extends the possibility of a woman's custody of her children up to age 16; removes adultery restriction.

Lectures for women established at Oxford.

1874 London Medical College for Women established.

Factory Act legislates a 56 hour work week.

1875 First woman elected as guardian of the poor in London.

1876 Medical licensing bodies empowered to examine women.

Manchester New College opened to women.

Women's Printing Society established.

1876 Annie Besant and Charles Bradlaugh tried for publication of pamphlet on birth control.

1878 *Matrimonial Causes Act* offers legal separation, child custody and maintenance orders for women whose husbands have been found guilty of assault against them.

1879 Lady Margaret Hall, Somerville Hall established at Oxford.

Invention of Mensinga Diaphragm.

1880 *Compulsory Elementary Education Act* makes school compulsory for children aged 7 to 10.

1881 Cambridge permits women to take honours examinations.

1882 *Married Women's Property Act* legislates women's right to all property earned or acquired before and after marriage.

1884 Third *Reform Act* extends franchise to all male householders.

1885 *Criminal Law Amendment Act* raises age of consent for girls from 13 to 16. Labouchiere's Amendment to the act makes illegal all sexual acts between men, consensual or not, an offence. The Act is also known as the Blackmailer's Charter.

National Vigilance Association founded in response to W.T. Stead's exposé of "white slavery" or child prostitution in his journal, the *Pall Mall Gazette.*

1886 *Contagious Diseases Acts* repealed in UK.

Infant Custody Act legislates mother's right to custody of her children if their father dies (prior to this a father's will could name any guardian).

1887 Queen's Golden Jubilee.
Rational Dress Campaign.

1889 *Prevention of Cruelty and Protection of Children Act* (Children's Charter) passes into law.
Women's Trade Union League established.

1893 Women's lectures at Oxford no longer chaperoned.

1897 Queen's Diamond Jubilee.
National Union of Women's Suffrage Societies founded. Millicent Garrett Fawcett presides.
Lobbying of Parliament for suffrage intensifies.

1899 First milk depot for the distribution of sterilised milk for infant feeding established in London.

1901 Death of Queen Victoria.
Factory Act forbids the employment of children under 12 in any factory or workshop.

1903 Women's Social and Political Union (WSPU) founded by Emmeline and Christabel Pankhurst. Militant feminism embraces new political strategies to achieve suffrage.

1907 WSPU's first major public demonstration.

1909 First hunger strike by suffrage activists in prison.

1911 *National Insurance Act* includes establishment of maternity benefits.

1918 *Woman Suffrage Act* passes into law. Women householders or wives of householders who are over 30 gain the vote. The act enfranchises approximately one-half the female population of UK.
Maternity and Child Welfare Act offers grants to local authorities for a variety of services for mothers and children, including midwives, health visitors, doctors, meals and daycare.

1919 First woman Member of Parliament takes her seat.
Sex Disqualification Removal Act passes into law.

1928 Women over 21 gain the franchise.

A Note on the Text

The essays here have been organized according to birthdates of authors, forming three cohorts of Victorian women writers. Wherever more than one article by any one author has been reprinted, the essays have been arranged by date of publication. I have chosen not to footnote the many references to contemporary personages, events, publications, etc., that characterise these essays. Many of the references are to well-known persons or events that require no further comments. The significance of the other often historically obscure references are generally quite clear from the context of the essay itself. I have also chosen not to provide translations for the many foreign phrases and tags scattered through these essays when, as is so often the case, the author has provided a free translation of her own. Adding additional footnoting to all of these references would, I think, be unduly cumbersome in a collection aimed at the general reader.

ANNA BROWNELL JAMESON
(1794-1860)

"THE MILLINERS"

Report and Appendices of the Children's Employment Commission.
Presented to both Houses of Parliament, by Command of Her Majesty

How little do people dream of the incidents and ills of that wide world of industry, with all its deeply interesting varieties of craft, skill, and condition, which surrounds and sustains our daily existence, unheeded and unseen by the throng of society! How fearful is the pain, toil, disease, and vice, convulsing the very class who supply some of the costliest pageantries of life! It is not so with all the trades which minister to pleasure; but some of the extremes of pain of production, and luxury of enjoyment, are fantastically and horribly coupled.

The Report before us was last week presented to Parliament. It is an outpouring of facts full of warning; teeming with graphic narratives and discoveries of horror, which ought to have been long since known and remedied, and which, being to the world as novel as they are interesting, are a stigma on the mind and soul of our generation. There is something to us unintelligible, and almost contradictory, in the present growth and inactivity of intellect. Nobody questions this growth, and yet we see no fruits equal to the progressive sense of the need, as well as power, of improving society and the sources of its weal. Nevertheless, this is the use and design of all mental power. But it is our purpose to pourtray, and not to philosophize:

We mean to gather from these leviathan revelations the most striking and interesting of the descriptive passages relating to a variety of employments, of which the circumstances almost form a romance unlooked-for in the regions of labour, even by those who dwell in them. The very seats of fashion and easy opulence in this voluptuous London, present the worst instances of excessive toil in their service, of which the industry of the empire has afforded any evidence throughout the whole scope of this very searching inquiry, in the case of

THE MILLINERS

After reading Mr. Grainger's Report, and the body of evidence he adduces, we can well appreciate the remark made to us by an individual, acquainted with the facts, on the morning of the last Court Fancy Ball,—"I shall have no more pleasure there: I shall have before my eyes a score of the makers of those gay dresses in their coffins."

1

We gather from the Report that there are about 15,000 milliners and dress-makers in the metropolis. They commence work usually at from 14 to 16,—that is to say, at an age when the future health and constitution is determined by the care it then receives. A very large portion of these girls are boarded and lodged by their employers, and they often come from the country healthy and strong during the busy seasons—ie., from April to August, and from October to Christmas—the regular hours of work "at all the principal houses" are, *on the average, eighteen hours daily!* "Long as these hours are," adds Mr. Grainger, "they are very often exceeded." Sometimes fifty of these girls work together in a room almost always insufficiently ventilated. The sleeping apartments are generally overcrowded. In one instance, five slept in a single bed, and often ten in one room. They are fed chiefly, says an experienced witness, on cold mutton; but they subsist mostly on tea and bread and butter. Stimulants are often applied to keep them awake.

"Miss O'Neill, of Welbeck-street, (who has been a dress-maker and milliner several years, and employed in several of the London homes, is now in business for herself,) states, that the hours of work in the spring season are unlimited. The common hours are from 6 a.m. till 12 at night; sometimes from 4 a.m. till 12. Has herself often worked from 6 a.m. till 12 at night for 2 or 3 months together. It is not at all uncommon, especially in the dress-making business to work all night; just in the 'drive of the season' the work is occasionally continued all night, 3 times-a-week. Has worked herself twice in the week all night."

Cases, such as follows, are not uncommon. Miss H. Baker says that—"On the occasion of the general mourning for His Majesty William IV, she worked without going to bed from 4 o'clock on Thursday morning till half-past 10 on Sunday morning; during this time witness did not sleep at all: of this she is certain. In order to keep awake she stood nearly the whole of Friday night, Saturday, and Saturday night, only sitting down for half an hour for rest. Two other young persons dozed occasionally in a chair. Witness, who was then 19, was made very ill by this great exertion; and when on Sunday she went to bed, she could not sleep."

We will now extract a few facts from the evidence of some of the girls themselves. For obvious reasons the names are not given. Miss —, in the establishment, we are informed, of a first-rate milliner, states that—

"On special occasions, such as drawing-rooms, general mournings, and very frequently wedding orders, it is not uncommon to work all night: has herself worked 20 hours out of the 24 for 3 months together; at this time she was suffering from illness, and the medical attendant remonstrated against the treatment she received. He wished witness to remain in bed at least one day longer, which the employer objected to, required her to get up, and dismissed the surgeon."

X.Y., in the same house, "was told she ought to take her breakfast standing"; and "M.D. has known several young persons so much exhausted that they were obliged to lie down either in the work-room or in their bed-room for an hour before they could undress."

In consequence of giving this evidence, which Mr. Grainger was, owing to the interruptions of the mistress, obliged to obtain elsewhere,—

"M.D. was grossly abused before 3 or 4 persons; accused of improper motives in meeting the Sub-Commissioner to give evidence, and at a moment's notice, turned out of doors without a character. She has reason to believe that her employer has made false representations to her relations. These circumstances have caused witness deep mental suffering and anguish, and have also seriously interfered with her future prospects in life. She is at this time out of a situation. M.D. is ready to corroborate the truth of the whole of these statements on oath."

It must not, however, be imagined that there are no instances of considerate humanity. "In houses," says one of the witnesses, "where they profess to *study the health of* their young people, they begin at 8 a.m. and leave off at 11 p.m. Never earlier"! And houses which are "regulated," Miss Baker informed the Commissioner, "mean those where they do not work all night." How comforting to philanthropy to find health sometimes studied, by a limitation of labour in a close room to fifteen hours per diem *only*! The humanities among *modistes* occasionally assume even a higher range; and the benevolence of superintendents sometimes even exceeds the tender mercies of the regulations themselves. A witness says:—"If they get very sleepy they lie on the floor, on the cuttings if there are any. This indulgence depends on the kindness of the head of the room!"

Mr. Grainger, though he feels bound to state that his Report in some respects, owing to intimidation of witnesses, falls short of the truth, yet maintains "that there is a strong desire on the part of many of the employers to promote the comfort of their workwomen, as far as the long hours permit." But do they permit of comfort, or any approach to it? Are they not hours universally protracted to an extent necessarily painful at the time, and utterly destructive of future health and welfare? The effects on general health are so disastrous, that one only had retained it out of the whole number, known to witness, who had been for years in the business. Indigestion, constitutional derangement, heart diseases, and, at last, consumption, seem to prevail in nearly every case. It is, in fact, a slow death.

One witness accounted for her approaching death by her excessive hours of work, and colds caught, at Bath, where her time for sleep was so short, that she used frequently to sleep on the rug, it not being "worth while to go to bed." Another, aged 25—

"Has been in the millinery business 8 years, in London. In the busy season, she began to work at 7 a.m., and went on till 12 or 1 in the morning. She was so unwell she could not begin before 7: *but the principal wished it. Lately has not gone to bed before 2 or 3 in the morning,* for a good while has been in a bad state of health."

This girl was ill at home, when the Commissioner visited here with her medical attendant. "In fact," says he, "such was her state, that it seemed as if I were taking, not her evidence, but her dying declaration. It is very doubtful if she will recover."

Medical evidence is not wanting to complete this picture, and authenticate its truth. Sir James Clark says, in his written evidence, of these poor girls:—

"—worked from 6 in the morning till 12 at night, with the exception of the short intervals allowed for their meals, in close rooms and passing the few hours allowed for rest in still more close and crowded apartments;—a mode of life more completely calculated to destroy human health could scarcely be contrived, and this at a period of life when exercise in the open air, and a due proportion of rest, are essential to the developement of the system."

Dr. Devonald states that he—

"Is convinced that in no trade or manufactory whatever is the labour to be compared to that of the young dress-makers; no men work so long. It would be impossible for any animal to work so continuously with so little rest."

Those who work at the great Mourning Establishments frequently lose their eyesight, and their tragic fate is closed in blindness.

Mr. Tyrrell, surgeon of the Ophthalmic Hospital, after elaborate evidence on this point, gives the following additional instances of the ravages made by this branch of the business:—

"A fair and delicate girl, about 17 years of age, was brought to witness in consequence of total loss of vision. Recovery was hopeless. She had been an apprentice as a dress-maker. The immediate cause of the disease in the eye was excessive and continued applications to making mourning. She states that she had been compelled to remain without changing her dress for nine days and nights consecutively; that during this period she had been permitted only occasionally to rest on a mattress placed on the floor for an hour or two at a time; and that her meals were placed at her side, cut up, so that as little time as possible should be spent in their consumption."

He has, he states, "often" seen cases of total loss of sight from the same cause. Mr. Dalrymple, of the Moorfields Ophthalmic Hospital, gives similar evidence; and, in one instance, succeeded in rescuing a young victim from total blindness (who was *then* required to work 18 hours per day only,) by threat of appeal to the Lord Mayor, to force her mistress to cancel the girl's indentures.

The portion of the work done in making mourning which is so peculiarly hurtful to the sight, is embroidery on black. A Court mourning is calculated to cause the loss of eyesight to at least thirty of these girls.

To the Misses Ollivier, in Pall Mall, credit is due for an endeavour to alleviate the evils of the system. They have drawn up regulations, by observing which, much time may be saved. Miss Ricks, of Mount-street, equally desirous of benefiting the objects of the Inquiry, sensibly remarks that she—

"Has found by experience that by having more moderate hours she derives quite as much benefit in her business as when they worked much longer. If young persons are kept up night after night very late, they become languid, exhausted, and unfit for proper application to the work."

But what, after all, is the moderation recommended? This—"the restriction of the *work* of young persons under 18 to 12 hours a-day, to be taken between half-past 5 a.m. and half-past 8 p.m., which would not interfere with the efficiency of the business." We dare say not. The question which the humanity of this country has to settle, is how far it may interfere with the efficiency of health, for a young girl, under 18, to be confined at work for 12 hours a-day to a close sedentary occupation. Where really humane employers deem this "moderation," it is manifest that less moderate mercies must interpose to save the victims. Miss Ricks says that—

"One of the principal causes of the late hours is the influx of orders and the short time which is allowed to execute them. A considerable amelioration would result if the ladies would be more considerate, and allow more time for their orders."

Well may Dr. James Johnson exclaim in his evidence:—

"The fashionable world know not how many thousand females are annually sacrificed, during each season, in this metropolis, by the sudden demand and forced supply of modish ornaments and ephemeral habiliments. They know not that, while they conscientiously believe they are patronizing trade and rewarding industry, they are actually depriving many thousand young women of sleep, air, and exercise."

Such is the condition of 15,000 of the inhabitants of London; a body, moreover, so quickly mouldering away, that during the span of an ordinary life full two generations have passed through the horrors of the craft, and perished in its services. Now, supposing these 15,000 beings, instead of being scattered over and lost sight of in the vortex of our Metropolitan millions, constituted the whole of a town, and a separate community, as large, for instance as Canterbury, or Dover, or Halifax, what outcries of indignation, what lamentations of sympathy, what a hurricane of virtuous reproach, would burst forth of the breadth and length of the land! And yet these towns of Canterbury, Dover, or Halifax, contain no larger population than that of the London milliners, and there would be not an atom more suffering than there is already.

The refinement and wealth of London is ever commemorating events, and efforts, and epochs; great men and great doings have their mementos in every square and nook; we erect palaces for our private pleasures, temples for our public pieties, galleries for art, and pillars and pedestals, great and small, for every sort and kind of hero; but oh, for a monument to remind us of our crushing crimes,—our thousands and tens of thousands of fellow beings, the doomed slaves of our glittering grandeur, living a deathly life of torment for the gratification of wealth, which immolates them almost without a thought or care in the service of its paltry pomp, and silly pageantry. Of all the vanities of life, that of dress is at once the most inane and mindless, and its gratification the least defensible, if purchased at the cost of pain to any human being. We shall consider that this Report has done valuable service if, henceforth, where plumes wave and diamonds sparkle, and fashion disports herself in all the galaxy of her costliest trappings, a thought be now and then bestowed on the mass of suffering from which that splendour sprung. If the bloodless cheeks and attenuated frames of these poor milliner girls passed in array before the beauty their lives are sacrificed to adorn, it might, perhaps, induce them to abate a little of the brilliance of our ball-rooms, for the preservation of the souls and bodies of fifteen thousand of our fellow beings.

Source: Reprinted from *The Athenaeum* (4 March 1843).

BIOGRAPHICAL NOTE

Born in Dublin on 19 May 1794, Anna Jameson was the eldest of five daughters born to the artist and miniaturist, Denis Murphy. Little is known about her mother. The family moved to England in 1798, settling in London in 1806. Though Anna's father had a successful career, becoming Painter-in-Ordinary to Princess Charlotte, he was never able to provide adequately for his large family. Anna became a governess at the age of sixteen, and continued in this line of work for fifteen years. In 1821, she announced her engagement to Robert Jameson, a barrister, but broke it off shortly after. After much hesitation, she resumed the engagement and they were married in 1825.

The marriage was not successful. Despite shared artistic and literary interests, there were fundamental differences in temperament between the two; there is some evidence that the marriage was never consummated. Financial worries also caused problems, and in 1829 Robert Jameson accepted an appointment as a judge on the Island of Dominica, initiating a separation that eventually became permanent.

In the meantime, Anna Jameson established herself as a writer. In 1826, her fictionalized travel biography, based on a tour she had taken as a governess, was published. *The Diary of an Ennuyee* was well-received, and she became a celebrity. Her next books, *Loves of the Poets* (1829) and *Celebrated Female Sovereigns* (1831), displayed the growing interest in biographies of women in literature and women's wielding of power that characterizes much of her writing. A later book, *Characteristics of Women* (1832), later re-titled *Shakespeare's Heroines*, was highly acclaimed and established her reputation as a critic worldwide.

In 1832, Robert Jameson returned to England for a few months, during which time he and Anna lived together. He soon left to take up the appointment of Attorney General of Upper Canada. Anna Jameson remained in England until 1836 when she joined her husband in Canada, determined to "make another trial for happiness" despite serious misgivings. The reconciliation failed very quickly; she hated the isolation of a frontier society, and he seemed unable to give the affection and consideration she needed to make the marriage work. They agreed on a separation, he making her an allowance of £300 a year. She left Canada for England in 1837, and never saw her husband again. On her return, she published *Winter Studies and Summer Rambles in Canada* (1838), much of it based on a two-month excursion she made alone, accompanied only by copies of the Bible and Shakespeare and a stiletto for self-defence. It was also her first work to deal explicitly with the position of women, and earned her passionate denunciations from several reviewers and critics displeased by her negative comparison of the relative positions of European and Red Indian women in Canada.

Jameson settled in London, where she was financially responsible for a large family, including her mother, invalid father, two unmarried sisters, and a niece. Her husband's irregular payment of her allowance contributed to her difficulties. During the 1840s her feminist activity noticeably increased. Having read the 1842 Report of the Royal Commission on the Employment of Women and Young People in Mines, she wrote a review article for the *Athenaeum* calling for better educational facilities for women and urging public support for working women. A brief selection of her 1843 work on the Report, focussing on the plight of milliners and dressmakers, is reprinted here. Two later essays, "The Relative Position of Mothers and Governesses" and "Women's Mission and Women's Position," published in her *Memoirs and Essays* (1846) similarly demonstrate her interest in the Woman Question.

Jameson's literary reputation and financial security continued to be enhanced by the publication throughout the 1850s of numerous guide and handbooks to art galleries in England and abroad. In 1851, Robert Jameson, now a confirmed alcoholic, was retired from his position as Attorney General, and ceased payment of her allowance altogether. In 1854 he died, leaving her without any share in his estate. Friends arranged an annuity for her, and she received a civil list pension from the queen. Needing more in the way of financial support, Jameson undertook two public lectures, "Sisters of Charity, Catholic and Protestant, at Home and Abroad," and "The Communion of Labour: a lecture on the Social Employments of Women." Not believing in the strict equality of the sexes, Jameson laid out her thoughts on the different functions of men and women while still calling for more opportunities for women in society. Both lectures were later published.

During this time, Jameson became increasingly involved with the Langham Place circle, an organization of women, including Barbara Leigh Smith Bodichon and Bessie Rayner Parkes, interested in improving employment opportunities for women. The circle's petition in support of the Married Women's

Property Bill was presented in the names of Anna Jameson and Mary Howitt, though it was not until 1893 that the proposed legal reforms were finally passed. Her connection and activities with this group continued until her death from pneumonia in 1860.

SECONDARY SOURCES

Adams, Kimberley VanEsveld. *Our Lady of Victorian Feminism: the Madonna in the work of Anna Jameson, Margaret Fuller, and George Eliot.* Athens, OH: Ohio UP, 2000.

Johnson, Judith. *Anna Jameson: Victorian, Feminist, Woman of Letters.* Brookfield, VT: Scolar Press, 1997.

Thomas, Clara. *Love and Work Enough: The Life of Anna Jameson.* London: Macdonald, 1967.

Harriet Martineau
(1802-1876)

"Female Industry"

ART.I.—1. *The Results of the Census of Great Britain in 1851.* By EDWARD CHESHIRE. London: 1853.
2. *Report of Assistant Poor-law Commissioners on the Employment of Women and Children in Agriculture.* 1843.
3. *Minutes of the Committee of Council of Education.* 1855-6.
4. *Reports of the Governesses' Benevolent Institution.*
5. *The Industrial and Social Position of Women in the Middle and Lower Ranks.* London: 1857.
6. *Women and Work.* By B.L. SMITH (Mrs. BODICHON). London: 1857.
7. *Two Letters on Girls' Schools, and on the Training of Working Women.* By Mrs. AUSTIN. 1857.
8. *Experience of Factory Life.* By M.M. 1857.
9. *The Lowell Offering.* Lowell, Massachusetts, United States.
10. *The Laws of Life, with Special Reference to the Physical Education of Girls.* By ELIZABETH BLACKWELL, M.D. New York: 1858.

There was a time when continental visitors called England 'the hell of horses, the purgatory of servants, and the paradise of women,' from the two former having everything to do, and the latter nothing. The lapse of centuries has materially altered this aspect of affairs. The railways have annihilated the hardest-worked class of horses; improvements in the arts of life have relieved our servants of a great amount of toil, while on the whole elevating their condition; whereas the women of the United Kingdom have been led forth from their paradise into a life of labour and care, more strongly resembling that of men than either the men or women of old times could have anticipated. Wearied as some of us are with the incessant repetition of the dreary story of spirit-broken governesses and starving needlewomen, we rarely obtain a glimpse of the full breadth of the area of female labour in Great Britain; and it requires the publication of the 'Results of the Census,' or some such exhibition of hard facts, to make us understand and feel that the conditions of female life have sustained as much alteration as the fortunes of other classes by the progress of civilisation. Sooner or later it must become known, in a more practical way than by the figures of the census returns, that a very large proportion of the women of England earn their own bread; and there is no saying how much good may be done, and how much misery may be saved, by a timely recognition of this simple truth.

The idea itself expressed by the form of words 'earning one's bread,' is somewhat modern,—except indeed in the primitive sense in which Adam was set to do it. In the modern sense of 'earning one's bread,' the position arose, for men first, and subsequently for women, after the creation of a middle class of society. The thing and the name have been recognised for some centuries in regard to men. Women have been more and more extensively involved in the thing, especially during the last half-century; but the name is new and strange; and the extent to which they work for a maintenance is a truth known scarcely to one in ten thousand of us. It is as well to know it; and timely attention to the fact is the best way of knowing it to practical purpose.

There is no reason to suppose that women's lives were less laborious than now, in the early days when they had no responsibility about their own maintenance. When there was no middle-class, and no shopping and marketing, the mere business of living was very hard work, both to men and women. They belonged to somebody, except the few who owned the rest; and the owners had perhaps as much on their hands as the dependents. The gentlewoman of ancient times had to overlook the preparation of every article of food, clothing and convenience, for a whole settlement, in days when the corn had to be grown, reaped, and dressed at home; and the wool and hemp the same; and all the materials of building, furnishing, and adorning. The low-born women had to grind the corn before they could make the bread; to spin the wool, and dye and weave it before they could make the clothes. Every process was gone through on every estate. Every step of daily life was laborious; and all working men and women were slaves. Not a few of them were called so in the days when the Irish used to purchase their workpeople from England. 'The spindle side' of the house, as King Alfred called the gentlewomen, ascertained how many hands were necessary to do the women's work of the establishment; and the useless were got rid of, by one method or another, and chiefly by sale to Ireland, or the estate suffered. In those times, there was no such idea afloat as that of self-dependence for subsistence. The maintenance was a matter of course; and hard work a common necessity everywhere outside of the convent.

The lot of the labourer seems to have been little lightened when the middle class began to grow, though more and more articles were to be had by purchase, and much toil and time were saved by new arts of life. It was a great matter when the mill saved the pounding of corn. It was a great matter when the first Flemish weavers came over with their looms, and spared the women a world of trouble about 'homespun.' Before that, the foreigners used to say that the English were scarcely anything but shepherds. and wool producers. More wool than ever was wanted; but the saving of the women's time and labour led to an increased production of poultry and eggs, butter and cheese, and many other good things. Still, the work must have been as hard as any that is known now. The days of the small yeomen had come on; the trading-class was beginning to appear; and all domestic matters rested on the women as entirely in the farmhouse and cottage as in the castle or mansion. 'To winnow all manner of corn, to make malt, to wash, and to make hay, shear corn, and in time of need, help her husband to fill the muck-wain or dung-cart, drive the plough, to load hay, corn, and such other, to market and sell butter or pigs, fowls or corn,'—such was the duty of the farmer's wife, according to Fitzherbert, in the first English work on husbandry. The women had to make the straw or flock beds, and the chaff pillows, when that luxury replaced the log of wood. They had to spin, weave, and dye the coverlets, and all the fabrics worn by the household, not being wealthy enough to employ the Flemings as the higher orders did. All the measuring and administration of the corn and pulse was the women's business, and the preparation of the winter food; that is, the salting and drying of the lean cows which were killed in autumn because no way was known of keeping cattle alive till the spring grasses were ready. The women made the candles and the salt, and the soap; and the mead from the beehives, and the cider from the orchard; and they spent no little time in collecting the finest inner bark in the forest, and the best herbs in the fields, to make bread of when corn and pulse failed. In all the intervals, the spinning was going on;—that art which has given a denomination to the unmarried women of Great Britain and the United States to this day. First, in keeping the cattle, sheep, and swine, the women plied the distaff, as we now see the Alpine girls plying it amidst their goats, and the Arab maidens near almost every well or moist *wady* in the desert; and then, when the spinning-wheel came in, its whirr was heard all over the land, all day and the last thing at night. 'It stops a gap, and so must needs be,' was the reason assigned by the men; and in every house or hovel, there stood the wheel for every woman to sit down to, in the intervals of other business.

The gentlewomen first exhibited the change wrought by the rise of a shop-keeping class. It gave them more time than English women ever had before. There were seasons when, in the absence of husband or father, they had to govern large households or small districts,—with millions of details to attend to; but even then, from the time when the miller ground the corn, and the vintner supplied the wine, and stuffs were to be had from the merchant, the mistress of an establishment had something of the leisure of a princess for doing what she had a fancy for;—and that was, for the most part, working tapestry. While the priest wrote the letters, and the steward kept the accounts and made the purchases, the lady could overlook the garden from her lattice, and the kitchen from the gallery, without much interruption to the grave labour of stitching the siege of Troy, or the finding of Moses, in coloured wools or silks. These coloured silks bring us to a point of view whence we can get a glimpse of a change in the life of those times. When shops were so established an institution as that laws were made from year to year to regulate measures and weights, and exportation and importation, a rabid hatred sprang up against the Lombards who brought in silk ready for use, ('deceitfully wrought') so as to destroy the mystery of the silkwomen and spinners, 'and all such virtuous occupations of women.' This was in 1455. Half a century later, the new prohibitions of small articles of wrought silk from abroad went by the name of enactments 'for silk-women;' and it seems as if there were really women who made 'knit articles,' girdles, cauls, nets, laces, &c., for profit, as well as for household use. While reading the pulpit censures aimed at the ladies' dress, in those days when silk was a bewitching novelty, the 'head-dresses, horns, tails, and ornaments of pomp,' we can easily imagine that there was a demand 'for silkwomen' beyond what separate households could supply; and hence the rise of one of the earliest branches of female industry.

We can, at this moment, recall very few others capable of yielding a subsistence. In all ages and all nations there has been a tendency to commit medical and surgical practice to old women. It is so now, in the heart of Africa, and in the backwoods of America, and in the South-sea islands, and in remote parts of some islands which lie in a northern sea. One of the earliest figures in the lengthening series of female bread-winners is that of the doctress, with her simples and her ointments, and her secrets, and her skill in dressing wounds. By a similar mysterious adaptation, the doctress has been, in all times, the fortune-teller, or the witch, or at lowest the match-maker,—vocations by any of which a good deal of money has been obtainable from age to age, In some analogy with these is, or was, the vocation of cook,—a profitable one also. Sending her messes from her own fire, or carrying her own saucepans and spices and herbs to the rich neighbour's kitchen, or the lady's still-room, the skilful cook was more patron than client, in times when English banquets were emerging from utter barbarism. There seems to have been little besides, in the way of paid industry. The occasional foster-mother took the infant home to be reared. The sick nurse was either one of the household, or the doctress. Orphans, or the daughters of impoverished gentlemen, entered the household of some great lady, as maids-of-honour did those of queens: but, beyond this, it does not appear that women sustained themselves by any other industry than the kinds we have indicated.

In those days, therefore, the supposition was true which has now become false, and ought to be practically admitted to be false;—that every woman is supported (as the law supposes her to be represented) by her father, her brother, or her husband. In those days, unmarried women were rare; and convents were the refuge of celibacy. It was not only in royal families that children were betrothed in their cradles. In all ranks, parents made matches for their children at any age that suited the family convenience; and the hubbub that ensued, when a daughter refused to marry at her parents' bidding, shows what a disaster it was considered to have a woman in the house who would neither marry nor become a nun. There was, in such a state of society, no call for female industry, except within the establishment,—whether it were the mansion, the farm, the merchant's dwelling, or the cottage. From that time (the uprising of a middle class) to this, the need and the supply of female industry have gone on increasing, and latterly at an unparalleled rate, while our ideas, our language, and our arrangements have not altered in any corresponding degree. We go on talking as if it were still true that every woman is, or ought to be, supported by father, brother, or husband: we are only beginning to think of the claim of all workers,—that their work should be paid for by its quality, and its place in the market, irrespective of the status of the worker:—we are only beginning to see that the time must come when such artificial depreciation must cease, under the great natural laws of society. We are (probably to a man) unaware of the amount of the business of life in England done by women; and if we do not attend to the fact in time, the knowledge will be forced upon us in some disadvantageous or disagreeable way. A social organisation framed for a community of which half stayed at home, while the other half went out to work, cannot answer the purposes of a society, of which a quarter remains at home while three-quarters go out to work. This seems to be clear enough. It does not follow that extensive changes in the law are needed; or that anybody is called upon to revolutionise his thoughts or his proceedings. The natural laws of society will do whatever has to be done, when once recognised and allowed to act. They will settle all considerable social points,—all the controversies of the labour-market, and the strifes about consideration and honour. All that we contend for at this moment is, that the case should be examined and admitted. Under a system like ours, in which the middle-class of society constitutes the main strength of the whole organisation, women have become industrial in the sense of being the supporters of themselves and of a large proportion of households: and their industrial production is rapidly on the increase. The census of 1851 affords some idea of how the matter stands. 'While the female population has increased (between 1841 and 1851) in the ration of 7 to 8, the number of women returned as engaged in independent industry has increased in the far greater ration of 3 to 4.' *(Industrial and Social Position of Women,* p. 219.) We are not very far from another census, which will afford the means of learning what that progress will have been in ten years. Meantime, we can hardly do better than prepare ourselves to estimate the next disclosure, by looking at the case as it stands to-day.

The first head of industry is always Agriculture. The Americans pride themselves on employing no women in agriculture, and are exceedingly scandalised at the sight of the peasantry in continental countries tilling their ground in family concert—the women and girls working there with their husbands and brothers. It may be questioned whether the yeoman's wife in New England, and the back settler's daughters, have an easier life of it than the German peasant-woman, or the Devonshire labourer's wife, or Highland lassies at a shearing. Considering the maple sugar-making, the soap-boiling, the corn- husking, &c., we should doubt whether any women work harder than some who would on no account be permitted to handle a hoe or a rake. However that may be, there seems to be no doubt of agricultural labour being relished by English women, and of its being, on the whole, favourable to health and morality. Health is morality, to begin with; and, if the woman's labour improves the family diet, and subscribes to the clothing club, while bacon and new shirts would be out of the question from the husband's labour alone, the fact may be less deplorable than a well-to-do young republic may consider it. If the children are not at school, they are with their mother in the field; and this is better than the fate of the town child, whose mother is out at work. It is not, then, to be regretted that the proportion of women employed in agriculture seems increasing in England. No census affords the means of more than an approximate estimate of the numbers, because we have not yet been told (as we must hope to be in 1861), how many of the rural labouring class become domestic servants. In the 'Industrial and Social Position of Women', we find this statement:—

'Going through the necessary calculation, we are led to the following conclusions, viz., that, of the whole number of domestic servants, nearly two-thirds are born in rural parts; that the agricultural class, although little more than half as numerous as the classes engaged in trade, commerce, and manufacture, sends out nearly twice as many domestic servants; that of the women of town families engaging in independent industry, about one-third become domestic servants; and that, of the women of country families engaging in independent industry, six-sevenths become domestic servants. To a great extent, therefore, the women of the rural classes monopolise that situation both in town and in the country.' (p. 192)

According to the census of 1841, there were then 66,329 women, above twenty years of age, employed in agriculture, without reckoning the widow-farmers (who are not few), or the farmers' wives. The late census gives 128,418 as the number so occupied, exclusive of the 'farmer's wives' and 'farmers' daughters,' who are specially, but perhaps not completely, returned as being 289,793. Of the independent female agricultural labourers, about one-half, or above 64,000, are dairy women. Neither in America, nor anywhere else, would dairy work be objected to as a feminine employment, conducted within doors, as it is, and requiring feminine qualities for its management: yet it is harder work, and more injurious to health, than hoeing turnips or digging potatoes. 'No end of work' is the complaint; and it is not an unreasonable one. On a dairy-farm, the whole set of labours has to be gone through twice a day, nearly the whole year round; and any one of our readers who has seen the vessels on a Cheshire farm, the width of the tubs, the capacity of the ladles, the strength of the presses, and the size of the cheeses, will feel no surprise at hearing from the doctors that dairywomen constitute a special class of patients, for maladies arising from over-fatigue and insufficient rest. There is some difference between this mode of life and the common notion of the ease and charm of the dairymaid's existence, as it is seen in a corner of a Duchess's park, or on a little farm of three acres and a paddock. The professional dairywoman can usually do nothing else. She has been about the cows since she was tall enough to learn to milk, and her days are so filled up, that it is all she can do to keep her clothes in decent order. She drops asleep over the last stage of her work; and grows up ignorant of all other knowledge, and unskilled in all other arts. Such work as this ought at least to be paid as well as the equivalent work of men; indeed, in the dairy farms of the West of England the same labour of milking the kine is now very generally performed by men, and the Dorset milkmaid, tripping along with her pail, is, we fear, becoming a myth. But even in Cheshire the dairymaids receive, it appears, only from 8*l.* to 10*l.* a-year, with board and lodging. The superintendent of a large dairy is a salaried personage of some dignity, with two rooms, partial or entire diet, coal and candle, and wherewithal to keep a servant—50*l.* a year or more. But of the 64,000 dairywomen of Great Britain, scarcely any can secure a provision for the time when they can no longer lean over the cheese tub, or churn, or carry heavy weights.

Ireland has to be treated separately in all these surveys, from her having had no place in the census; and yet, in considering the female industry of the United Kingdom, that of Ireland is the most prominent, and commands the most surprise. It will be ever memorable that during the transition period in which Ireland passed over from destitution and despair to comfort and progress, the nation was mainly supported by the industry of the women. Our readers may remember the 'Cottage Dialogues' of Mrs. Leadbeater,—a homely book which shows what rural life in Ireland was like before O'Connell broke up the good understanding formerly existing between the landlords and the peasantry. That book represented the ordinary life of the peasant women, spent in the field or the bog, and in managing the manure and the pig at home. In the succeeding period, and after the famine, the desire for the lowest-priced labour led to the employment of women and children; and the strange spectacle was then common of the women toiling on the farms or pastures, while the strong men were nursing the babies and the grannies at home. It was not only, nor chiefly, the agricultural labour however which fed the peasantry, before the men resumed their proper place. The Scotch merchants employed 400,000 women and girls in 'sewing,' or what English ladies call 'working' muslins. The Glasgow employers paid 90,000*l.* a week in wages for this Irish work. A good deal more was earned by other kinds of fine fabrics. On the whole, the change from outdoor labour to this seemed to be unfavourable to health in one direction, and favourable in another, while the social benefit was indisputable. The sedentary employment was less wholesome than the laborious one; but the homes became cleaner and more comfortable. There is nothing in needlework, any more than in dairy-work, to make a woman a good housewife; and the Irish peasant woman had yet another step upwards to make, to constitute her the labourer's wife that we may hope to see her; but the pig no longer shared the cabin, and the children were not tumbling about in the midden all day. The family diet is of a higher order than the old potato; and, as one consequence, there is a stronger demand for dairywomen. The land which used to be sub-let for potato grounds is more and more devoted to the service of the butter-merchants, causing an expansion of female industry in that direction. Whenever cheese is added, there will be still more for Irishwomen to do. It is odd that the innkeepers in the most rural districts of that island have to get every ounce of their cheese from England. Even without this prominent kind of women's work, the female industry of Ireland must be very great. It is not less now than when it nearly supported the population, though the men have again taken the lead in the toils of life, and their reward.

In connexion with agricultural labour we should consider the rearers of poultry, pigs and lambs; the makers of cider and perry; and the bee-mistresses, who gain a living by their honey in many rural districts. The enormous importation of eggs from the continent, and especially from France, shows that there is more work for women yet in this direction: but the reigning passion for poultry-yards must result in a great diffusion of the knowledge and skill which the upper classes are cultivating so diligently. In addition to the twenty thousand female farmers and land-owners of England, and the half-million and more of 'farmers' wives and daughters,' a separate class of poultry- women will soon be able to make a good subsistence out of eggs and chickens. Then there are the market-gardeners,—thousands of women, most admirably employed. There are the florists and nursery-gardeners,—not infrequently Quakers. It is a pretty sight,—a good nursery ground and set of conservatories, under the charge of a sensible Quakeress, whose shrewdness penetrates the whole management. There are the flax producers too,—not a small number, if we include the care of the crop, the pulling, steeping, beetling and dressing, and bringing to market; and, as 60,000 acres of Irish land are annually under flax, and as 500,000 acres would yield no more than is wanted; and as millions of pounds sterling (2,000,000l. in ten years) have been wasted in buying an impure seed from abroad when it might easily be obtained at home, we may conclude that flax-producing is, or might be, an extending branch of female industry. We may add that the demand for labour will increase, instead of diminishing, when the farmer consigns the preparation of the flax to establishments organised for the purpose, instead of insisting on doing it at home, and sinking in the market. At present, the women are in one place, poking in the ditch or pond at home, amidst an insufferable stench, and waiting on the weather for days or weeks; and then beetling with the old-fashioned instrument; while in another place they are about the same work in scotching-mills, to far greater advantage. The steeping, done without the stench of decay, and in a few hours or days in vats; and the dressing by patent machinery, are proper work for women, and will, no doubt, employ more and more of them,—especially as a great deal of seed is saved by the process. It is worth while to spend 170*l.* in labour to save 1,200*l.* in seed: and, as we spend 300,000*l.* in importing seed, the prospects of labour in the flax-producing department are well worthy of notice. When we have mentioned the itinerant classes of female agricultural labourers,—the hay-makers, reapers and binders, and the hop-pickers, we have reviewed, in a cursory way, the whole of that division of female industry.

On the whole, its prospects are good. The introduction of agricultural machinery does not at first please the Irish hay-maker, the Scotch reaper, the Berkshire bean-setter, or the Norfolk turnip-hoer: but neither did their grandfathers like the threshing-machines in the days of Farmer George. Time and patience show that the results of that particular change are two, among others,—an increased demand for labour, and an elevation of the character of the employment,—two very good things in view for the scores of thousands of our country-women who are engaged in agricultural processes of one kind or another.

Next to those who draw commodities from the surface of the land should come those who draw commodities from its depths,—the women engaged in mining processes. We are happily spared the dismal chapter of coal-pit life which we must have presented a few years ago. It is true, the desire for an independent maintenance,—the popular craving for wages,—causes a good deal of evasion of the law; and women do get down into the pits in disguise, or by connivance; but the employment of women in coal-pits is no longer a recognised branch of industry among us. Who then are the 7000 women returned in the census under the head of Mines?

They are, no doubt, for the most part, the dressers of the ores in the Cornish and Welsh mines. The work is dirty, but not too laborious;—less laborious than the work which may perhaps be included under the same head,—the supplying porcelain clay from the same regions of the country. Travellers in Devonshire and Cornwall are familiar with the ugly scenery of hillsides where the turf is broken up, and the series of clay-pits is overflowing, and the plastered women are stirring the mess, or sifting and straining, or drying and moulding the refined clay. The mineral interest is, however, one of the smallest in the schedule of female industry; and it is likely to contract rather than expand,—except the light labour of sorting the ores.

Next to the produce of the land comes that of the waters. Here again, scores of thousands of women find employment (otherwise than as fishermen's wives and daughters) within our four seas. It is true the amount of fish-eating in our country by the lower classes of the population is inexplicably small. No one seems yet to have accounted for the neglect of, or prejudice against, a kind of food so excellent and so abundant. But the demand created by railway carriage, and by the removal of various restrictions, bids fair now to restore something like the fish-eating of the old Catholic days. A few years since, tons of good fish were buried in the sands of the coast because they could not be disposed of while they were fresh, though the price in the neighbouring districts was so high that fish came to be considered a delicacy for the rich. The ponds of old abbeys and mansions had fallen into ruin; the river fish were dwindling in number and quality; and the uncertainty of the great coast and deep sea fisheries became so extreme as to render that branch of commerce a mere lottery. Through all this, the fisherwomen of all kinds stood their ground, with more or less difficulty. We do not mean only the sellers,—the celebrated Billingsgate fair, or the Musselburgh dames, and the Claddagh women. The shrill voices of the fishwomen all round the coast, and in all the ports, will for ever forbid their being forgotten when the independent industry of women is in question. They seem to be appointed to show how independent industrial women may be. A far larger number, however, are employed in the curing, and even in the catching of fish; and these held on through bad times and good times; but, it is supposed, in decreasing numbers till a new period set in. We need not describe the change wrought by the railway system, which scatters fresh fish all over the country, so that you may meet a man on the Yorkshire hills with a string of mackerel, or enjoying his haddock or fresh herring in the midst of a sporting county in the heart of England. The new arrangements for the protection of salmon, and for pisciculture, in imitation of the French practice, point to a steady growth of fish-eating at home; and the extension of our colonies, and of new settlements all over the globe ensures an increased demand for the staple of our great sea-fisheries. The pilchard fishery, confined (with pilchard-eating) to two counties and exportation to Italy, employs thousands of women. Jersey oysters alone employ 1000 women, and this may give us some idea of the amount of independent support afforded to women by our herring and cod fisheries (which last includes a variety of kindred sorts); the mackerel and oyster, and lobster fisheries, round our own coast,—to say nothing of the remote cod and turbot,—and the whale fisheries, in which the women take a part when the cargoes return. There are probably few of us who have not seen more of this direction of industry than of manufactures and commerce in which women are the labourers. In every seaside place we have seen the women and girls pushing their shrimping-nets through the little lagoons on the beach, or visiting the lobster traps at low water. In the Scotch islands, and on many an Irish promontory, we have seen the curing-houses where rows of women were at work in a way suggestive of Red Indian life, where the squaws sit cleaning their fish on the margin of Lakes Ontario or St. Clair. The further north we go in our own island the more we find the women habituated to marine industry, as well as to preparing its products for the markets. From Berwick to the Ord of Caithness the hardy race of men who fish the German Ocean are bred and nurtured by a race of women as amphibious as themselves, and busy all the year round in mending nets, vending fish, or salting and curing the 'crans' of autumnal herrings. They swarm along the bleak coast of Aberdeen, and they give at some seasons the activity of a vast manufactory to the little harbours of Helmsdale and Wick. In the sea-lochs and western islands of Scotland, it is common for the girls to ply the oar; whether at ferries or in the fishery. The art which young ladies now practise on the still waters of their fathers' pleasure-grounds, as an exercise to open the chest, the daughters of England all along her coasts, and yet more those of Scotland, have practised as naturally as walking, all their lives. Here the memory of Grace Darling will rise in all hearts,—as it ought; and with it the protest she made against being singled out for fame, on account of an act which she declared to be very common. Notwithstanding that protest, some of us prize above most of our cabinet treasures the statuette from the Northumberland monument which represents her sleeping after her battle with wind and tide, with her oar at rest upon her arm. Yet more do we prize the immaterial monument raised to her in that crypt within us wherein great deeds are laid by for eternal remembrance. Not the less, but the more, for her protest against her own fame is she become the type of a class of our hardy country-women, who are good angels in storm and shipwreck. As long as her monument remains, it should be remembered that she received her renown with grief and remonstrance, 'because,' as she said, 'there was scarcely a girl along the coast who would not have done as she did.'

Before we leave the margin of the sea, we must just glance at the smaller occupations pursued there by women. The most considerable of these was once the gathering and burning of kelp: but chemical science has nearly put an end to that. There is still a great deal of raking and collecting going on. In some counties, half the fields are manured with small fish, and the offal of larger, and seaweeds and sand. Then there is the gathering of jet and amber, and various pebbles, and the polishing and working them. The present rage for studies of marine creatures must afford employment to many women who have the shrewdness to avail themselves of it. Then there are the netting women, who supply that part of the fishermen's gear, and the bathing women, where visitors congregate. We have no means of learning the numbers engaged in such a variety of seaside occupations, but they must be considerable.

As nearly two-thirds of our maid-servants are country-born, that class presents itself next for review. There are some standing marvels in regard to the order; how it is that so few of them marry, and how they live in old age; both questions being pertinent to every inquiry into female industry.

The small proportion of marriages among domestic servants is no marvel if we consider that nearly half a million of our maid-servants have come from country places, where the proportion of the sexes was about equal, to towns where their numbers are added to the women's side, while a considerable percentage of the men are absent as soldiers, sailors, fishermen, commercial agents, &c. We find the following passage in. 'The Industrial and Social Position of Women':—

'Take for illustration the town of Edinburgh. In 1851 there were in that town (including Leith)—
Men above the age of 20. — 47,049
Women "   "   " — 64,638

the proportion being as three to four. In the same town the number of the sexes below the age of 20 was about equal. Turn then to the number of domestic servants. Of these there were no less than 12,449 above the age of 20, besides nearly half that number below the age of 20. In other words, 1 out of every 5 women in Edinburgh above the age of 20 is a domestic servant, while in Great Britain, on the average, 1 in 10 only is so. Even this large number of domestic servants does not suffice to account for the large disproportion of the female sex in the town in question. It is partly attributable to the seaport of Leith; and the even distribution of wealth in such a town as Edinburgh, besides drawing from rural districts an unusually large proportion of domestic servants, draws also many women from the same districts to the trade of millinery, and to other assignable and unassignable occupations. But, that the main cause of the disproportion of the sexes in Edinburgh is referable to domestic service, may be seen by comparing the statistics of that town with those of its rival Glasgow. Glasgow is in many respects a wealthier town than Edinburgh, but not in the same sense. In Edinburgh a large section of the population stand above the working ranks, and wealth is distributed. In Glasgow riches tend to accumulate in the hands of a smaller number of individuals; wealth is not distributed; a larger section of the population fall within the working ranks, and fewer persons can afford to have domestic servants. Hence, although Glasgow is one of the most extensive shipping ports, with many of its population absent at sea (an agency, however, that is probably counterbalanced by the influx of adventurers), the sexes in that town counted, in 1851, as follows:—

Men above the age of 20 — 83,455
Women "   "   " — 100,574

the proportion being as six to seven, or thereby, in place of three to four, as in Edinburgh. In Glasgow, the number of female domestic servants above the age of 20 is 9635; less than one in ten of the female population of the same age, less than the average of Great Britain, and about one-half the proportion obtaining in Edinburgh.' (pp. 194-6)

This explains a great deal of the celibacy of the class. In houses where men-servants are kept the housemaids and cooks marry; and so they do in country mansions, where they are considered good matches by the young labourers round; but in middle- class households, in towns, it is rather a remarkable circumstance when a servant marries from her place. This tends to establish the independence of female industry. The class is so large, and their earnings are so completely at their own disposal, that their industrial position is as determinate as that of men. The household, of which they form so useful and essential a part, becomes their home. Born for the most part in a cottage, and destined, if they marry, to struggle through married life in narrow circumstances and bitter privations, it is only in the houses of the middle and higher classes that they participate in those comforts and even luxuries of domestic life which capital, as well as labour, affords. There are few changes in the life of a woman more severe than that by which she transfers herself from the security and ease of domestic service to the precarious independence of married life; accordingly, this check operates with great power on the propensity to marriage among female domestic servants, and as we have seen, a very large proportion of them do not marry at all. As for the other question, how they are supported when past work, there may be several answers, none of which are very cheering. Our readers must be aware that this is one of the points on which we have found it necessary to consult the female members of the family council. They, and the clergy-man, and the physician, can, among them, afford some degree of satisfaction, though of a dismal quality. The physician says that, on the female side of lunatic asylums, the largest class, but one, of the insane are maids of all work (the other being governesses). The causes are obvious enough: want of sufficient sleep from late and early hours, unremitting fatigue and hurry, and, even more than these, anxiety about the future from the smallness of the wages. The 'general servant,' as the maid of all work is now genteelly called, is notoriously unfit for higher situations, from her inability to do anything well. She has to do everything 'somehow,' and therefore cannot be expected to excel in anything. At the same time, her wages are low, because it is understood that a servant of high qualification in any department would not be a maid of all work. Thus she has no prospect but of toiling on till she drops, having from that moment no other prospect than the workhouse. With this thought chafing at her heart, and her brain confused by her rising at five, after going to bed at an hour or two past midnight, she may easily pass into the asylum some years before she need otherwise have entered the work- house. 'This is horrible!' some of our readers will exclaim, 'but it relates to only a small proportion of one out of many classes of maid-servants,—a very small class, probably.' Not so. Little as the fact is generally understood, the maids of all work constitute nearly half of the entire number of female domestics, as computed at the last census, including the large class of charwomen, who amount to nearly 54,000. We are apt to forget that all the households in the land have not each a cook and housemaid at least, and a nursemaid where there are children; but if we would consider the vast tradesmen class, and the small manufacturers, and the superior artisans, we should not be surprised to find that in Great Britain (without Ireland) there are upwards of 400,000 maids of all work. Beginning upon five or six pounds wages in youth, they rarely rise beyond ten pounds. They have no time to take care of their clothes, which undergo excessive wear and tear, so that it is a wonder if there is any-thing left for the Savings' Bank at the year's end. Such is the aspect of one branch of independent industry in England.

How is it with the other classes of the sisterhood? What are their chances of escaping the workhouse?

The next in number to the 'general servants,' and rather more than one-eighth as many, are the charwomen, as we have just seen. In full practice, a charwoman makes from twenty to twenty-five pounds a year (at one shilling and sixpence a day, Sundays excepted), apart from her food. As 'advantages' of various kinds occur to occasional servants, she may obtain enough in that direction to provide her room and bed, and thus she can, if alone in the world, and at the head of her kind of service, lay by ten pounds a year: but the chances are much against it, and all the wives and widows, with children at home, must find it as much as they can do to live. Next in number, to our surprise, we find the housekeepers, who are scarcely short of 50,000. The wages of a housekeeper, in the proper sense of the term, are, we are assured, not less than forty or fifty pounds, provided she has nothing to do with cook-ing; but a 'cook and housekeeper' is a domestic officer of a lower grade. If, then, housekeepers wear out naturally, and are not heavily burdened, they may easily afford to purchase a small annuity (and, if a deferred annuity, a not very small one) from their savings. The cooks come next: and in no class are the wages so various. A middle-class household, in which two servants are kept, pays the cook ten pounds, and from that point the wages rise (we are informed) to about forty pounds, when the man cook assumes the command of the kitchen fire. Of the 47,000 women cooks in our kitchens, the larger proportion receive from twelve to eighteen pounds a year. The housemaids are fewer than the cooks, their number being under 42,000. Their work is eas-ier and lighter than that of any other class in domestic service, and it is some-what less highly paid. We are told that they, for the most part, have twelve pounds, almost as many having ten pounds, and few rising above fourteen pounds. Among the nursemaids the lady's-maids must be included, unless they come in with the house-maids in the tables before us, which seems improbable. The nursemaids are set down as amounting to 21,000. It is a sur-prise to fond papas, who think that their children are not made of the same clay as other people's, that their personal attendant, the guardian of such treasures, should be paid no higher than the woman who sweeps the cham-bers and polishes the grates; but the truth is, the best nursemaids are young girls, properly looked after by the mamma. So think the children, and they are good judges. The nursery girl begins with her five or six pounds, and if, in course of years, she becomes the elderly head nurse in a dignified place, her wages rise to perhaps four times the amount. Indeed, we have recently heard of a case in which the head nurse, guardian no doubt of babies of price, receives in wages no less than forty pounds: but we trust, for the sake of the nurseries of England, that the case is a rare one, and that our indiscreet disclosure of the fact will not be followed by a general strike in that department. To make up the half million, there are the gate-keepers in country mansions (between three and four hundred), and the 20,000 inn-servants, whose receipts are not, for the most part, in the form of regular wages.

Now, how can half a million of women, accustomed to the comforts of our households, provide for the time when they must go and seek a home for themselves? Most of them belong to poor families whom they must assist; but if not, what can they save in the way of a provision? Two or three pounds a year is as much as the larger proportion can possibly spare. Where the choice is offered them of a money payment, to provide themselves with tea and beer (about two guineas a year for each), the two or three pounds may be made four or five; and this, we are assured often happens. Still, with every advantage of good health and quality, and consequent continuous service, and with all aids of economy, it is apparently impossible for domestic servants to secure for their latter days anything like the comforts they have been accustomed to from their youth upwards. The clergyman can tell how shockingly thankful they often are, in the cold and bitter season which closes their lives, for the bounty which passes through his hands. Our wives say they encounter old servants in every almshouse they visit. Too often we find that the most imbecile old nurses, the most infirm old charwomen, are the wrecks and ruins of the rosy cooks and tidy housemaids of the last generation. This ought not to be. We are not alone in the wonder we have felt all our lives at the exceedingly low rate at which we obtain such a benefit as having the business of living done for us. There must be a change. When society becomes aware of the amount of industrial achievement performed by women, the chief impediment to an equalisation of wages for equal work will be removed, and domestic servants will then require higher wages, or leave service. In fact, this change has already begun. Wages are rising to unprecedented sums, is the cry we hear from the domestic exchequer; they have probably increased in the last twenty-five years more rapidly than the price of any other branch of female emoluments; they are increasing more rapidly in towns than in the country, and most rapidly in London. Unhappily the taste for expensive dress increases in the same ratio, and a very large portion of these legitimate earnings is squandered to procure a smart bonnet, a silk dress, a mantilla, and a parasol for Sundays. It is certainly a moral duty of no slight obligation on masters and employers to endeavour to assist the members of their household to make a judicious use of their earnings. It is not difficult for them to do justice, without running the risk of putting too much money into unprepared hands. There are Savings' Banks and many kinds of Assurance societies where distant annuities may be secured on various terms.

Under the head of 'service' several kinds of independent industry occur which need only be pointed out: as sick and monthly nurses, matrons and nurses in asylums and hospitals; women who go out to brew, to cook, to wash, and to sew; the searchers at police and custom-house offices; matrons of gaols; light-house keepers; pew-openers; waiters at railway refreshment rooms, and the like. These lead us, by a natural transition, to the commercial directions of female industry, some of which partake of the character of service.

In looking over the census returns, the occupations mark out the classes of women employed, the widows, wives, and maidens. The shopkeepers, like the farmers, are almost always the widows, who, as wives, assisted their husbands, and who now endeavour to keep up the business for the sake of the children. The same is the case with the 10,000 beershop keepers and victuallers, and the 9000 inn-keepers, and the 14,000 butchers and milk merchants, and the 8000 waggon or hack-carriage proprietors. Considerable as these numbers are, they would range higher if women were taught book-keeping in a proper style. So many are seen to decline in fortune, or to marry again, or in other ways to hand over the business to men, while in France, and in the United States, the same class prosper at least as well as men, that inquiry is provoked into the cause of the English failure; and it is usually found that the weakness lies in the financial ignorance of the women. The weak point is in the multiplication table;—in plain old English, they are bad at ciphering. This leads us to consider the wives. The 'shoemakers' wives' alone are nearly 94,000, their business being both shopkeeping and manufacturing. They serve ladies and children, and sell across the counter, and in the intervals do the lighter part of the shoemaking. Some other denominations are returned separately, as the 27,000 victuallers' wives, and the 26,000 butcheresses; but it is enough to say here that the industrial wives, specially so returned, amounted in 1851 to nearly half a million. It would be a prodigious benefit to their households if they were qualified to manage the accounts. That there is no good reason why they are not is proved by the recent rise of a class of female accountants in London, as well as by the instances in many of our large towns of the counting-house desk behind the shop, or in the manufactory, being occupied by women. We have never heard a doubt suggested as to the capacity of women for arithmetic; on the contrary, the girls in the Irish National Schools equal or excel the boys in mental arithmetic; and in every good girls' school of the middle-class there are some children who had rather cover their slates with sums for play than go for a walk. Elderly people remember, too, the old-fashioned sight, in unregenerate shops, of the wife or daughter, well-shawled, and in gloves with the finger-ends cut off, sitting from breakfast time till dinner, and from dinner till dusk, with the great books before her, and the pen always in hand; the light of a candle being observed till late on Saturday evenings, when the accounts of the week were posted up During the first period of the new style of shopkeeping, the desk class of women seemed to disappear; but they are evidently coming back again. And this fact leads us on to the employments of the single women.

The shopwomen (distinguished from shopkeepers) are surprisingly few. The figures seem scarcely credible. The shopkeepers being nearly 29,000, the shopwomen are only 1742. This fact will remind many people of the controversy about the dignity of shopmen, during and since the late war, when not only newspapers but a quarterly review attacked 'the men-milliners who smirk behind the counters of our shops,' and bade them be off to the army, and leave women's work to women. Our impression, on the whole, was that the shopmen exhibited a much better case than could have been anticipated by careless observers, though we are far from denying that, as a class, they are jealous of the competition of women, and act in the spirit of that jealousy. One or two of the facts of the case ought to be remembered; as, for instance, that the light business of 'dandling tapes and ribbons,' and exhibiting ornaments, &c., is usually coupled with work requiring bodily strength. In the shop where ribbons are sold, silk and velvet dresses are sold also; and it is more than most women can do to 'dandle' rollers of silk and whole pieces of velvet, at intervals for twelve hours per day. Where tapes are sold, there is demand for those very ponderous articles,—sheetings and shirtings, and table linen. In jewellery shops, men must attend, and a sufficiency of them, to deter thieves before whom such temptations are spread. Again, it seems to be proved, unexpected as is the fact, that our wives discourage the employment of women behind the counter. It is not very long since we met with the following illustration in the columns of a newspaper:—

'A large, well attended draper's and mercer's shop, in a good situation, became, by a sort of accident, the property of a benevolent and sensible person, who saw in the accident the means of employing female labour in a suitable department. He had always cried shame on the exclusion of women from the counter, where they could surely measure ribbons and cambrics as well as men. The well stocked shop was served by women, picked for their aptitude and experience, as well as their respectability. The old custom fell off, and the proprietor was assured that it was because there were only women behind the counter. It became necessary to introduce some shopmen, to reassure the ladies who could not trust the ability of their own sex. Two shopmen were introduced. It would not do. They were worked off their feet, while the shopwomen stood idle; for the ladies had no faith in female ability, even behind the counter.'

Such incidents as this disclose the true reasons of the shopwomen of Great Britain being (apart from the shopkeepers) only 1742. Now that girls, however few, are trained with a view to their becoming accountants, either as a separate profession, or as managers of the family business, we may expect to see the difference, from one ten years to another, in the census returns. The growing contrast between the recent and the coming time is exhibited in certain anecdotes now before us: one in 'Women and Work,' and the other in a Scotch newspaper. Mrs. Bodichon says:—

'There are now many trades open to women with good training in book-keeping and knowledge of some special branch of business, not difficult to acquire, if fathers would help their daughters as they help their sons. Two or three young women together might enter upon most shopkeeping businesses. But very few young women know enough arithmetic to keep accounts correctly.

We remember seeing two young women who kept a shop in a country village, slaving to answer the perpetual tinkle-tinkle of the shop-bell, dealing out halfpennyworths of goodies, bacon, or candles, who, when asked how much they were paid yearly for the hard work of attending the shop, hardly understood the question, and only knew that *generally* they did not have to pay more for their goods than they sold them for, and got their food into the bargain, week by week. "But how do you make your other expenses out?" "By letting lodgings," said they.' *(Women and Work, p. 15)*

'In taking a ticket the other day at the Edinburgh station of the Edinburgh, Perth, and Dundee Railway, we were pleasantly surprised on being waited upon by a blooming and bonnie lassie, who, along with an activity quite equal to, exhibited a politeness very rare in, railway clerks of the literally ruder sex. We observed that the department was entirely occupied by women, there being another giving out tickets, and a third telegraphing. This innovation thus far north is rather startling; but, instead of objecting to it, we think it highly commendable, and hope to see the employment of women in light occupations rapidly extended.' (*Scottish Press*, December, 1858.)

The mention of telegraphing in this passage reminds us of another example. The 'Times' gives the following account of the way in which it was enabled to supply London breakfast-tables with the speeches of Mr. Bright and others, on occasion of the Gibson and Bright festival at Manchester last December.

'It is only an act of justice to the Electric and International Telegraph Company, to mention the celerity and accuracy with which our report of the proceedings at Manchester on Friday night was transmitted to the "Times" office. The first portion of the report was received at the telegraph office at Manchester at 10:55 on Friday night, and the last at 1:25 on Saturday morning. It may be added that the whole report, occupying nearly six columns, was in type at a quarter to 3 o'clock on Saturday morning, every word having been transmitted through the wire a distance of nearly 200 miles. Some of our readers may be surprised to hear that this report was transmitted *entirely by young girls*. An average speed of twenty-nine words per minute was obtained, principally on the printing instruments. The highest speed on the needles was thirty-nine words per minute. Four printing instruments and one needle were engaged, with one receiving clerk each, and two writers taking alternate sheets. Although young girls in general do not understand much of politics, there was hardly an error in the whole report.'

In the United States, the telegraphing is largely consigned to women; and with it the kindred art of the compositor. From what we have heard in various directions within a few years, we believe that the manipulation of type by women is found to be such an advantage here that a great deal of our printing is likely to be done by them henceforth. Much was said beforehand about the impossibility of their enduring the smells of the office: but the same thing used to be said of oil-painting; and in both cases it is a mistake. If printing is on the increase among women, much more so is painting in oils and on glass. Printing reminds us of book-binding, which affords an admirable occupation to women. One well-known firm was, some few years since, employing 200 young women, under careful arrangements for their moral welfare, technical improvement, and daily comfort. Such means of instruction were provided as prevented their domestic qualities from being spoiled by their regular business. For the sake of quiet and respectability, little was said where so much was done; but the few who saw the workrooms, and followed the processes, from the folding of the sheets to the highest ornamentation of the covers, are not likely to forget that spectacle of cheerful and prosperous industry.

Before quitting the commercial department of female industry, we must remark that in all countries, and at all times, the fitness of assigning to women what may be called the hospitable occupations has been admitted. In metropolitan hotels the presence and authority of a master may be requisite; but, all through the country, the image of a good landlady presents itself when rural inns are in question. Throughout our literature, the country landlady is a pleasant personage; and we hope it may be so for ages to come. She makes the angler welcome, and gives him a luxurious home during his summer holiday; and she cooks his fish as no other woman knows how to do. Her sister in the sporting county has a similar abode to offer in autumn, among stubble fields, and near some choice covers; and she is as admirable at game as her sister in fish. A pleasant landlord is very well; but a widowed hostess is fully up to the duty, and seems rightfully to fill the place. And so it is where the scenery is the attraction. She is weatherwise for the advantage of her guests. She can tell them at what time of day they should see the waterfall with its rainbow or slanting sunbeam. She can fit up the boat comfortably for delicate ladies or dreaming poets. She puts up good luncheons for explorers and mountain climbers; and when they come home wearied and hungry, she has the bright little evening fire ready, and the tempting light supper, and the clean airy bedroom. The race of rural landladies ought never to die out; nor should woman's stake in institutions of hospitality ever be withdrawn.

We are told that boarding-house life will become more common than it has been. We have boarding-houses in London and Edinburgh, Liverpool, and Hull, and other towns, for foreigners accustomed to that mode of living at home. We see also, more and more, the tendency of our bachelors, young and old, to dine anywhere but at their lodgings. Some go to luxurious clubs; some to boarding-houses; some to chop-houses; and some to cooks' shops, of various grades. Bad cooking seems to be both cause and effect of the growing change. An ill-cooked dinner, repeated sufficiently often, sends the lodger elsewhere for his chief meal; and the want of daily practice on the lodger's dinner causes the landlady to lose any skill she might once have had. Thus is swelled the popular lamentation over the decay of the art of cookery among the working women of England, from the peasant's wife, who gives her household dry bread or watery potatoes, to the great lady of the first-class inn, who is as helpless among her own servants as if she had come from another planet.

This is a topic worth a pause;—if indeed it be a pause or interruption to speak of an art which would, any day, make the fortune of any working woman who was skilled in it. Some of us, it may be hoped, have wives who are not bent on inflicting on us, in our leisure hours, the kitchen troubles of our own or our neighbours' houses: yet every man of us is aware that one of the irksome cares of life at present is the difficulty of obtaining cooks who can send up wholesome meals to the nursery (a thing of superlative importance), or satisfy the most moderate tastes of the dining-room. We are constantly hearing that the art of domestic cookery is declining in this country, and almost gone. After some deep reflection, and comprehensive observation on this matter, we are disposed to think that there is a good deal of exaggeration in some directions, while the evil is plain enough in others. Count Rumford's Essays prove that cottage cookery was, throughout many counties, as bad in the last century as it is now. The contrast which he pointed out between the prisoners of war who made a warm, savoury dinner, out of a red herring and bread and water, and the natives round their prisons who ate up the same value in the shape of a slice of dry bread, and whose wives and mothers insisted that it must come to the same thing because it cost the same, was as striking as any cottage picture of a skill-less meal that we can offer now. Our religious tracts and other sermonising books for the poor tell us, as imaginative grandmothers used to do, of the labourer's home, where the wife made a good stew every day, and there was always the hot juicy rasher or the Welsh rabbit for the good man's supper; but Count Rumford's account was the true one; and the people (of more ranks than one) laughed to scorn his news that the process of cooking could alter the actual nourishment conveyed by a given portion of food. But there can be no doubt that the middle class of our countrywomen are far less skilled in the knowledge and practice of cookery than their grandmothers, who were themselves apparently inferior to *their* grandmothers. We are not going into the old controversy about how much time and thought the cares of the store room and kitchen used to occupy, and how much they ought to occupy. It is enough that the gentlewomen of a former century could not be said to be inferior in sense, intelligence, and manners to those of our own time; and that we have therefore every reason to believe that our wives and sisters would be no worse for understanding the business of the kitchen. The learning and graces of some of the ancient ladies of England compel us to suppose that, in each age, such narrowness or shallowness as exists is owing to restrictions on intercourse, by war or other influences; and that if the opportunities of our day had been granted to our ancestors, the dames would have been as accomplished as ours are, without being worse cooks. Well! is the art to be lost? or will an effort be made to recover it?

Our wives complain that they never had an opportunity of learning it. Their mothers took no notice of their natural wishes (every girl has an innate longing, we are confident, for the household arts, if nature had but her way); and the consequence is—a heavy weight of care on the heart in marrying, and many an hour of keen mortification afterwards, in addition to the constant sense of inability and dependence, and dread of shame and tacit reproach. Such is the wife's confession, when she can bring herself to make a clean breast of it. But what can be done for the daughters? There used to be means of instruction in cooking and in sewing, as there now are in drawing and music. Why is it not a branch of female industry now to give such instruction, instead of leaving those departments of knowledge a blank, while hundreds of governesses are starving or living on charity, in the workhouse or out of it? It may not be necessary or desirable for young ladies to spend so many hours in the still-room, among conserves and quackeries, as the damsels of three centuries ago, when kitchen cookery was gross and wholesale; and it might be better that they should learn from their mothers how to order and superintend the administration of food; but if their mothers have not the requisite knowledge, skill and ideas, it would be a great blessing to have a professional instructress within reach. By none, we fear, is such a training more needed than by the heads of boarding-houses in England. Our ordinary tables-d'hôte are almost as bad as the American, in regard to the cookery. How different are the German, where every lady is a trained cook! If the ladies of London complain that their husbands spend more and more time at the clubs, and take fewer meals at home; if boarding-house keepers find the business not a good one in England; if lodging-house keepers complain of the small gain of inmates who only sleep at home; let them all look to their consciences as to the table they offer, and say whether it is not reasonable that we should go for our dinner where we can have a good one for the same cost as a bad one.

A suggestion has been made and repeated, but not yet acted on, we believe, that lecturers should travel through the country with a portable kitchen, to give instruction in plain cookery, as improved by modern science and art, and especially by the discoveries of the lamented Soyer. Humble housewives were chiefly in the view of the adviser,—the wives and daughters of small tradesmen, artisans and cottagers, who might become convinced, by the evidence of their senses, of the economy and luxury of a good treatment of the commonest articles of food. It would be a great work if some educated woman would try the experiment. Its direct success is more than probable; and it might introduce into our towns a regular method of instruction in establishments where young women of almost every rank would thankfully become pupils. Is not this one of the undisclosed paths of industry in which there would be no interference by the jealousy of men?

If the complaint be well founded, that there are no good cooks to be had for middle-class households, why is such an evil permitted? If womankind has always had a faculty for that kind of achievement, how comes it to be in abeyance in England at present? Whose fault is it, if we are ill-supplied with cooks? The only use of asking the question is to learn how to supply the need. One mischief, no doubt, is the wrong- headedness with which we have gone to work in our popular schools, in our zeal to elevate the labouring classes. A letter on our desk,—from a lady who can cook and sew, after having been an excellent governess before her marriage,—indicates the case. She says:—

'I am in a state of periodical irritability on the government education schemes, owing to the visit of Mr. ——, the inspector. His tastes are philological; and he has written what, I have no doubt, is an excellent grammar for those who are worthy of it; and he seems to think that grammar in its uttermost niceties is to be the great intellectual engine in training our poor children. I have not a word to say against it in the case of the teachers (always provided they have made the elementary steps safe and sure), but I am quite certain that the highest class have learned far more practical grammar from me, indirectly, by conversation and writing, than by the scientific analysis on which such stress is laid. Mr. —— went through a sentence yesterday with girls who were made to point out predicate, extensions of predicate, classifying the latter, and other minutiæ, when I had in my pocket papers from these very girls, with shameful spelling, and the most elementary agreements of subject and verb disregarded.'

Some people will think, as we do, that this way of teaching girls whose business is to lie in domestic service, or something lower, is like insanity. Let us
see whether we can find better sense in other directions. In one, we light
upon what we want in the point of cooking; and in another we find the cooking so treated as to fill us with hope and cheer.

First, Mrs. Austin quotes, in her useful little tract, the prospectus of a
school, instituted by Miss Martineau of Bracondale near Norwich, for the
education of a few girls of the shopkeeping and artisan class, apparently. Two
old-fashioned adjoining houses are devoted to the object; and there is a good
playground. For sixpence a week a sound practical education is given.

'This is the skeleton of the scheme,' Mrs. Austin says of the prospectus,
'which differs in nothing from a common day school, save *in the things taught*,
and, above all, in the *direction* given to the tastes and habits of the pupils.
Without seeing it in operation, it is impossible to imagine the life and energy which Miss F. Martineau and her excellent assistants have infused into it.
The lessons on objects, which I heard, those on arithmetic, and the writing,
were excellent. The attention of the children never flagged. Their eyes were
fixed with eager inquiry on the cheerful animated face of their young mistress. But excellence in these branches is not rare. Miss Martineau, in a letter now before me, touches the true points of superiority in her school and
its mistress: "I think myself very fortunate in having a mistress so capable of
teaching the higher branches of knowledge, and yet so anxious to give an
interest to all home and useful duties. The idea of *taking pleasure* in cutting
out their own clothes, washing, &c., seems so new to the children."

'According to Miss F. Martineau's wise plan of feeling her way, and
attempting nothing on a large scale till she has proved its success on a small
one, the girls at present only wash for the mistress and the housekeeper, who
is their instructress in this department.

On the same principle of slow and cautious advance, cooking has, as yet,
not been attempted. This will come hereafter. Every needful appliance is
ready. Meantime, an important step in domestic education has been
gained. Those of the girls who live at a distance bring their dinners. Their
humble repast is set out and eaten with the nicest attention to cleanliness
and propriety. I saw the table exactly as it had been left by the girls who
had just dined. Not a thing was out of its place, nor was there a trace of
untidiness or disorder. The service of the table is performed by the girls in
turn. They clear away the dishes and plates, knives and forks, clean them,
and deposit them in their places. I saw one at her work washing the earth-
en vessels, wiping, *not smearing* them, and arranging them, dry and bright,
on pantry shelves of spotless whiteness. It was with peculiar satisfaction that
I soon afterwards saw the same girl come into the school and teach a class
of younger girls arithmetic.' (pp. 18-20.)

By an introduction of a subsequent date, we learn that at first the cooking was a difficulty,—the parents preferring sending the children with cold food of greater cost to paying a small sum which would enable them to have a warm meal, with the benefit of learning to cook it. But the opposition was gradually giving way.

A letter to the 'Times' (January 29, 1858), from the Vicar of Sandbach, Cheshire, exhibits the next scene of progress;—a scene which contrasts remarkably with that of a learned philological inspector, hammering his abstractions into girls who had no idea how to discharge any one duty in life, and were certainly not at all likely to learn it from him.

'The results of the Sandbach National School kitchen for the sick and aged poor, are—that with the sum of 77*l*. 12*s*. 6 1/2*d*., derived chiefly from the offertory collections, 852 dinners of roast mutton, 307 of mutton chops, &c., making in all 2,104 meat dinners, with 176 puddings, and 102 quarts of gruel, were supplied to the village, simply by the adoption of a judicious and economical system of cookery.'

Mr. Armistead adds,—

'It is a matter of thankfulness, though not of surprise, that a system so easy and simple of operation should have excited an amount of inquiry, personal and by letter, to an extent which leads to a well-grounded hope that in a few years a kitchen will form a necessary part of the National School of every large parish throughout the kingdom, a result no less beneficial to the sick poor than to the children themselves, thus early initiated in industrial employments well suited to their condition in after life.'

This topic leads us directly into the middle of the great question,—perhaps the most important of all the practical considerations connected with the subject of female industry;—the effect of manufacturing employment on the domestic qualities of women. We have no space here,—and it is no part of our present duty,—to discuss the pros and cons of factory life for our female population. We have to glance at the facts of the extent of that kind of occupation, and at the probabilities of its being reconciled with that domestic existence for which women are constituted, and to which they sooner or later return, after every experiment which the progress of civilisation inflicts, amidst its play of social changes.

The number of women employed in textile manufactures in 1851 were nearly 385,000. Under this head. are included cotton and its fabrics, woollen, flax, silk, straw, lace, and articles in fur, hair and hemp, and the paper manufacture. In the mechanical arts which usually rank in the same class, such as metal-works and earthenware, there were nearly 40,000. With these two classes may be united the third,—the women engaged in providing and treating Dress;—making, mending, and washing articles of dress. These are set down as above half-a-million. The three amount to within a fraction of a million. If we could include the women of Ireland, so largely engaged in the linen, cambric, and muslin manufactures of Ulster, and in the embroidery of muslins (as we have already shown), and in lace-making and knitted goods, the number would be greatly increased. Now, what a section of the nation this is,—a million and a quarter of women above twenty, earning an independent subsistence by manufacturing industry! The condition, claims, and prospects of such a section of the population ought to be as important and interesting to us as those of any class of men in the community.

The three sorts of employment need not here be considered separately. In the case of textile manufactures, the greater part of the work is done in factories; but not a little is carried on at home,—looms being set up in the cottage, or in the town lodging. In such old towns as Norwich, and in many a village in the eastern counties, the click and smack of the loom is heard in the narrow streets and over garden walls, as it is in the singular region of Spitalfields. A visitor will find the family engaged in winding, piecing and weaving,—father, mother, boys and girls all doing different parts of the work: and this is just the case of a large proportion of the Birmingham metal workers. They have a light room which they call a shop, where they work together at the articles which are to be completed by a certain time. So it is with the occupations which relate to dress. The lace maker is an old-fashioned figure in English life,—sitting at her door with her pillow before her, and her fingers busy among the bobbins. So it is with the straw-platter, and the clear-starcher and mender, and the artificial-flower maker, and the embroiderer, and, as we may see in every street, with the dress-maker. The 'Song of the Shirt' tells us that this is the way also with poor needlewomen. On the other hand, the factory, and gregarious occupation in many modes, is not now, as formerly, supposed to mean cotton or flax spinning. Silk, cotton, and flax mills may still be the representatives of the factory life of English women; but genuine factory-life can be seen at Birmingham as truly as at Manchester or Leeds. Long ranges of upper apartments in Birmingham factories are occupied by women, sitting in rows, quiet, diligent and skilful, putting together the links of cobweb gold chains, or burnishing silver plate, or cutting and polishing screws (a Manufacture mainly in their hands, because the Machinery requires delicate manipulation), or sorting needles, or painting papier-mâché trays. Of the 40,000 female workers in metals and clay, the greater portion now are factory-women, as much as any Lancashire or Yorkshire spinners or weavers. As for the third class, not only are the Nottingham and Leicester lace-makers and hosiery weavers of the genuine manufacturing class, but the London dress-makers may be called so; and the upholstresses too. They are collected, not always in large apartments alas! but in considerable numbers, and under a scheme of division of labour,—which is, we suppose, on an extensive scale, the distinction between domestic and factory labour; a distinction not interfered with by the distribution of portions of the work to different members of the family at home. Whatever may be the respective proportions of the factory and domestic workers who make up the million and a quarter of industrial women now under notice, it is a question of the deepest interest to us all, in every view, whether the factory-work is likely to increase or diminish in years to come.

At first sight, most of us are disposed to pronounce that the number will certainly increase. The demand for industry seems at present rather to exceed the supply,— generally speaking. We want more soldiers, more sailors, more agricultural labourers and rough workers, while emigration carries off tens of thousands every year. The rapid increase of labour-saving machinery indicates a want, rather than a superfluity, of hands; and so does the liberty to work which has been acquired by women within a few years. It is not very long since the Coventry men were as jealous and tyrannical about the women winding silks and weaving ribbons as they are still about their engraving watch plates; yet now many thousands of women are earning a subsistence in the ribbon and fringe manufacture. The increasing use of sewing-machines, at centres of dressmaking, tailoring, and blouse and shirt making, points in the same direction. In a community where a larger proportion of women remain unmarried than at any known period; where a greater number of women depend on their own industry for subsistence; where every pair of hands, moved by an intelligent head, is in request; and where improved machinery demands more and more of the skilled labour which women can supply, how can there be a doubt that the women will work more and more, and in aggregate ways, as combination becomes better understood and practised? Such is the first aspect of the case: but there are others. It will not be going out of our way to show by an example that factory-life is not everywhere the same; that it does not necessitate the evils of which too many of our manufacturing classes are examples. We conclude, as a matter of course in England, that a factory-girl cannot make her own clothes, cannot cook her father's dinner, cannot do the household marketing, or cleaning; is, in short, fit for nothing but the spinning or weaving, burnishing or sorting, in which her days are passed. If we can find good evidence that the occupation need not have these effects, it will be a great comfort. There are such evidences in abundance, and the facts work in opposite directions,—on the one hand, extending the inducements to factory labour for women, and, on the other, giving the women themselves a freer choice, and a stronger disposition to remain at home.

Twenty years ago, there were about 4000 women employed in the cotton-mills of Lowell, in Massachusetts. They worked seventy hours per week, earning their meals and from one to three dollars per week. They had built a church, and a Lyceum, and several boarding-houses; and in the winter they engaged the best lecturers in the state to instruct them in their Lyceum. These factory girls issued the periodical called the 'Lowell Offering,' which Mr. Knight reprinted in his series of Weekly Volumes, under the title of 'Mind among the Spindles.' Prefixed to that volume was a letter from Harriet Martineau, in which the factory life of these literary spinsters was described. They are the daughters and sisters of the yeomen of New England,—some aiming at disencumbering the farm, or educating a brother for the church, whilst others club their earnings to build a house in which to live under the sanction of some elderly aunt or widowed mother. Whole streets of pretty dwellings adorn the factory settlement; and books, music, and flowers within testify to the tastes of the young proprietors. The girls are well-dressed, weekdays and Sundays; and the Savings' Bank exhibits their provident habits. At the date of this account, in 1834, there were 5000 work-people at Lowell, of whom 3800 were women and girls; and the deposits, after all the public and private edifices were paid for, amounted to 114,000 dollars.

In a recent publication there is a contrasting view of the same class, employed in a silk-mill, under one of those dozen, or twenty, or fifty, or hundreds of good men who are each called by all who know them 'the best employer in England.' It is cheering to find how many 'best' there are. The writer was evidently taken aback at first, confounded by the 'yelling and screaming' of the women in the lane, which she supposed to mean some terrible accident, and astonished at the universal supposition that everybody was purely selfish, and bent upon cheating everybody else. The experiment of inducing a more womanly mode of life among the girls is described in a very interesting way in the tract called 'Experience of Factory Life,' which is in the list at the head of our article. The passage is too long for quotation; but it is to be hoped that our readers will turn to it, if they have any desire to see what the differences between the factory girls of Old and New England really are, and to ascertain whether any part of what is repulsive and lamentable here is owing to the occupation, or to any mode of life which it necessitates. We believe that the conclusion of the best observers will be that it is not the labour of the factory which hardens and brutalizes the minds of men or women, but the state of ignorance in which they enter upon a life of bustle and publicity. The Lowell factory girls are great reciters, and even writers, of poetry: the Sunday sermon is quite a pursuit to them,—as in puritan New England generally. Literature and music are the recreations of many of the factory girls of the mills. Now—can the chasm be bridged over which divides these conditions of factory life? Can the English factory girl be made as womanly as other people? If so, what is the effect on the industrial aspect of affairs?

We find something like an answer to this in such accounts as we can obtain of the operation of evening schools on this class of people. There was a narrative published in 'Household Words,' we remember, some years ago, which afforded great encouragement. In that case, the girls were eager to learn to write, above everything, one explanation began 'Hur wants to write to hur chap,' who was gone to Australia; but, where it was possible to deceive themselves about their own ignorance, they did so. No girl could pretend to write when she did not know a letter; but whenever they could fancy themselves treated like children, they put on airs of resentment,—as when one, who had to spell *ox* and say what it meant, exclaimed 'As if everybody didn't know 'that a *hox* is a cow!' They fancied they could sew till a pull at the thread undid half a yard at a time. They were averse to bringing clothes to mend, but liked making new smart gowns. They were partly interested and partly offended at the instruction given about the human frame and its health—one, who was laced up into the shape and stiffness of a tree-stem, exclaiming that she had 'got only six-and-twenty whalebones.' Some of them had witnessed a sad misfortune,—the first and fatal quarrel of a married couple from the bride having rendered her husband's one white shirt unwearable, the first Sunday after their marriage, by starching it all over, 'as stiff as a church.' She had spent two days on the job: neither of them knew how to get the starch out: and the bridegroom cursed his spouse as a good-for-nothing slattern. Such cases were coming before them every day. The handsome shawl which the lover so admired on Sundays was found to be pawned on Monday mornings, and redeemed on Saturday nights. All clothes had to be bought ready- made, and all food prepared, as far as it could be. The bread and the ham,—a shilling plate at the time,—were obtained on credit at the huckster's shop; and, to obtain that credit, every article of every sort had to be bought at that miscellaneous shop. The wives could not boil potatoes, nor mend stockings, nor wash a garment, nor even scrub the floor. These deficiencies sent pupils— married women as well as single—to the evening school, eager to learn. What was the consequence? A vast complacency in carrying home a garment of their 'own making,' and a desperate set-to at arithmetic in its ordinary form. The sorters could reckon by grosses, miraculously; but had no notion of pounds, shillings and pence: and, sooner or later, the notion dawned that it might be *worth while* to be comfortable at home, and that their teachers meant to show them how to manage it. At a more advanced period, came further discoveries. The wife who locked her door before daylight, and turned her back upon her home till dark, except on Sundays, obtained a good deal of money: for at that time women's factory wages had risen twenty-percent., and were still rising: but yet there was never any cash left over, and generally more or less debt at the huckster's shop. When able to keep accounts, even in the humblest way, the wife occasionally found a penny set down in. the shilling column,—not necessarily from dishonesty, for the small shopkeepers themselves are often very ill-educated. This discovery led to inquiry and thought; till the grand idea presented itself that it might answer better, even in regard to money, to stay at home than to work at the factory. No more

plates of ham or light loaves! no more expensive washing-bills, or heavy purchases of ready-made clothes, or fancy head-dresses which cost nearly a week's
wages! No more hard potatoes, smoky fires, and tea smoked accordingly! No
more damp, half-grimy floors on Saturday nights; nor husbands driven elsewhere in search of comfort! If they earned twelve shillings a week less, they
saved twelve shillings a week, and much of more valuable things that no
money can buy.

Since those early attempts at schools for wives were instituted, great
improvements in particular cases have become common: but there has not
yet been that distinct step in civilisation which gives every woman in a manufacturing town the clear understanding that she has to choose between being
an earner of money in a way which precludes her being a housewife, or being
qualified for a housewife, at the expense of some of her power of earning, but
with great power of saving her husband's earnings. We need not despair of
seeing girls so educated as that they may be capable of both employments;
and this is well, as there can be no expectation that, within any time we can
look forward to, the employment of women in factories will cease. If it is ever
superseded, it will not be by the labour of men, but by new inventions: and in
the interval, it will do no good to declaim, and exhort, and lament. We must
take in hand the evils of the case, and improve its conditions. We must see
whether we cannot make needlewomen and plain cooks of the little girls, and
sensible housewives as they grow up. This done, we suspect that not even the
best paid factory labour will throw them back to the point from which many
of the class are now rising.

This leads us on to the class of manufacturing operations which can be carried on by women in their own homes. As the era of female industrialism has
set in, indisputably and irreversibly, it is of the utmost importance to contemplate this phase of it, and to assist it as far as possible:—which means to
relieve it from oppression and hindrance. We need say nothing of the ordinary 'woman's work' which may be done at home,—the needlework of various kinds; nor of the weaving which men have long ceased to oppose. But
there are arts to which female faculties are particularly appropriate which
women cannot practise on account of the monopolising spirit of the men.
Take the watch-making business as an instance.

Watches are so dear in this country that labouring men, the working-class-
es generally, and young people of all but the wealthy orders, are placed at a
disadvantage about the use and economy of time, from the absence of the
means of measuring it. The dearness of watches is proved to be a gratuitous
evil, imposed by the mistaken selfishness of a small class of the community. In
this country 186,000 watches per annum are manufactured; and, as this goes
a very little way towards supplying the demand, there is a large importation
from Switzerland,—exceedingly profitable to somebody at our expense, as
the price of the article is kept up by the artificial scarcity at home. Now,—who

makes the watches that we import?—In the valleys of Switzerland, in the cot-
tages on the uplands, in the wildest recesses that men can inhabit, as well as
in the streets of the towns, there are women helping to make watches. We are
told that 20,000 women are actually so employed. Why not? The metal in the
inside of a watch costs about sixpence in its unwrought condition. By the
application of the fine touch so eminently possessed by women, guided by
their fine sight and observation, that sixpenny-worth of metal is so wrought
and adjusted as to become worth several pounds. If there are 20,000 Swiss
women at work at their own windows, with their children about them, and
their husband's dinner at the fire, making watches for Europe and America,
why are there not 40,000 Englishwomen helping the family independence in
the same way? Simply because the caste or guild of watchmakers will not permit it. We need not explain to our readers that the monopolists punish themselves, as well as the public, and tens of thousands of our countrywomen. In
Switzerland, the greater the number of women so employed, the greater the
number of men also. By simply meeting the demand for watches at home,
and yet more by preparing a due supply for America and our own colonies,
our watchmakers would open a new vein of employment and profit for themselves and their households. Instead of this, what do they do? One case which
fell under our own knowledge, is this:— The wife of a respectable watchmak-
er wished, as did her husband, that she should work with him at his special
division of the manufacture: but they dared not attempt it, under the eyes of
the craft. She therefore engraved the 'brass work,'—a commoner and easier
kind of work. As soon as the fact was discovered, an outcry was raised, and
intimidation was tried, to drive her from her occupation. She kept her husband steady to their household plan: but it was only by permitting their
friends to set up a plea of apprenticeship, on the ground of her father having
been seen to do that kind of work in her presence, that she obtained any
peace and quiet. She brought up her two daughters to the business, while
training them in housewifery as well. By this time we hope many daughters
and sisters are seen, as we have seen a few, enamelling the faces of watches,
polishing them, inscribing the hours, and conducting the nicest mysteries of
the art. If it is true, as we are assured, and as may well be, that the parts of
watches made by Swiss women are imported into this country, it seems impossible that our countrywomen should be long excluded from that province of
industry. It seems incredible that some thousands of foreign women should
be supported by making watches for us to buy dear, while thousands of needle women should be starving in London, for want of permission to supply us
with cheaper watches. Mr. Bennett's exertions seem to be making the case
clear to an increasing number of the public; and the time cannot be far distant when the tyranny of a virtual guild will be overthrown, like that of so
many actual guilds. As for the mode in which the change will be made,—we
may obtain a hint from the Swiss. The watchmakers are an educated class; and

the more highly they are educated the better are the watches they produce. The fact appears to be undisputed; and the lesson is sufficiently plain.

This last topic would naturally lead us to consider other arts, requiring a higher education, which women have found it difficult to get leave to practise: but we must first devote a few moments to the miserable class of poor needlewomen,—whether the makers of shirts and trowsers or of gowns and petticoats. The sempstresses are returned as nearly 61,000 at the time of the last census; and the milliners and dressmakers as nearly half a million.

The wretched dependents on the slop shops are suffering under the last struggles of their art with the improvements of the time. We see the sewing-machine coming into use. It will do great things; and it will bring in further methods which will extinguish the craft of the poor needlewoman. Already we hear of more than one establishment in London which uses seventy of these machines, each of which dispatches as much work as fifteen pairs of hands; and of provincial shops, where the introduction of one machine has caused the dismissal of thirty women and girls. At first, it was supposed that only long rows of plain work could be done in this way; but now we hear of shirt-collars, gloves, and other delicate pieces of stitching being done, as well as saddlery and harness- making, and shoes. Both the needle and the awl are largely superseded by it; and it can be managed by even young children. Thus is the case of poor needlewomen to be solved! They can scarcely be worse off than at present; and if the change should reintroduce the art of genuine sewing, our countrywomen will have reason to rejoice. At present, we hear it said, that the art of sewing seems wellnigh lost in England, except among the ladies who have a taste for it, or who were trained by an unfashionable grandmother. The superiority of French *lingères* to English sempstresses is most remarkable, and proves that the handiwork of sewing is far better taught and practised in France than in England.

No machinery can supersede sewing altogether, though it may, and ought to, extinguish slopmaking at fourpence a day: and whereas scarcely a good sempstress can now be obtained, for love or money, we may hope to witness so much restoration of the art as is needed for economy and neatness. It is not desirable to wear out eyes, and spend precious time in marking letters, with a fine needle and coloured thread, on a cambric handkerchief, when we are in possession of marking inks, and practised in drawing with a free hand: but we must have a release from the ragged edges, loose buttons, galling shirt-collars, and unravelled seams and corners which have come up as the quality of needlewomen has gone down. Let our wives undertake the case of the remnant of the poor sempstress,—the last, we hope, of their sort. Many may be retained for the management of sewing-machines. Many may emigrate, under careful arrangements. The younger may possibly be even yet taught to sew properly, or to do something else that is useful; and all might, by a sufficient and well-concerted effort, be kept out of the hands of the middleman.

That department of the industrial market is undergoing vital changes. If some thousands of suffering women are to see their loathed occupation extinguished, the ladies of England should see that the two or three millions of girls who are soon to be maintaining themselves by their industry shall be exercised in all household arts, (and the needle, not last nor least) as the proper foundation of all others. In order to justify our estimate of the value of good needlework, and also to give pleasure to our readers, we cite a passage from a Report of one of the Inspectors of Schools, Rev. J.P. Norris, in the Privy Council Minutes for 1855.

'It appears to me that girls' schools have a great advantage over boys' schools, in the fact that nearly half the day is spent in industrial work. Independently of the practical value of skill in needle work, it would be well worth while, for the sake of the effect on the girls' characters, to occupy half their time at school in this way. No one can have marked the quiet domestic aspect of one of our better girls' schools when arranged for needlework, the scrupulous cleanliness which their work necessitates, the continual interchange of kindly offices and that most wholesome union, which a boys' school seldom presents, of industry with repose, of a cheerful relaxation of mind, with the most careful and decorous order, without seeing at once that it is here rather than during the morning lessons that the character of the future woman is formed. When we add to these considerations the paramount importance of skill in needlework, picturing to ourselves the contrast that a few short years will show between the slattern, in her cheap tawdry show-finery, and the white-aproned tidy housewife, with her knitting in her hands, or a shirt for her husband in her lap, we shall, I think, be more than ever anxious that this most valuable department of schoolwork should not be neglected. It has often occurred to me that one serious objection to mixed schools is the great probability of the needlework being slighted. The girls, thus brought into competition with the boys, regret the time spent away from their books. And, besides, the afternoon sempstress will appear to disadvantage when compared with the more intellectual morning teacher; her authority will come to be slighted, and the discipline will be impaired. I have often found that in these schools the girls get a notion that the needlework is of little or no consequence; and, with few exceptions, all the schools that produce the best needlewomen in my district are separate girls' schools.' (pp. 480, 481.)

To return to the difficulties created by the jealousy of men in regard to the industrial independence of women:—it shows itself with every step gained in civilisation; and its immediate effect is to pauperise a large number of women who are willing to work for their bread; and, we need not add, to condemn to perdition many more who have no choice left but between starvation and vice. The jealousy which keeps Coventry women from the employment of engraving the brass work of a watch, and from pasting patterns of floss-silk upon cards, for trade purposes, long kept the doors of the School of Design in London closed against female pupils, and renders it still almost impossible for an Englishwoman to qualify herself for treating the diseases of women and children. The same jealousy cost many lives in the late war, by delaying the reception of the nurses into the hospitals in the East, and by restricting their action when there. In the Staffordshire potteries women are largely employed in painting porcelain,—an art which they are better qualified to practise than men. It will hardly be credited, but we can vouch for the fact, that such is the jealousy of the men that they compel the women *to paint without a rest for the hand,* and the masters are obliged by their own workmen to sanction this absurd act of injustice.

The immediate and obvious consequence is, that women who must earn their bread are compelled to do it by one of two methods,—by the needle or by becoming educators. Often and emphatically as this has been said, we must say it again in this place; but we need not go into the description either of the miseries of needle women or of the tremendous mischief done by driving shoals of incompetent persons into the ranks of educators. Good and qualified governesses are as sensible of the evil as the employing class; and they are perhaps as keenly afflicted by it. The only certain remedy is to leave open every possible way to employments of the most various kinds that are suitable to the abilities of women. The merely incompetent instructress would never have placed herself in a position so painful and precarious if a way had been open to support herself by something that she could do better. The injury to the qualified governesses is cruel. The reputation of the whole class suffers by the faults of its lowest members; the emolument is depressed, first by the low average quality of the work done, and again by the crowded condition of that field of labour. The wretched condition of many of these unfortunate persons can hardly be exaggerated. We find under our eyes the following passage in one of the Reports of the 'Governesses' Benevolent Institution':—

'On a recent occasion, there were one hundred and twenty candidates for three annuities of twenty pounds each. One hundred and twenty ladies, many reared in affluence, and all accustomed to the comforts and luxuries of at least our middle ranks—all seeking an annuity of twenty pounds! Of these, ninety-nine were unmarried; and, out of this number, fourteen had incomes of, or above, twenty pounds (eleven of which were derived from public institutions or private benevolence, and *three* from their own savings); twenty-three had incomes varying from one pound to seventeen pounds; and eighty-three had absolutely *nothing.* It will be recollected that all these ladies are above fifty years of age; and, of the utterly destitute, forty-nine were above sixty.'

One way out of the desperate position is obvious and open. It is now a recognised truth that education is an art requiring instruction and training, as much as the function of the divine, the physician, and the lawyer; and the unprepared are cast out, more and more every day. The immediate misery thus caused is dreadful. It is that of the hand-loom weaver, and the slop-makers, with the aggravation that the sufferers' are, generally speaking, gentlewomen by birth, and universally accustomed to the comforts, and many of the luxuries, of life. It would open a dismal chapter to show how many of them have reversed the old rule of woman's destiny,—that of being supported by father, brother or husbands,—having given all their earnings to pay a father's debts, to sustain an idle or struggling brother's professional appearance, or to indulge the vices, or to neutralise the shiftlessness, of a husband. Facts seem to show that the proportion of governesses who have the advantage and use of their own earnings is very small. Instead of such just and pleasant results of their industry as a small independence at a time of life when some power of gratuitous usefulness and of enjoyment of ease is left, we read, till sheer pain of heart stops us, of the cases which come before the Governesses' Institution:—old age, or impaired health in middle age, amidst perfect destitution; failing sight, paralysed limbs, over-wrought brain, and no resource or prospect whatever; though (or because) the sufferers have supported orphans, saved a father from bankruptcy, educated brothers, or kept infirm and helpless relatives off the rates.We need not go on. The evil is plain enough. The remedies seem to be equally clear;—to sustain and improve the modern tests of the quality of educators; and to open broad and new ways for the industrial exertions of women; or at least to take care that such as open naturally are not arbitrarily closed.

The function of industry which might be supposed to be always standing wide for women is not in fact so,—the nursing function in all its directions, in private dwellings, in work-houses, in hospitals and in lunatic asylums, where it is at least as much wanted as anywhere else. We shall not argue it, or plead for it here. Florence Nightingale and her disciples have inaugurated a new period in the history of working-women, and the manifest destiny of the nursing class will fulfil itself.

There may be more difficulty about the kindred function,—that of the physician and surgeon: but it cannot long be a difficulty. The jealousy of the medical profession is, to be sure, proverbial: but it is not universal. From our youth up, some of us have known how certain of the wisest and most appreciated of physicians have insisted that the health of women and their children will never be guarded as it ought to be till it is put under the charge of physicians of their own sex. The moral and emotional considerations involved in this matter need no discussion. What has been done in the most advanced of the United States of America, where social conditions most nearly resemble those of England, shows what will be done here, and very soon. Some of the medical colleges have, after long opposition, or protracted deliberation, admitted ladies as students, and have conferred degrees; so that several of the cities have the blessing of highly qualified female physicians. The thing could not have been done without the sanction and practical encouragement of some of the first professional men in the community. That sanction and encouragement have been freely rendered, and are still continued, so that there is now a history of the change to be told. There are charters and grants of money by state legislatures for dispensaries, and medical colleges, and attendant hospitals, for the training and practice of female physicians, an increasing number of whom are established in the great cities from year to year. Dr. Elizabeth Blackwell, whose excellent work on the 'Laws of Health' is one of the list which heads this article, led the way; and by the influence of her high character, attainments, and success, she has conquered prejudice, and established the enterprise. In our country, more time will, no doubt, be required. Prejudices are stronger; the capabilities of women are less tested and understood; and social service is not so earnest as in the younger country: but, if English physicians of two generations ago desired and foretold the change, it is for us to reckon confidently on it. In the branch of practice too much encroached upon by ignorant poor women, a few desultory efforts have been made, with no other success than preparing the way for more. Mrs. Hockley was a professional accoucheur for many years, and in excellent reputation. Dr. Spencer, of Bristol, educated his daughter for the same office; but the prejudice was too strong for her endurance, and she entered the ranks of governesses, where her honour and success indicated what her career as a physician might have been. The institution of the medical profession as a career for women in any one country facilitates its opening every where else; and we have no doubt whatever of the approaching conversion or supersession of such opponents as would deny the means of special training to educated women who demand it.

There remain the classes which speak so well for themselves as to leave others little to say;—the artists and authors. Here nature indicates the path of action; and all that we are practically concerned with is that her behests are not disobeyed,—her guidance not perverted,—her elect not oppressed, through our mismanagement. A Jenny Lind cannot be stopped in her singing, nor a Siddons in her dramatic career, nor a Currer Bell in her authorship, by any opposition of fortune: but none of us can tell how many women of less force and lower genius may have been kept useless and rendered unhappy, to our misfortune as much as their own. We have adverted to the opposition made to opening Schools of Design to female students. We must permit no more obstruction of that kind, but rather supply the educational links that are wanted, if we would render the powers and the industry of women available to the welfare of society. For one instance;—it is a good thing to admit students freely to Schools of Design, and to train them there:

and it is a good thing that manufacturers of textile and metal productions employ women at rising wages, in proportion to their qualifications. But there is a chasm between the training and the work which requires bridging. The greater part of the higher order of designs are practically unavailable, for want of knowledge on the part of the designer of the conditions of the particular manufacture in question. The economic possibility and aptitude are not studied; and hence, the manufacturers say, an enormous waste of thought, skill, and industry. This want supplied, a field of industry practically boundless would be opened to female artists, as well as artisans; and it would be an enlightened policy to look to this, while the whole world seems to be opening its ports to our productions.

It seems not very long ago that the occupation of the Taylor family, of Ongar, was regarded as very strange. The delightful Jane Taylor of Ongar and her sisters paid their share of the family expenses by engraving. Steel engravings were not then in very great demand; yet those young women were incessantly at work,—so as to be abundantly weary of it,—as Jane's letters plainly show. For a quarter of a century past, many hundreds of young women, we are assured, have supported themselves by wood engraving, for which there is now a demand which no jealousy in the stronger sex can intercept. The effort to exclude the women *was* made, in this as in other branches of art; but the interests of publishers and the public were more than a match for it. One of the most accomplished 'hands' in this elegant branch of art has built herself a country house with the proceeds of her chisel; and will no doubt furnish it by those of her admirable paintings on glass.

Strangely enough, the Report before us lumps together the female artists, authors, and teachers, so that we have no means of knowing the numbers of each. They are set down collectively at 644,336. The artists have an unlimited field before them; and the annual exhibition of the works of female artists proves the disposition to occupy it. The contributors have it now in their power to ascertain whether there is any other than an educational barrier in the way of their attainment of excellence in painting and sculpture. Lord Lyndhurst said the other day, in stating to the House of Lords the claim which the Royal Academy of Arts undoubtedly has to the respect and gratitude of the public, that all Her Majesty's subjects have a right to the gratuitous instruction afforded by the first artists in the country to the students who attend its classes, on the simple condition of good moral character and a competent knowledge of elementary drawing. But women are not at present included in this our principal National School of Arts, though, from the use they make of the National Gallery, no class of students would derive greater advantage from it. This deficiency should be remedied. Photography has annihilated the secondary class of miniature-painting, which a considerable number of female artists practised with success. But photography itself has opened an enlarged field to their industry, both in the operations of that art and in the application of painting to it.

We look to cultivated women also for the improvement of our national character as tasteful manufacturers. It is only the inferiority of our designs which prevents our taking the lead of the world in our silks, ribbons, artificial flowers, paper-hangings, carpets and furniture generally. Our Schools of Design were instituted to meet this deficiency: and they have made a beginning: but the greater part of the work remains to be done; and it is properly women's work. There is no barrier of jealousy in the case, for our manufacturers are eager to secure good designs from any quarter.

For the rest, the female artists can take very good care of themselves. Music will be listened to, if it is good; and sculpture and painting must assert their own merits. Miss Herschel sat unmolested in her brother's observatory, discovering comets; and Mrs. Somerville became a mathematician in a quiet way, and after her own fashion. Our countrywomen have the free command of the press; and they use it abundantly. Every woman who has force of character enough to conceive any rational enterprise of benevolence is sure to carry it through, after encountering more or less opposition. For a Catherine Mompesson, supported by her husband's companionship in a plague-stricken village two centuries ago, we have had a Mary Pickard doing exactly the same work, but alone, within our own century. Mrs. Fry in Newgate, Florence Nightingale and Mrs. Bracebridge at Scutari; Miss Dix reforming lunatic asylums; Sarah Pellatt reclaiming the Californian gold-diggers from drink; Mary Carpenter among her young city Arabs: all these, and several more, are proofs that the field of action is open to women as well as men, when they find something for their hand to do, and do it with all their might.

Out of six millions of women above twenty years of age, in Great Britain, exclusive of Ireland, and of course of the Colonies, no less than half are industrial in their mode of life. More than a third, more than two millions, are independent in their industry, are self-supporting, like men. The proceedings in the new Divorce Court, and in matrimonial cases before the police-magistrates, have caused a wide-spread astonishment at the amount of female industry they have disclosed. Almost every aggrieved wife who has sought protection, has proved that she has supported her household, and has acquired property by her effective exertions. It is probable that few of our readers have ever placed this great fact before their minds for contemplation and study: yet it is one which cannot safely be neglected or made light of. The penalty of such neglect or carelessness is an encroachment of pauperism at one end of the scale, and the most poisonous of vices at the other. How do we meet the conditions which stare us in the face? Mr. Norris's Report supplies us with the answer.

'But I much fear the chief reason that more is not done in this direction, is the very general apathy that prevails in the matter of girls' education. Why is it that, where you find three or four good boys' schools, you will find barely one efficient girls' school? Why is it that in pamphlets, and speeches, and schemes of so-called national education, they are almost uniformly ignored? The reasons are twofold: a very large number of the people who are interested in the progress of education think of it only in connexion with our national wealth; they mean by education the extension of skill and knowledge as essential elements of productiveness, and, therefore, with them, girls' schooling is a matter of little or no moment. Another still larger class of persons, who, from native illiberality of mind, are opposed to all education, though ashamed to confess this generally, do no blush to own it with respect to girls. So that on either hand the girls' school is neglected. And what is the result? For want of good schools for girls three out of four of the girls in my district are sent to miserable private schools, where they have no religious instruction, no discipline, no industrial training; they are humoured in every sort of conceit, are called "Miss Smith" and "Miss Brown," and go into service at fourteen or fifteen, skilled in crochet and worsted work, but unable to darn a hole or cut out a frock, hating household work, and longing to be milliners or ladies' maids. While this is called education, no wonder that people cry out that education is ruining our servants, and doing more harm than good!

But there are other evil results arising from the neglect of girls' education, far more serious than the want of good servants;—as the girl is, so will the woman be; as the woman is, so will the home be; and as the home is, such, for good or for evil, will be the character of our population. My belief is, that England will never secure the higher benefits expected to result from national education, until more attention is paid to girls' schools. No amount of mere knowledge, religious or secular, given to boys, will secure them from drunkenness or crime in after life. It may be true that knowledge is power, but knowledge is not virtue. It is in vain for us to multiply the means of instruction, and then sit down and watch the criminal returns in daily expectation of seeing in them the results of our schooling. If we wish to arrest the growth of national vice, we must go to its real seminary, *the home.* Instead of that thriftless untidy woman who presides over it, driving her husband to the gin palace by the discomfort of his own house, and marring for life the temper and health of her own child by her own want of sense, we must train up one who will be a cleanly careful housewife, and a patient skilful mother. Until one or two generations have been improved, we must trust mainly to our schools to effect this change in the daughters of the working classes. We must multiply over the face of the country girls' school of a sensible and practical sort. The more enlightened women of England must come forward and take the matter into their own hands, and do for our girls what Mrs. Fry did for our prisons, what Miss Carpenter has done for our reformatories, what Miss Nightingale and Miss Stanley are doing for our hospitals.' (*Minutes on Education,* 1855-6, pp. 482, 283.)

Further illustrations may be found in the group of good books with which we have prefaced these remarks. The volume on the 'Industrial and Social Position of Women,' and the Reports of the Census and the School Inspectors, are written by men; and the rest are even more worthy of attention as being by women, who best know their own case, though they must appeal to us to aid them in obtaining free scope for their industry. The tale is plain enough,—from whatever mouth it comes. So far from our countrywomen being all maintained, as a matter of course, by us 'the breadwinners,' three millions out of six of adult Englishwomen work for subsistence; and two out of the three in independence. With this new condition of affairs, new duties and new views must be accepted. Old obstructions must be removed; and the aim must be set before us, as a nation as well as in private life, to provide for the free development and full use of the powers of every member of the community. In other words, we must improve and extend education to the utmost; and then open a fair field to the powers and energies we have educed. This will secure our welfare, nationally and in our homes, to which few elements can contribute more vitally and more richly than the independent industry of our countrywomen.

Source: Reprinted from *Edinburgh Review* (April 1859).

BIOGRAPHICAL NOTE

Harriet Martineau, journalist, sociologist and historian, was one of eight children born to Thomas Martineau, a Norwich textile manufacturer, and Elizabeth Rankin, daughter of a wholesale grocer and sugar refiner. By her own account, her childhood was grimly unhappy as it was dominated by a stern, demanding mother. Although emotionally deprived, Martineau benefitted from her parents' Unitarianism which supported education for girls. She was taught at home, mainly by her older brothers and sisters, and became a serious student of Political Economy, the classical economic and social theory underpinning Utilitarian philosophy.

Martineau's first publication, "Female Writers of Practical Divinity" (1820) for the Unitarian journal *Monthly Repository*, was quickly followed by her first published book, *Devotional Exercises for the Use of Young Persons* (1823). When her father's death in 1826 plunged the family into a financial crisis, Martineau continued the writing she loved as a means to support herself, her mother, and her aunt. Unable to turn to governessing because of her deafness, she moved to London to live with an aunt and uncle, doing needlework by day and writing by night. Her book reviews for the *Monthly Repository* gave her a much needed supplementary income. Suddenly recalled to Norwich by her mother, Martineau's literary career was briefly threatened by domestic obligations, but she was soon writing prize-winning essays on Unitarianism in the *Monthly Repository*. Permitted by her mother to spend three months of the year in London, Martineau was quickly engrossed in a project to illustrate political economy for the ordinary reader. After enormous difficulties finding a publisher, her *Illustrations of Political Economy*, a series of twenty-five monthly parts appearing from 1832-1834, catapulted her to financial independence and enormous literary success.

On the proceeds of her series, Martineau travelled to America. Her return to England in 1836 ushered in a period of quite intense literary production. Her two books, *Society in America* (1837) and *Retrospect of Western Travel* (1838), explored America's failure to live up to its democratic ideals. The chapter, "The Political Non-Existence of Women," from *Society in America* is notable as an extremely early argument for women's full political rights. Her novel, *Deerbrook* (1839) was also published. Later in that same year, she became seriously ill and moved to Tynemouth in order to be under the care of her brother-in-law physician, Thomas Greenhow. It has been suggested that Martineau's illness was psychological, an unconscious attempt to avoid family responsibilities. However, after her death, an autopsy revealed a twelve-inch long uterine tumour.

Her five years at Tynemouth were characteristically productive, despite the acute pain caused by her illness. She wrote *Life in the Sickroom* (1844), an unusual account of the effects of long-term illness. She also published *The Crofton Boys*, one of four stories for children later collected and published as *The Playfellow* (1841-1843). During this time she agreed to be mesmerized for relief from her pain. She considered the process successful, though the relief was probably due to a shift in the position of the tumour. She wrote up her faith in mesmerism in "Six Letters on Mesmerism," published in the *Athenaeum* in 1844. Many of her family considered these letters a public insult to her brother-in-law. He retaliated with a pamphlet, *A Medical Report of the Case of Miss H—— M——*, offering a detailed gynecological description of her symptoms in support of his case.

The controversy caused a great rift between Martineau and the rest of her family. To escape it she moved to The Knoll, Ambleside, the home she had newly built for herself. Here she lived, pain free and active, for ten years. The first book written here, *The History of the Peace* (1849), a history of England between 1816-1846 was very popular, and she was soon travelling again, this time to the Middle East. Her *Eastern Life Past and Present* (1848) was followed by *Letters on the Laws of Man's Nature and Development* (1851), an account of her rejection of religion. Throughout this time at Ambleside, Martineau aimed to put her ideas and theories into day-to-day practice, presenting a series of lectures on sanitation, the principle of building societies, the stomach and the brain, and temperance to local working families.

She also became leader writer on the London *Daily News*, writing some sixteen hundred leaders, letters, and obituaries in her sixteen years there. Her journalism played a particularly significant role in the blossoming women's movement. Her 1859 article for the prestigious *Edinburgh Review*, "Female Industry" reprinted here, prompted the poet and feminist Adelaide Proctor to establish the Society for the Promotion of the Employment of Women. The essay was singled out by Emily Faithfull in the *English Woman's Journal* as "a fuller account of the actual state of female industry in this country than had perhaps ever been previously brought before the notice of the public" (*EWJ* 6 [1860]: 121]. Other writings in the *Daily Mail* on the Contagious Diseases Acts, which permitted the compulsory examination and treatment for venereal disease of any woman in a garrison town believed to be a prostitute, warned against the threat to women's liberty. Martineau's name later headed the memorial from the newly organized Ladies National Association for the Repeal of the Contagious Diseases Act, inaugurating a campaign that was to last another twenty-three years.

The onset of deteriorating health in 1855 convinced Martineau that she was about to die, and prompted her to begin writing her autobiography. In fact she lived for nearly twenty more years; her autobiography, *Harriet Martineau's Autobiography, with Memorials by Maria Weston Chapman* (1877) was published after her death in 1876.

Selected Secondary Sources

David, Deirdre. *Intellectual Women and Victorian Patriarchy*. Ithaca: Cornell UP, 1987.

Harper, Lisa Marz. *Solitary Travellers: Nineteenth-Century Women's Travel Narratives and the Scientific Vocation*. Madison: Fairleigh Dickinson UP, 2001.

Hoecker, Susan Drysdale. *Harriet Martineau: First Woman Sociologist*. London: St. Martin's Press, 1992.

Pichanick, Valerie Kossew. *Harriet Martineau: The Woman and her Work, 1802-1876*. Ann Arbor: U of Michigan P, 1980.

FRANCES POWER COBBE
(1822-1904)

"CELIBACY V. MARRIAGE"

How to be Happy though Married, was the rather significant title of a quaint little treatise of the seventeenth century, still to be perused in old libraries. "Le mariage," says Fénelon, "est on état de tribulation très pénible auquel il faut se préparer en esprit de penitence quand on s'y croit appellé"*[1] Between these views of holy matrimony and those popularly attributed to Belgravian mothers, there exists so vast a difference that we cannot but suggest (considering the importance of the subject), that the Social Science Association should appoint a special department to examine the matter. Male and female reformers would find topics for many interesting papers in debating the relative benefits to society of "selfish domestic felicity," and sublimely "disinterested celibacy," as now inculcated from many quarters. An able article has lately appeared in a contemporary periodical, entitled "Keeping up Appearances." It propounds, in brief, the following doctrine:—"That it is not a question of appearances, but of very substantial realities, whether a family in the rank of gentlefolk have to live on three or four hundred a year in England; that where this is the case it is impossible but that Paterfamilias, be he lawyer, doctor, divine, or man of letters, must needs, in all his ways and works, regard, *not* the pure aim of his profession, but the pecuniary interests involved therein. His wife is oppressed with household cares, and his children have hardly the means of health and suitable education. Under these circumstances, no man with common feelings can act with the same disregard of mercenary considerations as he might do were he living alone on an income sufficient to supply his bachelor necessities." He must needs "keep an eye to the main chance," and consider at all moments, how will it pay for me to act in this manner? Can I afford to offend this influential man, to write this outspoken book, to preach this unpopular doctrine? Thus we arrive at the very awkward conclusion that all the most gifted and devoted men who do not happen to inherit £1,000 a year, or to fall in love with an heiress, are bound in honour never to marry, at least until that goodly maturity of years when their professional earnings may have realized such an income. In a word, all our best men must be celibates—all our women who marry at all must put up with rather mercenary husbands (always excepting elder sons), and all the children of the next generation must be born of parents the least likely to convey to them any remarkable faculties or exalted principles. Ragnarok, of course, may be expected in the ensuing century.

---

* Marriage is a state of such painful tribulation that it is necessary to prepare oneself in a spirit of penitence when one is called upon [Editor's note].

Now this argument is much too cogent in itself, and much too well urged from really noble points of view, not to deserve serious investigation. If it be indeed true that no married man with small means can be perfectly disinterested, than we have come upon a new and most important item to be added to that sum of objections to wedlock, which the present order of things is daily bringing forward. As the expediency system of ethics is passing out of men's minds, the notion gains ground that all true work must be *disinterested* work. We begin dimly to perceive the truth that in human nature there are too great forces, one all noble and generous; the centrifugal force of LOVE, which carries us out of and above ourselves; the other, all base and narrow, the centripetal force of SELFISM, which brings us back to our own personal interests and desires. Every profession may be followed in one or other of these ways. Statescraft, war, science, art, philanthropy, may be pursued from pure love of our country or our kind, pure devotion to truth, or beauty, or justice. Or, on the other hand, they may be followed from selfish ambition, personal interest, and vanity. Our *affections* obey the same law, for we may love our friends for their own sakes, and be willing to give our happiness for theirs; or we may love them merely for our selfish gratification in their intercourse, striving not to make them better and happier, but to narrow them heart and soul to ourselves. Our *moral* natures are in the same case, for we may obey the law of duty from simple allegiance to the eternal right, with the motto in our hearts, *Fais ce que doit advienne que pourra;** or we may be just, and true, and charitable, for the sake of human reward on earth or celestial payment in heaven. And, finally, even *religion* may be pure, or may be selfish. We may love God himself because He is supremely, infinitely good, and worthy of the love of all the hearts He has made; or we may serve Him with souls filled with servile fears and selfish hopes, favoured servants in a disfavoured universe, offering to the holy Lord of Good the homage which Ecloge and Actè paid to Nero.

Yes! If anything good, or noble, is ever to be done on earth, it must be done *disinterestedly*. The man of action and the man of thought must alike work because they love the true, the good, the beautiful, and genuinely desire (each in his own way) to realize them on earth. If their own interest cannot be wholly forgotten, yet it must be entirely subordinated to the nobler aim. The clergyman must preach what he finds to be true; the statesman legislate as he thinks right; the poet write what he feels to be beautiful; and none of them deign to consider —Will this sermon stop my preferment? Will the Act of Parliament offend my party? Will this book draw on me the lash of such a Review? He who truly achieves any good on earth, must surely do it in this spirit of disinterested devotion.

Now is it true that marriage without wealth must curb and check all these nobler impulses? Must the husband and father be a baser man, at all events a less true and brave one, than he was as a bachelor? If not selfish for himself,

---

* Do what should be done, come what may [Editor's note].

must he now grow wife-selfish, child-selfish, interested for those who belong to him, as he would disdain to be for himself?

It must be admitted this is a difficult question. There seems no small danger that the answer must be one which would land us in the monstrous conclusion that the condition which God has appointed as the natural one for human beings, is calculated inevitably to debase their purest aspirations. To find a less deplorable solution, let us go further back on our problem. What have we assumed a wife to be? A wholly passive medium of expenditure, like a conservatory or a pack of hounds?

The author of the article under debate admits with astonishing candour, that the *woman's* interest and happiness are necessarily sacrificed by the proper fulfilment of the man's destiny. He quotes Kingsley's aphorism with approbation—

Man must work and woman must weep.

Truly this conclusion, whereby no inconsiderable portion of the human race is consigned to the highly unprofitable occupation of "weeping," might have excited some doubts of the accuracy of the foregoing ratiocinations. It is not easy, we should suppose, for women generally to accept this matter of "weeping" as the proper end of their creation! At all events, if they occasionally indulge henceforth in the solace of tears, we cannot believe they will shed them for the loss of the connubial felicity to be enjoyed with those "workers," who so readily appoint them such a place in the order of the world.

Leaving aside, however, this piece of "muscular sociology," let us seriously inquire whether the true destiny of woman, if rightly understood, would not serve to make right this puzzle of life, and show that *if the wife were what the wife should be*, the husband would not need to grow more mercenary and more worldly to supply her wants, but would rather find her pure and religious influence raise him to higher modes of thinking, and a nobler and more devoted life, than either man or woman can attain alone.

The *actual* fact must, alas! be admitted. The cares of a family have a tendency to make a man interested; and what is much worse, the wife too frequently uses her influence the wrong way, and prompts her husband even to more worldly and prudential considerations than he would be inclined spontaneously to entertain.

Woman's natural refinement leads her to give too high a value to outward polish, and, consequently, to tend always to seek social intercourse above her own natural circle. It is nearly always the *wives* of shopkeepers, merchants, professional men, and the smaller gentry, who are found pushing their families into the grade a step higher, and urging the often-recalcitrant husband to the needful toadyism and expenditure. Woman is Conservative, or rather feudal, by instinct, if she be not by some accident vehemently prejudiced the other way;

and her unacknowledged but very real political influence is constantly exercised to check aspirations after progress of the rational kind

> Of Freedom slowly broadening down
> From precedent to precedent.

Worse than all, the education she now receives, makes her a bigot in religion. To *her*, the sources of wider and broader thought on the greatest of all subjects, are usually closed from childhood. The result is, that a timid and narrow creed constantly fetters the natural religious instincts of her heart, and she can exercise in no degree the influence over her husband's soul which her genuine piety might otherwise effect. If he venture to speak to her of the limits of his belief, she gives him reproach instead of sympathy; if he tell her he doubts the conclusions of her favourite preacher, she bursts into tears! Men have kept women from all share in the religious progress of the age, and the deplorable result is, that women are notoriously the drags on that progress. Instead of feeling like their Teuton forefathers, that their wives were "in nearer intercourse with the divinity than men," the Englishmen of to-day feel that their wives are the last persons with whom they can seek sympathy on religious matters. Half with tenderness for their good hearts, half with contempt for their weak minds, they leave them to the faith of the nursery, and seek for congenial intercourse only among men, hardheaded and honest, perhaps, in the fullest degree, yet without a woman's native spring of trust and reverence.

All these things tend to make wives fail in performing their proper part of inspiring feelings of devotion to noble causes. And further, a woman's ignorance of real life leads her to attach to outward show a value which it actually bears only in the opinion of other women as foolish as herself, and by no means in the eyes of anything which deserves to be called society at large. The *real* world—"the world of women and men,"

> Alive with sorrow and sin,
> Alive with pain and with passion,

does *not* concern itself so very earnestly with the number of the domestics and the antiquity of the millinery of its friends, as these ladies fondly imagine. Mrs. Grundy *lives*—she is a fact; but she is a very small and unimportant fact in life. Anybody with an ounce of pluck may cut Mrs. Grundy dead in the street, and never be troubled by her again. People do want some few things to make up their ideas of a gentleman or a lady, but they are not exactly what may be bought for even twice as many hundreds a year as our author has supposed, nor yet forfeited by the loss of any amount of stock in the Bank. A friend long resident in Italy, on reading these formidable statements, asked us ironically, "Pray, how many hundreds a year does it take to make a gentleman in England, and how many more go to making a lady?" No! we are not fallen so low as all this. Let a man or woman be honourable, refined, well-bred, agreeable in conversation: then there is little chance they will be turned out of the sphere to which they were born, because they keep two servants instead of a dozen, and use a hired cab instead of a carriage. It is miserable odious "flunkeyism" which attaches such infinite importance to these things; and the books of our day which represent them as holding the most prominent place in the thoughts of men, are utterly false to the realities of our social state. *Vanity Fair* is one stage of Pilgrim's Progress, but there are fifty others. To represent English social life as if it were the ineffable mass of meanness these books would make it, is a libel against human nature at which it is marvellous men do not rise in scorn and indignation.

"Ay—but," observed to us once a well-known writer, "all this meanness *is* a part of life! It is competent, then, to an author, if he please, to make it the staple of his fictions."

"And give them as true pictures of human nature?" we demanded. "Yes, surely."

"We were in Egypt this year," we answered. "Suppose we gave an account of our *impressions de voyage*, and omitted all mention of the Nile, the Pyramids, the Sphinx, the palm-trees, and only described accurately certain small nocturnal troublers of our repose? Would that be a fair description of grand old Egypt? You know it would be quite *true?* There *were* those Becky Sharps!"

It is needless to discuss at any length how a wife's belief that these outward "appearances" are of real importance, must unfit her for properly meeting the problems of a limited income. She thinks it a good investment to expend on show, what would suffice to procure very substantial comforts. There *is* a great truth in the *Times*' observation—"All the meaner and more miserable part of economical cares and discussions refers to 'appearances;' for the sense of pettiness and shame cannot attach to the actual needs of health and comfort, but only to the aspect our poverty may bear in the eyes of those whom we are senseless enough to wish should suppose us to be rich." In particular, the wives of poor gentlemen seem almost invariably to make it a point of conscience to dress with more richness and variety than those of wealthy men. Delicate taste and a generally ladylike appearance will not suffice,—they must *prove* they are not poor, precisely because all their acquaintances know that they are so. Moire antique is the invariable uniform of the wives of unsuccessful physicians, briefless barristers, and younger sons.

But supposing these mistakes of women removed; suppose (what ought to be the ordinary course of the marriages of professional men) that the wife brings a portion which covers her added share of the joint household, and that she expends the common income judiciously. Here is the material basis for a well-ordered life. Now, does it appear that the husband in such a case is likely to be less disinterested than he was when he was single? There is only one answer. It depends on the wife's own character. If she encourage him in every noble aim and disinterested action, it will hardly happen but that he will keep up to his former standard—nay, rise far above it. On the other hand, if she urge selfish considerations at every turn; if she palliate meanness and deprecate self-sacrifice;—then indeed the natural temptations of avarice and selfish ambition *have* a most powerful, almost an invincible ally in the wife, faithless to her holy duty of sustaining her husband's soul in life's great battle.

It is little understood how in all human relations the moral influences we begin by exercising, go on re-acting *ad infinitum* from one to the other in proportion to the closeness of the relationship. A (we will suppose) starts, by a little weak fondness, encouraging B to some small piece of selfishness or indolence, because he is fatigued. B cannot well help returning the compliment shortly, and making excuses for A not performing some duty on account of the weather. Next day it is an unkind sentiment, which passes unchecked; then a harsh word; and so on and so on. On the other hand, if, with whatever effort, the one encourage the other to exert himself—to sacrifice comfort for duty—to think kindly of disagreeable people—to speak only what is right and sincere,—then from that side also comes an influence raising step by step the virtue of the other. In higher ways still, the same truth holds good. Any two people who live much together (even in less tender connexion than husband and wife), cannot fail most importantly to colour each other's views of the great purposes of life. Live with one to whom the centripetal force of Selfism is paramount, and it is hardly possible to avoid contemplating everything from a selfish point of view. Live with one for ever carried beyond his own interests by the centrifugal force of pure Love for truth, for right, for man, for God, and it is impossible but that the divine fire in such a breast will kindle the embers in our own, till we blush to remember we have lived for lower aims and our own poor paltry happiness.

These discussions on the moral aspects of marriage assume a special significance at this moment, since from many other quarters obstacles are arising which must all tend towards rendering (for a long time, at least) celibacy more and more common and desirable. We have heard, perhaps, more than enough of these obstacles on the *man's* side. Let us, therefore, turn for a moment to consider those which must render women less willing than formerly to enter into such relation.

In the first place, till lately the condition of an unmarried woman of the upper classes was so shackled by social prejudices that it was inevitably a dreary and monotonous one. Mostly, the "old maid" lived in a small house or lodging, out of which she rarely dared to sally on any journey, and where, with a few female friends as closely limited as herself, she divided her life, as the Frenchman has it, between "*la médisance, le jeu, et la dévotion.*"* A society of these unhappy ones was once not inappropriately nicknamed by a witty noblemen

---

* Gossip, amusement, and devotion [Editor's note].

"the Bottled Wasps." It is half piteous, half ridiculous, to hear of the trifles which occupy these poor shrivelled hearts and minds. We once called on a very worthy and even clever member of the sisterhood residing in Bath. Her features were discomposed—her voice somewhat shriller than usual. We inquired considerately of the cause of affliction.

"I am going to leave my lodgings."

"I am sorry to hear it. They seem very nice."

"Yes, yes; but I can bear it no longer! Do you not observe there are two mats in the passage—one at the hall-door, one at the door of my room?" "It escaped my notice."

"Well, there they are. And for seven-and-twenty times—I have counted them!—seven-and-twenty times the people of the house have passed by the mat at the hall door and come and wiped their feet on my mat, and made me think visitors were coming, and get off the sofa and take off my spectacles; and then nobody came in! I am going away tomorrow."

I think, however, this sort of existence will probably end with the present generation. The "old maid" of 1861 is an exceedingly cheery personage, running about untrammelled by husband or children; now visiting her relatives' country houses, now taking her month in town, now off to a favourite *pension* on Lake Geneva, now scaling Vesuvius or the Pyramids. And, what is better, she has found not only freedom of locomotion, but a sphere of action peculiarly congenial to her nature. "My life, and what shall I do with it?" is a problem for which she finds the happiest solution ready to her hand in schools and hospitals without number. No longer does the Church of Rome monopolize the truth, that on a woman who has no husband, parent, or child, *every* sick and suffering man, every aged childless woman, every desolate orphan, has a claim. She has not fewer duties than other women, only more diffused ones. The "old maid's" life may be as rich, as blessed, as that of the proudest of mothers with her crown of clustering babes. Nay, she feels that in the power of devoting her *whole* time and energies to some benevolent task, she is enabled to effect perhaps some greater good than would otherwise have been possible. "On n'enfante les grandes oeuvres que dans la virginité."

And further, if a woman have but strength to make up her mind to a single life, she is enabled by nature to be far more independently happy therein than a man in the same position. A man, be he rich or poor, who returns at night to a home adorned by no woman's presence and domestic cares, is at best dreary and uncomfortable. But a woman makes her home for herself, and surrounds herself with the atmosphere of taste and the little details of housewifely comforts. If she have no sister, she has yet inherited the blessed power of a woman to make true and tender friendships, such as not one man's heart in a hundred can even imagine; and while he smiles scornfully at the idea of friendship meaning anything beyond acquaintance at a club, or the intimacy of a barrack, she enjoys one of the purest of pleasures and the most unselfish of all affections.

Nor does the "old maid" contemplate a solitary age as the bachelor must usually do. It will go hard but she will find a *woman* ready to share it. And more!—(but it is a theme we may not treat of here). She thinks to *die,* if without having given or shared some of the highest joys of human nature, yet at least without having caused one fellow-being to regret she was born to tempt to sin and shame. We ask it in all solemn sadness—Do the *men* who resolve on an unmarried life, fixedly purpose also so to die with as spotless a conscience?

And on the other hand, while the utility, freedom, and happiness of a single woman's life have become greater, the *knowledge* of the risks of an unhappy marriage (if not the risks themselves) has become more public. The Divorce Court, in righting the most appalling wrongs to which the members of a civilized community could be subjected, has revealed secrets which must tend to modify immensely our ideas of English domestic felicity. Well it is that these hideous revelations should take place, for, as Carlyle says, "To nothing but error can any truth be dangerous;" and the fatal error of hasty marriage is constantly due to ignorance of the possibilities of some forms of offence among the apparently respectable classes of society. It has always been vaguely known, indeed, that both husbands and wives sometimes broke their most solemn vows and fell into sin; but it was reserved for the new law to show how many hundreds of such tragedies underlie the outwardly decorous lives, not only of the long-blamed aristocracy, but of the middle ranks in England. But beside that most grievous wrong, who imagined that the wives of English *gentlemen* might be called on to endure from their husbands the violence and cruelty we are accustomed to picture exercised only in the lowest lanes and courts of our cities, where drunken ruffians, stumbling home from the gin-palace, assail the miserable partners of their vices with curses, kicks, and blows? Who could have imagined it possible, that well-born and well-educated men, in honourable professions, should be guilty of the same brutality? Imagine a handsomely-furnished drawing-room, with its books, and flowers, and lights, and all the refinements of civilized life, for the scene of similar outrages. Imagine the offender a well-dressed gentleman, tall and powerful as English gentlemen are wont to be; the victim shrinking from his blows—a gentle, high-bred English *lady!* Good God! does not the picture make every true man set his teeth, and clench his hand?

Now these things *are* so. The Divorce Court has brought dozens of them to light; and we all know well that for one wife who will seek public redress for her wrongs, there are always ten, who, for their childrens' sakes, will bear their martyrdoms in silence. True martyrs they are—the sorest tried, perhaps, of any in the world—God help and comfort them! But single women can surely hardly forget these things, or fail to hesitate to try a lottery in which there may be one chance in a thousand of such a destiny. Thus, then, on the man's side, we have got arrayed against marriage all the arguments we have heard so often—economy, independence, freedom of risk of an uncongenial, a bad-tempered, a sickly, or an unfaithful wife; and, lastly, this new principle, that, to pursue his calling disinterestedly, he must be untrammelled by the ties of a dependent family. And, on the woman's side, we have got a no less formidable range of objections; the certainty now offered to her of being able to make for herself a free, useful, and happy life alone, and the demonstrated danger of being inexpressibly miserable should she choose either an unfaithful or a cruel husband.

The conclusion seems inevitable, that marriage will become more and more rare, in spite of all Belgravian or other mothers can do. Instead of all young men intending, at some time or other, to marry, and all young women looking forward to be wives, we shall find many of them both resolving on a celibate life.

But the tide must turn at last. Marriage was manifestly the Creator's plan for humanity, and therefore we cannot doubt that it will eventually become the rule of all men and women's lives. When that time arrives, both sexes will have learned weighty lessons. 'The Englishman of the twentieth century will abandon those claims of marital authority, whose residue he still inherits from days when might made right, and from lands of Eastern sensuality, where woman is first the slave of her own weakness, and then inevitably the slave of man. When the theory of the "Divine Right of Husbands" has followed to limbo that of the "Divine Right of Kings," and a precedency in selfishness is no longer assumed to be the sacred privilege of masculine strength and wisdom, then will become possible a conjugal love and union nobler and more tender by far than can ever exist while such claims are even tacitly supposed. Of all true, holy, human love, as distinguished from the love of the hound and the slave, Chaucer said right well—

When mastery cometh, then sweet Love anon
Flappeth his nimble wings, and soon away is gone.

And abandoning his authority (save such as real wisdom and power of nature must ever secure), man will also abandon that direful licence of which we hear so much—the licence to be less pure and faithful than a woman while escaping the same penalty of disgrace. Then will the husband bring to his wife feelings as fresh as those which now are too often her contribution alone to their joint happiness.

And the Englishwoman of the twentieth century will, on her part, learn to rise above her present pitiful ambitions of social advancement and petty personal vanity—the thousand childish foibles in which she now thinks it her right to indulge. She will be ready to cope with poverty, and encourage her husband cheerfully to bear it for life, rather than sully the noblest of his aspirations. She will learn that no longer must morality be divided between them; Truth and Courage for him, and Chastity and Patience for her; but that she, too, must be true as an honourable *man* is true and brave in her own sphere of duty as he is brave in his, if she would exchange his half-contemptuous gallantry for genuine respect. And, finally, she will share her husband's religion, she will boldly confront the doubts of his understanding by the intuitions of her heart; she will help him to *love*, as he will help her to *knowledge*. And thus together may they reach a nobler and a warmer faith than the world yet has seen.

Source: Reprinted from *Fraser's Magazine* (February 1862).

NOTE

1   Sentimens et Avis Chrétiens, chap. 1.

"'WHAT SHALL WE DO WITH OUR OLD MAIDS?'"

In the Convocation of Canterbury for this year of 1862, the readers of such journals as report in full the sayings and doings of that not very interesting assembly, were surprised to find the subject of Protestant Sisterhoods, or Deaconesses, discussed with an unanimity of feeling almost unique in the annals of ecclesiastic parliaments. High Churchman and Low, Broad Churchman and Hard, all seemed agreed that there was good work for women to do, and which women *were* doing all over England; and that it was extremely desirable that all these lady guerillas of philanthropy should be enrolled in the regular disciplined army of the Church, together with as many new recruits as might be enlisted. To use a more appropriate simile, Mother Church expressed herself satisfied at her daughters 'coming out,' but considered that her chaperonage was decidedly necessary to their decorum.

Again, at the Social Science Congress of this summer, in London, the Employment of women, the Emigration of women, the Education of women, and all the other rights and wrongs of women, were urged, if not with an unanimity equal to that of their revered predecessors, yet with, at the very least, equal animation. It is quite evident that the subject is not to be allowed to go to sleep, and we may as well face it valiantly, and endeavour to see light through its complications rather than attempt to lecture the female sex generally on the merits of a 'golden silence,' and the propriety of adorning themselves with that decoration (doubtless modestly declined, as too precious for their own use, by masculine reviewers), 'the ornament of a meek and quiet spirit.' In a former article ('Celibacy *v.* Marriage'—*Fraser's Magazine* for February, 1862) we treated the subject in part. We now propose to pursue it further, and investigate in particular the new phases which it has lately assumed.

The questions involved may be stated very simply.

It appears that there is a natural excess of four or five per cent of females over the males in our population. This, then, might be assumed to be the limits within which female celibacy was normal and inevitable.

There is, however, an actual ratio of thirty per cent of women now in England who never marry, leaving one-fourth of both sexes in a state of celibacy. This proportion further appears to be constantly on the increase. It is obvious enough that these facts call for a revision of many of our social arrangements. The old assumption that marriage was the sole destiny of woman, and that it was the business of her husband to afford her support, is brought up short by the statement that one woman in four is certain not to marry, and that three millions of women earn their own living at this moment in England. We may view the case two ways: either—

1st, We must frankly accept this new state of things, and educate women and modify trade in accordance therewith, so as to make the condition of celibacy as little injurious as possible; or—

2nd, We must set ourselves vigorously to stop the current which is leading men and women away from the natural order of Providence. We must do nothing whatever to render celibacy easy or attractive; and we must make the utmost efforts to promote marriage by emigration of women to the colonies, and all other means in our power.

The second of these views we shall in the first place consider. It may be found to colour the ideas of a vast number of writers, and to influence essentially the decision made on many points—as the admission of women to university degrees, to the medical profession, and generally to free competition in employment. Lately it has met a powerful and not unkindly exposition in an article in a contemporary quarterly, entitled, 'Why are Women Redundant?' Therein it is plainly set forth that all efforts to make celibacy easy for women are labours in a wrong direction, and are to be likened to the noxious exertions of quacks to mitigate the symptoms of disease, and allow the patient to persist in his evil courses. The root of the malady should be struck at, and marriage, the only true vocation for women, promoted at any cost, even by the most enormous schemes for the deportation of 440,000 females. Thus alone (and by the enforcing of a stricter morality on men) should the evil be touched. As to making the labours of single women remunerative, and their lives free and happy, all such mistaken philanthropy will but tend to place them in a position more and more false and unnatural. Marriage will then become to them a matter of 'cold philosophic choice,' and accordingly may be expected to be more and more frequently declined.

There is a great deal in this view of the case which, on the first blush approves itself to our minds, and we have not been surprised to find the article in question quoted as of the soundest common-sense. All, save ascetics and visionaries, must admit that, for the mass of mankind, marriage is the right condition, the happiest, and the most conducive to virtue. This position fairly and fully conceded, it *might* appear that the whole of the consequences deduced followed of necessity, and that the direct promotion of marriage and discountenancing of celibacy was all we had to do in the matter.

A little deeper reflection, however, discloses a very important point which has been dropped out of the argument. Marriage is, indeed, the happiest and best condition for mankind. But does anyone think that all marriages are so? When we make the assertion that marriage is good and virtuous, do we mean a marriage of interest, a marriage for wealth, for position, for rank, for support? Surely nothing of the kind. Such marriages as these are the sources of misery and sin, not of happiness and virtue, nay, their moral character, to be fitly designated, would require stronger words than we care to use. There is only one kind of marriage which makes good the assertion that it is the right and happy condition for mankind, and that is a marriage founded on free choice, esteem, and affection—in one word, on love. If, then, we seek to promote the happiness and virtue of the community, our efforts must be directed to encouraging *only* marriages which are of the sort to produce them—namely, marriages founded on love. All marriages founded on interest, on the desire for position, support, or the like, we must discourage to the utmost of our power, as the sources of nothing but wretchedness. Where now, have we reached? Is it not to the conclusion that to make it a woman's *interest* to marry, to force her, by barring out every means of self-support and all fairly remunerative labour, to look to marriage as her sole chance of competency, is precisely to drive her into one of those sinful and unhappy marriages? It is quite clear we can never drive her into *love*. That is a sentiment which poverty, friendlessness, and helplessness can by no means call out. Nor, on the contrary, can competence and freedom in any way check it. It will arise under its natural conditions, if we will but leave the matter alone. A *loving* marriage can never become a matter of 'cold philosophic choice.' And if *not* a loving one, then, for Heaven's sake, let us give no motive for choice at all.

Let the employments of women be raised and multiplied as much as possible, let their labour be as fairly remunerated, let their education be pushed as high, let their whole position be made as healthy and happy as possible, and there will come out once more, here as in every other department of life, the triumph of the Divine laws of our nature. Loving marriages are (we cannot doubt) what God has designed, not marriages of interest. When we have made it *less* women's interest to marry, we shall indeed have less and fewer interested marriages with all their train of miseries and evils. But we shall also have more *loving* ones, more marriages founded on free choice and free affection. Thus we arrive at the conclusion that for the very end of promoting marriage—that is, such marriage as it is alone desirable to promote—we should pursue a precisely opposite course to that suggested by the Reviewer or his party. Instead of leaving single women as helpless as possible, and their labour as ill-rewarded—

instead of dinning into their ears from childhood that marriage is their one vocation and concern in life, and securing afterwards if they miss it that they shall find no other vocation or concern;—instead of all this, we shall act exactly on the reverse principle. We shall make single life so free and happy that they shall have not one temptation to change it save the only temptation which *ought* to determine them—namely, love. Instead of making marriage a case of 'Hobson's choice' for woman, we shall endeavour to give her such independence of all interested considerations that she may make it a choice, not indeed 'cold and philosophic,' but warm from the heart, and guided by heart and conscience only.

And again, in another way the same principle holds good, and marriage will be found to be best promoted by aiding and not by thwarting the efforts of single women to improve their condition. It is a topic on which we cannot speak much, but thus far may suffice. The reviewer alludes with painful truth to a class of the community whose lot is far more grievous than either celibacy or marriage. Justly he traces the unwillingness of hundreds of men to marry to the existence of these unhappy women in their present condition. He would remedy the evil by preaching marriage to such men. But does not all the world know that thousands of these poor souls, of all degrees, would never have fallen into their miserable vocation had any *other* course been open to them, and they had been enabled to acquire a competence by honest labour? Let such honest courses be opened to them, and then we shall see, as in America, the recruiting of that wretched army becoming less and less possible every year in the country. The self-supporting, and therefore self-respecting woman may indeed become a wife, and a good and happy one, but she will no longer afford any man a reason for declining to marry.

It is curious to note that while, on the one hand, we are urged to make marriage the sole vocation of women, we are simultaneously met on the other by the outpourings of ridicule and contempt on all who for themselves, or even for their children, seek ever so indirectly to attain this vocation. Only last year all England was entertained by jests concerning 'Belgravian mothers;' and the wiles and devices of widows and damsels afford an unending topic of satire and amusement in private and public. Now we ask, in all seriousness, Wherefore all this ridicule and contempt? *If* marriage be indeed the one object of a woman's life—*if* to give her any other pursuit or interest be only to divert her from that one object and 'palliate the symptoms while fostering a great social disease'— then, we repeat, *why* despise these match-making mothers? Are they to do nothing to help their daughters to their only true vocation, which if they should miss, their lives *ought* to be failures, poverty-stricken and miserable? Nay; but if things be so, the most open, unblushing marketing of their daughters is the *duty* of parents, and the father or mother who leaves the matter to chance is flagrantly neglectful. Truly it is a paradox passing all limits of reason, that society should enforce marriage on woman as her only honourable life, and at the same time should stigmatize as dishonourable the efforts of her parents to settle her in marriage.

The spontaneous sentiment of mankind has hit a deeper truth than the theories of economists. It *is* in the nature of things disgraceful and abominable that marriage should be made the aim of a woman's life. It can only become what it is meant to be, the completion and crown of the life of either man or woman, when it has arisen from sentiments which can never be bespoken for the convenient fulfilment of any vocation whatsoever.

But it is urged, and not unreasonably—If it be admitted on all hands that marriage is the best condition, and that only one-fourth of the female sex do not marry, how can we expect provision to be made for this contingency of one chance in four by a girl's parents and by herself in going through an education (perhaps costly and laborious) for a trade or profession which there are three chances in four she will not long continue to exercise?

It must be admitted here is the great knot and difficulty of the higher branches of woman's employment. It does require farseeing care on the part of the parent, perseverance and resolution of no mean order on that of the daughter, to go through in youth the training which will fit her to earn her livelihood hereafter in any of the more elevated occupations. Nay, it demands that she devote to such training the precise years of life wherein the chances of marriage are commonly offered, and the difficulties of pursuing a steady course are very much enhanced by temptations of all kinds. If she wait till the years when such chances fail, and take up a pursuit at thirty merely as a *pis aller*, she must inevitably remain for ever behindhand and in an inferior position.

The trial is undoubtedly considerable, but there are symptoms that both young women and their parents will not be always unwilling to meet it, and to invest both time and money in lines of education which *may* indeed prove superfluous, but which likewise may afford the mainstay of a life which, without them, would be helpless, aimless, and miserable. The magnitude of the risk ought surely to weigh somewhat in the balance. At the lowest point of view, a woman is no worse off if she marry eventually, for having first gone through an education for some good pursuit; while if she remain single, she is wretchedly off for not having had such education. But this is in fact only a half view of the case. As we have insisted before, it is only on the standing-ground of a happy and independent celibacy that a woman can really make a free choice in marriage. To secure this standing ground, a pursuit is more needful than a pecuniary competence, for a life without aim or object is one which, more than all others, goads a woman into accepting any chance of a change. Mariana (we are privately convinced) would have eloped out of the Moated Grange not only with that particular 'he' who never came, but with any other suitor who might have presented himself. Only a woman who has something else than making love to do and to think of will love really and deeply. It is in *real lives*—lives devoted to actual service of father or mother, or to work of some kind for God or man—that alone spring up *real feelings*. Lives of idleness and pleasure have no depth to nourish such plants.

Again, we are very far indeed from maintaining that *during* marriage it is at all to be desired that a woman should struggle to keep up whatever pursuit she had adopted beforehand. In nine cases out of ten this will drop naturally to the ground, especially when she has children. The great and paramount duties of a mother and wife once adopted, every other interest sinks, by the beneficent laws of our nature, into a subordinate place in normally constituted minds, and the effort to perpetuate them is as false as it is usually fruitless. Where necessity and poverty compel mothers in the lower ranks to go out to work, we all know too well the evils which ensue. And in the higher classes doubtless the holding tenaciously by any pursuit interfering with home duties must produce such Mrs. Jellabys as we sometimes hear of. It is not only leisure which is in question. There appear to be some occult laws in woman's nature providing against such mistakes by rendering it impossible to pursue the higher branches of art or literature or any work tasking mental exertion, while home and motherly cares have their claims. We have heard of a great artist, saying that she is always obliged to leave her children for a few weeks before she can throw herself again into the artist-feeling of her youth, and we believe her experience is corroborated on all hands. No great books have been written or works achieved by women while their children were around them in infancy. No woman can lead the two lives at the same time.

But it is often strangely forgotten that there are such things as widows left such in the prime of life and quite as much needing occupation as if they had remained single. Thus, then, another chance must fairly be added to our one in four that a woman may need such a pursuit as we have supposed. She may never marry, or having married she may be left a childless widow, or a widow whose few children occupy but a portion of her time. Suppose, for instance, she has been a physician. How often would the possibility of returning to her early profession be an invaluable resource after her husband's death! The greatest female mathematician living, was saved from despairing sorrow in widowhood, by throwing herself afresh into the studies of her youth.

It may be a pleasantly romantic idea to some minds, that of woman growing up solely with the hope of becoming some man's devoted wife, marrying the first that offers, and when he dies, becoming a sort of moral Suttee whose heart is supposed to be henceforth dead and in ashes. But it is quite clear that Providence can never have designed any such order of things. All the infinite tenderness and devotion He has placed in women's hearts, though meant to make marriage blessed and happy, and diffusing as from a hearth of warm affections, kindness and love on all around, is yet meant to be subordinated to the great purposes of the existence of all rational souls—the approximation to God through virtue. With reverence be it spoken, God is the only true centre of life for us all, not any creature he has made. 'To live unto God' is the law for man and woman alike. Whoever strives to do this will neither spend youth in long-ing for happiness which may be withheld, nor age in despair for that which may be withdrawn.

To resume. It appears that from every point of view in which we regard the subject, it is desirable that women should have other aims, pursuits, and inter-ests in life beside matrimony and that by possessing them they are guaranteed against being driven into unloving marriages, and rendered more fitted for lov-ing ones; while their single life, whether in maidenhood or widowhood, is made useful and happy.

Before closing this part of the subject, we cannot but add a few words to express our amused surprise at the way in which the writers on this subject con-stantly concern themselves with the question of *female* celibacy, deplore it, abuse it, propose amazing remedies for it, but take little or no notice of the twenty-five per cent old bachelors (or thereabouts) who needs must exist to match the thirty per cent old maids. *Their* moral condition seems to excite no alarm, their lonely old age no foreboding compassion, their action on the community no reprobation. Nobody scolds them very seriously, unless some stray Belgravian grandmother. All the alarm, compassion, reprobation, and scoldings are reserved for the poor old maids. But of the two, which of the parties is the chief delinquent? The *Zend Avesta*, as translated by Anquetil du Perron, contains somewhere this awful denunciation:—'That damsel who having reached the age of eighteen, shall refuse to marry, must remain in hell till the Resurrec-tion!' A severe penalty, doubtless, for the crime, and wonderful to meet in the mild creed of Zoroaster, where no greater punishment is allotted to any offence whatsoever. Were these Guebre young ladies so terribly cruel, and *mazdiesnans* (true believers) so desperately enamoured? Are we to imagine the obdurate damsels despatching whole dozens of despairing gentlemen in conical caps to join the society in the shades below—

Hapless youths who died for love,
Wandering in a myrtle grove!

It takes a vivid stretch of imagination in England, in the nineteenth century, to picture anything of the kind. Whatever other offences our young ladies may be guilty of, or other weaknesses our young gentlemen, obduracy on the one hand, and dying for love on the other, are rarities, at all events. Yet one would suppose that Zoroaster was needed over here, to judge of the manner in which old maids are lectured on their very improper position. 'The Repression of Crime,' as the benevolent Recorder of Birmingham would phrase it, seems on the point of being exercised against them, since it has been found out that their offence is on the increase, like poaching in country districts and landlord shooting in Ireland. The mildest punishment, we are told, is to be transporta-tion, to which half a million have just been condemned, and for the terror of future evil doers, it is decreed that no single woman's work ought to be fairly remunerated, nor her position allowed to be entirely respectable, lest she exercise 'a cold philosophic choice' about matrimony. No false charity to criminals! Transportation or starvation to all old maids!

Poor old maids! Will not Reformatory, Union, or some other friends of the criminal, take their case in hand? They are too old for Miss Carpenter. Could not Sir Walter Crofton's Intermediate System be of some use? There is reason to hope that many of them would be willing to adopt a more honest way of life were the chance offered them.

If the reader should have gone with us thus far, we shall be able better to follow the subject from a point of view which shall in fact unite the two leading ideas of which we made mention at starting. We shall, with the *first*, seek earnestly how the condition of single women may be most effectually improved; and with the *second*, we shall admit the promotion of marriage (*provided it be disinterested and loving*) to be the best end at which such improvements will tend.

In one point there is a practical unanimity between the schemes of the two parties, and this we should desire to notice before proceeding to consider the ways in which the condition of single women may be improved as such. This scheme is that of emigration for women to the colonies. Here we have multitudes of women offered in the first place remunerative employment beyond anything they could obtain at home; and further, the facilitation of marriage effected for large numbers, to the great benefit of both men and women. What there might appear in the plan contradictory to the principles we have laid down above, is only apparent and not real. The woman who arrives in a colony where her labour, of head or hands, can command an ample maintenance, stands in the precise condition we have desired to make marriage—a matter of free choice. She has left 'Hobson's choice' behind her with the poverty of England, and has come out to find competence and freedom, and if she choose (but *only* if she choose), marriage also.

It is needless to say that this scheme has our entire sympathy and good wishes, though we do not expect to live to see the time when our reviewer's plans will be fulfilled by the deportation of women at the rate of thirty or forty thousand a year.[1]

An important point, however, must not be overlooked. However far the emigration of women of the working classes may be carried, that of educated women must at all times remain very limited, inasmuch as the demand for them in the colonies is comparatively trifling. Now, it is of educated women that the great body of old maids' consists; in the lower orders celibacy is rare. Thus, it should be borne in mind that emigration schemes do not essentially bear on the main point, 'How shall we improve the condition of the thirty per cent of single women in England?' The reviewer to whom we have so often alluded, does indeed dispose of the matter by observing that the transportation he fondly hopes to see effected, of 440,000 women to the colonies, will at least *relieve the market* for those who remain. We cannot but fear, however, that the governesses and other ladies so accommodated will not much profit by the large selection thus afforded them among the blacksmiths and ploughmen, deprived of their proper companions. At the least we shall have a quarter of a million of old maids *in esse* and *in posse* left on hands. What can we do for them?

For convenience we may divide them into two classes. One of them, without capital or high cultivation, needs employment suitable to a woman's powers, and yet affording better remuneration than woman's work has hitherto usually received. Here we find the efforts of Miss Faithfull, Miss Crowe, Miss Rye, and the other ladies in combination with the society founded by Miss Parkes, labouring to procure such employment for them by the Victoria Printing Press, the Law Copying Office, and other plans in action or contemplated for watch-making, hair-dressing, and the like. We may look on this class as in good hands; and as the emigration of women will actually touch it and carry away number of its members, we may hope that its destinies are likely henceforth to improve.

The other and higher class is that of which we desire more particularly to speak, namely, of ladies either possessed of sufficient pecuniary means to support themselves comfortably, or else of such gifts and cultivation as shall command a competence. The help these women need is not of a pecuniary nature, but a large portion of them require aid, and the removal of existing. restrictions, to afford them the full exercise of their natural powers, and make their lives as useful and happy as Providence has intended. Of *all* the position is at the present moment of transition worthy of some attention, and suggestive of some curious speculations regarding the future of women. Channing remarks that when the negro races become thoroughly Christianized we shall see a development of the religion never known before. At least equally justly may we predict that when woman's gifts are at last expanded in an atmosphere of freedom and happiness, we shall find graces and powers revealed to us of which we yet have little dreamed. To the consideration, then, of the condition and prospects of women of the upper classes who remain unmarried, we shall devote the following pages.

All the pursuits of mankind, beside mere money-getting, may be fitly classed in three great orders. They are in one way or another the pursuit of the True, the Beautiful, or the Good. In a general way we may say that science, literature, and philosophy are devoted to Truth; art in all its branches (including poetic literature) to the Beautiful; and politics and philanthropy to the Good. Within certain limits, each of these lines of action are open to women; and it is in the aspect they bear as regards women's work that we are now to regard them. But before analysing them further, I would fain be allowed to make one remark which is far too often forgotten. Each of these pursuits is equally noble in itself; it is our fitness for one or the other, not its intrinsic sanctity or value, which ought to determine our choice; and we are all astray in our judgements if we come to the examination of them with prejudices for or against one or the other. In these days, when 'the icy chains of custom and of prejudice' are somewhat loosened, and men and women go forth more freely than ever of old to choose and make their lives, there is too often this false measurement of our brother's choice. Each of us asks his friend in effect, if not in words—'Why not follow my calling rather than your own? Why not use such a gift? Why not adopt such a task?' The answer to these questions must not be made with the senseless pedantry of the assumption, that because to *us* art or literature, or philanthropy or politics, is the true vocation, therefore for all men and women it is the noblest; and that God meant Mozart to be a statesman, and Howard a sculptor, and Kant a teacher in a ragged school. The true, the beautiful, and the good are all revelations of the Infinite One, and therefore all holy. It is enough for a man if it be given him in his lifetime to pursue any one of them to profit—to carry a single step further the torch of humanity along either of the three roads, every one of which leads up to God. The philosopher, who studies and teaches us the laws of mind or matter—the artist, who beholds with illumined eyes the beauty of the world, and creates it afresh in poetry or painting—the statesman or philanthropist, who labours to make Right victorious, and to advance the virtue and happiness of mankind,—all these in their several ways are God's seers, God's prophets, as much the one as the other. We could afford to lose none of them, to undervalue none of them. The philosopher is not to be honoured only for the goodness or the beauty of the *truth* he has revealed. All truth is good and beautiful, but it is to be prized because it is *truth*, and not merely for its goodness or beauty. The artist is not to be honoured only for the truth or the goodness of the *beautiful* he has revealed. The beautiful is necessarily good and true, but it is to be loved because it is *beautiful*, and not merely for its truth or goodness.[2] Like the old Athanasian symbol, we may say, 'The Truth is divine, the Beautiful is divine, and the Good is divine. And yet they are not three divine things, but three revelations of the One Divine Lord.' If men would but feel this each in his own pursuit, and in judging of the pursuits of others, how holy and noble would all faithful work become! We are haunted yet with the Romish thought that a life of asceticism, of preaching, of prayer, of charity, is altogether on a different plane of being from a life devoted to other tasks. But it is not so. From *every* field of honest human toil there rises a ladder up into heaven. Was Kepler further from God than any Howard or Xavier when, after discovering the law of the planetary distances, he bowed his head and exclaimed in rapture, 'O God, I think Thy thoughts after Thee!' Was Milton less divine than any St. Theresa locked in her stony cell, when his mighty genius had soared 'upon the seraph wings of ecstasy' over the whole beautiful creation, and he poured out at last his triumphant Psalm—

These are Thy glorious works, Parent of Good—
Almighty!

Of these three great modes of Divine manifestation, it would appear, however, that, though equal in sanctity and dignity, the pursuit of the True and of
the Beautiful were designed for comparatively few among mankind. Few possess the pure abstract love of Truth in such fervour as to fit them to become the
martyrs of science or the prophets of philosophy. Few also are those who are
endowed with that supreme sense of the Beautiful, and power to reproduce it
in form, colour, or sound, which constitute the gifts of the artist. Especially does
this hold good with women. While few of them do not feel their hearts warmed
with the love of goodness, and the desire to relieve the sufferings of their fellows, a mere fraction, in comparison, interest themselves to any extent in the
pursuit of the abstract truths of philosophy or science, or possess any powers to
reproduce the Beautiful in Art, even when they have a perception of its presence in nature. We may discuss briefly, then, here the prospects of the employment of women in the departments of Truth and Beauty, and in a future paper
consider more at length the new aspect of their philanthropic labours and
endeavours to do Good.

Till of very late years it was, we think, perfectly justifiable to doubt the possibility of women possessing any creative artistic power. Receptive faculties they
have always had, ready and vivid perception of the beautiful in both nature and
art, delicate discrimination and refined taste, nay, the power (especially in
music and the drama) of reproducing what the genius of man had created. But
to originate any work of even second-rate merit was what no woman had done.
Sappho was a mere name, and between her and even such a feeble poetess as
Mrs. Hemans, there was hardly another to fill up the gap of the whole cycle of
history. No woman has written the epics, nor the dramas, nay, nor even the
national songs of her country, if we may not except Miriam's and Deborah's
chants of victory. In music, nothing. In architecture, nothing. In sculpture,
nothing. In painting, an Elisabetta Sirani, a Rosalba, an Angelica Kauffman—
hardly exceptions enough to prove the rule. Such works as women did accom-
plish were all stamped with the same impress of feebleness and prettiness. As
Mrs. Hemans and Joanna Baillie and Mrs. Tighe wrote poetry, so Angelica
Kauffman painted pictures, and other ladies composed washy music and Min-
erva-press romances. If Tennyson had spoken of woman's *Art*, instead of
woman's passions, he would have been as right for the one as he was wrong as
regards the other. It *was*

As moonlight is to sunlight
And as water is to wine.

To coin an epithet from a good type of the school—it was all 'Angelical,'
no flesh and blood at all, but super-refined sentiments and super-elongated
limbs.

But there seem symptoms extant that this state of things is to undergo a change, and the works of women become remarkable for other qualities beside softness and weakness. It may be a mere chance conjunction, but it is at least remarkable, that the same age has given us in the three greatest departments of art—poetry, painting, and sculpture—women who, whatever be their faults or merits, are pre-eminently distinguished for one quality above all others—namely, strength. *Aurora Leigh is* perhaps the least 'Angelical' poem in the language, and bears the relation to *Psyche* that a chiselled steel corslet does to a silk boddice with lace trimmings. The very hardness of its rhythm, its sturdy wrestlings and grapplings, one after another, with all the sternest problems of our social life—its forked-lightning revelations of character -and finally, the storm of glorified passion with which it closes in darkness (like nothing else we ever read since the mountain-tempest scene in *Childe Harold*)—all this takes us miles away from the received notion of a woman's poetry.

And for painting, let us look at Rosa Bonheur's canvas. Those droves of wild Highland black cattle, those teams of tramping Norman horses—do they belong to the same school of female art as all the washed-out saints, and pensive ladies, and graceful bouquets of Mesdemoiselles and Signorine Rosee, and Rosalba, and Panzacchi, and Grebber, and Mérian, and Kauffman? We seem to have passed a frontier, and entered a new realm wherein Rosa Bonheurs are to be found.

Then for Sculpture. Will woman's genius ever triumph here? We confess we look to this point as to the touchstone of the whole question. Sculpture is in many respects at once the noblest art and the one which tasks highest both creative power and scientific skill. A really good and great statue is an achievement to which there must contribute more elements of power and patience than in almost any other human work, and it is, when perfected, one of the most sublime. We know generally very little of this matter in England. We possess pictures by the great masters sufficient in number and excellence to afford a fair conception (though of course an incomplete one) of the powers of painting. But notwithstanding the antique treasures in the Elgin and Arundel Collections, and a few fine modern statues to be found in private houses in this country, it is, I believe, to every one a revelation of a new agency in art when he first visits Italy and beholds the 'Laocöon,' the 'Apollo,' the 'Niobe,' and the 'Psyche' of Praxiteles. Hitherto sculpture has appeared to be merely the production of beautiful forms, more or less true to nature. Now it is perceived to be genius breathing through form, the loftiest thoughts of human souls. 'Apollo Belvidere' is not the mere figure of a perfect man in graceful attitude, as we thought it from casts and copies in England. It is Power itself, deified and made real before our eyes. The 'Laocöon' is not the hapless high-priest writhing in the coil of the serpent. It is the impersonation of the will of a giant man, a Prometheus struggling with indomitable courage against the resistless Fate in whose grasp meaner mortals are crushed helplessly. The 'Niobe' is not merely a woman of noblest mould inspired by maternal anguish. She is glorified MOTHERHOOD, on whose great bosom we could rest, and round whose neck we could throw our arms. And the 'Psyche' in the Museo Borbonico?—is this a poor fragment of a form, once perhaps graceful and fair, but now a mere ruin? No! It is the last gleam of the unknown glory of ancient art, the one work of human hands which we forget to admire because we learn to love it—the revelation to each of us of our innermost ideal of friend or wife, the sweetest, purest of our dreams made real before our eyes.

Not untruly has sculpture been named the *Ars Divinior.* A deep and strange analogy exists between it and the highest we know of the Supreme Artist's works. Out of the clay, cold and formless, the sculptor slowly, patiently, with infinite care and love, moulds an image of beauty. Long the stubborn clay seems to resist his will, and to remain without grace or proportion, but at last the image begins, faintly and in a far-off way, to reflect that prototype which is in the sculptor's mind. The limbs grow into shape, and stand firmly balanced, the countenance becomes living and radiant. And last of all, the character of true sculpture appears; there is calm and peace over it all, and an infinite divine repose, even when the life within seems higher and fuller than that of mortality. The moulding is done, the statue is perfected.

But even then, when it should seem that the sculptor's great work is achieved, and that his image should be preserved and cherished evermore, what does he in truth do with his clay? Return hither, oh traveller, in a few short days, and the image of clay is gone, its place knows it no more. It has returned to the earth whence it was taken, thrown by, perchance for ever, or else kneaded afresh in some new form of life. Did he make it, then, but for destruction, and mould it so carefully but to crush it out at last in dust? Look around with illumined eyes! In the great studio of the universe the Divine image is still to be found, not now moulded in clay and ready to perish, dull of hue and dead in lustre, but sculptured in eternal marble, white, and pure, and radiant; meet to stand for ever in the palaces on high.

Sculpture is the noblest of the arts; nay, it is above all others in this very thing which has been pointed at as its bane and limitation. Its aim must ever be the expression of calmness and repose. No vehement wildness of the painter's dream, no storm of the musician's harmony, no ecstasy of the poet's passion; but the stillness and the peace of which earth knows so little. To bring our souls into sympathy with a great work of sculpturesque repose, is to bring them into the serener fields of the upper air, where the storms approach not, nor any clouds ascend. We do not naturally in the earlier moral life feel in union with things calm and still like these. The struggle in our own breasts, the lordly will wrestling with the lower powers for mastery, leaves us rather able to sympathize with all nature's warfare of wind and wave, all human death-battles, than with the repose in which the saint's soul rests, loving the cloudless sky and waveless sea, and the smile of a sleeping child nestled in the long sweet grass of summer. To reach that rest of the whole nature, which is at the same time absolute repose and absolute action of every power and every faculty in perfect balance, is the 'Beulah land,'

> Where blessed saints dwell ever in the light
> Of God's dear love, and earth is heaven below.
> For never doubt nor sin may cloud their sight,
> And the great PEACE OF GOD calms every human woe.

The art which is the idealizing, the perpetuation of repose is, then, the divinest art—the art to be practised only by great souls—great races of men. Egyptians and Greeks were races of sculptors; Hindoos and Mexicans stone cutters of goblins. We repeat that the sharpest test to which the question of woman's genius can be put is this one of sculpture. If she succeed here, if a school of real sculptresses ever arise, then we think that in effect the problem is solved. The greater includes the less. They may still fall below male composers in music, though we have seen some (in edited) music of wonderful power from a female hand. They may produce no great drama—perhaps no great historical picture. Yet if really good statues come from their studios, statues showing at once power of conception and science of execution, then we say, women can be artists. It is no longer a question whether the creative faculty be granted to them.

Now, we venture to believe that there are distinct tokens that this solution is really to be given to the problem. For long centuries women never seem to have attempted sculpture at all; perhaps because it was then customary for the artist to perform much of the mechanical labour of the marble-cutter himself; perhaps because women could rarely command either the large outlay or the anatomical instructions. But in our time things are changed. The Princesse Marie d'Orleans, in her well-known Joan of Arc, accomplished a really noble work of sculpture. Others have followed and are following in her path, but most marked of all by power and skill comes Harriet Hosmer, whose Zenobia (now standing in the International Exhibition, in the same temple with Gibson's Venus) is a definite proof that a woman can make a statue of the very highest order. Whether we consider the noble conception of this majestic figure, or the science displayed in every part of it, from the perfect *pose* and accurate anatomy, to the admirable truth and finish of the drapery, we are equally satisfied. Her is what we wanted. A woman—aye, a woman with all the charms of youthful womanhood—can be a sculptor, and a great one.

Now we have arrived at a conclusion worthy of some little attention. Women a few years ago could only show a few weak and washy female poets and painters, and no sculptors at all. They can now boast of such true and powerful artists in these lines as Mrs. Browning, Rosa Bonheur, and Harriet Hosmer.

What account can we give of the rise of such a new constellation? We confess ourselves unable to offer any solution, save that proposed by a gifted lady to whom we propounded our query. Female artists hitherto always started on a wrong track; being persuaded beforehand that they ought only to compose sweet verses and soft pictures, they set themselves to make them accordingly, and left us Mrs. Hemans' Works and Angelica's paintings. *Now*, women who possess any real genius, apply it to the creation of what they (and not society for them) really admire. A woman naturally admires power, force, grandeur. It is these qualities, then, which we shall see more and more appearing as the spontaneous genius of woman asserts itself.

We know not how this may be. It is at all events a curious speculation. One remark we must make before leaving this subject. This new element of *strength* in female art seems to impress spectators very differently. It cannot be concealed that while all true artists recognise it with delight, there is no inconsiderable number of men to whom it is obviously distasteful, and who turn away more or less decidedly in feeling from the display of this or any other power in women, exercised never so inoffensively. There is a feeling (tacit or expressed) 'Yes, it is very clever, but somehow it is not quite feminine.' Now we do not wish to use sarcastic words about sentiments of this kind, or demonstrate all their unworthiness and ungenerousness. We would rather make an appeal to a better judgement, and entreat for a resolute stop to expressions ever so remotely founded on them. The origin of them all has perhaps been the old error that clipping and ferreting every faculty of body and mind was the sole method of making a woman—that as the Chinese make a lady's foot, so we should make a lady's mind; and that, in a word, the old ale-house sign was not so far wrong in depicting 'The Good Woman' as a woman without any head whatsoever. Earnestly would we enforce the opposite doctrine, that as God means a woman to *be* a woman and not a man, every faculty he has given her is a woman's faculty, and the more each of them can be drawn out, trained, and perfected, the more *womanly* she will become. She will be a larger, richer, nobler woman for art, for learning, for every grace and gift she can acquire. It must indeed be a mean and miserable man who would prefer that a woman's nature should be pinched, and starved, and dwarfed to keep on his level, rather than be nurtured and trained to its loftiest capacity, to meet worthily his highest also.

Thus we quit the subject of woman's pursuit of the Beautiful, rejoicing in the new promise of its success, and wishing all prosperity to the efforts to afford female students of art that sound and solid training, the lack of which has been their greatest stumblingblock hitherto. The School of Art and Design in London is a good augury with its eight hundred and sixty-three lady pupils!

But for woman's devotion to the True in physics and metaphysics, woman's science and woman's learning, what shall we venture to say? The fact must be frankly admitted—women have even more rarely the powers and tastes needful to carry them in this direction than in that of art. The love of abstract truth as a real passion is probably antithetic in some measure to that vivid interest in persons which belongs to the warm sympathies and strong affections of women. Their quickness of perception militates against the slow toil of science, and their vividness of intuitive faith renders them often impatient of the discussions of philosophy. Many women love truth warmly enough, and for religious truth female martyrs have never been wanting since the mother of the Maccabees. But few women complete their love of truth by such hatred of error as shall urge them to the exertion of laboriously establishing and defining the limits of the truths they possess. These natural causes again have been reinforced by endless artificial hindrances. The want of schools and colleges, the absence of such rewards as encourage (though they cannot inspire) the pursuit of knowledge, popular and domestic prejudices rendering study disfavoured, difficult access to books or leisure from household duties, the fluctuating health fostered by the unwholesome habits of women; and lastly, the idleness and distractions of those very years of youth in which education can rise above the puerile instruction of a girl's school-room.

Far be it from us to wish to force all women into courses of severe study—to put (as has been well said of late) Arabian horses to the plough, and educate directly against the grain; only we desire thus much, that those women who do possess the noble love of knowledge and are willing to undergo the drudgery of its acquirement, should have every aid supplied and every stumblingblock removed from their paths. The improvements which in our time are making in these directions may be briefly stated. First, popular prejudice against well-educated women is dying away. It is found they do *not* 'neglect infants for quadratic equations,' nor perform in any way less conscientiously the various duties of life after reading Plato or even Kant. Secondly, the opening of ladies' colleges, such as Bedford-square and Harley-street, where really sound and solid instruction is given by first-rate teachers at a cost not equal to half that of the shallow and superficial boarding-school of twenty years ago. Thirdly, women have benefited even more than men by the general progress of the times, the facilitation of travelling (formerly impossible to them without protection), the opening of good lending-libraries, cheap books and postage. The dead sea of ennui in which so many of them lived is now rippled by a hundred currents from all quarters of heaven, and we may trust that the pettiness of gossip which has been the standing reproach of the sex will disappear with the narrowness of life which supplied no wholesomer food for conversation or thought. To cramp every faculty and cut on all large interests, and then complain that a human being so treated is narrow-minded and scandal-loving, is precisely an injustice. parallel to that of some Southern Americans whom we have heard detail those vices of the negroes *which slavery had produced*, as the reason why they were justified in keeping so degraded a race in such a condition. It would be indeed a miracle often if a woman manufactured on some not unpopular principles were anything else than a very poor and pitiful piece of mechanism. The further improvements which may be sought in these directions are of various kinds. The standard of ordinary female education cannot perhaps be elevated above that of the ladies' colleges already mentioned, but *this* standard will become not (as now) the high-water mark for a few, but the common tide-line for classes supposed to be fairly educated. Above this high standard, again, facilities and encouragements may be given to women of exceptionally studious tastes to rise to the levels of any instruction attainable. One important way in which this last end may be reached—namely, the admission of women to the examinations and honours of the London University—has been lately much debated. The arguments which have determined its temporary rejection by the senate of the University (a rejection, however, only decided by the casting vote of the chairman), seem to have been all of the character discussed a few pages ago,—the supposed necessity of keeping women to their sole vocation of wives and mothers, and so on. The benefits which would accrue from the measure were urged by the present writer before the Social Science Congress,[3] and were briefly these—that women need as much or more than men a stimulus to carry their education to a high pitch of perfection and accuracy; that this stimulus has always been supplied to men by university examinations and rewards of honour; that it ought to be offered to women, as likely to produce on them the same desirable results; lastly, that the University of London requiring no collegiate residence, and having its examinations conducted in special apartments perfectly unobjectionable for women's use, it constitutes the one university in the kingdom which ought to admit women to its examinations.

Intimately connected with this matter is that of opening to women the medical profession, for which university degrees would be the first steps. The subject has been well worn of late; yet we must needs make a few remarks concerning it, and notably to put a question or two to objectors. Beloved reader (male or female, as the chance may be), did it ever happen to you to live in a household of half a dozen persons in which some woman was *not* the self-constituted family physician, to whom all the other members of the party applied for advice in the ninety-nine cases out of a hundred? A cold, a cough, a rheumatism, a sprain, a cut, a burn, bile, indigestion, headaches and heartaches, are they not all submitted to her counsel, and the remedies she prescribes for them devoutly taken? Usually it is the grandmother or the housekeeper of the family who is consulted; but whichever it may chance to be, mistress or servant, it is always a *woman*. Who ever dreamed of asking his grandfather or his uncle, his butler or footman, 'what he should do for this bad cold,' or to 'be so kind as to tie up this cut finger'? We can hardly imagine the astonishment of 'Jeames' at such a request; but any woman abovestairs or below would take it as perfectly natural. Doctoring is one of the 'rights of women,' which albeit theoretically denied is practically conceded so universally that it is probable that all the MD.'s in England, with the apothecaries to boot, do not order more drugs than are yearly 'exhibited' by their unlicensed female domestic rivals. It is not a question whether such a state of things be desirable; it exists, and no legislation can alter it. The two differences between the authorized doctors and unauthorized doctoresses are simply these—that the first are paid and the second unpaid for their services, and the first have *some* scientific knowledge and the second none at all. It behooves us a little to consider these two distinctions. First, if patients choose to go for advice to women, and women inspire them with sufficient confidence to be consulted, it is a piece of interference quite anomalous in our day to prevent such services being rewarded, or in other words, to prevent the woman from qualifying herself legally to accept such reward. A woman may or may not be a desirable doctor, just as a dissenter may or may not be a desirable teacher; but unless we are to go back to paternal governments, we must permit patients and congregations to be the judges of what suits them best, and not any medical or ecclesiastical corporation. It is not that *women* are called on to show cause why they should be permitted to enter the medical profession and obtain remuneration for their service, but the *doctors*, who are bound to show cause why they should exclude them and deprive them of the remuneration which there are abundance of patients ready to bestow. This is the side of the rights of the doctor. But are we not still more concerned with the second point of difference, which involves the safety of the patient? As we have said, men and women *will* go continually to women for medical advice in all those thousand contingencies and minor maladies out of which three-fourths of the mortal diseases of humanity arise. There is no use scolding, and saying they *ought* to go to the apothecary or the M.D. People will *not* do so, least of all will delicate women do so when it is possible to avoid it. The only question is, whether the advice which in any case they will get from a woman will be good advice or bad advice—advice founded on some scientific knowledge, or advice derived from the wildest empiricism and crassest ignorance.

We have sometimes lamented that we have lacked the precaution of making memoranda of the wonderful remedies which have become known to us in the course of time, as applied by that class of domestic doctoresses of which we have spoken. They would have afforded a valuable storehouse of arguments to prove that, if 'the little knowledge' of medicine (which we are told is all women could hope to acquire in a college) is 'a dangerous thing,' the utter absence of all knowledge whatever which they at present display, is a hundred times more perilous still. Well can we recall, for instance, in the home of our childhood, a certain admirable old cook who was the oracle in medical matters of the whole establishment. Notwithstanding the constant visits of an excellent physician, it was to her opinion that recourse was had on all emergencies; and the results may be imagined when it is avowed that in her genius the culinary and therapeutic arts were so assimilated, that she invariably *cooked* her patients as well as their dinners. On one occasion a groom having received an immense laceration and excoriation of the leg, was treated by having the wound *rubbed with salt, and held before a hotfire!*

At the opposite end of the social scale we can remember a lady of high degree and true Lady Bountiful disposition pressing on us, in succession, the merits of Morison's pills, hydropathy, and brandy and salt; 'and if none of them cure your attack, there is St. John Long's remedy, which is *quite* infallible.' It would not be easy to calculate how often such practitioners might incur the same chance as a grandmother of our own, who, asking an Irish labourer his name, received the *foudroyante* reply—'Ah! and don't you know me, my lady? And didn't your ladyship give the dose to my wife, and she died the next day?— *long life to your ladyship!*

All this folly and quackery—nay, the use of quack medicines altogether— would be vastly diminished, if not stopped, by the training of a certain number of women as regular physicians, and the instruction derived through them of females generally, in the rudiments of physiology and sanitary science. It is vain to calculate whether individual lady physicians would be as successful as the ordinary average of male doctors. To argue about an untried capacity, à *priori*, seems absurd; and such experience as America has afforded us appears wholly favourable. But the point is, not whether women will make as good doctors as men, but how the whole female sex may be better taught in a matter of vital importance, not only to themselves, but to men whose health is modified through life by their mother's treatment in infancy. As the diffusion of physio-logical knowledge among women *generally* must unquestionably come from the instruction of a few women *specially* educated, the exclusion of females from courses of medical study assumes the shape of a decree that the sex on whom the health of the community peculiarly depends shall for ever remain in igno-rance of the laws by which that health is to be maintained.

With the highest possible education for women in ladies' colleges, with Uni-versity examinations and the medical profession opened to them, we have little doubt that a new life would enter into many, and the pursuit of knowledge become a real vocation, where it has been hitherto hardly more than an amuse-ment. Many a field of learning will yield unexpected flowers, to a woman's fresh research, and many a path of science grow firm and clear before the feet which will follow in the steps of Mrs. Somerville. Already women have made for them-selves a place, and a large one, in the literature of our time; and when their gen-eral instruction becomes deeper and higher, their works must become more and more valuable. Whether doctoresses are to be permitted or not, may be a question; but authoresses are already a guild, which, instead of opposition, has met kindliest welcome. It is now a real profession to women as to men, to be writers. Let any one read the list of books in a modern library, and judge how large a share of them were written by women. Mrs. Jameson, Mrs. Stowe, Miss Brontë, George Eliot, Mrs. Gaskell, Susan and Katherine Winkworth, Miss Mar-tineau, Miss Bremer, George Sand, Mrs. Browning, Miss Procter, Miss Austen, Miss Strickland, Miss Pardoe, Miss Mulock, Mrs. Grey, Mrs. Gore, Mrs. Trollope, Miss Jewsbury, Mrs. Speir, Mrs. Gatty, Miss Blagden, Lady Georgiana Fullarton,

Miss Marsh, and a dozen others. There is little need to talk of literature as a field for woman's future work. She is ploughing it in all directions already. The one thing is to do it thoroughly, and let the plough go deep enough, with good thorough drainage to begin upon. Writing books ought never to be thought of slightly. In one sense, it is morally a serious thing, a power of addressing many persons at once with somewhat more weight than in common speech. We cannot without offence misuse such a power, and adorn vice, or sneer at virtue, or libel human nature as all low, and base, and selfish. We cannot without offence neglect to *use* such a power for a good end; and if to give pleasure be the object of our book, make it at least to the reader an ennobling and refining pleasure. A book ought always to be the high water-mark of its author—his best thoughts, his clearest faith, his loftiest aspiration. No need to taunt him, and say he is not equal to his book. His book ought not to be merely the average of his daily ebb and flow, but his flood-line—his spring-tide, jetsam of shells and corallines, and all 'the treasures of the deep.'

And again, writing is an Art, and as an art it should be seriously pursued. The true artist spirit which grudges no amount of preparatory study, no labour of final completion,—this belongs as much to the pen as to the pencil or the chisel. It is precisely this spirit which women have too often lacked, fondly imagining their quickness would do duty for patience, and their tact cover the defect of study. If their work is (as we hope and believe) to be a real contribution to the happiness and welfare of mankind hereafter, the first lesson to be learned is this—conscientious preparatory study, conscientious veracity of expression, conscientious labour after perfection of every kind, clearness of thought, and symmetry of form. The time will come, we doubt not, when all this will be better understood. Writing a novel or a book of travels will not be supposed to come to a lady by nature, any more than teaching children to a reduced gentlewoman. Each art needs its special study and careful cultivation; and the woman who means to pursue aright either literature or science, will consider it her business to prepare herself for so doing, *at least* as much as if she purposed to dance on the stage or make bonnets in a milliner's shop.

Then, we believe we shall find women able to carry forward the common progress of the human race along the path of the True, as well as of the Beautiful and the Good; nay, to give us those views of truth which are naturally the property of woman. For be it remembered, as in optics we need two eyes to see the roundness and fullness of objects, so in philosophy we need to behold every great truth from two stand-points; and it is scarcely a fanciful analogy to say, that these stand-points are provided for us by the different faculties and sentiments of men's and women's natures. In every question of philosophy there enters the intuitive and the experimental, the arguments à *priori* and à *posteriori*. In every question of morals there is the side of justice and the side of love. In every question of religion there is the idea of God as the Father of the world—the careful Creator, yet severe and awful Judge; and there is the idea of God as the Mother, whose tender mercies are over us all, who is grieved by our sins as our mothers were grieved by them, and in whose infinite heart is our only refuge. At the highest point all these views unite. Absolute Philosophy is both intuitive and experimental; absolute Morality is both justice and love; absolute Religion is the worship (at once full of awe and love) of the 'Parent of Good, Almighty,' who is both parents in One. But to reach these completed views we need each side by turns to be presented to us; and this can hardly be better effected than by the alternate action of men's and women's minds on each other.

NOTES

1   We rejoice to hear that Miss Maria S. Rye, who has already done so much for this cause, is on the point of sailing to Otago with one hundred female emigrants, to superintend personally the arrangements for their welfare. This is doing woman's work in working style truly.
2   See Victor Cousin, Du Vrai, du Beau, et du Bien.
3   Female Education, and how it would be affected by University Education. A Paper read before the Social Science Congress. Published by Emily Faithfull and Co., Great Coram-street. Price ad.

Source: Reprinted from *Fraser's Magazine* (November 1862).

"THE EDUCATION OF WOMEN, AND HOW IT WOULD BE AFFECTED BY UNIVERSITY EXAMINATIONS"

A Paper Read by the Author,
before the Social Science Association, London, 1862.

The subject of the Education of Women of the higher classes is one which has undergone singular fluctuations in public opinion. There have been times when England and Italy boasted of the literary attainments of a Lady Jane Grey and a Vittoria Colonna, and there have been times when the Chinese proverb seemed in force, and it was assumed that "the glory of a man is knowledge, but the glory of a woman is to renounce knowledge." For the last half-century, however, the tide seems to have set pretty steadily in the direction of female erudition. Our grandmothers understood spelling and writing, Blair's sermons and long whist. Our mothers to these attainments added French and the pianoforte, and those items (always unimportant in a woman's education), history and geography. In our own youth we acquired, in a certain shadowy way peculiar to the boarding-schools of that remote period, three or four languages and three or four instruments, the use of the globes and of the dumb-bells, moral philosophy and Poonah-painting. How profound and accurate this marvellous education (usually completed at the mature age of sixteen) it is needless to remark. A new generation has appeared, and he who will pursue the splendid curriculum of one of the Ladies' Colleges, of Bedford Square, of Harley Street, for instance, will perceive that becoming an accomplished young lady is a much more serious affair now than it was in "the merry times when we were young."

The question now arises, This wider and deeper education, how far is it to go? Have we reached its reasonable limit, or shall we see it carried much farther? If it be found desirable to push it into higher branches of study and greater perfection of acquirements, how will this best be accomplished? In particular, the grave query has lately been mooted, "Will those University examinations and academical honours, which have long been reckoned all-powerful in advancing the education of men, be found equally efficacious in advancing the education of women? Ought they to be opened to female competition, and a Free Trade in knowledge established between the sexes? Or, on the contrary, does there appear just cause why this door, at all events, should for ever be closed to the possible progress of women?

Before offering a few suggestions on this subject, I crave permission to make some general observations on the present condition of young women of the higher classes, and their special wants at this moment. A knowledge of these wants alone has induced me to obey the request to give such little aid as may be in my power to their efforts after a better state of things. Few indeed can be unaware that they are passing through a transitory period of no small difficulty, and that there is urgent need for revision of many of the old social regulations regarding them. No class has felt more than they the rise in the atmosphere of modern thoughts; and where their mothers lived healthily enough in closed chambers, they are stifling. New windows must be opened to the light, new air of heaven admitted, and then we shall see bloom in women's cheeks, and light in their eyes, such as they have never worn before.

The miseries of the poor are doubtless greatest of all, but there are other miseries besides theirs which it behoves us to consider. The wretchedness of an empty brain is perhaps as hard to bear as an empty purse, and a heart without hope is as cheerless as a fireless grate. As society is now constituted, no inconsiderable portion of women's lives are aimless and profitless. There are Eugenie Grandets by hundreds in all our towns, and Marianas in Moated Granges in the country, whose existence is no better than that of "the weed on Lethe's banks," and yet who were given by Providence powers whereby they might have become sources of happiness to all around them. For (let us hope it will some time or other be recognised) there *are* purposes in the order of Providence for the lives of single women and childless wives, and they too are meant to have their share of human happiness. Most people prefer to ignore their existence as a class to be contemplated in the education of women, but it is as vain to do so as it is cruel. All of us know enough of those hapless households where the wife, having no children and few home duties, undergoes the most deplorable depreciation of character for want of employment of heart and mind; and her nature, if originally weak and small, shrivels up in petty vanities and contentions; and if strong and high, falls too often blasted by the thunderstorms of passion accumulated in the moveless and unwholesome atmosphere. All of us know those other households, none less hapless, where grown-up daughters, unneeded by their parents, are kept from all usefulness or freedom of action, frittering away the prime of their days in the busy idleness of trivial accomplishments; till, when all energy to begin a new course is gone, the parents die at last, and each one sinks into the typical "Old Maid," dividing her life henceforth in her small lodgings, between "*la médisance, le jeu et la dévotion.*"

All this is pitiful enough. We may laugh at it; but it is not the less a miserable destiny, and one, moreover, which it is often almost impossible for a young woman to shake off. If she be a Roman Catholic, she may leave her home and go into a nunnery in all honour and credit; but the exchange is perhaps no great gain. If she be a Protestant, friends, parents, neighbours, and all her little world cry out lustily if she think of leaving her father's roof for any end, however good or noble, save only that one sacred vocation of matrimony, for which she may lawfully leave a blind father and dying mother, and go to India with Ensign Anybody. These curiosities of public opinion need surely to be set right. Let me plead with those men and women whose lives are rich and full, whose every hour has its duty of its pleasure, who can say,

"How beautiful it is to be alive!
To wake each morn as if the Maker's grace
Did us afresh from nothingness derive,"

to think of these poor, narrow, withered existences, and not say, "How can we keep women just what we would like—images set up in a niche?" but, "What can we do to give to a vast number of our fellow-creatures all the joys of a useful and honourable life?" Again, there are numbers of young women who are free, so far as the wishes of their parents go, to devote themselves to practical usefulness. But the employment of women of the upper classes is one of the most difficult of achievements. At nearly every door they knock in vain; and, what is worse, they are sometimes told they are unfit for work (even for philanthropic work), *because* they are not soundly educated, or possessed of steady business habits. Yet when they seek to obtain such education, here again they meet the bolted door!

It is needless to go on farther. Enough has been said, I trust, to show that young women (both those possessed of the means of independent mainte-nance, and those desiring to support themselves by intelligent labour) are sadly in need of some further improvements in their condition. Among the ways in which it may be possible to effect such improvements, a high education mani-festly stands foremost—a great good in itself, and needful for nearly all further steps of advance. On this subject also I must say a few words, and notably, to refute some popular misconceptions regarding it.

The idea that there is a natural incompatibility between classical studies and feminine duties, and that a highly-educated lady is necessarily a bad wife and mother, is indeed an idea venerable from its antiquity and wide diffusion. "I would rather make women good wives than teach them Latin," is a favorite species of apothegm, whose parallel, however, (for all the sense it possesses), might be found in saying, "I would rather make women good wives than make them eat their breakfasts!" Storing the mind with declensions, or the mouth with tea and toast, are neither of them, in the nature of things, antithetic to becoming a careful housewife and an affectionate companion. As Sydney Smith remarked, "A woman's love for her offspring hardly depends on her ignorance of Greek, nor need we apprehend that she will forsake an infant for a quadratic equation." A pri-ori, the thing is not probable, and actually we see that a very different doctrine holds good. Few of us, I think, would fail to cite in their own circles the best culti-vated women as precisely those whose homes are the happiest, who exercise there-in that spirit of order and love of beauty, and, above all, that sense of the sacred-ness of even the smallest duties, which comes of true culture of mind. These private examples of moral excellence in studious women we cannot often quote on such occasions as the present. I may be permitted, however, to name two of them who have become household words among us all, and both of whom it has been my rare fortune to know very intimately. They are examples respectively of the two great lines in which a woman's virtue may be best displayed: the home duties of the wife and mother, and the out-of-door duties of the philanthropist.

The woman whose home was the happiest I ever saw, whose aged husband (as I have many times heard him) "rose up and called her blessed" above all, and whose children are among the most devoted, was the same woman who in her youth outstripped nearly all the men of her time in the paths of science, and who in her beloved and honoured age is still studying reverently the won-ders of God's creation,—that woman is Mary Sommerville.

And the woman whose philanthropy has been the most perfect, who has done more than any beside to save the criminal and vagrant children of our land, and whose whole time and heart are given to their instruction, that woman is the same who taught Homer and Virgil as assistant in her father's school at eighteen,—that woman is Mary Carpenter.

We now proceed a step farther in our argument. After the examples cited, it may perhaps be assumed as proved that a high education does not in itself unfit women from performing either domestic or philanthropic duties; but that, on the contrary, it is a thing to be desired on every account. Our next position obviously is this: If a high education is to be desired for women, ought it not to be sought for them in those same University studies and honours which have so long proved efficacious in the case of men? Here another objection straightway rises up against us: "A *high* education (it is said) may be desirable for women, but not a *University* education; for that would be to assimilate the training of the two sexes, and any step in such a direction must be fatal, as tending to obliterate the natural differences between them."

A most weighty objection indeed would this be, were it founded on fact.

No *man* can possibly less desire any obliteration of the mental characteristics of the two sexes, than does every woman who has an intelligent care for the welfare of her own. But is such erasure indeed *possible?* Is it not clear enough that the Creator has endowed men and women with different constitutions of mind as of body? and need we be under the slightest apprehension that any kind of education whatever will efface those differences? Education is, after all, only what its etymology implies—the educing, the drawing out; of the powers of the individual. If we, then, draw out a *woman's* powers to the very uttermost, we shall only educe her *womanliness.* We cannot give her a man's powers any more than we can give a man a woman's brilliancy or intuition, or any other gift. We can only educe her God-given *woman's* nature, and so make her a more perfect woman. These differences will, I affirm, come out in every line of woman's expanding powers—in study, quite as much as in all beside. If a woman apply herself to Art, it will be a fresh type of beauty she will reveal. If she devote herself to philanthropic labours, she will not work like a man, from *without*—by the outward legislation, but as a woman, from *within*—by the influence of one heart on another. Not by force of will, not by despotic volition does a woman ever do any good. She has abandoned somewhat of her womanhood when she exerts such powers. Even in teaching a class of little children, she rules not by authority, but by winning each little heart to voluntary submission. And in every other work it is the same. Her true victory must ever be an inward one,—a greater and more perfect victory, therefore, than was ever gained by conqueror's sword. And in matters of study it will be the same. Woman learns differently from man; and when she is able to teach, she teaches differently and with different lessons. If ever the day arrives when women shall be able to deal worthily with the subjects of our highest interests, we shall all be the better, I believe, for completing man's ideal of religion and morals by that of woman, and learning to add to his Law of Justice her Law of Love, and to his faith in God's fatherly care, her faith in His motherly tenderness,—that blessed lesson forgotten too long: that "as a woman hath compassion on the son of her womb, even so the Lord hath pity on us all"!

The differences between men and women are coextensive with their whole natures. A man and a woman are *parallel* to each other, but never *similar.* He is the Right Hand of humanity, and she is the Left. They are *equivalents* to each other, but never *equals.* He is the pound in gold, she is the twenty shillings in silver. All these differences are innate, unchangeable, ineradicable. It is a perfect caricature of them to represent that some kinds of knowledge are fit for men, and other kinds for women. As well we might say that some kinds of food were fit for one and not the other. It is not *in the truths to be acquired,* but in the *assimilation* of those truths in the mind which receives them, that the difference consists. It is as absurd to try to keep a woman feminine in mind by making her learn French because a man learns Latin, as it would be to try to keep her so in person by making her eat mutton because a man eats beef! Endless are the absurdities of this kind extant upon us. Men ought to be well-informed: let women, then, know nothing but trivial accomplishments. Men ought to be strong and healthy: let a woman's cheek (as Burke expresses it) display the charming *morbidezza* of partial disease. A man ought to be brave: let a woman be instructed to dread all things in heaven and earth, from thunder-storms to spiders. Thus it is fondly imagined we are helping Providence to keep women women, and securing the universe against the disorder of their turning into men. Now, however, by narrowing and clipping every faculty—not by pinching her in mental stays, shall we make a true woman. Such processes produce Dolls, not Women; figures very suitable to be set up in haberdashers' shops, to show off bonnets and crinolines, but not such forms as sculptors copy as types of womanly beauty. Our affair is to give nature its fullest, healthiest play and richest culture, and then the result will be what the Lord of Nature has designed— a true Woman; a being, not artificially different from a man, but radically and essentially, because *naturally* different—his *complement* in the great sum of human nature, not a mere *deduction* from his own share of that sum.

If these views be true, it follows that the highest education we can give will never efface, in the slightest degree, the natural characteristics of a woman's mind. Another argument, however, is here urged against us. It is said, "Let it be granted that you will not make women *masculine* by teaching them Greek and Euclid; yet it may still appear that Greek and Euclid are very inappropriate studies for women—useless in themselves, if not detrimental in the way supposed. A woman's mind has natural *affinities* to the lighter studies, and *repulsions* to the heavier ones. Let us have an entirely different course of studies, suited to the feminine soul, and then, perhaps, the form of a University education may be beneficial."

Now, that anyone will aver that the subjects of study in any one University are actually the very best possible subjects for women, or even for men, I do not suppose we shall find. But the point is, Who is to decide what is fit for a woman's brain save the owner of the brain herself? Who has the right to decree that the curriculum for the *goose* ought not be the same as that which collegiate wisdom has appointed for the *gander?* If we were told that soldiers, artisans, or any other class of the community had sought instruction in arithmetic, or any such study, we should hardly think it is our business to lay down the law for them: "Thus is fit for you to learn, and this is unfit; your Bœotian brains may have *affinities* for the multiplication table, but they certainly have *repulsions* for the rule of three." The proof of this particular description of pudding lies exclusively in the eating!

It may be found, indeed, hereafter, that opening up other studies for examination than those at present used, and leaving the option among them free, may be a desirable change, specifically beneficial to women. This is quite possible; but in any case the highest masculine studies ought to be left free to a woman, *if* she feel the power and perseverance to undertake them. As Herbert Spencer remarks, "That a woman has *less* powers than a man, is a poor argument why she should be forbidden to use such powers as she *has*." It is a grave mistake to assume that what we judge is the proper pursuit for women in general is the proper for each in particular, and that we have any just authority to crush individuality displayed in the choice of unusually arduous studies.

The three great revelations of the Infinite One—the True, the Beautiful, and the Good—are all alike in sanctity in themselves. To devote life to the pursuit of any one of them is a noble thing. With respect to the Good we all feel this, and admit that to promote the virtue and happiness of our neighbours is a holy destiny for man or woman. And again, with respect to the Beautiful, we in a degree admit the same for women; and if they display the gifts of Jenny Lind, or Mrs. Browning, or Rosa Bonheur, or Harriet Hosmer, we permit them to study music, or poetry, or painting, or sculpture. But with respect to the True, the rare and noble love of it, the readiness to devote life to its acquirements in abstract and abstruse studies—this is a thing we can hardly bring ourselves to sanction in a woman. Most women care only for the concrete and the personal, and the widest generalizations of philosophy too often interest them only as they concern the small affairs of families and neighbours. Therefore, *because* few women rise to the level of abstract truth, *no* women are to be permitted to do so? This is utterly absurd. Instead of striving to bring all to the same dead level, we should welcome heartily all earnest devotion to Truth, Beauty, or Goodness, and rejoice in every diversity of gift whereby women may bring their special characteristics into play, and so enrich us all.

If I may hope that by these observations I have removed, in a measure, the objections to women pursuing the solid studies of a University education, I may now proceed to the positive side of the argument, which seems to have received far too little attention from men; namely, that the natural constitution of the female mind renders a solid education peculiarly desirable, and even necessary, to bring out all womanly powers and gifts in proper balance and usefulness. I verily believe that a *man* can infinitely better dispense with sound mental training than a woman. Among the essential differences between the mental constitution of the two sexes, one of the most obvious is the preponderance in the latter of the intuitive over the reasoning faculties. As it has been facetiously expressed, "When a man has laboriously climbed up step by step to the summit of his argument, he will generally find a woman standing before him on the top. But of how she got there, neither he nor she can give the smallest explanation." This rapid institution of women may or may not prove a defect. Properly trained and balanced by that carefulness of truth which comes of conscientious study, it is no defect at all, but a great advantage; but unregulated quickness is a peril and misfortune. Jumping at conclusions is a favorite species of feminine steeplechase, with whose sad results we are probably too familiar. I recollect an instance of it, in which that imperviousness to reason, which affords apparently so much pleasure to spectators when manifested by young ladies, must have been rather trying to the person principally concerned. It happened that an elderly lady, a "true woman" on weak-minded principles, discovered that the gentleman in whose house she resided had kindly paid the insurance for her personal property along with his own at his fire-office. Rousing herself in great indignation, she exclaimed, "He insure my property? He insure *getting my property after my death*? No such thing! I meant to leave him a good legacy, now I will do nothing of the kind—I will alter my will and leave him nothing at all!" Vainly did the unfortunate gentleman endeavor to explain that fire insurances did not insure inheritance of property. Vainly did his friend, a Queen's Counsel of eminence, who had convinced a hundred juries, argue for hours with that irate old lady. Her will was altered, and the legacy revoked! I should like to know the sincere opinion of that gentleman on the desirability of giving a better cultivation of the reasoning faculties of women.

Again, women need solid mental training, not only to amend their reasoning and open their minds to argument, but also to correct the terribly inaccurate and superficial knowledge they now usually think sufficient. If the ladies of the present day proceed in geography too far to ask the celebrated query of one of the grandmothers, "Was Hyder Ali an island or a continent?" and if in physical science they no longer (like another old lady) confine their knowledge of flowers to the Aurora Borealis and the delirium tremens, yet abundance of them are to be found whose ideas of Hyder Ali are of the most hazy description, and whose physical science might be expressed in the exhaustive analysis of another lady: "Plants are divided by botanists into monandria, bulbous roots, and weeds." Modern languages are excellent studies, especially for us women, to whom enforced silence, whether in England or on the Continent, is not supposed to be particularly tasteful. Often I have rejoiced for myself and my fellows, in finding ourselves all over Europe and the East, not only chattering away gaily on our own account, but able to assist our countrymen out of the multitudinous dilemmas to which their ignorance consigned them. Indeed, if any one particular branch of education be liable to the charge of giving ladies an inconvenient degree of independence of, and even power over the lordly sex, it is precisely this one of modern languages, which on all hands is given as our *specialité*. A certain old saw concerning the "Grey Mare," and her superiority to her masculine companion in harness, is never so forcibly brought to recollection as when we behold the intelligent mother of a family at a railway station or hotel door in Italy or Germany, making all needful payments and arrangements with the utmost fluency and *savoir faire*, while at the rear of her brood of pretty chickens comes Paterfamilias, able to do nothing except carry the umbrellas and "Bradshaws" of the party.

But these same delightful modern languages, does their acquirement afford any mental training similarly beneficial to that which a boy's mind undergoes over his Latin grammar? Speaking from my own sad experience, I must avow it does nothing of the kind, and that it is possible to talk three or four of them while remaining in pristine innocence regarding the cases and tenses of any one.

Lastly, the one noble science which would be the very best corrective of the slovenliness of female instruction, the science of geometry, is nearly utterly neglected. I verily believe that to gain only the idea of what constitutes a mathematical demonstration, and how mathematical reasoning proceeds, would be to many of our minds a clearing up of fog and haze which would brighten the rest of our days.

Now to bring women's education out of the stage of imperfection in which it stops, it seems evident that some test and standard of perfection is needful. And this test to be sought and applied must be made a goal to which women will strive as ensuring some sort of prize. Scholarships and similar rewards are already used with much benefit at Bedford and other Ladies' Colleges. But the prize which naturally belongs to perfection of attainment is simply its *recognition*,—such public and secure recognition of it as shall make it available for all subsequent purposes. Herein will women find (as men have long found) the sufficient stimulus to strain up to that point, without which, in fact, education must ever be most incomplete. With the education of Oxford and Cambridge would be were there no such things as "Little-go" and "Great-go," no examinations or strivings for degrees, women's education has hitherto been—nay, it has been worse, for it has been stopped at an age earlier than the collegiate education of men begins, and all the best years of study have been lost to her. We would now alter these things. We would obtain for women the right to such academic honours as would afford a sufficient motive and stimulus for thorough, accurate, and sustained study by young women past mere girlhood, and able to acquire the higher branches of knowledge. This *general* and great benefit would be the first object—the raising for *all* women the standard of education. But, beside this general utility, we believe that great special use would accrue to certain classes of women (and through them to the community) from thus opening to them the benefit of University education.

First, as regards those intending to be governesses. Here will be first provided an exceedingly high standard, held out with due encouragements for those who seek the chief places in the profession. An entirely new class of instructresses will, we believe, be thence created. Secondly, mothers, whether themselves well taught or ignorant, will know on what they depend when they engage such governesses; and not, as now, find themselves constantly deceived by shallow pretence, and references to ill-judging employers. Thirdly, and above all, a few dozen *accurately* trained governesses would, I am convinced, do much to revolutionize the present state of female education in the country, by giving to their pupils the same habits of solid and accurate study they have themselves acquired. The slovenly lessons, the half-corrected exercises, will then we hope, be at an end; and the young lady's schoolroom become a mental gymnasium, where health and soundness of mind will be gained for life, instead of what now is too often—a place where ineradictable habits are acquired of mental scrambling and shuffling, of shallowness and false show. And again, these certificates will be of importance as preliminary steps to the introduction of women into the medical profession. On this great subject I have no space worthily to speak, and can therefore only refer to it as one of improvements most to be desired. Such little experience as I have myself had of such matters has lain among a class the most piteous assuredly in the community—the sufferers of incurable disease. I can only record my conviction that a large number of women among them would have been saved from agonizing deaths had they been able in the first stages of their disorder to obtain the advice of female doctors. There are other employments beside those governesses and physicians—clerkships, secretaryships, and the like, to which the admission of women will be universally facilitated by the proposed degrees. These matters are, however, sufficiently obvious to require no discussion.

I hope I have now in some measure demonstrated—first, that some improvement is needed in the condition of young women, and that a better education is one of the stages of such improvement. Secondly, that a high education does not make women *less* able and willing to perform their natural duties, but better and more intelligently able and willing to do so. Thirdly, that to assimilate the *forms* of a women's education to that of a man by means of examinations and academical honours, and also the *substance* of it by means of classical and mathematical studies, will in nowise tend to efface the natural differences of their minds, which depend not on any accidental circumstances, to be regulated by education, but on innate characteristics given by the Creator. Fourthly, that there are many positive benefits, general and particular, to be expected from such Examinations and Honours, such classical and mathematical studies being opened to women.

Now it happens that there is one institution in this country which seems especially qualified to afford the advantages we have supposed—namely, the London University. In the older Universities the rule of collegiate residence necessarily excludes women; but in London, the examinations being open to all, wheresoever educated, there is no reason why young ladies studying in the various female colleges, or in their homes, should not be admitted to share all the benefits of the institution.

As most of my readers are no doubt aware, the proposal that women should be thus admitted has been lately under debate in the Senate of the University—

the occasion of a new charter offering a convenient opportunity for the change. A clause (it was suggested) should be inserted, extending the present terms, "all classes and denominations of her Majesty's subjects, without any exception whatever," to that *small* class, including half the human race, to which her Majesty herself belongs. This proposition, after much debate, was negatived, but only by the casting-vote of the chairman. Not unreasonably, therefore, may we hope that on the next occasion a fresh consideration will be given to the case, and another decision obtained: That so startling a proposal received on its first suggestion the votes of ten members of the Senate out of twenty, is much more surprising than that it should have been ultimately rejected. The long list of eminent names which has been obtained in favour of the movement, is guarantee for an amount of public opinion which may well inspire confidence in eventual success.

Should it so prove, and the University of London open its doors to women, the time will not be far distant when the innovation, which some may now regard as a derogation from its dignity, will be boasted of as no inconsiderable claim to public gratitude and respect. Those inadequacies of the two sexes which place women at a disadvantage during ages when might makes right, are altered in happier times, when the strong heart is seen to be worth as much as the strong head. The tide has turned for women, and by and by the credit of helping their progress will not be lightly esteemed. Even were this otherwise, however, the University of London would hardly suffer, I think, from following in the course of the schools of Alexandria, where the martyr Hypatia held the first chair of philosophy then existing in the world; or in that of the University of Padua, where women learned and taught by the side of Galileo, Petrarch, and Colombus.

In conclusion, I would venture to make one appeal: do not let us in this, or any other matter connected with women's claims, allow ourselves to be drawn aside by those prejudices which on both sides distract us. To a woman of refined feeling, that popular Ogress, the Strong-minded Female, is so distasteful, that she is inclined rather to leave her whole sex to mental starvation than contribute to the sustenance of one specimen of the genus. To a man with a spark of fun in his composition, the temptation to perpetrate jokes about Mistresses of Arts and Spinsters of Arts is perfectly irresistible. But, after all, refined women will best prevent the growth of strong-mindedness, in its obnoxious sense, by bringing their own good taste to help their sisters, whom the harsh struggles of life under a woman's disadvantages have perhaps somewhat hardened and embittered. And men who laugh at the absurdities (incident, alas! in some mysterious way to all the doings of women), will also in graver moments feel that there is another side to the subject, not a ludicrous one; and that the answer of the poor frogs to the boys in the fable might often be made by human sufferers: "throwing stones may be fun to you, but it is death to us." To aid a woman in distress was deemed in the old days of chivalry the cheifest honour of the bravest knight; it is assuredly no less an honour now for wise and generous men to aid the whole sex to a better and nobler life, and to the developing more perfectly, because more fully and freely, that Womanhood which God has also made in His own image—a divine and holy thing.

"'CRIMINALS, IDIOTS, WOMEN, AND MINORS'"

There was an allegory rather popular about thirty years ago, whose manifest purpose was to impress on the juvenile mind that tendency which Mr. Matthew Arnold has ingeniously designated 'Hebraism.' The hero of the tale descends upon earth from some distant planet, and is conducted by a mundane cicerone through one of our great cities, where he beholds the docks and arsenals, the streets and marts, the galleries of art, and the palaces of royalty. The visitor admires everything till he happens to pass a grave-yard. 'What is that gloomy spot?' he asks of his companion. 'It is a cemetery,' replies the guide.

'A—what did you say?' inquires the son of the star.

'A grave-yard; a place of public interment; where we bury our dead,' reiterates the cicerone.

The visitor, pale with awe and terror, learns at last that there is in this world such a thing as *Death*, and (as he is forbidden to return to his own planet) he resolves to dedicate every moment left to him to prepare himself for that fearful event and all that may follow it.

Had that visitor heard for the first time upon his arrival on earth of another incident of human existence—namely, *Marriage*, it may be surmised that his astonishment and awe would also have been considerable. To his eager inquiry whether men and women earnestly strove to prepare themselves for so momentous an occurrence, he would have received the puzzling reply that women frequently devoted themselves with perfectly Hebraistic singleness of aim to that special purpose; but that men, on the contrary, very rarely included any preparation for the married state among the items of their widest Hellenistic culture. But this anomaly would be trifling compared to others which would be revealed to him. 'Ah,' we can hear him say to his guide as they pass into a village church. 'What a pretty sight is this! What is happening to that sweet young woman in white who is giving her hand to the good-looking fellow beside her, all the company decked in holiday attire, and the joy-bells shaking the old tower overhead? She is receiving some great honour, is she not? The Prize of Virtue, perhaps?'

'Oh, yes,' would reply the friend; 'an honour certainly. She is being Married.' After a little further explanation the visitor would pursue his inquiry:

'Of course, having entered this honourable state of matrimony, she has some privilege above the women who are not chosen by anybody? I notice her husband has just said, "With all my worldly goods I thee endow." Does that mean that she will henceforth have the control of his money altogether, or only that he takes her into partnership?

'*Pas précisément*, my dear sir. By our law it is *her* goods and earnings, present and future, which belong to him from this moment.'

'You don't say so? But then, of course, his goods are hers also?'

'Oh dear, no! not at all. He is only bound to find her food; and truth to tell, not very strictly or efficaciously bound to do that.'

'How! do I understand you? Is it possible that here in the most solemn religious act, which I perceive your prayer book calls "The Solemnisation of Holy Matrimony," every husband makes a generous promise, which promise is not only a mockery, but the actual reverse and parody of the real state of the case: the man who promises giving nothing, and the woman who is silent giving all?'

'Well, yes; I suppose that is something like it, as to the letter of the law. But then, of course, practically—'

'Practically, I suppose few men can really be so unmanly and selfish as the law warrants them in being. Yet some, I fear, may avail themselves of such authority. May I ask another question? As you subject women who enter the marriage state to such very severe penalties as this, what worse have you in store for women who lead a dissolute life, to the moral injury of the community?'

'Oh, the law takes nothing from them. Whatever they earn or inherit is their own. They are able, also, to sue the fathers of their children for their maintenance, which a wife, of course, is not allowed to do on behalf of *her* little ones, because she and her husband are one in the eye of the law.'

'One question still further—your criminals? Do they always forfeit their entire property on conviction?'

'Only for the most heinous crimes; felony and murder, for example.'

'Pardon me; I must seem to you so stupid! Why is the property of the woman who commits Murder, and the property of the woman who commits Matrimony, dealt with alike by your law?

Leaving our little allegory and in sober seriousness, we must all admit that the just and expedient treatment of women by men is one of the most obscure problems, alike of equity and of policy. Nor of women only, but of all classes and races of human beings whose condition is temporarily or permanently one of comparative weakness and dependence. In past ages, the case was simple enough. No question of right or duty disturbed the conscience of Oriental or Spartan, of Roman or Norman, in dealing with his wife, his Helot, his slave, or his serf. 'Le droit du plus fort' was unassailed in theory and undisturbed in practice. But we, in our day, are perplexed and well nigh overwhelmed with the difficulties presented to us. What ought the Americans to do with their Negroes? What ought we to do with our Hindoos? What ought all civilised people to do with their women? It is all very easy to go on driving down the 'high à *priori*' road of equal rights for all human beings, but as it is quite clear that children and idiots cannot be entrusted with full civil and political rights, the question always resolves itself into the further one, Where shall we draw the line? When has a human being fairly passed out of the stage of pupilage and attained his majority?

At the head of this paper I have placed the four categories under which persons are now excluded from many civil, and all political rights in England. They were complacently quoted this year by the *Times* as every way fit and proper exceptions; but yet it has appeared to not a few that the place assigned to Women among them is hardly any longer suitable. To a woman herself who is aware that she has never committed a Crime; who fondly believes that she is not an Idiot; and who is alas! only too sure she is no longer a Minor, there naturally appears some incongruity in placing her, for such important purposes, in an association wherein otherwise she would scarcely be likely to find herself. But in all seriousness, the question presses, Ought Englishwomen of full age, at the present state of affairs, to be considered as having legally attained majority? or ought they permanently to be considered, for all civil and political purposes, as minors? This, we venture to think, is the real point at issue between the friends and opponents of 'women's rights,' and it would save, perhaps, not a little angry feeling and aimless discussion, were we to keep it well in view and not allow ourselves to be drawn off into collateral debates about equality and abstract rights. Let us admit (if it be desired) that the pupilage in which women have been hitherto kept has been often inevitable, and sometimes salutary. The question is, should it be prolonged indefinitely?

In the present paper we shall attempt to consider the most striking instance wherein the existing principle presses upon women, and where its injustice appears most distinctly,—namely, in the regulation of the Property of Married Women under the Common Law. We shall endeavour to do this with all possible fairness and equanimity. The acrimony which too often creeps into arguments on this subject is every way needless and mischievous. Of course it is not pleasant to women to be told they are 'physically, morally, and intellectually inferior' to their companions. The humblest individual is neither more contented, nor (we believe) much the better for being reminded of congenital defects which he can never hope to overcome; and for a proud and gifted woman to be told that she is in every possible respect inferior to the footman who stands behind her chair, can hardly be thought pleasing intelligence. Nevertheless, women are foolish to be angry with the man who in plain words tells them straightforwardly that in his opinion such is the case. After all he pays them a better compliment than the fop who professes to adore them as so many wingless angels, and privately values them as so many dolls. In any case all such discussion is beside our present aim. We shall endeavour, in these pages, neither to talk with one party, as if all instinct and feeling were the creatures of law, and could be altered by 'An Act to Review the Constitution of Human Nature;' nor with another, as if the particular sentiment of our age and country about 'woman's sphere' were the only possible standard of legislation for all time. If, as Pope said, 'the world were inhabited by Men, Women, and Herveys,' we should endeavour to write like a Hervey, to do justice to both the other parties!

Mr. G. Shaw Lefevre has this summer carried through two readings in Parliament, and obtained a favourable report upon, 'A Bill to Amend the Law with respect to the Property of Married Women.' Let us briefly state what is the existing law which it is proposed to amend; what may be urged in its behalf; and what may be said against it.

By the common law of England a married woman has no legal existence, so far as property is concerned, independently of her husband. The husband and wife are assumed to be one person, and that person is the husband. The wife can make no contract, and can neither sue nor be sued. Whatever she possess of personal property at the time of her marriage, or whatever she may afterwards earn or inherit, belongs to her husband, without control on her part. If she possess real estate, so long as her husband lives he receives and spends the income derived from it, being only forbidden to sell it without her consent. From none of her property is he bound to reserve anything, or make any provision for her maintenance or that of her children. This is the law for all, but practically it affects only two classes of women, viz. those who marry hurriedly or without proper advisers, and those whose property at the time of marriage is too small to permit of the expense of a settlement; in other words, the whole middle and lower ranks of women, and a certain portion of the upper ranks. Women of the richer class, with proper advisers, never come under the provisions of the Common Law, being carefully protected therefrom by an intricate system elaborated for the purpose by the courts of Equity, to which the victims of the Common Law have for years applied for redress. That system always involves considerable legal expenses, and an arrangement with trustees which is often extremely inconvenient and injurious to the interests of the married couple; nevertheless it is understood to be so great a boon that none who can afford to avail themselves of it, fail to do so.

What then is the principle on which the Common Law mulets the poorer class of women of their property and earnings, and entails on the rich, if they wish to evade it, the costs and embarrassment of a marriage settlement? There is, of course, a principle in it, and one capable of clear statement. There are grounds for the law; first of Justice, then of Expediency, lastly (and as we believe) most influential of all, of Sentiment. Let us briefly describe them as best we can.

First, the grounds of Justice.

Man is the natural bread-winner. Woman lives by the bread which man has earned. Ergo, it is fit and right that the man who wins should have absolute disposal, not only of his winnings, but of every other small morsel or fraction of earning or property she may possess. It is a fair return to him for his labour in the joint interests of both. He supports her, pays any debts she has incurred before or after marriage, and provides for the children which are hers as well as his. For all this, it is but just he should receive whatever she has to give. The woman's case is that of a pauper who enters a workhouse. The ratepayers are bound to support him; but if he have any savings they must be given up to the board. He cannot both claim support and keep independent property.

Then for Expediency. 'How can two walk together except they be agreed?' says the Bible. 'How can they walk together except one of them have it all his own way?' says the voice of rough and ready practicality. Somebody must rule in a household, or everything will go to rack and ruin; and disputes will be endless. If somebody is to rule it can only be the husband, who is wiser, stronger, knows more of the world, and in any case has not the slightest intention of yielding his natural predominance. But to give a man such rule he must be allowed to keep the purse. Nothing but the power of the purse—in default of the stick—can permanently and thoroughly secure authority. Besides, for the good of the whole family, for the children and the wife herself, it is far more expedient that all the resources of the family should be directed by a single hand, and that hand the one that can best transact business of all kinds. Equally then, as a matter of justice to the husband, and of expediency for the interests of the family at large, the law of England has decreed, as aforesaid, that all a woman's present and prospective property becomes on marriage the property of her husband.

But where women are concerned, English law ceases to be a dry system, regardful only of abstract justice and policy. Themis, when she presides at the domestic hearth, doffs her wig, and allows herself to be swayed by poetical, not to say romantic, considerations. We are rarely allowed in debating it to examine accurately the theory of conjugal justice. We are called upon rather to contemplate the beautiful ideal of absolute union of heart, life, and purse which the law has provided for, and which alone it deigns to recognise. If it so happen that happy married couples do not want the law to provide for them, and that the troubles of unhappy ones are greatly aggravated by the law *not* providing for them, it is an inconvenience to be regretted; but it is counterbalanced to the minds of all sensible persons by the great public benefit of the existing system. That the legislative judgement of England should hold up before the world a perfect picture of what it understands that married life *ought* to be, is of much more consequence than that it should try to mend cases which must be bad at the best.

Now let us admit heartily that there is much sense in these arguments of justice and expediency, and much beauty in this ideal of absolute union of interests. In what may fairly be taken as typical marriages, where the man labours all day in the field or the office, and the woman provides for the household at home, the woman *has* no earnings independently of her husband, and what she has earned or inherited before marriage is employed for some purpose common to the family. There is no injustice here. When we remember the thousands of husbands and fathers who thus labour all their lives long for their wives and children—so commonly that it is only the exceptional selfishness we notice, never the rule of manly unselfishness—it may appear the plainest justice, that he on whom all depends (the 'houseband' as our ancestors well called him) should have all the power as well as the toil. True that men have other motives for work beside the love of their families; they have interest in their pursuits, ambition, and pride. Many a bachelor, with none to come after him to inherit his store, labours as sedulously to increase it as the most devoted of parents. But with how many hundreds and thousands is it otherwise! How many men long and pine to cast down the spade or the pen, to leave the bleak field for the fireside, the gloomy shop or office for the streets and the hills; and *could* do so in a moment and live in comfort with a quarter of their present toil, were it not for the thought of the wife who is sitting at home rocking the cradle, or the young daughters who are asking for all the luxuries and fripperies of fashion! We have heard a boy remark, that when he grew up he would never marry, because he noticed that when men married their wives enjoyed everything, and they had only to work harder than before. There was a good deal of truth in the remark— as doubtless the *Saturday Review* would readily corroborate. In the large sense and the common run of life, men are wonderfully unselfish towards women; and the general feeling of society has actually constituted it a rule that they should be expected to be so. Is it not, then, plainly just that he who plants the vineyard should eat—or at least have the distribution—of *all* the fruit thereof?

Then, again, for Expediency. How ignorant are most women in money concerns! How little they understand the commonest transactions, and how liable they are to be cheated, when they flatter themselves they do understand them! In the lower classes, as a general rule, women are more stupid than men; the feminine brain, such as it is, less well bearing rough usage, and the education of girls being inferior to that of boys. For the benefit of both husband, wife, and children, is it not every way expedient to make the wiser of the two keep the common purse?

Lastly, for the sentimental view. How painful is the notion of a wife holding back her money from him who is every day toiling for her support! How fair is the ideal picture of absolute concession on her part of all she possesses of this world's dross to the man to whom she gives her heart and life! How magnificent in its unreserve is Portia's endowment of Bassanio, as quoted by Mr. Lefevre:

Myself and what is mine, to you and yours
Is now converted. But now I was the lord
Of this fair mansion, master of my servants,

Queen o'er myself; and even now, but now,
This house, these servants, and this same myself
Are yours, my lord!

And in the humbler ranks, how sweet is the corresponding idyllic picture! The young man and maiden, after years of affection, and careful laying by of provision for the event, take each other at last, to be henceforth no more twain, but one flesh. Both have saved a little money, but it all now belongs to the husband alone. He lays it out in the purchase of the cottage where they are henceforth to dwell. Day by day he goes forth to his labour, and weekly he brings home his earnings, and places them in his wife's lap, bidding her spend them as she knows best for the supply of their homely board, their clothing which her deft fingers will make and many a time repair, and at last for their common treasures, the little children who gather around them. Thus they grow old in unbroken peace and love, the man's will having never once been disputed, the wife yielding alike from choice and from necessity to his superior sense and his legal authority.

Surely this ideal of life, for which the Common Law of England has done its utmost to provide, is well worth the pondering before we attempt to meddle with any of its safeguards? Who will suggest anything better in its room?

Alas, there are other scenes besides idylls of domestic peace and obedience promoted by the law we are considering. We must look on the dark side as well as on the bright, before we determine that its preponderating influence is beneficial. But of these we shall speak hereafter. Before doing so we must traverse once more, and a little more carefully, the ground we have gone over. Is the Justice, is the Expediency, is the Sentiment of the Common Law all that appears at first sight?

What, in the first place, of the Justice of giving all a woman's property to her husband? The argument is that the wife gets an ample *quid pro quo. Does* she get it under the existing law? That is the simple question.

In the first place, many husbands are unable, from fault or from misfortune, to maintain their wives. Of this law takes no note, proceeding on reasoning which may be reduced to the syllogism:

A man who supports his wife ought to have all her property;
Most men support their wives;
Therefore, all men ought to have all the property of their wives.

Let us suppose the managers of a public institution to engage with a contractor, to pay him 1,000*l.* on the nail for the supply of the institution with provisions for a year. At the end of a month the contractor has spent the 1,000*l.* on his own devices and is bankrupt. The institution starves accordingly. What, in such case, do we think of the managers who gave the 1,000*l.* without security for the fulfilment of the contract, and what do we think of the contractor? But are not hundreds of husbands in the position of the contractor, yet rather pitied than blamed by public opinion? And is not the law in such cases precisely in the position of the reckless managers? When all that a woman possesses in the present and future is handed over unreservedly by the law to her husband, is there the smallest attempt at obtaining security that he on his part can fulfil that obligation which is always paraded as the equivalent, namely, the obligation to support her for the rest of her life? Nay, he is not so much as asked to promise he will reserve any portion of her money for such purpose, or reminded of his supposed obligation. If he spend 10,000*l.* of her fortune in a week in paying his own debts, and incapacitate himself for ever from supporting her and her children, the law has not one word to say against him.

But waiving the point of the *inability* of many husbands to fulfil their side of the understood engagement, one thing, at all events, it must behove the law to do. Having enforced her part on the woman, it is bound to enforce his part on the man, *to the utmost of his ability.* The legal act by which a man puts his hand in his wife's pocket, or draws her money out of the savings' bank, is perfectly clear, easy, inexpensive. The corresponding process by which the wife can obtain food and clothing from her husband when he neglects to provide it— what may it be? Where is it described? How is it rendered safe and easy to every poor woman who may chance to need its protection? When we are assured that men are always so careful of the interests of the women for whom they legislate, that it is quite needless for women to seek political freedom to protect themselves, we might be inclined to take it for granted that here, if anywhere, here where the very life and subsistence of women are concerned, the legislation of their good friends and protectors in their behalf would have been as stringent and as clear as words could make it. We should expect to find the very easiest and simplest mode of redress laid open to every hapless creature thus reduced to want by him to whom the law itself has given all she has ever earned, or inherited. Nay, seeing the hesitation wherewith any wife would prosecute the husband with whom she still tries to live, and the exceeding cowardice and baseness of the act of maltreating so helpless a dependant, it might not have been too much had the law exercised as much severity in such a case as if the offender had voluntarily starved his ass or his sheep, and the Society for the Prevention of Cruelty to Animals were his prosecutors.

But this is the imaginary, what is the actual fact? Simply that the woman's remedy for her husband's neglect to provide her with food, has been practically found unattainable. The law which has robbed her so straightforwardly, has somehow forgotten altogether to secure for her the supposed compensation. Since 1857, if the husband altogether forsake his home for years together, the wife may obtain from the magistrate a protection order, and prevent him from seizing her property. But, if he come back just often enough to keep within the technical period fixed as desertion, and take from her everything she may have earned, or which charitable people may have given her, then there is absolutely no resource for her at all. The Guardians of her Union, if she ask to be admitted into the workhouse, may, if they please, receive her and prosecute her husband at the petty sessions for putting the parish to the expense of supporting his wife. But the guardians are not obliged to admit her, and the trouble and cost of prosecution is an argument which frequently weighs with them against doing so. Then, as if to add insult to injury, when the poor wretch, driven from the shelter of the workhouse, and perhaps on the point of bearing a child to the wretch who is starving her, goes to the magistrate to implore protection,— what answer does she receive? She is told that he cannot hear her complaint; that she cannot sue her husband, as he and she are one in the eye of the law.[1]

Again, the Common Law fails to secure justice to the wife, not only during her husband's life, but after his death. The following story was published many years ago in the *Westminster Review* as having then recently occurred. We cannot vouch otherwise for its veracity, and must quote from memory, but if it be only taken as a hypothetical case, what a lesson does it convey! A gentleman of landed estate in the north of England became involved in debt and finally ruined and reduced to actual want. His wife, a lady of ability and spirit, finding him incapable of any effort for their joint support, opened a little shop for millinery in the county town. Her old friends gave her their custom, and her taste and industry made it a thriving business. For many years she maintained her husband and herself, till at last having realised a little competency, and grown old and feeble, she sold her shop and retired to spend, as she hoped, in peace with her husband the remaining years of her life. After a short time, however, the husband died, duly nursed and tended to the last by his wife. When he was dead he was found to have left a will by which he bequeathed every shilling of his wife's earnings to a mistress he had secretly maintained. Either the wife had originally married without a settlement, or her settlements had not contemplated so singular a fact as her earning a fortune. The husband's will therefore was perfectly valid, *and was executed.*

So much for the justice of the Common Law. What now shall we say to its Expediency? The matter seems to lie thus. Men are generally more wise in worldly matters; more generally able and intelligent, and their wives habitually look up to them with even ridiculously exaggerated confidence and admiration. Such being the case, it would naturally happen, were there no law in the case, that the husband should manage all the larger business of the family, The law then *when the husband is really wise and good* is a dead letter. But for the opposite cases, exceptions though they be, yet alas! too numerous, where the husband is a fool, a gambler, a drunkard, and where the wife is sensible, frugal, devoted to the interests of the children,—is it indeed expedient that the whole and sole power should be lodged in the husband's hands; the power not only over all they already have in common, but the power over all she can ever earn in future?

Such a law must paralyse the energy of any woman less than a heroine of maternal love. How many poor wives has it driven to despair, as one time after another they have been legally robbed of their hard won earnings, who can calculate?[2] One such hapless one, we are told,[3] when her lawful tyrant came home as usual, drunk with the spoils of her starving children, took up some wretched relic of their ruined household and smote him to death. She was a murderess. In former times she would have been burnt alive for 'petty treason' for killing her lord and master. But what was the law which gave to that reckless savage a power the same as that of a slave-holder of the South over his slave?

It is continually repeated *in this connection only* that laws cannot take note of exceptional cases; they must be laid down to suit the majority, and the minority must do as best they can. But is there any other department of public justice in which the same principle is applied? What else is law *for*, but to be 'a terror to evil doers'?—always, as we trust, in a minority in the community. The greater number of people are honest, and neither steal their neighbours' goods nor break into their houses. Yet the law takes pretty sharp account of thieves and burglars.

Setting up an ideal of perfect marriage union sounds very well. But what would it be to set up an ideal, say, between rich and poor, and to assume that what ought to be their relation in a Christian country actually is so? A new Poor Law based on the hypothesis that the Sermon on the Mount forms the rule of English life, to which the exceptions were too trifling to be regarded, would be at all events a novelty in legislation. Or rather, would it not correspond in spirit with the law we have been considering? The poor woman whose husband has robbed her earnings, who leaves her and her children to starve and then goes unpunished because the law can only recognise the relation of husband and wife as it ought to be, and he and she are one before the law,—that poor soul's case would resemble closely enough that of a pauper who should be told that the law can only recognise the relation of rich and poor as it ought to be, and that as every one who had two coats must be assumed to give to him who has none, and from him that would borrow nobody can be supposed to turn away, the striking of a Poor's Rate in a Christian land must be wholly superfluous.

It is one of the numerous anomalies connected with women's affairs, that when they are under debate the same argument which would be held to determine other questions in one way is felt to settle theirs in another. If for instance it be proved of any other class of the community, that it is peculiarly liable to be injured, imposed on, and tyrannised over (e.g. the children who work in factories), it is considered to follow as a matter of course, that the law must step in for its protection. But it is the alleged *helplessness* of married women which, it is said, makes it indispensable to give all the support of the law, *not* to them, but to the stronger persons with whom they are unequally yoked. 'Woman is physically, mentally, and morally inferior to man.' Therefore it follows—what?—that the law should give to her bodily weakness, her intellectual dulness, her tottering morality, all the support and protection which it is possible to interpose between so poor a creature and the strong being always standing over her? By no means. Quite the contrary of course. The husband being already physically, mentally, and morally his wife's superior must in justice receive from the law additional strength by being constituted absolute master of her property. Do we not seem to hear one of the intelligent keepers in the Zoological Gardens explaining to a party of visitors:

'This, ladies and gentlemen, is an inoffensive bird, the *MulierAnglicana.* The beak is feeble, and the claws unsuited for grubbing for worms. It seems to be only intelligent in building its nest, or taking care of its young, to whom it is peculiarly devoted, as well as to its mate. Otherwise it is a very simple sort of bird, picking up any crumbs which are thrown to it, and never touching carrion like the vulture or intoxicating fluids like the maccaw. Therefore you see, ladies and gentlemen, as it is so helpless, we put that strong chain round its leg, and fasten it to its nest, and make the bars of its cage exceptionally strong. As to its rudimentary wings we always break them early, for greater security; though I have heard Professor Huxley say that he is convinced it could never fly far with them, under any circumstances.'

Such is the argument from the feebleness of women to the expediency of weakening any little independent spirit they might possibly found on the possession of a trifle of money. 'To him that hath shall be given, and he shall have more abundantly; but from her that hath not, shall be taken away even that which it seemeth she has a right to have.' The text is a hard one, in an ethical point of view.

But the great and overwhelming argument against the Expediency of the Common Law in this matter is the simple fact that no parent or guardian possessed of means sufficient to evade it by a marriage settlement ever dreams of permitting his daughter or ward to undergo its (supposed) beneficial action. The parent who neglected to demand such a settlement from a man before he gave him his daughter, would be thought to have failed in the performance of one of his most obvious and imperative duties. Even the law itself in its highest form in the realm (that of the Court of Chancery) invariably requires settlements for its wards. How then can it be argued that the same rule is generally considered expedient, yet invariably evaded by all who have means to evade it?

Again. There is the test of experience. Are married couples with settlements obviously less harmonious, are they less united in affection, are their children less well brought up than those who undergo the action of the law? When a woman has money of her own so settled that she really has it for her separate use, do we find her always opposing her husband, and do her children seem to suffer from parental dissensions? nay, let us go to the countries where no Common Law like ours exists at all, or where it has been repealed. In Russia marriage makes no difference in a woman's possession of property, to which also are attached the same political and municipal rights as belong to male proprietors. All that we know of Russian households is their peculiar harmony and mutual good feeling. And in the State of New York, where the Common Law was repealed in 1860, in Vermont, where it was changed in 1847, in Pennsylvania, where it was changed in 1848, and in Massachusetts, where it was changed in 1855, the report of the action of the new law, whereby the woman holds her own property and earning, is entirely satisfactory. The following are some of the testimonies to the fact, collected by the Parliamentary Committee:

> Mr. Washbourne, formerly Governor of Massachusetts, and now Professor of Law at Harvard University, and who allows that he viewed the change with apprehension that it would cause angry and unkind feelings in families, and open the door for fraud, now admits that he is so far convinced to the contrary, that he would not be one to restore the common law if he could. Any attempt to go back to it would meet with little favour at this day. 'The oral evidence we have received from members of the Vermont and Massachusetts bars, from Mr. Cyrus Field of New York, and from the Hon. J. Rose, Finance Minister of Canada, is to the same effect. They state that the change has given entire satisfaction; that it has not caused dissension in families'.... that the benefit has chiefly accrued to women of small means.' Mr. Wells, Judge of the Supreme Court of Massachusetts, says: 'That for which the law seems to me most commendable is the power which it gives to women of the poorer classes to control the fruits of their own labour. Many women of that class are left to struggle against the hardships of life, sometimes with a family of children, abandoned by their husbands, or, still worse, with a drunken, thriftless, idle vagabond of a man, claiming all the rights of a husband, and fulfilling none of the duties of the relation. When such men could take the hard earnings of their wives from service in the mills, and waste it upon their indulgences, no woman could have courage to struggle long in such a useless effort. In our manufacturing towns there are a great many women thus situated, who are saved from the most hopeless poverty and slavery by this most just provision, which gives them the right to receive and to hold the wages of their own labour. The misfortune has been, that the more ignorant and degraded men were, the more rigorously they insisted upon and exercised their marital rights.... The law, by this change in the relative rights of husband and wife, has brought to the women of the poorer classes a relief which touches the spring of hope and energy.' Mr. Dudley Field says of it: 'Scarcely one of the great reforms which have been effected in this State have given more satisfaction than this.'[4]

With such examples before us it truly seems wanton to talk of Expediency.[5] The only persons for whom the existing law is expedient are fortune-hunters, who, if they can befool young women of property so far as to induce them to elope, are enabled thereby to grasp all their inheritance. Were there no such law as the cession of the wife's property on marriage, there would be considerably fewer of those disgusting and miserable alliances where the man marries solely to become possessed of his wife's money.

But, as we have said already, there is an argument which has more force in determining legislation about marriage than either considerations of Justice or of Expediency. It is the sentiment entertained by the majority of men on the subject; the ideal they have formed of wedlock, the poetical vision in their minds of a wife's true relation to her husband. Legislators. talk in Parliament with a certain conviction that the principles of fairness and policy are the only ones to be referred to *there*. But whenever the subject is freely discussed, in private or in a newspaper, there is sure to burst out sooner or later the real feeling at bottom. Nothing can be more amusing than to watch such spontaneous outbreaks of the natural man in the dignified columns of the Times, or the hard-hitting periods of a well-known writer in the *Pall Mall Gazette*. Let us try to fathom this sentiment, for till we understand it we are but fighting our battles in the dark. Is it not this— that a woman's whole life and being, her soul, body, time, property, thought, and care, ought to be given to her husband; that nothing short of such absorption in him and his interests makes her a true wife; and that when she is thus absorbed even a very mediocre character and inferior intellect can make a man happy in a sense no splendour of endowments can otherwise do? Truly I believe this is the feeling at the bottom of nearly all men's hearts, and of the hearts of thousands of women also. There is no use urging that it is a gigantic piece of egotism in a man to desire such a marriage. Perhaps it is natural for him to do so, and perhaps it is natural for a great number of women to give just such absorbed adoring affection. Perhaps it is a tribute to the infinite nature of all love, that for those who know each other best, as a wife knows her husband, there is no limit to human affection. At all events it seems a fact that the typical Man (if we may call him so), desires such love, and the typical Woman is ready to give it to him. He is impatient at the notion of a marriage in which this conception of absolute absorption of his wife's interests in his own shall not be fulfilled; and, so far as legislation can create such an ideal, he is resolved that it shall do so.

So far all is plain and natural, but the question is this: Supposing such marriages to be the most desirable, do men set the right way about securing them, by making such laws as the Common Law of England? Is perfect love to be called out by perfect dependence? Does an empty purse necessarily imply a full heart? Is a generous-natured woman likely to be won or rather to be alienated and galled by being made to feel she has no choice but submission? Surely there is great fallacy in this direction. The idea which we are all agreed ought to be realised in marriage is that of the highest possible Union. But what *is* that most perfect Union? Have we not taken it in a most gross commercial sense, as if even here we were a nation of shopkeepers? Let us go into this matter a little carefully. It is rather instructive.

Husband and wife, in the eye of the poet, the divine, and—shall we say, the Judge of the Divorce Court? are 'not twain, but one flesh' I know not whether

Mr. Darwin will sanction that theory concerning the Origin of Species, which tells us that

> Man came from Nothing, and by the same plan,
> Woman was made from the rib of a man;

or whether Dr. Carpenter and Professor Huxley have verified the anatomical doctrine instilled by our nurses, that in consequence of Adam's sacrifice of his rib, men have ever since had one rib fewer than women. Still, however learned physiologists may decide this obscure problem, we shall all agree that it is a noble Oriental metaphor, to describe a wife's relation to her husband as 'bone of his bone, and flesh of his flesh.' But the union of two human beings may, as preachers say, be considered three ways. Firstly, there is the sort of union between any friends who are greatly attached to one another; a union oftenest seen, perhaps, between two sisters, who each have full liberty to come and go, and dispose of their separate resources, but who yet manage commonly to live in harmony and affection, and not unfrequently to bring up a whole batch of little nephews and nieces in their common abode. Two such we know, who for many years have kept the same account at their banker's, and say that they find only one serious objection to the plan—they can never make each other a present!

Secondly, there is the Union of the celebrated Siamese twins, who are tied together—not by Mother Church but by Mother Nature—so effectually that Sir William Fergusson and Sir William Wilde are equally powerless to release them. Each of them has, however, the satisfaction of dragging about his brother as much as he is dragged himself and if either have a pocket, the other must needs have every facility of access thereto.[6]

Lastly, for the most absolute type of Union of all, we must seek an example in the Tarantula Spider. As most persons are aware, when one of these delightful creatures is placed under a glass with a companion of his own species a little smaller than himself, he forthwith gobbles him up; making him thus, in a very literal manner, 'bone of his bone' (supposing tarantulas to have any bones) 'and flesh of his flesh.' The operation being completed, the victorious spider visibly acquires double bulk, and thenceforth may be understood to 'represent the family' in the most perfect manner conceivable.

Now, of these three types of union, it is singular that the only one which seems to have approved itself, in a pecuniary point of view, to the legislative wisdom of England should be that of the Tarantula. Unless a man be allowed to eat up the whole of a woman's fortune, there is apparently no union possible between their interests. Partnerships, limited liabilities, and all other devices for amalgamation of property are here considered inadmissible. The way in which brothers and sisters settle their affairs when they reside under the same roof would never suffice, it seems, to keep things straight between those who hold a yet more tender and trustful relationship.

Englishmen have, perhaps beyond all men, generous hearts and chivalrous natures. They delight in such glorious lines as that of their own poet:

Yet were life a charnel, where
Love lay coffined with Despair;
Yet were Truth a sacred lie,
Love were lust—if Liberty
Lent not life its soul of light,
Hope its iris of delight,
Truth its prophet's robe to wear,
Love its power to give and bear.[7]

Is it possible that one of them, whose eye kindles over such words, seriously believes that his own mother, sister, daughter, is made of such different clay from himself, as that for *her*, abject dependence is calculated to create and foster love, while for *him* it would be gall and wormwood, turning his affection into bitterness and revolt?

Truly I am persuaded it is not *thanks* to the Common Law, but in *spite* thereof, that there are so many united and happy homes in England.

To sum up our argument. The existing Common Law is not *Just*, because it neither can secure nor actually even attempts to secure for the woman the equivalent support for whose sake she is forced to relinquish her property.

It is not *Expedient*, because while in happy marriages it is superfluous and useless, in unhappy ones it becomes highly injurious; often causing the final ruin of a family which the mother (if upheld by law) might have supported single-handed. It is also shown not to be considered expedient by the conduct of the entire upper class of the country, and even of the legislature itself in the system of the Court of Chancery. Where no one who can afford to evade the law fails to evade it, the pretence that it is believed to be generally expedient is absurd. Further, the classes which actually evade it, and the countries where it is non-existing, show in no degree less connubial harmony than those wherein it is enforced.

Lastly, it does not tend to fulfil, but to counteract, the *Sentiment* regarding the marriage union, to which it aims to add the pressure of force. Real unanimity is not produced between two parties by forbidding one of them to have any voice at all. The hard mechanical contrivance of the law for making husband and wife of one heart and mind is calculated to produce a precisely opposite result.

The proposal, then, to abolish this law seems to have in its favour Justice, Expediency, and even the Sentiment which has hitherto blindly supported the law. As the Parliamentary Committee report, they are strongly of opinion 'that the Common law of this country, which gives the wife's property to her husband, should be repealed, and that the wife should have control over her property and earnings; and that her disability to contract and sue and be sued in respect of them should be removed.'

That certain difficulties must arise in carrying out so extensive a change is obvious, yet they are probably less than might be supposed; and a brief trial of the working of a new law would enable the legislature to find out the weak point (if any) of their present work. As the Committee remark:

> Questions of importance arise in settling details of such a matter. Whether, for instance, the poor law liability of the father for the maintenance of the children should be extended to the mother; whether the change should be confined to future marriages only, or should be applied to existing marriages where other property is acquired, &c.

One thing, however, was unanimously agreed upon, and it is an important point in question.

> It does not appear to be necessary to make any alteration in the liability of a husband to maintain his wife in consequence of such a change in the law with regard to the property of married women. A married woman living apart from her husband can only bind him for what is necessary, and the possession of property of her own *pro tanto* negatives the authority arising from necessity. A married woman living with her husband has an authority which, in spite of some fluctuations and uncertainty of judicial decisions, seems to be regulated by the general principle of the law of agency. Agency is a mixed question of law and fact, and the courts will give due weight to such a fact as the possession of property by a married woman without any express statutable direction.[8]

That such a change could not entail injurious consequences is guaranteed by two facts: first, there follow no injurious consequences to the richer classes in England, by whom the law is practically set aside; second, there have followed no injurious results, but very beneficial ones, to the lower classes in the American States, by whom the law has been repealed. We have already cited the testimony of the distinguished American lawyers, Mr. Dudley Field, judge Welles, Governor Washbourne, and others, to this point.

Justice, Expediency, a truly guided Sentiment, and such Experience as is yet attainable—all these then point unanimously to the repeal of the existing Common Law, as it touches the Property of Married Women.

But leaving this special, though typical case of the property of married women, may we not for a moment try to answer, if it be but vaguely, the larger question in which it is involved: What ought to be the general tone of legislation, the general line of policy pursued in these days by English men towards English women? It is clear enough that we have come to one of those stages in human history which, like a youth's attainment of majority, makes some change in the arrangements of past time desirable, if not imperative. There is no use reverting, on the one side with pertinacious dogmatism, and on the other with scorn and indignation, to old Eastern, or classic, or feudal relations between men and women. Any one who has lived in southern and eastern lands can perfectly understand, from the nature of the women of those passionate races, how such states of things arose at first, and have been maintained ever since without blame or cruelty. In feudal times, also, the blended chivalry and tyranny of men towards women was rather to be admired, for the chivalry then condemned a tyranny which probably fell more lightly on women than on any inferior class of men in the social scale. But all these things are changed for us. Our Teuton race, from the days of Tacitus, has borne women whose moral nature has been in more than equipoise with their passions; and who have both deserved and obtained a freedom and a respect unknown to their sisters of the south. As the ages of force and violence have passed away, and as more and more room has been left for the growth of gentler powers, women (especially in England) have gradually and slowly risen to a higher place. It is indeed quite possible still to point out thousands who are unfit for any important exercise of freedom, who are mere dolls, or something worse. Half the discussions which go on about women would be stopped at the outset, if the speakers could settle *what* women they are going to talk of—the women of strong characters, or the women who have as little character as their own looking-glasses. One woman lives for affection, for duty, for elevated and refined pleasures of taste and intellect; not incapable of devoted love yet not living with love alone in her thoughts; pleased to adorn her person, yet not dreaming and chattering of dress from morning till night. Another woman lives for admiration and passion, for low pleasures of vanity and sense; having for her sole ambition to befool the men who surround her, and for her sole serious employment to deck herself for their gaze. To one the society of men and women is equally interesting, provided each be equally intelligent. To the other, the presence of a man, be he almost an idiot, is so exciting and delightful that every woman in company is forgotten, and the most ludicrous changes of tastes and opinions are effected at a moment's notice, to fall in with his pleasure, as if they were the furniture of a lodging-house, to be moved to suit a new lodger. As a French wit says; if the minds of such women have received any impression over night, it is carefully smoothed down next morning, like a gravel walk, *avec le rateau*, to be quite ready to receive a fresh impression from the next visitor.

Such are the differences, the contrasts rather, between two orders of women; and it is not unnatural that when 'women's rights' are under discussion and one interlocutor is thinking of one sort of woman and the other of the other, they should not readily agree to what is either just or expedient to be done for them. It seems equally out of question to withhold the franchise from Florence Nightingale when she asks for it,[9] or to grant it to the 'Girls of the Period.' Unfortunately, as strong-minded women are apt to associate only with the strong of their own sex, and as men are apt to be a good deal more familiarised with the man-adoring type of women than with them, it is common when they argue for each to go on contradicting the other without the slightest hope of coming to an understanding.

But it must be granted, we think, that the numbers of those of whom Pope could affirm that

Most women have no characters at all,

has a tendency to diminish year by year; and the numbers of the women with characters to increase. How much faster the alteration will go on under improved education, if such splendid schemes as that of Miss Davies and Madame Bodichon's College can be carried out, is hard to judge. Already the classification of which we have already spoken, with the 'idiots' and the 'minors,' seems hardly such as the scientific intellect would be satisfied with in other departments of zoology. Shall we say it resembles the botanical scheme of the governess who informed her pupils that 'plants are divided into Monandria, Bulbous roots, and Weeds'?

We wish that we could persuade men more often to try and realise for themselves what is actually the life of a woman. Not as an appeal for compassion. It is very much to be questioned whether the warm affections and simple hearts of the better sort of women do not make life sweeter to them than to most men. 'Happiness,' says Paley, 'is to be found no less with the purring cat, than with the playful kitten.' Enjoyment is a hardy little plant which grows at all altitudes above the level of actual starvation. There are glories of the nursery and ambitions of the kitchen which fill human hearts no less than the contests of the senate and the triumphs of the battle field. To the majority of men the life of a woman with its narrow household cares, its small social emulations, and its slightly flavoured pleasures, seems dull and insipid to the verge of disgust. Very few would hesitate to repeat the thanksgiving of the Rabbins for 'being born of the human race, and not a brute; a Jew, not a Gentile; a man, and not a woman.' Yet happiness is quite sufficiently elastic to shrink into the narrow circle of domestic life even while it is capable of stretching itself to the wide bounds of imperial power. Maria Theresa, and Catherine the Great might have made themselves content, the one perhaps as the mistress of a well frequented inn, or the other as an actress at a provincial theatre. Women who are not utterly ground down by the sordid cares of poverty, are perhaps quite as cheerful and a good deal more resigned to the decrees of Providence than their lords. It is therefore with a pity not dashed with compassion, but partaking of the tenderness wherewith we watch a child pleased with its doll and its baby-house, that men usually regard the lives of those dearest to them in the world. Were they ever to ask themselves how such an existence would suit *them*, they might perhaps be startled at the reflections which would suggest themselves. Any way I believe they would thenceforth carefully endeavour that none of the little patrimony of woman's pleasures should be retrenched, none of the bounds of their interests and duties made narrower than nature herself has drawn them by the laws of their physical constitutions and their domestic affections.

Last summer the *Times* remarked that 'when working men desired to have votes *they* threw down the park palings, but that women have not shown their wish for the same privilege by any such proceedings.' Were we not on that same enchanted ground whereon all arguments are turned topsy turvy, we should have supposed that the mob who attacked the police and spoiled the public park, and the women who stopped at home and signed Mr. Mill's petition, had respectively shown the one their *un*fitness, the other their fitness for the franchise of a law-respecting nation. But, in truth, women very rarely throw down *any* palings, either material or only imaginary; and they generally hurt themselves cruelly when they do so. Not for that reason ought men to refuse to them whatever rights may seem for them fairly established. Among these I trust, in the present paper, I have placed that of Married Women to the use of their own earnings and inheritances.

In conclusion, I would make one remark on the general question. Much time and more temper have been lost in debating the sterile problem of the 'equality' of men and women, without either party seeming to perceive that the solution either way has no bearing on the practical matters at issue, since civil rights have never yet been reserved for 'physical, moral, and intellectual' equals. Even for political rights, among all the arguments eagerly cited last year against extending the franchise, no one thought it worth while to urge that the class proposed to be admitted to them was, or was not, physically, intellectually, or morally inferior to the classes which already possessed it. As for civil rights—the right to hold property, to make contracts, to sue and be sued—no class, however humble, stupid, and even vicious, has ever been denied them since serfdom and slavery came to an end. If men choose to say that women are their inferiors in *everything*, they are free and welcome then to say so. Women may think that they are the equivalents if not the equals of men; that beauty is as great a physical advantage as the strength which man shares with the ox; that nimble wits and quick intuitions are on the whole as brilliant, though not as solid intellectual endowments as the strong understanding and creative imaginations of men; and finally, that for morality,[10] that old man is happy whose conscience as he leaves the world is as void of grave offence as that of the majority of old women. But whatever a woman may think on these subjects, she has no need to argue, much less to grow shrill and angry about it. 'Granted,' she answers to all rebuffs; 'let me be physically, intellectually, and morally your inferior. So long as you allow I possess moral responsibility and sufficient intelligence to know right from wrong (a point I conclude you will concede, else why hang me for murder?) I am quite content. It is *only* as a Moral and Intelligent Being I claim my civil rights. Can you deny them to me on that ground?'

Source: Reprinted from *Fraser's Magazine* (December 1868).

NOTES

1   A horrible instance in point occurred near Gainsborough, in Lincolnshire. The evidence given on the inquest was published in the *Lincolnshire Chronicle*, July 5, 1863.
The parish surgeon wrote thus to the clergyman of the parish, who was also a magistrate:—

> 'Dear Sir,—I have to-day seen Mrs. Seymour. I found her in a wretchedly weak state. She is nursing a baby, which office she is not able to perform effectually from her exhausted condition. Her husband, she says, does not allow her the necessaries of life, which he, in his position, could find if he liked. Without some means be taken to provide her with good diet, &c., or to make her husband do so, she must die of starvation at no very distant period. If you could, in your official capacity, help the poor creature, you would confer a great blessing on the poor woman., and oblige yours faithfully,
> J.C. Smallman.'

The clergyman found, however, that he had no power as a magistrate to take cognisance of the case, unless the guardians would give the wife relief, and prosecute the husband; and this they declined to do. In vain did the poor half-starved wretch appear before them, and pray to be admitted into the workhouse. She was refused admission on the ground that her husband earned good wages; and so she went home, and after lingering awhile, probably fed now and then by her neighbours, she died. The husband escaped without any punishment whatever. The jury who tried him [*men*, of course!] gave him the benefit of a doubt as to the cause of his wife's death, and acquitted him.—*Illustrations of the Operations of our Laws*, p. 8.

2   See the overwhelming evidence on this point given before the Parliamentary Committee this last session, by the Rev. S. Hansard, rector of Bethnal Green; J.L. Nansfield, Esq., police magistrate of Marylebone; Mr. Ormerod, president of the Co-operative Society at Rochdale; and Rev. Thomas Fowle, rector of Hoxton.—*Minutes of Evidence*, pp. 63-70.

3   *Illustrations of the Operations of our Laws*, p. 13.

4   *Special Report of Parliamentary Committee* on *Married Women's Property Bill*.

5   It is satisfactory to know that separate property and the right of contract has been accorded to married women by the new law of India, compiled by some of the ablest lawyers in this country: Lord Romilly, Sir W. Erle, Mr. Justice Willes, Sir Edward Ryan and Mr. Lowe.

6   Since the above was written it has been announced that even *this* Union is likely to be severed—by M. Nélaton!

7   Shelley's *Hellas*.

8   *Special Report from the Select Committee on Married Women's Property—Bill*, p. vii.

9   As she has done, along with such women as Mrs. Somerville, Harriet Martineau, and Anna Swanwick, &c.

10   It must be confessed that, to a woman, the claim of superior *morality* for men sounds supremely strange. Looking at the three most hateful forms of vice—cruelty, drunkenness, unchastity—are they most common in women or in men? Watch for the first-the devil—vice of cruelty—among children. See how the little girl tends her birds and animals, and, as Chaucer describes her, 'all conscience and tendre heart,' 'greting' when any one strikes her dog. See how her brother (brought up just as tenderly) begins in the nursery to pull flies to pieces, to worry the cat; then to terrify the sheep, to lay traps in the snow for sparrows. Observe how it is always his *mother's* soft words, his sister's tears which win him at last, and make of him that really tender-hearted being, a perfect English gentleman. It is never his schoolfellows who correct him, rarely his master. Watch in the class below. Is it the poor wild street girls who persecute and stone to death the hapless lost dogs of London? Read the reports of the Society for the Prevention of Cruelty to Animals, and observe whether it be men or women who are commonly prosecuted for torturing domestic creatures. Would any *woman's* devotion to science (does the reader think) lead her to practise vivisection? Nay, but it is hard for a man to tell the misery and disgust, rising almost to revolt against the order of the world, which fills many a women's heart when she sees daily around her the instances of man's wanton and savage cruelty to the harmless creatures for whom she can only plead, and pleas usually in vain. As I have been actually writing these pages, some dozen young men of the labouring class have passed under my window, pursuing with volleys of heavy stones a hapless little canary, which had escaped out of its cage, and in its feeble flight was striving to find shelter among the trees below. Is it needful to say there was no woman among the gang, and that the appeal of other women beside myself to give up their cruel chase was unheeded? '*It ought to be killed!*' shouted one young ruffian in reply. A canary worthy of death! I sit down to pursue the theme of woman's moral inferiority. But where was I? Did I hear anybody say that women were more cruel than men?—or perhaps that cruelty is not the very crown of—shall we call it, Moral Superiority?

"WIFE-TORTURE IN ENGLAND"

It once happened to me to ask an elderly French gentleman of the most exquisite manners to pay any attention she might need to a charming young lady who
was intending to travel by the same train from London to Paris. M. de ——
wrote such a brilliant little note in reply that I was tempted to preserve it as an
autograph; and I observe that, after a profusion of thanks, he assured me he
should be "trop heureux de se mettre au service" of my young friend. Practically, as I afterwards learned, M. de —— did make himself quite delightful, till,
unluckily, on arriving at Boulogne, it appeared that there was some *imbroglio*
about Miss ——'s luggage and she was in a serious difficulty. Needless to say, on
such an occasion the intervention of a French gentleman with a ribbon at his
button-hole would have been of the greatest possible service; but to render it
M. de —— would have been obliged to miss the train to Paris; and this was a
sacrifice for which his politeness was by no means prepared. Expressing himself
as utterly *au désespoir*, he took his seat, and was whirled away, leaving my poor
young friend alone on the platform to fight her battles as best she might with
the impracticable officials. The results might have been annoying had not a
homely English stranger stepped in and proffered his aid; and, having recov-
ered the missing property, simply lifted his hat and escaped from the lady's
expressions of gratitude.

In this little anecdote I think lies a compendium of the experience of hundreds of ladies on their travels. The genuine and self-sacrificing kindness of
English and American gentlemen towards women affords almost a ludicrous
contrast to the florid politeness, compatible with every degree of selfishness,
usually exhibited by men of other European nations. The reflection then is a
puzzling one—How does it come to pass that while the better sort of Englishmen are thus exceptionally humane and considerate to women, the men of the
lower class of the same nation are proverbial for their unparalleled brutality, till
wife-beating, wife-torture, and wife-murder have become the opprobrium of
the land? How does it hoppen (still more strange to note!) that the same gen-
erous-hearted gentlemen, who would themselves fly to render succour to a lady
in distress, yet read of the beatings, burnings, kickings, and "cloggings" of *poor*
women well-nigh every morning in their newspapers without once setting their
teeth, and saying, "This must be stopped! We can stand it no longer"?

The paradox truly seems worthy of a little investigation. What reason can be
alleged, in the first place, why the male of the human species, and particularly
the male of the finest variety of that species, should be the only animal in creation which maltreats its mate, or any female of its own kind?[1]

To get to the bottom of the mystery we must discriminate between assaults
of men on other men; assaults of men on women who are not their wives; and

assaults of men on their wives. I do not think I err much if I affirm that, in common sentiment, the first of these offences is considerably more heinous than the second—being committed against a more worthy person (as the Latin grammar itself instructs boys to think); and lastly that the assault on a woman who is *not* a man's wife is worse than the assault on a wife by her husband. Towards this last or *minimum* offence a particular kind of indulgence is indeed extended by public opinion.[2] The proceeding seems to be surrounded by a certain halo of jocosity which inclines people to smile whenever they hear of a case of it (terminating anywhere short of actual murder), and causes the mention of the subject to conduce rather than otherwise to the hilarity of a dinner party. The occult fun thus connected with wife-beating forms by no means indeed the least curious part of the subject. Certainly in view of the state of things revealed by our criminal statistics there is something ominous in the circumstance that "Punch" should have been our national English street-drama for more than two centuries. Whether, as some antiquarians tell us, Judas Iscariot was the archetypal Policinello, who, like Faust and Don Juan, finally meets the reward of his crimes by Satanic intervention, or whether, as other learned gentlemen say, the quaint visage and humour of the Neapolitan vintager Puccio d'Aniello, originated the jest which has amused ten generations, it is equally remarkable that so much of the enjoyment should concentrate about the thwacking of poor Judy, and the flinging of the baby out of the window. Questioned seriously whether he think that the behaviour of Punch as a citizen and *père de famille* be in itself a good joke, the British gentleman would probably reply that it was not more facetious than watching a caster flogging a horse. But invested with the drollery of a marionette's behaviour, and accompanied by the screeches of the man with the Pan-pipe, the scene is irresistible, and the popularity of the hero rises with every bang he bestows on the wife of his bosom and on the representative of the law.

The same sort of half-jocular sympathy unquestionably accompanies the whole class of characters of whom Mr. Punch is the type. Very good and kind-hearted men may be frequently heard speaking of horrid scenes of mutual abuse and violence between husbands and wives, as if they were rather ridiculous than disgusting. The "Taming of the Shrew" still holds its place as one of the most popular of Shakespeare's comedies; and even the genial Ingoldsby conceived he added a point to his inimitable legend of "Odille," by inserting after the advice to "succumb to our she-saints, videlicet wives," the parenthesis, "that is, if one has not a 'good bunch of fives.'" Where is the hidden fun of this and scores of similar allusions, which sound like the cracking of whips over the cowering dogs in a kennel?

I imagine it lies in the sense, so pleasant to the owners of superior physical strength, that after all, if reason and eloquence should fail, there is always an *ultima ratio*, and that final appeal lies in their hands. The sparring may be all very well for a time, and may be counted entirely satisfactory *if they get the better*. But then, if by any mischance the unaccountably sharp wits of the weaker creature should prove dangerous weapons, there is always the club of brute force ready to hand in the corner. The listener is amused, as in reading a fairy tale, wherein the hero, when apparently completely vanquished, pulls out a talisman given him by an Afreet, and lo! his enemies fall flat on the ground and are turned into rats.

Thus it comes to pass, I suppose, that the abstract idea of a strong man hitting or kicking a weak woman—*per se, so* revolting—has somehow got softened into a jovial kind of domestic lynching, the grosser features of the case being swept out of sight, just as people make endless jests on tipsiness, forgetting how loathsome a thing is a drunkard. A "jolly companions" chorus seems to accompany both kinds of exploits. This, and the prevalent idea (which I shall analyze by-and-by) that the woman has generally deserved the blows she receives, keep up, I believe, the indifference of the public on the subject.

Probably the sense that they must carry with them a good deal of tacit sympathy on the part of other men has something to do in encouraging wife-beaters, just as the fatal notion of the good fellowship of drink has made thousands of sots. But the immediate causes of the offence of brutal violence are of course very various, and need to be better understood than they commonly are if we would find a remedy for them. First, there are to be considered the class of people and the conditions of life wherein the practice prevails; then the character of the men who beat their wives; next that of the wives who are beaten and kicked; and finally, the possible remedy.

Wife-beating exists in the upper and middle classes rather more, I fear, than is generally recognized; but it rarely extends to anything beyond an occasional blow or two of a not dangerous kind. In his apparently most ungovernable rage, the gentleman or tradesman somehow manages to bear in mind the disgrace he will incur if his outbreak be betrayed by his wife's black eye or broken arm, and he regulates his cuffs or kicks accordingly. The dangerous wife-beater belongs almost exclusively to the artisan and labouring classes. Colliers, "puddlers," and weavers have long earned for themselves in this matter a bad reputation, and among a long list of cases before me, I reckon shoemakers, stonemasons, butchers, smiths, tailors, a printer, a clerk, a bird-catcher, and a large number of labourers. In the worst districts of London (as I have been informed by one of the most experienced magistrates) four-fifths of the wife-beating cases are among the lowest class of Irish labourers—a fact worthy of more than passing notice, had we time to bestow upon it, seeing that in their own country Irishmen of all classes are proverbially kind and even chivalrous towards women.

There are also various degrees of wife-beating in the different localities. In London it seldom goes beyond a severe "thrashing" with the fist—a sufficiently dreadful punishment, it is true, when inflicted by a strong man on a woman; but mild in comparison of the kickings and tramplings and "purrings" with hobnailed shoes and clogs of what we can scarcely, in this connection, call the "dark and true and *tender* North." As Mr. Serjeant Pulling remarks,[3] "Nowhere is the ill-usage of woman so systematic as in Liverpool, and so little hindered by the strong arm of the law; making the lot of a married woman, whose locality is the 'kicking district' of Liverpool, simply a duration of suffering and subjection to injury and savage treatment, far worse than that to which the wives of mere savages are used." It is in the centres of dense mercantile and manufacturing populations that this offence reaches its climax. In London the largest return for one year (in the Parliamentary Report on Brutal Assaults) of brutal assaults on women was 351. In Lancashire, with a population of almost two millions and a-half, the largest number was 194. In Stafford, with a population of three-quarters of a million, there were 113 cases. In the West Riding, with a million and a-half, 152; and in Durham, with 508,666, no less than 267. Thus, roughly speaking, there are nearly five times as many wife-beaters of the more brutal kind, in proportion to the population, in Durham as in London. What are the conditions of life among the working classes in those great "hives of industry" of which we talk so proudly? It is but justice that we should picture the existence of the men and women in such places before we pass to discuss the deeds which darken it.

They are lives out of which almost every softening and ennobling element has been withdrawn, and into which enter brutalizing influences almost unknown elsewhere. They are lives of hard, ugly, mechanical toil in dark pits and hideous factories, amid the grinding and clanging of engines and the fierce heat of furnaces, in that Black Country where the green sod of earth is replaced by mounds of slag and shale, where no flower grows, no fruit ripens, scarcely a bird sings; where the morning has no freshness, the evening no dews; where the spring sunshine cannot pierce the foul curtain of smoke which overhangs these modern Cities of the Plain, and where the very streams and rivers run discoloured and steaming with stench, like Styx and Phlegethon, through their banks of ashes. If "God made the country and man made the town," we might deem that Ahrimanes devised this Tartarus of toil, and that here we had at last found the spot where the Psalmist might seek in vain for the handiwork of the Lord.

As we now and then, many of us, whirl through this land of darkness in express trains, and draw up our carriage windows that we may be spared the smoke and dismal scene, we have often reflected that the wonder is, *not* that the dwellers there should lose some of the finer poetry of life, the more delicate courtesies of humanity, but that they should remain so much like other men, and should so often rise to noble excellence and intelligence, rather than have developed, as would have seemed more natural, into a race of beings relentless, hard, and grim as their own iron machines—beings of whom the Cyclops of the Greek and the Gnomes of the Teuton imaginations were the foreshadowings. Of innocent pleasure in such lives there can, alas! be very little; and the hunger of nature for enjoyment must inevitably be supplied (among all save the few to whom intellectual pursuits may suffice) by the grosser gratifications of the senses. Writers who have never attempted to realize what it must be to hear ugly sounds and smell nauseous odours and see hideous sights, all day long, from year's end to year's end, are angry with these Black Country artisans for spending largely of their earnings in buying delicate food—poultry and salmon, and peas and strawberries. For my part, I am inclined to rejoice if they can content themselves with such harmless gratifications of the palate, instead of the deadly stimulants of drink, cruelty, and vice.

These, then, are the localities wherein Wife-torture flourishes in England; where a dense population is crowded into a hideous manufacturing or mining or mercantile district. Wages are usually high though fluctuating. Facilities for drink and vice abound, but those for cleanliness and decency are scarcely attainable. The men are rude, coarse, and brutal in their manners and habits, and the women devoid, in an extraordinary degree, of all the higher natural attractions and influences of their sex. Poor drudges of the factory, or of the crowded and sordid lodging-house, they lose, before youth is past, the freshness, neatness, and gentleness, perhaps even the modesty of the woman, and present, when their miserable cases come up before the magistrate, an aspect so sordid and forbidding that it is no doubt with difficulty he affords his sympathy to them rather than to the husband chained to so wretched a consort. Throughout the whole of this inquiry I think it very necessary, in justice to all parties, and in mitigation of too vehement judgement of cases only known from printed reports, to bear in mind that the women of the class concerned are, some of them woefully unwomanly, slatternly, coarse, foul-mouthed—sometimes loose in behaviour, sometimes madly addicted to drink. There ought to be no idealizing of them, *as a class*, into refined and suffering angels if we wish to be just. The home of a Lancashire operative, alas! is not a garden wherein the plants of refinement or sensitiveness are very likely to spring up or thrive.

Given this direful milieu, and its population, male and female, we next ask, What are the immediate incitements to the men to maltreat the women? They are of two kinds, I think,—general and particular.

First, the whole relation between the sexes in the class we are considering is very little better than one of master and slave. I have always abjured the use of this familiar comparison in speaking generally of English husband and wives, because as regards the upper orders of society it is ridiculously overstrained and untrue. But in the "kicking districts," among the lowest labouring classes, Legree himself might find a dozen prototypes, and the condition of the women be most accurately matched by that of the negroes on a Southern plantation before the war struck off their fetters.[4] To a certain extent this marital tyranny among the lower classes is beyond the reach of law, and can only be remedied by the slow elevation and civilization of both sexes. But it is also in an appreciable degree, I am convinced, enhanced by the law even as it now stands, and was still more so by the law as it stood before the Married Women's Property Act put a stop to the chartered robbery by husbands of their wives' earnings. At the present time, though things are improving year by year, thanks to the generous and far-seeing statesmen who are contending for justice to women inside and out of the House of Commons, the position of a woman before the law as wife, mother, and citizen, remains so much below that of a man as husband, father, and citizen, that it is a matter of course that she must be regarded by him as an inferior, and fail to obtain from him such a modicum of respect as her mental and moral qualities might win did he see her placed by the State on an equal footing.

I have no intention in this paper to discuss the vexed subject of women's political and civil rights, but I cannot pass to the consideration of the incidental and minor causes of the outrages upon them, without recording my conviction that the political disabilities under which the whole sex still labours, though apparently a light burden on the higher and happier ranks, presses down more and more heavily through the lower strata of society in growing deconsideration and contempt, unrelieved (as it is at higher levels) by other influences on opinion. Finally at the lowest grade of all it exposes women to an order of insults and wrongs which are never inflicted by equals upon an equal, and can only be paralleled by the oppressions of a dominant caste or race over their helots. In this as in many other things the educating influence of law immeasurably outstrips its direct action; and such as is the spirit of our laws, such will inevitably be the spirit of our people. Human beings no longer live like animals in a condition wherein the natural sentiments between the sexes suffice to guard the weak, where the male brute is kind and forbearing to the female, and where no Court of Chancery interferes with the mother's most dear and sacred charge of her little ones. Man alone claims to hold his mate in subjection, and to have the right while he lives, and even after he dies, to rob a mother of her child; and man, who has lost the spontaneous chivalry of the lion and the dog, needs to be provided with laws which may do whatever it lies with laws to effect or form a substitute for such chivalry. Alas! instead of such, he has only made for himself laws which add legal to natural disabilities, and give artificial strength to ready-constituted prepotence.

I consider that it is a very great misfortune to both sexes that women should be thus depreciated in the opinion of that very class of men whom it would be most desirable to impress with respect and tenderness for them; who are most prone to despise physical infirmity and to undervalue the moral qualities wherein women excel. All the softening and refining influences which women exert in happier conditions are thus lost to those who most need them,—to their husbands and still more emphatically to their children; and the women themselves are degraded and brutified in their own eyes by the contempt of their companions. When I read all the fine-sounding phrases perpetually repeated about the invaluable influence of a good mother over her son,—how the worst criminals are admitted to be reclaimable if they have ever enjoyed it,—and how the virtues of the best and noblest men are attributed to it, as a commonplace of biography,—I often ask myself, "Why, then, is not something done to lift and increase, instead of to depreciate and lower, that sacred influence? Why are not mothers allowed to respect themselves, that they may fitly claim the respect of their sons? How is a lad to learn to reverence a woman whom he sees daily scoffed at, beaten, and abused, and when he knows that the laws of his country forbid her, ever and under any circumstances, to exercise the rights of citizenship; nay, which deny to her the guardianship of *himself*—of the very child of her bosom—should her husband choose to hand him over to her rival out of the street?"

The general depreciation of women *as a sex* is bad enough, but in the matter we are considering, the special depreciation of *wives* is more directly responsible for the outrages they endure. The notion that a man's wife is his PROPERTY, in the sense in which a horse is his property (descended to us rather through the Roman law than through the customs of our Teuton ancestors), is the fatal root of incalculable evil and misery. Every brutal-minded man, and many a man who in other relations of life is not brutal, entertains more or less vaguely the notion that his wife is his *thing*, and is ready to ask with indignation (as we read again and again in the police reports), of any one who interferes with his treatment of her, "May I not do what I will *with my own?*" It is even sometimes pleaded on behalf of poor men, that they possess *nothing else* but their wives, and that, consequently, it seems doubly hard to meddle with the exercise of their power in that narrow sphere.[5]

I am not intending to discuss the question of the true relation between husbands and wives which we may hope to see realized when

"Springs the happier race of human kind"

from parents "equal and free"—any more than the political and social rights of women generally. But it is impossible, in treating of the typical case wherein the misuse of wives reaches its climax in Wife-beating and Wife-torture, to avoid marking out with a firm line where lies the underground spring of the mischief. As one of the many results of this *proton pseudos*, must be noted the fact (very important in its bearing on our subject) that not only is an offence against a wife condoned as of inferior guilt, but any offence of the wife against her husband is regarded as a sort of *Petty Treason*. For her, as for the poor ass in the fable, it is more heinous to nibble a blade of grass than for the wolf to devour both the lamb and the shepherd. Should she be guilty of "nagging" or scolding, or of being a slattern, or of getting intoxicated, she finds usually a short shrift and no favour—and even humane persons talk of her offence as constituting, if not a justification for her murder, yet an explanation of it. She is, in short, liable to capital punishment without judge or jury for transgression which in the case of a man would never be punished at all, or be expiated by a fine of five shillings.[6]

Nay, in her case there is a readiness even to pardon the omission of the ordinary forms of law as needlessly cumbersome. In no other instance save that of the Wife-beater is excuse made for a man taking the law into his own hands. We are accustomed to accept it as a principle that "lynching" cannot be authorized in a civilized country, and that the first lesson of orderly citizenship is that no man shall be judge, jury, and executioner in his own cause. But when a wife's offences are in question this salutary rule is overlooked, and men otherwise just-minded, refer cheerfully to the *circonstance atténuante* of the wife's drunkenness or bad language, as if it not only furnished an excuse for outrage upon her, but made it quite fit and proper for the Queen's peace to be broken and the woman's bones along with it.

This underlying public opinion is fortunately no new thing. On the contrary, it is an idea of immemorial antiquity which has been embodied in the laws of many nations, and notably, as derived from the old Roman *Patria Potestas*, in our own. It was only in 1829, in the 9th George IV., that the Act of Charles II., which embodied the old Common Law, and authorized a man "to chastise his wife with any reasonable instrument," was erased from our Statute-Book. Our position is not retrograde, but advancing, albeit too slowly. It is not as in the case of the Vivisection of Animals, that a new passion of cruelty is arising, but only that an old one, having its origin in the remotest epochs of barbarian wife-capture and polygamy, yet lingers in the dark places of the land. By degrees, if our statesmen will but bring the educational influence of law to bear upon the matter, it will surely die out and become a thing of the past, like cannibalism,—than which it is no better fitted for a Christian nation.

Of course the ideas of the suffering wives are cast in the same mould as those of their companions. They take it for granted that a Husband is a Beating Animal, and may be heard to remark when extraordinarily ill-treated by a stranger,—that they "never were so badly used, no not by their own 'usbands." Their wretched proverbial similarity to spaniels and walnut-trees, the readiness with which they sometimes turn round and snap at a bystander who has interfered on their behalf, of course affords to cowardly people a welcome excuse for the "policy of non-intervention," and forms the culminating proof of how far the iron of their fetters has eaten into their souls. A specially experienced gentleman writes from Liverpool: "The women of Lancashire are *awfully fond* of bad husbands. It has become quite a truism that our women are like dogs, the more you beat them the more they love you." Surely if a bruised and trampled woman be a pitiful object, a woman who has been brought down by fear, or by her own gross passions so low as to fawn on the beast who strikes her, is one to make angels weep?[7]

To close this part of the subject, I conceive then, that the common idea of the inferiority of women, and the special notion of the rights of husbands, form the undercurrent of feeling which induces a man, when for any reason he is infuriated, to wreak his violence on his wife. She is, in his opinion, his natural *souffre-douleur*.

It remains to be noted what are the principal incitements to such outbursts of savage fury among the classes wherein Wife-beating prevails. They are not far to seek. The first is undoubtedly *Drink*—poisoned drink. The seas of brandy and gin, and the oceans of beer, imbibed annually in England, would be bad enough, if taken pure and simple,[8] but it is the vile adulterations introduced into them which make them the infuriating poisons which they are—which literally *sting* the wretched drinkers into cruelty, perhaps quite foreign to their natural temperaments. As an experienced minister in these districts writes to me, "I have known men almost as bad as those you quote (a dozen wife-murderers) made into most kind and considerate husbands by total abstinence." If the English people will go on swallowing millions' worth yearly of brain poison, what can we expect but brutality the most hideous and grotesque? Assuredly the makers and vendors of these devil's philtres are responsible for an amount of crime and ruin which some of the worst tyrants in history might have trembled to bear on their consciences; nor can the national legislature be absolved for suffering the great Drink interest thus foully to tamper with the health—nay, with the very souls of our countrymen. What is the occult influence which prevents the Excise from performing its duty as regards these frauds on the revenue?

2. Next to drunkenness as a cause of violence to women, follows the other "great sin of great cities," of which it is unnecessary here to speak. The storms of jealousy thence arising, the hideous alternative *possession* of the man by the twin demons of cruelty and lust—one of whom is never very far from the other—are familiar elements in the police-court tragedies.

3. Another source of the evil may be found in that terrible, though little recognized passion, which rude men and savages share with many animals, and which is the precise converse of sympathy, for it consists in anger and cruelty, excited by the signs of pain; and impulse to hurt and destroy any suffering creature, rather than to relieve or help it. Of the widespread influence of this passion (which I have ventured elsewhere to name *Heteropathy*), a passion only slowly dying out as civilization advances, there can, I think, be no doubt at all. It is a hideous mystery of human nature that such feelings should lie latent in it, and that cruelty should grow by what it feeds on; that the more the tyrant causes the victim to suffer the more he hates him, and desires to heap on him fresh sufferings. Among the lower classes the emotion of Heteropathy unmistakably finds vent in the cruelty of parents and step-parents to unfortunate children who happen to be weaker or more stupid than others, or to have been once excessively punished, and whose joyless little faces and timid crouching demeanour, instead of appeals for pity, prove provocations to fresh outrage. The group of his shivering and starving children and weeping wife is the sad sight which, greeting the eyes of the husband and father reeling home from the gin-shop, somehow kindles his fury. If the baby cry in the cradle, he stamps on it. If his wife wring her hands in despair, he fells her to the ground.[9]

4. After these I should be inclined to reckon, as a cause of brutal outbreaks, the impatience and irritation which must often be caused in the homes of the

working classes by sheer *friction*. While rich people, when they get tired of each other or feel irritable, are enabled to recover their tempers in the ample space afforded by a comfortable house, the poor are huddled together in such close quarters that the sweetest tempers and most tender affections must sometimes feel the trial. Many of us have shuddered at Miss Octavia Hill's all-too-graphic description of a hot, noisome court in the heart of London on a fine summer evening, with men, women, and children "pullulating," as the French say, on the steps, at the windows, on the pavement, all dirty, hot, and tired, and scarcely able to find standing or sitting room. It is true the poor are happily more gregarious than the rich. Paradoxical as it sounds, it takes a good deal of civilization to make a man love savage scenery, and a highly cultivated mind to find any "pleasure in the pathless woods" or "rapture in the lonely shore." Nevertheless, for moral health as much as for physical, a certain number of cubic inches of space are needed for every living being.

It is their interminable, inevitable propinquity which in the lower classes makes the nagging, wrangling, worrying women so intolerably trying. As millers get accustomed, it is said, to the clapping of their mill, so may some poor husbands become deaf to their wives' tongues; but the preliminary experience must be severe indeed.

These, then, are the incentives to Wife-beating and Wife-torture. What are the men on whom they exert their evil influence?

Obviously, by the hypothesis, they are chiefly the drunken, idle, ruffianly fellows who lounge about the public-houses instead of working for their families. Without pretending to affirm that there are no sober, industrious husbands goaded to strike their wives through jealousy or irritation, the presumption is enormous against the character of any man convicted of such an assault. The cases in which the police reports of them add, "He had been bound over to keep the peace several times previously," or "He had been often fined for drunkenness and disorderly behaviour," are quite countless. Sometimes it approaches the ludicrous to read how helplessly the law has been attempting to deal with the scoundrel, as, for example, in the case of William Owen, whom his wife said she "met for the first time beside Ned Wright's Bible-barrow," and who told the poor fool he had been "converted." He was known to Constable 47 K as having been convicted *over sixty times* for drunkenness and violent assaults; and the moment he left the church he began to abuse his wife.

The pitilessness and ferocity of these men sometimes looks like madness. Alfred Stone, for example, coming home in a bad temper, took his wife's parrot out of its cage, stamped on it, and threw it on the fire, observing, "Jane! it is the last thing you have got belonging to your father!" In the hands of such a man a woman's heart must be crushed, like the poor bird under his heel.

Turn we now from the beaters to the beaten. I have already said that we must not idealize the women of the "kicking districts." They are, mostly, poor souls, very coarse, very unwomanly. Some of them drink whenever they can procure drink. Some are bad and cruel mothers (we cannot forget the awful stories of the Burial Clubs); many are hopelessly depraved, and lead as loose lives as their male companions. Many keep their houses in a miserable state of dirt and disorder, neglect their children, and sell their clothes and furniture for gin. Not seldom will one of these reckless creatures pursue her husband in the streets with screams of abuse and jeers. The man knows not where to turn to escape from the fury. When he comes home at night, he probably finds her lying dead drunk on the bed, and his children crying for their supper. Again, in a lesser degree, women make their homes into purgatories by their bad tempers. There was in old times a creature recognized by law as a "Common Scold," for whom the punishment of ducking in the village horse-pond was formally provided. It is to be feared her species is by no means to be reckoned among the "Extinct Mammalia." Then comes the "nagging" wife, immortalized as "Mrs. Caudle;" the worrying, peevish kill-joy, whose presence is a wet blanket—nay, a wet blanket stuck full of pins; the argumentative woman, with a voice like a file and a face like a ferret, who bores on, night and day, till life is a burden.[10]

These are terrible harpies. But it is scarcely fair to assume that every woman who is accused of "nagging" necessarily belongs to their order. I have no doubt that every husband who comes home with empty pockets, and from whom his wife needs to beg repeatedly for money to feed herself and her children, considers that she "nags" him. I have no doubt that when a wife reproaches such a husband with squandering his wages in the public-house, or on some wretched rival, while she and her children are starving, he accuses her to all his friends of intolerable "nagging," and that, not seldom having acquired from him the reputation of this kind of thing, the verdict of "Serve her Right" is generally passed upon her by public opinion when her "nagging" is capitally punished by a broken head.

But *all* women of the humblest class are not those terrible creatures, drunken, depraved, or ill-tempered; or even addicted to "nagging." On the contrary, I can affirm from my own experience, as well, I believe, as that of all who have had much to do with the poor of great cities, there are among them at least as many good women as bad—as many who are sober, honest, chaste, and industrious, as are the contrary. There is a type which every clergyman, and magistrate, and district visitor will recognize in a moment as very common: a woman generally small and slight of person, but alert, intelligent, active morning, noon, and night, doing the best her strength allows to keep her home tidy, and her children neat and well fed, and to supply her husband's wants. Her face was, perhaps, pretty at eighteen: by the time she is eight-and-twenty, toil and drudgery and many children have reduced her to a mere rag, and only her eyes retain a little pathetic relic of beauty. This woman expresses herself well and simply: it is a special "note" of her character that she uses no violent words, even in describing the worst injuries. There is nothing "loud" about her in voice, dress, or manners. She is emphatically a "*decent*," respectable woman. Her only fault, if fault it be, is that she will insist on obtaining food and clothing for her children, and that when she is refused them she becomes that depressed, broken-spirited creature whose mute, reproachful looks act as a goad, as I have said, to the passions of her oppressor. We shall see presently what part this class of woman plays in the horrible domestic tragedies of England.

We have now glanced at the conditions under which Wife-beating takes place, at the incentives immediately leading to it, the men who beat, and the women who are beaten. Turn we now to examine more closely the thing itself.

There are two kinds of Wife-beating which I am anxious the reader should keep clearly apart in his mind. There is what may be called *Wife-beating by Combat*, and there is Wife-beating properly so called, which is only wife, and not wife-and-husband beating. In the first, both parties have an equal share. Bad words are exchanged, then blows. The man hits, the woman perhaps scratches and tears. If the woman generally gets much the worst of it, it is simply because cats are weaker than dogs. The man cannot so justly be said to have "beaten" his wife as to have vanquished her in a boxing-match. Almost without exception in these cases it is mentioned that "both parties were the worse for liquor." It is in this way the drunken woman is beaten, *by the drunken man*, not by the ideal sober and industrious husband, who has a right to be disgusted by her intoxication. It is nearly exclusively, I think, in such drunken quarrels that the hateful virago gets beaten at all. As a general rule she commands too much fear, and is so ready to give back curse for curse and blow for blow, that, in cold blood, nobody meddles with her. Such a termagant is often the tyrant of her husband, nay, of the whole court or lane in which she lives; and the sentiments she excites are the reverse of those which bring down the fist and the clogs of the ruffian husband on the timid and meek-faced woman who tries, too often unsuccessfully, the supposed magic of a soft answer to turn away the wrath of such a wild beast as he.

One word, however, must be said, before we leave this revolting picture, even for that universally condemned creature, the drunken wife. Does any save one, the Great Judge above, ever count how many of such doubly-degraded beings have been *driven* to intemperance by sheer misery? How many have been lured to drink by companionship with their drunken husbands? How many have sunk into the habit because, worn out in body by toil and child-bearing, degraded in soul by contempt and abuse, they have not left in them one spark of that self-respect which enables a human being to resist the temptation to drown care and remembrance in the dread forgetfulness of strong drink?

The second kind of Wife-beating is when the man alone is the striker and the woman the stricken. These are the cases which specially challenge our attention, and for which it may be hoped some palliative may be found. In these, the husband usually comes home "the worse for liquor," and commences, sometimes without any provocation at all, to attack his wife, or drag her out of the bed where she is asleep, or has just been confined. (See cases p. 149.) Sometimes there is preliminary altercation, the wife imploring him to give her some money to buy necessaries, or reproaching him for drinking all he has earned. In either case the wife is passive so far as blows are concerned, unless at the last, in self-defence, she lays her hand on some weapon to protect her life—a fact which is always cited against her as a terrible delinquency.[11]

Such are the two orders of Wife-beating with which a tolerably extensive study of the subject has made me familiar. It will be observed that neither includes that ideal Wife-beater of whom we hear so much, the sober, industrious man goaded to frenzy by his wife's temper or drunkenness. I will not venture to affirm that the Ideal Wife-beater is as mythical as the griffin or the sphinx, but I will affirm that in all my inquiries I have never yet come on his track.

I have insisted much on this point, because I think it has been strangely over-looked, and that it ought to form a most important factor in making up our judgment of the whole matter and of the proper remedies. It will be found, I believe, on inquiry that it is actually surprising how very seldom there is anything at all alleged by the husband against the wife in the worst cases of wife-torture—except the "provocation" and "nagging" of asking him for money; or, as in the case of poor Ellen Harlow, of refusing him twopence out of her own earnings when he had been drinking all day and she had been working.[12] In thirty-eight cases taken at random, five were of the class of drunken combats; and in thirty nothing was reported as alleged against the victims. In many cases strong testimony was given of their good conduct and industry: *e.g.* the wife of William White, who was burnt to death by the help of his paraffin lamp, was a "hard-working industrious woman." The wife of James Lawrence, whose face bore in court tokens of the most dreadful violence, "said that her husband had for years done nothing for his livelihood, while she had bought a shop, and stocked it out of her own earnings." The wife of Richard Mountain had "supported herself and her children." The wife of Alfred Etherington, who has been dangerously injured by her husband kicking and jumping on her, had been supporting him and their children. The wife of James Styles, who was beaten by her husband till she became insensible, had long provided for him and herself by charwork; and so on.

Regarding the extent of the evil it is difficult to arrive at a just calculation. Speaking of those cases only which come before the courts,—probably, of course, not a third of the whole number,—the elements for forming an opinion are the following:—

In the Judicial Statistics for England and Wales, issued in 1877 for 1876, we find that of Aggravated Assaults on Women and Children, of the class which since 1853 have been brought under Summary Jurisdiction there were reported,

In 1876	2,737
In 1875	3,106
In 1874	2,841

How many of these were assaults made by husbands on wives there is no means of distinguishing, but, judging from other sources,[13] I should imagine they formed about four-fifths of the whole.

Among the worst cases, when the accused persons were committed for trial or bailed for appearance at Assizes or Sessions (coming under the head of Criminal Proceedings), the classification adopted in the Parliamentary Return does not permit of identifying the cases which concerned women only. Some rough guess on the matter may perhaps be formed from the preponderance of male criminals in all classes of violent crime. Out of 67 persons charged with Murder in 1876, 49 were men. Of 41 charged with Attempt to Murder, 35 were males. Of 157 charged with Shooting, Stabbing, &c., 146 were men. Of 232 charged with Manslaughter, 185 were men; and of 1,020 charged with Assault inflicting bodily harm, 857 were men. In short, out of 1,517 persons charged with crimes of cruelty and violence, more than five-sixths were males, and only 235 females. Of course the men's offences include a variety of crimes besides Wife-beating and Wife-torture.

The details of the crimes for which twenty-two men who were capitally convicted in 1876 suffered death are noteworthy on this head. (Criminal Statistics p. xxix.) Of these:—

Edward Deacon, shoemaker, murdered his wife by cutting her head with a chopper.
John Thomas Green, painter, shot his wife with a pistol.
John Eblethrift, labourer, murdered his wife by stabbing.
Charles O'Donnell, labourer, murdered his wife by beating.
Henry Webster, labourer, murdered his wife by cutting her throat.

Beside these, five others murdered women with whom they were living in vicious relations, and three others (including the monster William Fish) murdered children. In all, more than half the convicted persons executed that year were guilty of wife-murder,—or of what we may term *quasi*-wife-murder.

A source of more accurate information is to be found in the abstracts of the Reports of Chief Constables for the years 1870-1-2-3-4, presented to the Home Secretary, and published in the "Report on Brutal Assaults" (p. 169, et seq.). In this instructive table Brutal Assaults on Women are discriminated from those on men, and the total number of convictions for such assaults for the whole five years is 6,029; or at the average of 1,205 per annum. This is, however, obviously an imperfect return. In Nottinghamshire, where such offences were notoriously common, the doings of the "Lambs" have somehow escaped enumeration. "The Chief Constable states that he is unable to furnish a correct return." From Merionethshire no report was received in reply to the Home Office Circular; and from Rutland, Salop, Radnor, and Cardiganshire, the Chief Constables returned the reply that there were no brutal assaults in those counties during the five years in question,—a statement suggesting that some different classification of offences must prevail in those localities, since the immunity of Cardiganshire and Salop for five years from such crimes of violence would be little short of miraculous, while Flint alone had sixteen convictions. Thus I conceive that we may fairly estimate the number of brutal assaults (*brutal* be it remembered, not ordinary) committed on women in England and Wales and actually brought to justice at about 1,500 a year, or more than four *per diem*, and of these the great majority are of husbands on wives.

Let us now proceed from the number to the nature of the offences in question. I have called this paper English *Wife-torture* because I wish to impress my readers with the fact that the familiar term "wife-beating" conveys about as remote a notion of the extremity of the cruelty indicated as when candid and ingenuous vivisectors talk of "scratching a newt's tail" when they refer to burning alive, or dissecting out the nerves of living dogs, or torturing ninety cats in one series of experiments.

Wife-*beating* is the mere preliminary canter before the race,—the preface to the serious matter which is to follow. Sometimes, it is true, there are men of comparatively mild dispositions who are content to go on beating their wives year after year, giving them occasional black-eyes and bruises, or tearing out a few locks of their hair and spitting in their faces, or bestowing an ugly print of their iron fingers on the woman's soft arm, but not proceeding beyond these minor injuries to anything perilous. Among the lower classes, unhappily, this rude treatment is understood to mean very little more than that the man uses his weapon—the fists—as the woman uses hers—the tongue—and neither are very much hurt or offended by what is either done by one or said by the other. The whole state of manners is what is deplored, and our hope must be to change the bear-garden into the semblance of a civilized community, rather than by any direct effort to correct the special offence. Foul words, gross acts, drink, dirt, and vice, oaths, curses, and blows, it is all, alas! *in keeping*—nor can we hope to cure one evil without the rest. But the unendurable mischief, the discovery of which has driven me to try to call public attention to the whole matter, is this—Wife-*beating* in process of time, and in numberless cases, advances to Wife-*torture*, and the Wife-torture usually ends in Wife-maiming, Wife-blinding, or Wife-murder. A man who has "thrashed" his wife with his fists half-a-dozen times, becomes satiated with such enjoyment as that performance brings, and next time he is angry he kicks her with his hob-nailed shoes. When he has kicked her a few times standing or sitting, he kicks her down and stamps on her stomach, her breast, or her face. If he does not wear clogs or hob-nailed shoes, he takes up some other weapon, a knife, a poker, a hammer, a bottle of vitriol, or a lighted lamp, and strikes her with it, or sets her on fire;—and then, and then only, the hapless creature's sufferings are at an end.

I desire specially to avoid making this paper more painful than can be helped, but it is indispensable that some specimens of the tortures to which I refer should be brought before the reader's eye. I shall take them exclusively from cases reported during the last three or four months. Were I to go further back for a year or two, it would be easy to find some more "sensational," as, for example, of Michael Copeland, who threw his wife on a blazing fire; of George Ellis, who murdered his wife by pitching her out of the window; of Ashton Keefe, who beat his wife and thrust a box of lighted matches into his little daughter's breast when she was too slow in bringing his beer; and of Charles Bradley, who, according to the report in the *Manchester Examiner*, "came home, and after locking the door, told his wife he would murder her. He immediately set a large bulldog at her, and the dog, after flying at the upper part of her body, seized hold of the woman's right arm, which she lifted to protect herself, and tore pieces out. The prisoner in the meantime kept striking her in the face, and inciting the brute to worry her. The dog dragged her up and down, biting pieces out of her arms, and the prisoner then got on the sofa and hit and kicked her on the breast."

But the instances of the last three or four months—from September to the end of January—are more than enough to establish all I want to prove; and I beg here to return my thanks for a collection of them, and for many very useful observations and tabulations of them, to Miss A. Shore, who has been good enough to place them at my disposal.

It is needful to bear in mind in reading them, that the reports of such cases which appear in newspapers are by no means always reliable, or calculated to convey the same impressions as the sight of the actual trial. In some of the following instances, also, I have only been able to obtain the first announcement of the offence, without means of checking it by the subsequent proceedings in court. *Per contra*, it should be remembered that if a few of these cases may possibly have been exaggerated or trumped up (as I believe the story of the man pouring Chili vinegar into his wife's eyes proved to have been), there are, for every one of these *published* horrors, at least three or four which *never are reported at all*, and where the poor victim dies quietly of her injuries like a wounded animal, without seeking the mockery of redress offered her by the law.

James Mills cut his wife's throat as she lay in bed. He was quite sober at the time. On a previous occasion he had nearly torn away her left breast.

J. Coleman returned home early in the morning, and, finding his wife asleep, took up a heavy piece of wood and struck her on the head and arm, bruising her arm. On a previous occasion he had fractured her ribs.

John Mills poured out vitriol deliberately, and threw it in his wife's face, because she asked him to give her some of his wages. He had said previously that he would blind her.

James Lawrence, who had been frequently bound over to keep the peace, and who had been supported by his wife's industry for years, struck her on the face with a poker, leaving traces of the most dreadful kind when she appeared in court.

Frederick Knight jumped on the face of his wife (who had only been confined a month) with a pair of boots studded with hobnails.

Richard Mountain beat his wife on the back and mouth, and turned her out of her bed and out of their room one hour after she had been confined.

Alfred Roberts felled his wife to the floor, with a child in her arms; knelt on her, and grasped her throat. She had previously taken out three summonses against him, but had never attended.

John Harris, a shoemaker, at Sheffield, found his wife and children in bed; dragged her out, and, after vainly attempting to force her into the oven, tore off her night-dress and turned her round before the fire "like a piece of beef," while the children stood on the stairs listening to their mother's agonized screams.

Richard Scully knocked in the frontal bone of his wife's forehead.

William White, stonemason, threw a burning paraffin lamp at his wife, and stood quietly watching her enveloped in flames, from the effects of which she died.

William Hussell, a butcher, ran a knife into his wife several times and killed her. Had threatened to do so often before.

Robert Kelly, engine-driver, bit a piece out of his wife's cheek.

William James, an operative boilermaker, stabbed his wife badly in the arm and mouth, observing afterwards, "I am sorry I did not kill both" (his wife and her mother).

Thomas Richards, a smith, threw his wife down a flight of fourteen steps, when she came to entreat him to give her some money for her maintenance. He was living with another woman—the nurse at a hospital where he had been ill.

James Frickett, a ratcatcher. His wife was found dying with broken ribs and cut and bruised face, a walking-stick with blood on it lying by. Frickett remarked, "If I am going to be hanged for you, I love you."

James Styles beat his wife about the head when he met her in the City Road. She had supported him for years by char-work, and during the whole time he had been in the habit of beating her, and on one occasion so assaulted her that the sight of one of her eyes was destroyed. He got drunk habitually with the money she earned.

John Harley, a compositor, committed for trial for cutting and wounding his wife with intent to murder.

Joseph Moore, labourer, committed for trial for causing the death of his wife by striking her with an iron instrument on the head.

George Ralphy Smith, oilman, cut his wife, as the doctor expressed it, "to pieces," with a hatchet, in their back parlour. She died afterwards, but he was found Not Guilty, as it was not certain that her death resulted from the wounds.

Fletcher Bisley, a clerk, struck his wife violently on the head with a poker, after having tried to throw a saucepan of boiling soup at her son. Both had just returned home and found Bisley in bed.

Alfred Cummins, tailor, struck his wife so as to deprive her of the sight of an eye.

Thomas Page, laundryman, knocked down his wife in the street and kicked her till she became insensible, because she refused to give him money to get drink.

Alfred Etherington, shoemaker, kicked his wife in a dangerous way, and a week later dragged her out of bed, jumped on her, and struck her. He said he would have her life and the lives of all her children. He gave no money for the support of his family (six children), and he prevented her from keeping the situations she had obtained for their maintenance. She had summoned him six or seven times.

Jeremiah Fitzgerald, labourer, knocked down his wife and kicked her heavily in the forehead. He had been twice convicted before. The woman appeared in court with her face strapped up.

Patrick Flynn, violently kicked his wife after he had knocked her down, and then kicked a man who interfered to save her. Had already undergone six months' hard labour for assaulting his wife.

Here is a case recorded from personal observation by a magistrate's clerk:—

"I attended a dying woman to take her deposition in a drunkard's dwelling. The husband was present in charge of the police. The poor wretched wife lay with many ribs broken, and her shoulder and one arm broken, and her head so smashed that you could scarcely recognize a feature of a woman. She, in her last agony, said that her husband had smashed her with a wooden bed-post. He, blubbering, said, 'Yes, it is true, but I was in drink, or would not have done it.'"

And here is one that has come in while I have been writing:—

"At the Blackburn police-court, yesterday, John Chamock was committed for trial on a charge of attempted murder. It was stated that he had fastened his wife's head in a cupboard and kicked her with his iron clogs, and that he had deliberately broken her arm." (Feb. 3, 1878)

And here another (reported in the *Manchester Courier*, February 5th) so instructive in its details of the motives for Wife-murder, the sort of woman who is murdered, the man who kills, and the sentiment of juries as to what constitutes "provocation" on the part of a wife, that I shall extract it at length:—

MANSLAUGHTER AT DUKINFIELD.

"Thomas Harlow, 39, striker, Dukinfield, was indicted for the manslaughter of his wife, Ellen Harlow, 45 years old, at Dukinfield, on 30th November,

1877. The prisoner was committed by the magistrates on the charge of wilful murder, but the grand jury reduced the indictment to that of manslaughter. Mr. Marshall prosecuted; and the prisoner, who was undefended by counsel, stated, in his plea, that he had no intention of killing his wife when he struck her.

"The prisoner, who was employed in and about Dukinfield, lived with his wife and three children in Waterloo Street, in that town. On the morning of the 30th November the deceased went out hawking as usual, and returned shortly after twelve o'clock. During the time she was away the prisoner remained in the house sitting by the fire, and for the most part drinking beer. When she returned she busied herself in preparing dinner, and the prisoner went out for a short time. In the afternoon the prisoner laid himself down, and slept for two or three hours. About five o'clock the deceased, and a lodger named Margaret Daley, and several others, were sitting in the house, when the prisoner came in and asked his wife for twopence. She replied that she had not twopence, and that she had had trouble enough with being out hawking all day in the rain and hungry. He then began to abuse her, and asked her for something to eat. She gave him some potatoes and bacon; after eating the greater part of which he again began to abuse her. He once more asked her for two-pence, and Margaret Daley, seeing there was likely to be a disturbance, gave him the twopence, and told him he had better get a pint of beer. Instead of getting beer, however, he sent a little girl to purchase a quantity of coal, and then recommenced abusing his wife. Shortly afterwards he was heard to exclaim, 'There will be a life less to-night, and 1 will take it.' At this time the persons who were sitting in the house when the prisoner came in went out, leaving Harlow, his wife, and their son Thomas, and Daley together. The prisoner had some further altercation with his wife, which ended with him striking her a violent blow under the right ear, felling her to the floor. She died in a few minutes afterwards; the cause of death being concussion of the brain. The prisoner subsequently gave himself into custody, and made a statement attributing his conduct to the provocation his wife had given him.

"The jury found the prisoner guilty, and recommended him to mercy *on account of the provocation* he received. Sentence was deferred."

I think I may now safely ask the reader to draw breath after all these horrors, and agree with me that they cannot, *must* not, be allowed to go on unchecked, without some effort to stop them, and save these perishing and miserable creatures. Poor, stupid, ignorant women as most of them are, worn out with lifelong drudgery, burdened with all the pangs and cares of many children, poorly fed and poorly clothed, with no pleasures and many pains, there is an enormous excuse to be made for them even if they do sometimes seek in drink the oblivion of their misery—a brief dream of unreal joy, where real natural happiness is so far away.[14] But for those who rise above these temptations, who are sober where intoxication holds out their only chance of pleasure; chaste in the midst of foulness; tender mothers when their devotion calls for toilsome days and sleepless nights,—for these good, industrious, struggling women who, I have shown, are the chief victims of all this cruelty,—is it to be borne that we should sit patiently by and allow their lives to be trampled out in agony?

What ought to be done?

First, what has been done, or has been proposed to be done, in the matter?

In June, 1853, an Act was passed (16th Victoria, c. 30) entitled "An Act for the Better Prevention and Punishment of Aggravated Assaults upon Women and Children, and for Preventing Delay and Expense in the Administration of the Criminal Law." In the preamble to this Act it is stated that "the present law has been found insufficient for the protection of women and children from violent assaults;" and the measure provides that assaults upon any female or any male child—occasioning actual bodily harm—may be punished by summary conviction before two justices of the Peace in Petty Sessions, or before any Police or Stipendiary Magistrate. The penalty to be inflicted is not to exceed imprisonment for six months with or without hard labour, or a fine not exceeding 20. The offender may also be bound to keep the peace for any period not exceeding six months from the expiration of his sentence. Failing to enter into recognizances, the offender may be kept in prison for a period not exceeding twelve months.

Since this Act was passed twenty-five years ago, no further legislation has taken place on the subject except the Consolidating Act (24. and 25 Vict. c. 100), which simply re-enacts the Act as above stated.

Beside this Act on their behalf, wives are able to obtain relief in certain cases, under the Divorce Act. That is to say, those women who are able to apply to the Divorce Court may obtain, under section 16 of the Act (20th and 21st Vict. c. 85), on proof of cruelty, a sentence of Judicial Separation, which shall have the effect of a divorce à mensâ et thoro.

In the case of the ignorant, friendless, and penniless women, who are the chief victims of Wife-torture, such relief as this court affords is practically unattainable; but another clause of the same Act (the twenty-first) is of great value to them. It provides that a wife deserted by her husband may, at any time after such desertion, apply to a Police Magistrate in the metropolitan district, or to Justices in Petty Sessions if in the country, for an order to protect any money or property she may acquire; and if such Protection Order be made, the wife shall, during its continuance, "be in all respects in the same position, with regard to property and contracts, and suing and being sued, as she would have been under the Act if she had obtained a decree of Judicial Separation."

For reasons to be hereafter noticed, this clause in the Divorce Act is of the utmost importance in establishing the principle that a Police Magistrate, or two Justices of the Peace in Session, may pronounce, on proof of the minor offence of desertion by the husband, a sentence which is tantamount, so far as property is concerned, to a Judicial Separation. The clause is, I am informed, brought very frequently indeed into action, and the magistrates not unfrequently interpret "desertion" to signify an absence of three months without cause, albeit in the Divorce Court such absence must exceed two years to enable the wife to obtain a judicial separation.

It was doubtless believed by the benevolent promoters of these Acts that their provisions would have done a good deal to check the ill-usage of wives. But the offence appears to have diminished very little, if at all, during the twenty years which have since intervened, and at last one well-meaning, though somewhat eccentric member of the House of Commons felt himself moved to speak on the subject.

On the 18th May, 1874, Colonel Egerton Leigh made a vehement appeal for some increased punishment for aggravated assaults on women. He said that England had been called the Paradise of Women, and he brought forward his motion to prevent it from becoming a Hell of Women. After a speech, in which Colonel Leigh appeared overcome by emotion, he ended by saying that he "was sure the women of England would not appeal in vain to the House of Commons" and Mr. Disraeli answered him in the same vein of cheerful confidence which that Honourable House always expresses in its own eagerness to do justice to women. The House "must have sympathized," he said, "with Colonel Leigh, for it was a subject on which there could not be any differences of opinion." He hoped "his honourable and gallant friend would feel he has accomplished his object in directing the attention of the country to the subject, and that he would allow his right honourable friend, the Secretary of State for the Home Department, whose mind is now occupied with this and similar subjects, time to reflect as to the practical mode in which the feeling of the country can be carried out." Colonel Leigh was requested to be "satisfied that after the address he has made, Her Majesty's Government will bear in mind what is evidently the opinion of the House;" and, of course, Colonel Leigh expressed himself as perfectly satisfied, and withdrew his amendment (authorizing flogging) with one of the jokes, which are so inexpressibly sickening in connection with this subject, about "fair play for the fairer sex."[15]

On the 15th October, 1874, six months after Colonel Leigh had thus broken a lance in defence of the tortured women, the Home Office issued a Circular inquiring the opinion of the Judges, Chairmen of Quarter Sessions, Recorders, Stipendiary Magistrates of Metropolitan Police Courts, and Sheriffs of Scotch Counties, respecting five points connected with brutal assaults, the principal being whether the existing law was sufficiently stringent, and whether flogging should be authorized, "especially in cases of assaults on women and children."

The replies to these questions were published in a Parliamentary Blue Book entitled "Reports on the State of the Law relating to Brutal Assaults," in 1875, and the following is a summary of the results:—

There was a large consensus of opinion that the law as it now stands is insufficient to effect its purpose. Lord Chief Justice Cockburn says, "In my opinion the present law against assaults of brutal violence is not sufficiently stringent" (p. 5), and Mr. Justice Lush, Mr. Justice Mellor, Lord Chief Baron Kelly, Baron Bramwell, Baron Pigott, and Baron Pollock, express the same judgment in almost the same words (pp. 7-19).

Several of these, and also other judges, who do not directly say that they consider the present law insufficient, manifest their opinion that it is so by recommending that (under various safeguards) the penalty of flogging be added thereto. The agreement of opinion of these great authorities on this point appears (to the uninitiated) as if it must have been sufficient to carry with it any measure which had such weighty recommendation.

The following are the opinions in favour of flogging offenders in cases of brutal assaults:—

Lord Chief Justice Cockburn, Mr. Justice Blackburn, Mr. Justice Mellor, Mr. Justice Lush, My Justice Quain, Mr. Justice Archibald, Mr. Justice Brett, Mr. Justice Grove, Lord Chief Baron Kelly, Baron Bramwell, Baron Pigott, Baron Pollock, Baron Cleasby, and Baron Amphlett. The opinions of Lord Coleridge and Mr. Justice Denman were hesitating, and the only decided opponent of flogging at that time on the judicial bench in England was Mr. Justice Keating.

The Chairmen of Quarter Sessions and magistrates in Sessions were in *sixty-four* cases out of the sixty-eight from whence responses came to the Home Office, in favour of flogging:—Leftwich, Oxford (county), Stafford (county), and the North Riding being the only exceptions.

The Recorders of *forty-one* towns were likewise in favour of flogging, and only those of Lincoln, Nottingham, and Wolverhampton were opposed to it. The Recorders of Folkestone and of Newcastle-on-Tyne added the recommendation that a husband who had been flogged for a brutal assault on his wife should be divorced from her.

On reading this summary it will doubtless to many persons appear inexplicable that three years should have elapsed since so important a testimony was collected at the public expense, and at the trouble of so many eminent gentlemen whose time was of infinite value; and that, so far as can be ascertained, absolutely nothing has been done in the way of making practical use of it. During the interval scores of Bills, on every sort and kind of question *interesting to the represented sex*, have passed through Parliament; but *this* question, on which the lives of women literally hang, has never been even mooted since Lord Beaconsfield so complacently assured its solitary champion that "Her Majesty's Government would bear in mind the evident feeling of the House on the subject." Something like 6,000 women, judging by the judicial statistics, have been in the intervening years "brutally assaulted"—that is, maimed, blinded, trampled, burned, and in no inconsiderable number of instances murdered outright—and several thousand children have been brought up to witness scenes which might, as Colonel Leigh said, "infernalilize a whole generation." Nevertheless, the newspapers go on boasting of elementary education, and Parliament busies itself in its celebrated elephant's trunk fashion, alternately rending oaks and picking up sixpences; but *this* evil remains untouched!

The fault does not lie with the Home Office—scarcely even with Parliament, except so far as Parliament persists in refusing to half the nation those political rights which alone can, under our present order of things, secure attention to any claims. We live in these days under *Government by Pressure,* and the Home Office *must* attend first to the claims which are backed by political pressure; and Members of Parliament *must* attend to the subjects pressed by their constituents; and the claims and subjects which are not supported by such political pressure *must* go to the wall.

Nevertheless, when we women of the upper ranks,—constitutionally qualified by the possession of property (and, I may be permitted to add, naturally qualified by education and intelligence at least up to the level of those of the "illiterate" order of voters), to exercise through the suffrage that pressure on Parliament,—are refused that privilege, and told year after year by smiling senators that we have no need whatever for it, that we form no "class," and that we may absolutely and always rely on men to prove the deepest and tenderest concern for everything which concerns the welfare of women, shall we not point to these long-neglected wrongs of our trampled sisters, and denounce that boast of the equal concern of men for women as—a falsehood?

Were women to obtain the franchise to-morrow, it is morally certain that a Bill for the Protection of Wives would pass through the legislature before a Session was over. I have yet hopes that even before that event takes place, some attention may be directed to the miserable subject, and that it may be possible to obtain some measure, holding out a prospect of relief to the wretched victims—if not of repression of the crime of Wife-torture. What measure ought we to ask for the purpose?

Of the desirability that any step should be taken in the direction of inflicting the lash for aggravated assaults on women, I shall not presume in the face of such authorities as have been cited above, to offer any opinion whatever.

One thing is manifest at all events. It is, that if flogging were added to the present penalties of wife-beating, the great difficulty which meets all efforts to stop the practice would be doubled. That difficulty is the inducing of the women (whose evidence is in most instances indispensable) to bear testimony against their husbands. It is hard enough to lead them to do so when the results will be an imprisonment to end in one month or in six, after which the husband will return to them full of fresh and more vindictive cruelty, and when in short, bringing him "up" means abandoning the last ray of hope of ever making a happy home. This sentiment, half prudence, half perhaps in some cases lingering affection, cannot be overcome (even were it desirable to do so), as the law now stands, and causes endless failures of justice and perplexity to the always well-meaning magistrates. As a general rule it is said the wives will often tell their stories to the constables at the moment of the arrest, and can frequently be induced to attend in court the day or two after their injuries and while still smarting from their blows, and kicks, and "cloggings." But if a week be allowed to elapse, still more if the case be referred to the Quarter Sessions or Assizes, the wife is almost certain in the interval to have relented, or to have learned to dread the consequence of bearing testimony, and, instead of telling her true story, is constantly found to narrate some poor little fable, whereby the husband is quite exonerated, and, perhaps the blame taken on herself, as in the pitifully ludicrous case cited by Colonel Egerton Leigh in the House of Commons—of the woman who appeared without a nose, and told the magistrate she had *bitten it off herself!* On this subject, and on the defects of our whole procedure in such cases, some just remarks were made by Mr. Serjeant Pulling in a paper read before the Social Science Congress at Liverpool, published in the Transactions for 1876, p. 345. He says—

"No one who has gained experience of wife-beating cases, can doubt that our present system of procedure seems as if it were designed not to repress crime, but to discourage complaints. A woman after being brutally assaulted by her husband, and receiving a sufficient number of kicks and blows to make her think she is being murdered, calls out for the aid of the police; and if her statements were there and then authentically recorded, and afterwards, on the commitment and trial of the aggressor, allowed to form part of the formal proof against him (subject of course to the right of the accused to refute it by cross-examination), there can be little doubt that the ends of justice would oftener be attained. In practice, however, the course is for the police to hear the loose statements of the scared victim and bystanders; and the subsequent proceedings are left very much to depend on the influences brought to bear on the poor wife in the interim (before the trial). She may relent before morning comes, or be subjected to so much sinister influence on the part of the husband and his friends as to be effectually prevented from disclosing the whole truth at all; or if doing so in the first stage of the proceedings she may be easily made so completely to neutralize its effect, that conviction becomes impracticable. The lesson taught to the ruffian is that if he ill-uses his dog or his donkey he stands a fair chance of being duly prosecuted, convicted, and punished; but that if the ill-usage is merely practised on his wife, the odds are in favour of his own entire immunity, and of his victim getting worse treatment if she dare appear against him."

To avoid these failures of justice, and the consequent triumph of the callous offenders, magistrates are generally very anxious to have these cases summarily disposed of, and to strike while the iron is hot. But of course there hence arises another evil, namely, that the greater offences, which ought to be tried in the higher courts, and were intended to receive the heaviest penalty which the law allows, are punished only to the extent of the powers of the summary jurisdiction, of which the maximum is six month's imprisonment. Occasionally there is reason to believe the magistrates mend matters a little by the not unfair device of ordering the offender to find security for good behaviour, which, as he is generally unable to discover anybody foolish enough to give it for him, involves his incarceration in jail, possibly for a year. And, again, magistrates kindly endeavour to make the period of detention serve the process of reclaiming the man to better feelings about his wife, by allowing her entreaty to weigh importantly in any application to curtail his sentence, and letting him know that any repetition of offence will be closely watched and doubly severely punished.[16] But all these humane devices, though sometimes, it is to be hoped, successful, yet leave the mournful fact patent to observation that the existing law, even worked with the extremest care and kindness, cannot and does not prevent the repetition, year after year, of all the frightful cruelties, beatings, burnings, cloggings, and tramplings of which we have given some pages back a few awful samples.

The relief which I most earnestly desire to see extended to these women, and from which I would confidently hope for *some* alleviation of their wretched condition, though its entire cure is beyond hope, is of a very different sort. It is this. A Bill should, I think, be passed, *affording to these poor women, by means easily within their reach, the same redress which women of the richer classes obtain through the Divorce Court.* They should be enabled to obtain from the Court which sentences their husbands a Protection Order, which should in their case have the same validity as a judicial separation. In addition to this, the *Custody* of *the Children should be given to the wife,* and an order should be made for *the husband to pay to the wife such weekly sum for her own and her children's maintenance as the Court may see fit.*

The following are the chief clauses in a Bill, which has been prepared by Alfred D. Hill, Esq., J.P., of Birmingham, and the principle of which has been approved by many eminent legal authorities:—

BILL

Intitled *An Act, for the Protection of Wives whose Husbands have been convicted of assaults upon them.*

Whereas it is desirable to make provision for the protection of wives whose husbands have been convicted of assaults upon them: Be it enacted by the Queen's Most Excellent Majesty, by and with the advice and consent of the Lords Spiritual and Temporal and of the Commons in this present Parliament assembled, and by the authority of the same, as follows:—

1. In any case where a husband has been convicted summarily or otherwise of an assault upon his wife, and has been sentenced to imprisonment therefor

without the option of a fine in lieu of such imprisonment, it shall be competent for the Court by which such sentence has been pronounced, either at the time of such conviction or at any time afterwards, upon proof thereof, to make and give to the wife upon her application an order protecting her earnings and property acquired since the date of such order from her husband and all creditors and persons claiming under him; and such earnings and property shall belong to the wife as if she were a *feme sole*; and if any such order of protection be made, the wife shall, during the continuance thereof, be an be deemed to be in the like position in all respects with regard to property and contracts, and suing and being sued, as she would be if she had obtained a decree of judicial separation from the Court for Divorce and Matrimonial Causes.

2. The police magistrate orjustices shall include in such order as aforesaid an injunction restraining the husband from going to or visiting the wife without her consent; and if any husband against whom any such injunction shall be made shall commit any act of disobedience thereto, such act shall be deemed to be a misdemeanour, upon due proof of which any Court which would have been competent to make such order and injunction may commit him to the common gaol or house of correction of the city, borough, or county within the jurisdiction of such Court for any period not exceeding three months with or without hard labour.

3. And any Court which would have been competent to make such order as aforesaid may further include in such order a provision that the wife shall have the legal custody of the children of her husband and herself. And the same Court which would have been competent to make such order may further include in such order a provision directing that the husband shall pay to the wife a weekly sum not exceeding shillings per week for the maintenance of herself and of such children, which provisions of the order shall, if the payments required by it be in arrear, be enforced in the manner prescribed by the Act of the 11th and 12th Vict. C. 43, for the enforcing of orders orjustices requiring the payment of a sum of money.

4. Every such order as aforesaid shall, within ten days after the making thereof, be entered with the registrar of the county court within whose jurisdiction the wife is resident, and a copy of such order shall, within such ten days, or within a reasonable time in that behalf, be served upon the husband. And it shall be lawful for the husband to apply to the Court for Divorce and Matrimonial Causes, or to the magistrate or justices by whom such order was made, for the discharge thereof, and they may (if they think fit) discharge the same. And the said Court for Divorce and Matrimonial Causes, or magistrate, or justices, is or are hereby authorized to discharge such order if it, he, or they shall deem fit.

(Here follows Schedule.)

The reasons which may be urged on behalf of this measure are manifold. They rest at all points on admitted principles of legislation.

In the first place, the Divorce Laws offering to women *who care avail themselves of them* the remedy of Judicial Separation in cases of the cruelty of their husbands, it is a matter of simple justice that the same remedy should be placed within the reach of those poor women who are subjected to tenfold greater cruelties than those which the court always rules to constitute a ground for such separation. It is impossible to imagine a matter in which the existence of "one law for the rich and another for the poor" is more unrighteous and intolerable than this. At the same time, except by some such machinery as has been suggested,— namely, that the police magistrate or petty sessions court should be given the power to pronounce the separation,—it is difficult to conceive of any way in which the very humble and ignorant class of women, with whom we are concerned, could ever obtain the decree which is *in principle* at present their *right*.

A second reason for such a measure is that, as above stated, Magistrates are already empowered, in cases of *desertion*, to give Protection Orders which are expressly stated to be (so far as property is concerned) equivalent to a Judicial Separation—and which (very frequently given as they are) practically act as Judicial Separations in all respects. The objection which has been raised by some hasty readers of the Bill, that it proposes to give an unheard-of power to one or two Magistrates, thus falls to the ground. They already practically exercise the same power every day in the minor case of desertion. The husband is also afforded by the Bill every facility for obtaining a discharge of the Order should it appear to have been unjustly given.

Finally, a most important reason for adopting such a measure is, that it—or something like it—is indispensable to induce the victims of such outrages to apply for legal redress.[17] The great failure of justice which has so long gone on in this matter, is chiefly due, as I have said before, to the fact that the existing law *discourages* such applications,—adds penalties to the husband's offence without providing the suffering wife with any protection from his renewed violence when that penalty has been endured. Under the Wives Protection Bill, should it become law, the injured wife would have the *very thing she really wants*, namely, security against further violence, coupled with the indispensable custody of her children (without which, no protection of herself would offer a temptation to the better sort of women), and some small (though probably precarious) contribution to their maintenance and her own. With this real relief held out to them by the law, I should have little doubt that we should find the victims of brutal assaults and of repeated aggravated assaults very generally coming forward to bear testimony and claim their release, and the greatest difficulty attendant on the case would be at an end.

Even were there but a few who availed themselves of the boon, I still think it would be fitting and right that the law should hold it out to them. In many instances no doubt the mere fact that the wife had such a resource open to her would act very effectually on the husband as a deterrent to violence.

As to the justice and expediency of giving the custody of the children (both boys and girls of all ages) to the wife, there can be, I should think, little hesitation. The man who is, *ex hypothesi*, capable of kicking, maiming, and mutilating his wife, is even less fit to be the guardian of the bodies and souls of children than the lord and master of a woman. They are no more safe under his roof than in the cage of a wild beast, and the guilt of leaving them in the one place is little less than that of placing them in the other. When a child is killed by one of these drunken savages,—as the illegitimate child of George Hill, whom he knocked on the head with a hammer in revenge for having an affiliation order made on him; or as the child of six years old whom James Parris murdered because its mother failed to keep an appointment,—or when a child is cruelly injured, as the poor little girl into whose breast Ashton Keefe thrust a box full of ignited matches because she had been slow in fetching his beer,—when these outrages occur we are indignant enough with the offenders; but, if they had previously betrayed their tiger instincts, is there no guilt attaching to those who *left* these defenceless creatures in their dens? For both the children's sakes and the mothers' this clause of the Bill, then, appears of paramount importance—in fact, a *sine quâ non* of any measure possessing practical value.

Lastly, as regards the alimony for the wife, and the maintenance for the children, to be paid by the husband after the term of his imprisonment, I presume the justice of the provision will not be disputed. The man obviously cannot wipe away his natural obligations by the commission of a deed of cruel violence, and it would be a most dangerous lesson to let him think he could do so. The difficulty of course lies in enforcing such an order in the case of those lowest classes of artisans and labourers who can move freely from place to place, obtaining employment anywhere with the help of a bag of tools, or tramping the country from workhouse to workhouse. In the case of affiliation orders it is, I understand, found pretty uniformly that the small tradesmen, and men having a fixed business, pay their weekly dole fairly regularly, thereby minimizing the scandal; but the lower and looser sort of men decamp, and are lost sight of sooner or later, the Poor-law authorities rarely troubling themselves to look after them. The same measure of escape will undoubtedly be sought by not a few separated husbands should the Bill before us become law. The evil is serious, but perhaps not so serious or irremediable as it may appear. In the first place the Poor-law authorities or the police might surely be stirred to put in motion the machinery which lies ready to hand in case of greater crimes. A man was whipped last January by order of the Recorder of Hereford, under the Act 5 George IV., C. 83, for leaving his wife and children four times, and throwing them on the Union. It would be a useful lesson to impress pretty generally the fact that such legal responsibilities cannot be shirked in England with impunity.[18]

Secondly, there are few of these beaten wives who would not be far better off separated from their husbands *even if they never received a farthing of maintenance* than they are under their present condition, or would be under liability to their occasional raids and incursions. Such women (as I have maintained so often) are nearly always the bread-winners of the family. They have usually been for months or years earning their children's subsistence and their own, and very often that of their husbands beside. The withdrawal of this supposed conjugal "support" accordingly means the withdrawal of minus quantity. They will find themselves where they were, with this difference, that they will not see their husbands reeling home to empty their scanty cupboards—chartered robbers, as scores of such husbands are. It is true the sole charge of their children will devolve on them, but (and this is a reflection which goes far further into the matter than I can pursue it) they will have no *more* children than those already born. Women never reach the bottom of the abyss of their misery save when the pangs and weaknesses of child-bearing and child-nursing are added to their burdens, and when to the outrage of their tyrant's blows is joined the deeper degradation of bearing him children year by year, to furnish fresh victims of his cruelty, and to rivet their chains. The subject is too revolting to be dwelt upon here.

Of course it is not difficult to find objections to the proposed measure. I have already referred to, and I hope satisfactorily answered, that which rests on the supposed difficulty of entrusting a single Police Magistrate or Justices in Petty Sessions with such powers as are given them in the Bill. As no complaints have ever been published of their frequent use of analogous power in cases of Desertion, I know not why we should anticipate them in those of Brutal Assault.

Again, objections have been taken to the Bill on the ground that cases of collusion might occur under its provisions. It has been suggested, for example, that a wife desiring to get rid of her husband might designedly provoke him to beat her, and that she might prefer taking the beating, and so obtaining both his money and release from. his presence. Or again, it is said that a wife who had given a man cause for jealousy, and had been beaten by him in consequence, would thus obtain her object of separation and freedom to live with her paramour. Or again, that a wife who drank and "sold up" her husband's goods might have practically done him much more grievous injury than he has done her by the thrashing he gives her, and yet, under such an Act as is proposed, the husband would be compelled to give a share of his wages to her, and to see his children in her custody possibly starving and ill-treated. To all these hypothetical cases I have only to reply that, should they ever be realized, they would certainly form a failure of justice, and that I should sincerely regret that any man, even a wife-beater, should suffer wrongfully, or a jot more than he deserves. But I confess I am more concerned to protect the *certainly* beaten wives than their hypothetically ill-used beaters; and that most of the suggestions above named appear to me exceedingly far-fetched; and unlikely ever to be verified.

The real and valid objection to the Bill—which I cannot blink—is the same which necessarily adheres to every severance of married couples which does not sanction their marrying again—in short, to every divorce à *mensâ et thoro*, which is not a divorce *à vinculo*. The latter kind of divorce—though we have the opinion of Mr. Lonsdale and Mr. Digby Seymour that it ought to be given to the wife in such cases of brutal assault—seems too dangerous a resource, seeing that it might often act as an incentive to commit the assault in the case of a husband, and an incentive to provoke one in the case of the wife. The *quasi*-judicial separation, on the other hand, which is all the Bill proposes, of course leaves the separated man and woman liable each to fall into vicious courses since marriage is closed to them, and thus to contribute to the disorder of the community. The evil, I think, must be fairly weighed against the benefits anticipated from the measure; but the reflection that the wife-beater is almost always *already* a man of loose and disorderly life will tend to diminish our estimate of that evil's extent. The decent respectable wife, such as I hope I have shown a large class of beaten wives to be, would of course live like a well-conducted widow.

I entreat my readers not to turn away and forget this wretched subject. I entreat the gentlemen of England,—the bravest, humanest, and most generous in the world,—not to leave these helpless women to be trampled to death under their very eyes. I entreat English ladies, who, like myself, have never received from the men with whom we associate anything but kindness and consideration, and who are prone to think that the lot of others is smooth and happy as our own, to take to heart the wrongs and agonies of our miserable sisters, and to lift up on their behalf a cry which must make Parliament either hasten to deal with the matter, or renounce for very shame the vain pretence that it takes care of the interests of women.

[NOTE.—Copies of the Bill advocated in the foregoing article may be had from Mr. King, Parliamentary Publisher, Canada Buildings, King Street, Westminster. Price 6*d*.]

NOTES

1 With the exception, perhaps, of the Seal. Mr. Darwin gives a sad picture of amphibious conjugal life: "As soon as a female reaches the shore ('comes out,' as we should say in 'society'), the nearest male goes down to meet her, making meanwhile a noise like the clucking of a hen to her chickens. He bows to her and coaxes her, until he gets between her and the water so that she cannot escape him. Then his manner changes, and with a harsh growl he drives her to a place in his harem."—*Descent of Man*, vol. ii. p.269. What an "o'er true tale" is this of many a human wooing and of what comes later; the "bowing and coaxing" first, and the "harsh growl" afterwards! I am surprised Mr. Darwin did not derive from it an argument for the Descent of Man from the Seal.

It is very instructive to watch the behaviour of a big male dog undergoing the experience which is understood to surpass the limits of a man's endurance; namely, being "nagged" by a little vixen who stands opposite to him in an attitude exactly corresponding to the "arms akimbo" of her human prototype, and pours out volleys of barking which would, obviously, in the police courts be reported as "abusive language." The much-tried dog—let us say a Retriever or Newfoundland—who could annihilate his little female assailant—a toy Terrier or Pomeranian, perhaps—in two mouthfuls, and who *would* do so in the case of an enemy of his own sex—always on these occasions starts aside with well-feigned surprise, as if astonished at the reception of his advances; lifts his ears as a gentleman raises his hat, and presently bounds away, lightly: "I beg your pardon, madam! I am the last dog in the world, I assure you, to offend a lady!" Be it noted that if that dog had retreated before the bullying of another male dog, he would have slunk off with his tail between his legs, ashamed of his own poltroonery. But from the female termagant he retires with all the honours of war; and with his tail held aloft like a standard; quite conscious that he is acting as becomes a dog and a gentleman.

2   Not universally I am glad to hear. In Yorkshire and several other counties a very old custom exists, or did exist as late as 1862, called "Riding the Stang" or "Rough Music," which consists in giving a serenade with cows' horns, and warming-pans, and tea-kettles to a man known to have beaten his wife or been unfaithful to her. See a very curious account of it and of its good effects, in Chambers' Book of Days, vol. ii. p.510. A correspondent kindly sends further details, from which it appears that there is always a sort of herald or orator on the occasion, who, when the procession halts before the delinquent's house, recites verses in this style: —

> "There is a man in this place,
> (*piano*) Has beat his wife [a pause]
> (*fortissimo*) Has beat his wife!!
> " 'tis a very great shame and disgrace
> To all who live in the place," &c.

The custom derives its name from the old Scottish "Stange"—a long pole on which the culprit is sometimes made to take a very disagreeable ride.

3   Transactions Social Science Association, 1876, p. 345.

4   Let it be noted that while they *were* slaves, these negroes were daily subjected to outrages and cruelties of which it thrilled our blood to hear. Since they have been emancipated their white neighbours have learned at least so far to recognize them as human beings, that these *tortures* have become comparatively rare.

5   Stripped of the euphemisms of courtesy wherewith we generally wrap them up, it cannot be denied that the sentiments of a very large number of men towards women consist of a wretched alternation of exaggerated and silly homage, and of no less exaggerated and foolish contempt. One moment on a pedestal, the next in the mire; the woman is adored while she gives pleasure, despised the moment she cease to do so. The proverbial difficulty of introducing a joke into the skull of a Scotchman is nothing to that of getting into the mind of such men that a woman is

a *human being*—however humble—not a mere adjunct and appendage of humanity; and that she must have been created, and has a right to live for ends of her own; not for the ends of another; that she was made, as the old Westminster Catechism says, "to glorify God and enjoy Him for ever," not primarily or expressly to be John Smith's wife and James Smith's mother. We laugh at the great engineer who gave as his opinion before a Royal Commission that rivers were created to feed navigable canals; and a farmer would certainly be treated as betraying the "bucolic mind" who avowed that he thought his horse was made to carry him to market, and his cat to eat his mice and spare his cheese; yet where women are concerned—beings who are understood to be at least *quasi*-rational, and to whom their religion promises an immortal life hereafter of good and glory—the notion that the Final Cause of Woman is Man seems never to strike them as supremely ridiculous.

6   Old English legislation embodied this view so far as to inflict the cruellest of all punishments—burning to death—on a woman guilty of *petty treason, i.e.*, the murder of her husband, while the husband was only liable to hanging for murdering his wife. A woman was burned to death under this atrocious law at Chester, in 1760, for poisoning her husband. The wretched creature was made to linger four months in jail under her awful sentence before it was executed.

7   And there are gentlemen who think there is something beautiful in this! The Rev. F.W. Harper, writing to the *Spectator* of January 26, says, "I make bold to believe that if ever I should turn into a wife I shall choose to be beaten by my husband to any extent (short of being slain outright), rather than it should be said a stranger came between us." After thus bringing to our minds the beatings, and kickings, and blindings, and burnings, and "cloggings," which sicken us, he bids us remember that the true idea of marriage is "the relation of Christ to his Church"! It is not for me to speak on this subject, but I should have expected that a minister of the Christian religion would have shuddered at the possibility of suggesting such a connection of ideas as these notions involve. Heaven help the poor women of Durham and Lancashire if their clergy lead them to picture a Christ resembling their husbands!

8   I doubt that, even if reduced to bestial helplessness by these drinks in a pure state, men would ever be goaded by them to the class of passions excited by the adulterated ones. I have myself seen in Savoy whole crowds of men returning from market, all more or less tipsy from the free use of the excellent Vin de Seychelles, but instead of quarrelling or fighting, or beating their horses and pigs, their demeanour was ludicrously good-humoured and affectionate.

9   *Hopes of the Human Race*, p.172 (the Evolution of the Social Sentiment). By Frances Power Cobbe. Williams and Norgate.

10   I have seen a woman like this tormenting a great, good-natured hobbledehoy, who unhappily belonged to Carlyle's order of "Inarticulate ones," and found it impossible to avoid being caught every five minutes in the Socratic *elenchus*,*

---

* The method pursued by Socrates of eliciting truth by means of short questions and answers [Editor's note].

which she set for him like a trap whenever he opened his mouth. At length when this had lasted the larger part of a rainy day, the poor boy who had seemed for some time on the verge of explosion, suddenly sprang from his chair, seized the little woman firmly though gently round the waist, carried her out into the hall, and came back to his seat, making no remark on the transaction. Who could blame him?

11 Such was the case of Susannah Palmer, a few years ago, whose husband had beaten her, and sold up her furniture again and again, blackened her eyes, and knocked out her five front teeth. At last on one occasion, with the knife with which she was cutting her children's supper, she somehow inflicted a slight cut on the man while he was knocking her about the head. He immediately summoned her for "cutting and wounding him," and she was sent to Newgate. I found her there, and afterwards received the very best possible character of her from several respectable tradespeople in whose houses she had worked as a charwoman for years. Friends subscribed to help her, and the admirable chaplain of Newgate interested himself warmly in her case and placed her in safety.

12 This, however, was a "provocation" on which a Chester jury founded a recommendation to mercy when they found him guilty of manslaughter. See p. 75.

13 *E.g.* the Report of the Society for the Protection of Women and Children, which has this significant passage: "Some of the cases of assaults were of a brutal and aggravated character, ... thirty-three by husbands on wives, five by fathers, and four by mothers on their children."

14 Few people reflect how utterly devoid of pleasures are the lives of the women of the working classes. An excellent woman, living near Bristol, having opened a Mothers Meeting, was surprised to find that not more than one out of forty of her poor friends had ever seen the sea, and not more than three had travelled on the railway. Of course their fathers, husbands, brothers, and sons had all seen these wonders, but they never. That good woman accordingly took the whole party one summer's day to the beach at Weston-super-Mare, and the sight of their enjoyment drew the tears from her eyes,—and from mine when she described it.

15 Hansard, vol. ccxix. p. 396.

16 I have before me a letter written by a man under these circumstances from Clerkenwell House of Detention to his wife. The writer (who was sent to jail for beating the aforesaid poor woman very cruelly) is wonderfully civil, and even condescends to coax. He regrets that it is long since he heard from her, but adds, "I hope you will not forget to try and get me out. If you will go to the magistrate, Mr. ***, I mean, it is very likely you can get my time reduced. I hope you will do all you can for me. I have quiet (*sic*) made up my mind to do what is right to everybody, more especially to you. I hope you will not be angery with me writing. I do hope and pray that you will do all you can for me. So good-bye, hoping to see and hear from you soon, and with your kind assistance to soon be out. So no more at present from your poor Petitioner, ***." The intelligent reader will perceive that there is not a single word of regret for his cruelty in this epistle. Still it

is a good point when the tyrant can be brought thus to sue his victim. All honour to the wise and kindly magistrate who brought it about.

17 Mr. W. Digby Seymour, Recorder of Newcastle-on-Tyne, in giving in his opinion on the desirability of adding flogging to the penalties of wife-beating, says—"If you flog the husband you will for ever degrade him as a married man. Let him be flogged by all means;—but why not amend the laws of divorce, and in cases of a conviction for 'brutal violence,' entitle the wife, on simple proof of conviction, to divorce *à vinculo?*"*—Returns, p. 90.

Mr. Lonsdale, Recorder of Folkestone, says practically the same: "I would not authorize flogging in cases of assaults upon wives unless that punishment were allowed to have the effect of a judicial separation."—Ibid. p. 82.

18 Perhaps the best plan as regards the maintenance for a wife would be (as suggested by an experienced magistrate) that the money should be paid through, and recoverable by, the Relieving Officer of the parish. This would afford her much greater security, and obviate the chance of collision with the husband.

Source: Reprinted from *Contemporary Review* (April 1878).

Biographical Note

Born on the family estate in Ireland, Frances Power Cobbe was the youngest of five children and the only daughter of Charles Cobbe, an Anglo-Irish landowner. By her own account, her childhood was a happy one; she had a warm affectionate relationship with her mother and her brothers. Educated at home until she was fourteen, she was then sent to a fashionable but frivolous finishing school for girls for two years. That period of her life is sharply criticized in her autobiography, *The Life of Frances Power Cobbe, By Herself* (1904).

By the time she was twenty, Cobbe showed clear signs of preferring serious study, especially on religious topics, over the idle round of social visiting characteristic of her class. Her first publication, *Essay on the Theory of Intuitive Morals* laying out her position on religion and morals, appeared in 1855 much to the disapproval of her father. He was already disappointed in her because she had confessed to him that her mother's death in 1847 had led her to question religion. In spite of this chilly relationship, Cobbe continued to act as her father's housekeeper until his death two years later.

With the £200 yearly allowance left to her from her father's estate, Cobbe moved to England, determined to find some way of making her own living. She first became involved with Mary Carpenter and her work with "ragged" or delinquent children in Bristol, though this proved unsuccessful due to differences in temperament between the two women. After this, she started visiting workhouses, which she wrote about in two of her earliest periodical publica-

---

* A judicial separation [Editor's note].

tions, "Workhouse Sketches" (1861) for *Macmillan's Magazine* and "Philosophy of the Poor Laws" (1864) for *Fraser's Magazine.*

Her interest in the "condition of women" dates from her work with Carpenter. Her many articles on the position of women—including "What Shall We do with Our Old Maids?" (1862), "Celibacy versus Marriage" (1862), "Criminals, Idiots, Women, and Minors" (1868), and "Wife Torture in England" (1878) reprinted here—made her reputation as an essayist on the women's movement. In addition to her writings for the periodical press, Cobbe also wrote the "social" article for the daily *Echo* newspaper, and was leader-writer on the *Standard* for some time.

Though always associated with the leading Victorian feminists of the day like Barbara Bodichon and Lydia Becker, and though she worked on many of the key feminist committees of the period like the women's suffrage committee and the Married Women's Property Committee, Cobbe was herself never a leader in Victorian feminist circles. This is partly due to her almost exclusive focus in the 1870s on animal rights rather than women's issues. She was the leading figure in the British anti-vivisection movement, from her first interest in that subject in 1870 through to her death in 1904. She was instrumental in passing the first Cruelty to Animals bill, and established in 1875 one of the first anti-vivisection societies in England, the Victoria Street Society, of which she was Honorary Secretary for ten years. Though her opposition to vivisection was based most strongly on her sympathy for suffering animals, and her suspicion of what she considered an increasingly materialist science, it would be incorrect to assume that her interest in vivisection indicated a decrease in concern for women's rights. Much of her work in the specialist periodicals of the anti-vivisection movement, like the *Zoophilist* which she edited until 1884, demonstrates strongly-felt connections between the two oppressions, as does her essay "Wife Torture in England."

In 1884, a testimonial of £1000 raised by the Victoria Street Society for the sixty-two year old Cobbe yielded an annuity of £100 per annum, a sum that allowed her to retire from journalism. She moved to Wales, where she spent the rest of her life with her long-time companion, sculptor Mary Lloyd, whom she had met in 1860. Cobbe continued to work for the animal rights cause she so dearly loved, writing many pamphlets and leaflets, and a number of books for the Victoria Street Society. When she died in 1904 she left her considerable fortune to that organization.

SELECTED SECONDARY SOURCES

Bauer, Carol and Lawrence Pitt, "'A husband is a beating animal'—Frances Power Cobbe confronts the wife-abuse problem in Victorian England," *International Journal of Women's Studies* 6 (1983): 99-118.

Caine, Barbara. *Victorian Feminists.* Oxford: Oxford UP, 1992.

French, Richard D. *Anti-vivisection and medical science in Victorian England.* Princeton: Princeton UP, 1975.

Hamilton, Susan. "Making History with Frances Power Cobbe: Victorian Feminism, Domestic Violence, and the Language of Imperialism." *Victorian Studies* 43.3 (2001): 437-460.

Peacock, Sandra, J. *The Theological and Ethical Writings of Frances Power Cobbe, 1822-1904.* Lampeter, Wales: Edwin Mellen Press, 2002.

ELIZA LYNN LINTON
(1822-1898)

"THE GIRL OF THE PERIOD"

Time was when the stereotyped phrase, "a fair young English girl," meant the ideal of womanhood; to us, at least, of home birth and breeding. It meant a creature generous, capable, and modest; something franker than a French-woman, more to be trusted than an Italian, as brave as an American but more refined, as domestic as a German and more graceful. It meant a girl who could be trusted alone if need be, because of the innate purity and dignity of her nature, but who was neither bold in bearing nor masculine in mind; a girl who, when she married, would be her husband's friend and companion, but never his rival; one who would consider their interest identical, and not hold him as just so much fair game for spoil; who would make his house his true home and place of rest, not a mere passage-place for vanity and ostentation to go through; a tender mother, an industrious housekeeper, a judicious mis-tress. We thought we had the pick of creation in this fair young English girl of ours, and envied no other men their own. We admired the languid grace and subtle fire of the South; the docility and childlike affectionateness of the East seemed to us sweet and simple and restful; the vivacious sparkle of the trim and sprightly Parisienne was a pleasant little excitement when we met with it in its own domain; but our allegiance never wandered from our brown-haired girls at home, and our hearts were less vagrant than our fancies. This was in the old time, and when English girls were content to be what God and nature had made them. Of late years we have changed the pattern, and have given to the world a race of women as utterly unlike the old insular ideal as if we had created another nation altogether. The girl of the period, and the fair young English girl of the past, have nothing in common save ancestry and their mother-tongue; and even of this last the modern version makes almost a new language, through the copious additions it has received from the cur-rent slang of the day.

The girl of the period is a creature who dyes her hair and paints her face, as the first articles of her personal religion; whose sole idea of life is plenty of fun and luxury; and whose dress is the object of such thought and intellect as she possesses. Her main endeavour in this is to outvie her neighbours in the extravagance of fashion. No matter whether, as in the time of crinolines, she sacrificed decency, or, as now, in the time of trains, she sacrifices cleanliness; no matter either, whether she makes herself a nuisance and an inconvenience to every one she meets. The girl of the period has done away with such moral muffishness as consideration for others, or regard for counsel and rebuke. It was all very well in old-fashioned times, when fathers and mothers had some authority and were treated with respect, to be tutored and made to obey, but she is far too fast and flourishing to be stopped in mid-career by these slow old morals; and as she dresses to please herself, she does not care if she displeases every one else. Nothing is too extraordinary and nothing too exaggerated for her vitiated taste; and things which in themselves would be useful reforms if let alone become monstrosities worse than those which they have displaced so soon as she begins to manipulate and improve. If a sensible fashion lifts the gown out of the mud, she raises hers midway to her knee. If the absurd structure of wire and buckram, once called a bonnet, is modified to something that shall protect the wearer's face without putting out the eyes of her companion, she cuts hers down to four straws and a rosebud, or a tag of lace and a bunch of glass beads. If there is a reaction against an excess of Rowland's Macassar, and hair shiny and sticky with grease is thought less nice than if left clean and healthily crisp, she dries and frizzes and sticks hers out on end like certain savages in Africa, or lets it wander down her back like Madge Wildfire's, and thinks herself all the more beautiful the nearer she approaches in look to a maniac or a negress. With purity of taste she has lost also that far more precious purity and delicacy of perception which sometimes mean more than appears on the surface. What the *demi-monde* does in its frantic efforts to excite attention, she also does in imitation. If some fashionable *dévergondée en evidence* is reported to have come out with her dress below her shoulder-blades, and a gold strap for all the sleeve thought necessary, the girl of the period follows suit next day; and then wonders that men sometimes mistake her for her prototype, or that mothers of girls not quite so far gone as herself refuse her as a companion for their daughters. She has blunted the fine edges of feeling so much that she cannot understand why she should be condemned for an imitation of form which does not include imitation of fact; she cannot be made to see that modesty of appearance and virtue ought to be inseparable, and that no good girl can afford to appear bad, under penalty of receiving the contempt awarded to the bad.

This imitation of the *demi-monde* in dress leads to something in manner and feeling, not quite so pronounced perhaps, but far too like to be honourable to herself or satisfactory to her friends. It lends to slang, bold talk, and fastness; to the love of pleasure and indifference to duty; to the desire of money before either love or happiness; to uselessness at home, dissatisfaction with the monotony of ordinary life, and horror of all useful work; in a word, to the worst forms of luxury and selfishness, to the most fatal effects arising from want of high principle and absence of tender feeling.The girl of the period envies the queens of the *demi-monde* far more than she abhors them. She sees them gorgeously attired and sumptuously appointed, and she knows them to be flattered, fêted, and courted with a certain disdainful admiration of which she catches only the admiration while she ignores the disdain. They have all for which her soul is hungering, and she never stops to reflect at what a price they have bought their gains, and what fearful moral penalties they pay for their sensuous pleasures. She sees only the coarse gilding on the base token, and shuts her eyes to the hideous figure in the midst, and the foul legend written round the edge. It is this envy of the pleasures, and indifference to the sins, of these women of the *demi-monde* which is doing such infinite mischief to the modern girl. They brush too closely by each other, if not in actual deeds, yet in aims and feelings; for the luxury which is bought by vice with the one is the thing of all in life most passionately desired by the other, though she is not yet prepared to pay quite the same price. Unfortunately, she has already paid too much—all that once gave her distinctive national character. No one can say of the modern English girl that she is tender, loving, retiring, or domestic. The old fault so often found by keen-sighted Frenchwomen, that she was so fatally *romanesque, so* prone to sacrifice appearances and social advantages for love, will never be set down to the girl of the period. Love indeed is the last thing she thinks of, and the least of the dangers besetting her. Love in a cottage, that seductive dream which used to vex the heart and disturb the calculations of prudent mothers, is now a myth of past ages. The legal barter of herself for so much money, representing so much dash, so much luxury and pleasure—that is her idea of marriage; the only idea worth entertaining. For all seriousness of thought respecting the duties or the consequences of marriage, she has not a trace. If children come, they find but a stepmother's cold welcome from her; and if her husband thinks that he has married anything that is to belong to him—a *tacens et placens uxor* pledged to make him happy—the sooner he wakes from his hallucination and understands that he has simply married some one who will condescend to spend his money on herself, and who will shelter her indiscretions behind the shield of his name, the less severe will be his disappointment. She has married his house, his carriage, his balance at the banker's, his title; and he himself is just the inevitable condition clogging the wheel of her fortune; at best an adjunct, to be tolerated with more or less patience as may chance. For it is only the old-fashioned sort, not girls of the period *pur sang*, that marry for love, or put the husband before the banker. But she does not marry easily. Men are afraid of her; and with reason. They may amuse themselves with her for an evening, but they do not take her readily for life. Besides, after all her efforts, she is only a poor copy of the real thing; and the real thing is far more amusing than the copy, because it is real. Men can get that whenever they like; and when they go into their mothers' drawing-rooms, to see their sisters and their sisters' friends, they want something of quite different flavour. *Toujours perdrix* is bad providing all the world over; but a continual weak imitation of *toujours perdrix* is worse. If we must have only one kind of thing, let us have it genuine; and the queens of St. John's Wood in their unblushing honesty, rather than their imitators and make-believes in Bayswater and Belgravia. For, at whatever cost of shocked self-love or pained modesty it may be, it cannot be too plainly told to the modern English girls that the net result of her present manner of life is to assimilate her as nearly as possible to a class of women whom we must not call by their proper— or improper—name. And we are willing to believe that she has still some modesty of soul left hidden under all this effrontery of fashion, and that, if she could be made to see herself as she appears to the eyes of men, she would mend her ways before too late.

It is terribly significant of the present state of things when men are free to write as they do of the women of their own nation. Every word of censure flung against them is two-edged, and wound those who condemn as much as those who are condemned; for surely it need hardly be said that men hold nothing so dear as the honour of their women, and that no one living would willingly lower the repute of his mother or his sisters. It is only when these have placed themselves beyond the pale of masculine respect that such things could be written as are written now; when they become again what they were once they will gather round them the love and homage and chivalrous devotion which were then an Englishwoman's natural inheritance. The marvel, in the present fashion of life among women, is how it holds its ground in spite of the disapprobation of men. It used to be an old-time notion that the sexes were made for each other, and that it was only natural for them to please each other, and to set themselves out for that end. But the girl of the period does not please men. She pleases them as little as she elevates them; and how little she does that, the class of women she has taken as her models of itself testifies. All men whose opinion is worth having prefer the simple and genuine girl of the past, with her tender little ways and pretty bashful modesties, to this loud and rampant modernization, with her false red hair and painted skin, talking slang as glibly as a man, and by preference leading the conversation to doubtful subjects. She thinks she is piquante and exciting when she thus makes herself the bad copy of a worse original; and she will not see that though men laugh with her they do not respect her, though they flirt with her they do not marry her; she will not believe that she is not the kind of thing they want, and that she is acting against nature and her own interests when she disregards their advice and offends their taste. We do not see how she makes out her account, viewing her life from any side; but all we can do is to wait patiently until the national madness has passed, and our women have come back again to the old English ideal, once the most beautiful, the most modest, the most essentially womanly in the world.

Source: Reprinted from *Saturday Review* (14 March 1868).

"The Modern Revolt"

The late remarkable outbreak of women against the restrictions under which they have hitherto lived—the Modern Revolt, as it may be called—has two meanings: the one, a noble protest against the frivolity and idleness into which they have suffered themselves to sink; the other, a mad rebellion against the natural duties of their sex, and those characteristics known in the mass as womanliness. And among the most serious problems of the day is, how to reconcile the greater freedom which women are taking with the restrictive duties of sex; how to bring their determination to share in the remunerative work of the world into harmony with that womanliness, without which they are intrinsically valueless—inferior copies of men, having neither the sweetness, the tenderness, the modesty of the one sex, nor the courage, the resolution, the power of the other.

Women have always been more or less riddles to men, whose stronger organization finds it difficult to understand the feverish impulses, the hysterical excitement by which they are swayed, and who cannot believe that the failings of slaves and the virtues of saints can co-exist in the same class. Hence they have taken extreme views: one, the cynical school, making them the authors of all the evil afloat, sly, intriguing, unreasonable, influenced only by self-interest, governed only by fear, cruel, false, and worthless; while another, more poetic and quite as untrue, paints them as seraphic creatures gliding through a polluted world in a self-evolved atmosphere of purity and holiness and ignorance of evil; creatures all heart and soul and compassion and love; embodiments of charity, bearing all things and believing all things, loving even their tyrants, kissing the rod wherewith they are struck, reforming bad men by the spectacle of their untainted virtues, and softening the rude by their ineffable grace. These are the two extremes: but no school has yet upheld them as sober, rational, well-informed beings—with brains to regulate their impulses, yet with more love than calculation; with strong instincts and intuitive perceptions, yet not devoid of reason; with courage to examine dark moral problems and to learn the truth of social conditions which they do not share, yet with purity surviving knowledge—women who do not care to make a fool's paradise of Arcadian innocence for themselves, but who are not content to let vice reign supreme while they stand loftily aside on the pleas of pitch and the defilement arising therefrom—women who are neither the slaves nor the rivals of men, and whose demand for equal rights does not include confusion of circumstance or identity of condition. And this is what the best of the revolters are aiming at becoming now. For the class which advocates indifference to the wishes and approbation of men is not one deserving serious consideration. This is the madness, the exaggeration which brings the whole question into disfavour; and no one who has woman's best interests at heart can thank the members of this class for their advocacy.

The first point in this modern revolt is the cry of women for leave to work. This surely is a mere cry, not a cause. There is work for them to do if they will do it; work waiting for them, and sadly needing their doing. But this is not the work they want to do. What they want is a share in that which men have appropriated, and which is undeniably better fitted for men than women. And in their attempt to get hold of this they are leaving undone that which Nature and the fitness of things have assigned to them, like children who quit their own tasks which are within their compass, while wanting those apportioned to the elders. Yet what have women to complain of in the way of wanting work? In reality very few careers are closed to them. To be sure the law and the church, the army, navy, and parliament, are crypts into which they may not penetrate, but all trades and commerce, and the financial world outside the Stock Exchange, are open to them: they may be merchants, bankers, traders of all kinds, shipowners and shipbuilders, artists, writers, teachers, farmers,[1] and they can practise medicine under restrictions, besides being nurses. All these and more modes of gaining a livelihood are free to them; and they have moreover their own more special work.

But let us confess it honestly, if sorrowfully—hitherto they have made no class mark in anything, and only a very few women, and those quite exceptional, have done what they might do. It is said that this want of class distinction is owing to the want of education. Granting the plea generally, who has educated women if not women themselves? No one has prevented women from giving to girls an education as broad and sound as that given by men to boys; the wretched thing called female education has not been men's doing, nor has the want of anything better been in deference to men's wishes. The education of her daughters is essentially the mother's care and a woman's charge: and as a proof of this, now that a desire for better things has sprung up among women, men help them to get the best that can be given. It has been because mothers have willed it so, that their daughters have been flimsily taught and flashily accomplished, and handed over to men neither intellectual companions nor useful house-managers.

Let us go over the list of what has been especially woman's work, and say candidly what she has made of her talent. All that concerns domestic and social life is hers—maternity and the care of the young, the education of the daughters, the management of the house, the arrangements of society, the regulation of dress and fashion. And whatever we may think about woman's right to a more extended sphere of action, we cannot deny that these are her principal duties; whatever we may add on to these, these must always remain her primary obligations.

But how are these duties performed?

In the question of maternity lies the saddest part of the Modern Revolt.

God alone knows what good is to come out of the strange reaction against the maternal instinct, which is so marked a social feature in America, and which is spreading rapidly here. Believing, for my part, in the progress of humanity, and in our unconsciously working to good ends even by crooked means, I find my faith in ultimate historic improvement severely exercised by this phenomenon. Formerly children were desired by all women, and their coming considered a blessing rather than otherwise: now the proportion of wives who regard them as a curse is something appalling, and the annoyance or despair, with the practical expression, in many cases, given to that annoyance as their number increases, is simply bewildering to those who have cherished that instinct as it used to be cherished. The thing is as I have said: the moral or historic end to be attained through it no one has yet discovered. It may mean an instinctive endeavour to check a superabundant population; but proximately it seems due to our artificial mode of life, and the high pressure under which we live, whereby we are taxed to the utmost we can bear, with no margin to spare: our civilization thus recurring to first principles and repeating the savage's dread of unnecessary mouths in his tribe. Still, however it may come about, or whatever it may mean, the modern revolt against the maternal instinct is something for the student of humanity to examine. Let us hope that before long he will explain to us the ultimate outcome of it.

The care of the young ranks as one of the most important of all things to the State and the race, and one on which no pains bestowed could be too much. Yet how many mothers understand the management of the young in any scientific sense? How many study the best modes of education, physical or moral, and bring their studies to good issue? How many mothers will even receive advice and not consider it interference in their own distinct domain? and how many are there who so much as doubt that maternity of itself does not give wisdom, and that by the mere fact of motherhood a woman is fully capable of managing her child without more teaching than that which she gets from instinct? We give less thought (not less love), less study, less scientific method, to the management of our own young than to the training of future racehorses or the development of the prize heifer on the farm. The wildest ideas on food, the most injudicious fashions in dress, amusements which ruin both body and mind, such as children's evening parties, theatres, and the like, make one often think that the last person to whom her children should be entrusted is the mother. Add to this a moral education, good or bad according to individual temperament, an ignorance of psychological laws as dense as that of the physiological and hygienic, and the personal care of the little ones delegated to servants, and we have the base on which the modern nursery is constructed. This delegation of the mother's duty to servants is as amazing in its contravention of instinct as the revolt against maternity. Every woman sees how nurses treat the children of other mothers, and every mother trusts her own nurse implicitly, and gives into the hands of a coarse and ignorant woman, the temper, the health, the nerves, the earliest mental direction, and the consequent permanent bias of the future of her child, while perhaps she goes out on a crusade to help people who need example rather than assistance. This is no overcharged picture. The unscientific management of children, and the absolute surrender of them while young, and therefore while most plastic, into the hands of servants, is too patent to be denied.

Of education we have already spoken, and because of the present better methods we need not go back on the past mistakes; but how about housekeeping?

The fashions of modern life are not favourable to good housekeeping. Here and there we meet with a woman who has made it an art, and carried it out to a beautiful perfection; but the number of those who have done so is small compared to the indifferent, the inefficient, those who interfere without organizing, and those who have given up their office to servants, retaining merely that symbol of authority called "keeping the keys." Few women above a very mediocre social position do anything in the house; and the fatal habit of fine-ladyism is gradually descending to the tradesman's and mechanic's classes; fewer still try to elevate the system of housekeeping altogether, and make it possible for ladies, even our artificial product, to take an active part in it with pleasure and profit to themselves. Yet French and German women keep house actively, and do not disdain the finer portions of the work. With the help of the machines which American need has fashioned for the home, this does not seem a very degrading task for women. One consequence wherever ladies of education are active housekeepers is, that a more scientific, compact, cleanly, and less rude and wasteful mode of cookery obtains. And indeed that cooking question is a grave one, belonging especially to women, and quite as important in its own way as the knowledge of drugs and the mixing up of pills. Women do not consider it so, and ladies are rather proud than otherwise of their ignorance of an art which is one of their elemental natural duties. But they want to be doctors, if they object to be cooks. Yet how it can be considered honourable to get meat by manipulating asafoetida,* and degrading to attend to the cooking of that meat when got—beneath the dignity of a woman's intellect to understand the constituent elements of food and what they make in the human frame, yet consistent with that dignity to understand the effects of drugs—why the power of bringing back to health should be a science fit for the noblest intellects to undertake, and the art of keeping in health an office fit only for the grossest and most ignorant to fill— is a nice distinction of honour, the quality of which I, for one, have never been able to understand; nor why that *imperium in imperio*, the kitchen, is a better institution than the centralization of authority dating from the draw-

---

* Bad-smelling gum resin used to treat illness or repel disease [Editor's note].

ingroom. Society in its simplest aspect is, as it were, the radical of our own more complex conditions; and do as we will, we cannot escape from the eternal fitness of this division of labour—the man to provide, the woman to prepare for use and to distribute. While, then, our housekeeping generally is bad because not undertaken with heart or intellect, and while our national cookery is still little better than "plain roast and boiled," we cannot say that we have gone through this lesson from end to end, or exhausted even this portion of our special acre.

The same complaint is true with respect to our absurd social arrangements and more absurd fashions. Yet both are in the hands of women only, and might be made as beautiful as they are now the reverse. The reform in the dinner-table that has taken place of late years has been heartily welcomed by men everywhere; so would a reform in the dinners themselves, if any one would undertake it. The adoption of a "day" has also been a boon in the matter of morning calls; but what can one say of the common sense shown in beginning our balls about midnight? or, indeed, of the common sense of most of our evening parties—at least in London—those mere crowds, successful in proportion to the discomfort of the guests, and brilliant only when a well-dressed mob overflows on to the stairs, unable to exchange even a greeting with the hostess? In face of such assemblies as these, it can scarcely be said that we have brought the art of human intercourse up to the highest artistic point to which it can reach.

Over dress and fashion one's dirges might be unending. And here again women are the arbiters, and dress only to please themselves, without any reference whatever to men or nature. Now the fashion is a steel balloon which gets into everybody's way, and in the vortex created by which lies disaster to all crockery and light furniture; now it is a long train, mainly useful in sweeping up dirt and tripping up human feet: sometimes we get headaches by overcrowding our heads, sometimes face-aches by leaving them wholly unprotected; high heels destroy the shape of the leg and the foot alike, as well as comfort in walking; and stays not only create deformity, but also disease, and maybe death. Still, though the need is so great no woman has yet cared to invent a perfectly beautiful, simple, and useful dress. She struck out Bloomerism, which was too hideous to be adopted by any woman holding to the religion of beauty and the need of looking charming; and she clings to trains, which, however graceful in line, are inconsistent with work or activity; but, save in the modern "costumes" which are overloaded with frills and ornaments, she has not come near to the desideratum—a dress which the peasant and the duchess could wear alike, graceful with the one, serviceable with the other, and beautiful in their degree with both. Much has been said and written of the cruelty of needlework, and of the precious lives which women have offered up to the Moloch of stitchery. Yet who has set the fashion of unnecessary stitches but women themselves? It is they who have crowded work upon work in all the garments which pass through their hands; and while bewailing the hard slavery of sewing, and considering it as one of the real curses of their condition, multiply frills and flounces, and gussets and seams and bands, as if the main object of a garment was to contain as much superfluous needlework as possible. Meanwhile, a tailor's work is simple, strong, and not fantastic, and a dressmaker's is flimsy and complicated; almost all body-linen is too elaborate, both in the shaping and the stitchery; and the greatest blessing of its kind, the sewing-machine, instead of lightening our labour has been the means of greatly increasing the complexity of sewed work.

Thus, in the duties special to women and the part in life apportioned to them, we find nothing brought to its possible perfection, nothing wrought out to its ultimate; and I cannot say it commends itself to one's calmer judgement, that while their own appointed duties are in such an unsatisfactory state, they should be clamorous to take from men work of an untried character, and which, if men perform only *tant bien que mal*, it cannot be asserted women will perform better.

There is more than a living, there is a fortune to be made by the woman of taste and refinement who will undertake the task of perfecting the womanly duties—of top-dressing the woman's acre. But no one will attempt it. The women who want to be clerks and apothecaries will not go out as lady-nurses, nor as lady-dressmakers, nor as lady-cooks. They flock to *take service* to tend wounded men, because of the excitement, the *kudos*, may be the instinct involved: but ask them to take service to nurse little children—ask them to exhibit so much enthusiasm for the perfecting of the future as they do for healing the present generation, and would you get a response? Yet the right management and noble nurture of the young is perhaps more important than the tender nursing, by women, of wounded men of whom their comrades would also be very tender! Again: ask them to be lady-dressmakers, teachers of taste and fashioners of beautiful garments; or ask them to make themselves first-rate cooks, and give lessons in the art, or go out as dinner superintendents,—will they do either? Yet they might thus make a good living by useful work which they discard, while they prefer a wretched pittance by fancy work which no one wants, by miserable art which breaks the hearts of kindly "hangers," by attempts at teaching where they have everything to learn. The woman who would copy this manuscript at twopence the folio would think herself degraded if advised to try to make a fortune as Soyer and Worth made theirs.

Many ladies of good but not immense incomes want this kind of help—and would pay for it. The "little" dressmaker cannot be trusted with anything better than a garden gown; Court dressmakers are simply ruinous; the women who go out to work have neither skill nor taste; and the maid wants the help of direction. A refined, tasteful, artistic woman to direct a maid, and give her ideas and patterns, is an institution as yet not established. Yet the woman who would do this first would open a new path for her sisters. So of cooking; but any help in the house beyond the charwoman and the day-worker, neither of whom is worth her salt, is, as every housekeeper knows, absolutely impossible in this great London of ours, where the cry goes up of "Work for women—for pity's sake, work!"

It must be owned that this disinclination of women with anything like culture, to work under women only richer, not intrinsically better bred than themselves, is mainly due to the scant courtesy with which many ladies treat those of their own sex whom they meet on paying terms. And they have not found out the way yet to enforce respect by what they are, independent of what they do. And as they themselves have degraded their natural work, consequently the position of the workers is held cheap and low. This can be reformed only when women of education and refinement shed their own lustre on their natural duties; and as old Antaeus gained strength when he touched his mother earth, so will they gain the womanly glory and the influence they have lost, when they turn back to the old sources and take up again the discarded work. All that they did in early times—things that kings' daughters did, that the noblest and stateliest lady did, and lost nothing of her nobleness in doing—they have degraded and relegated to the lower hand. Even the profession of medicine, about which there has been so much warm controversy, was once the lady's work, till she herself forsook it and let it fall from her hands into men's. All but one branch; and that she gave into the keeping of the coarsest and most ignorant old wife of the village. Only so late as Charles II midwives were "Dames" by legal right: we know what they are in the present day; though here also there has been great improvement and a wiser state of things begun.

What, then, I contend for in this question of woman's work is, that in her own world, which is so beautiful, so useful, she has unexplored tracts and unfulfilled duties; and that it is a fatal mistake in her not to put her intellect and an extended education into social and domestic details; so that she may make her own work perfect—not by lowering herself to the condition of a servant, but by raising her duties above the level of the servant.

But is not the truth something like this—that women crave public applause, an audience, excitement, notoriety, more than mere work? They want to be lecturers, professors, entitled to wear gowns and hoods, and to put letters after their names; and perhaps the desire is natural; but let us call it by its right name—personal ambition—and not be ashamed to confess the truth: and if they can do the work well, let them, in heaven's name! The Best is not a question of sex, though we may have our own ideas as to who is most likely to be the best. Still if women like to try their powers, why deny them the opportunity? Public opinion and the proof of experience would be sufficient to prevent an influx of weak incapacity in avenues already crowded by the capable and the strong; and the law of fitness would soon find them out and place them according to their deserving. Restrictions, which are hindrances of free-will only and not defence work against evil-doing, belong to a childish state of society; and the best thing that could be done for women would be to open all careers to them with men, and let them try their strength on a fair field, and no favour.

The second demand of the modern revolters is surely just—their right to the franchise. Stress is laid by the opposition on the difference between a natural right and a political privilege. They affirm that the franchise is not the natural right of every man, but a privilege accorded for purposes of polity to some men. Wherefore, they say, women cannot claim as an equal right what is not intrinsically any one's right. And so with this they set the claim aside, and will continue to do so till women are in earnest to enforce it. So long as the majority of women do not care for the franchise, the minority who do care for it will not get it; the argument being always at hand that to grant a political privilege for the purpose of creating a political conscience, would be the exact reverse of all the modes of government hitherto practised; and found to answer. The denial presses heavily on those who wish for it; but this too will pass away by the creation of a public opinion favourable to the demand: until then nothing will be done for the sake of equity, equality, or logic.

The third right of women on hand, but settled partially for the moment, is the right of married women to their own property. And the revolt of women against the virtual slavery of marriage, has not been without cause. Not that they have revolted, but that they have borne so long, is the wonder. A state of things which put them wholly in the power of a man when once he was the married master—which allowed him to ruin them without redress, and to treat them with every kind of cruelty, save an amount of personal brutality dangerous to life, yet held them to their bond, and held them close—was sure to produce misery, as it was sure also to create evil: human nature not being able to bear unchecked authority without letting it run into tyranny. Now, however, things have got somewhat put to rights in that quarter, and by and by more will be done, till it is all worked through, and the theory of marriage will be no longer based on the enslaving of one but on the equality of two.

Men say that this question of the rights of women to do such work and enter into such professions as they desire, to exercise the franchise, and to possess their own property, being wives, is eminently a peace question, and that if a war broke out we should hear no more of it. The time would then be the man's time, the hour of physical strength and of all other essentially masculine qualities, and these woman's rights, with other products of peace, would be trodden under foot forthwith. Granted: and the fact of its being a peace question proves its value. Nothing grows in wartime, and only weapons of destruction and strong hands to wield them are of value; so that to say a question is a peace question is to say that it belongs to the growing time of society, that it is part of its development, its improvement; and to ignore its claims on this ground, and because we should hear nothing about it if a war broke out, would be about as just and rational as to despise the fact of the corn-field, because the troops must trample down—the grain in passing to the front.

But there is also another reason, beside peace, why all these questions have arisen now, and the Modern Revolt has gained such head among us:—the immense disproportion of the sexes in England. There are not enough men to feed and protect all the women, so that some of them must work for themselves, and protect themselves as well—which, may be, is the harder thing of the two. And as they will not work in their own natural portion of the field of labour, and get money and dignity by raising the offices they have degraded to servants, they are clamorous to take the offices of men, and enter into competition with them on their own ground. And if they succeed, one result must inevitably arise—the further drainage from the country of men beaten out of the field by women. For though women never can compete with men in the amount of work turned out to time, and therefore never can make the same amount of wages, yet they may flood the market with cheaper work, and so ruin men by underselling them. This, and not "jealousy," is the reason why men look askance at the introduction of female hands in any branch of trade which they have hitherto kept to themselves; for we must remember that the man represents the family, a woman generally only herself, and that the workman's jealousy is as much for his wife and children as for himself. All things considered, would it not be wiser if women took their own work out of the lower hands and did it better and more beautifully than it is done now? And if the effect of this was to create an extensive emigration of good, honest, lower-class women, and of that miserable class next to them, neither ladies nor servants, who go out as shop-girls and nursery governesses, who do not marry early, and who know nothing by which they can make a sufficient income, it would be the best thing that could happen to England where women are redundant, and to the colonies where they are so sadly wanted.

But if we can do without so many women as we have, we cannot do without the womanly virtues. We want the purity and the love of women to refine the race which the magnanimity and justice of men ennoble. We want their power of sacrifice by which the future is preserved; their tenderness, their impulsiveness even; their sense of beauty, and their modesty. When women are bad, all is bad. Their vice poisons society at its roots, and their low estimate of morality makes virtue impossible; while the frivolous woman, devoted only to dress and pleasure, creates an atmosphere about her in which no sublimity of thought, no heroism can live. Yet some men admire only such women, and say that a woman's sole *raison d'être* is to be beautiful in person, graceful in manner, to dress well, look nice, and amuse men; and that it does not signify two straws whether she is good or bad so long as she is pleasant and pretty, and does the drawing-room business well. These men prefer these living dolls to real women out of fear—fear lest the future woman in losing her frivolity will lose also her grace, in gaining independence will gain also hardness and coarseness, and for every intellectual increase will lose correspondingly in womanliness and love.

Others, again, think that neither intellect nor reasonableness should be exclusively a masculine attribute, and that the wiser women are the nobler they will be, and the more likely to be faithful to them as well as true to themselves. And indeed it is not really the largest-minded women who swagger about, bad copies of a bad style of man, talking of everything they should not, reviling maternity, deriding woman's work, scorning the sweet instinctive reliance of the weaker, and affecting to despise the sex they ape. These are of the fools with which the world of women, as of men, abounds; and it is by a simple chance of physical organization that they are mannish fools rather than weak ones, given to slang and defiance rather than to slip-shod and frivolity. And these, though they form undeniably a part, are not the main body of the Modern Revolters.

In this main body the desire to enlarge the circle of women's activities springs from a lofty motive. If it is taking a wrong direction, it will put itself right before long, and by its recognitions of error will repair the evil it may have done. It can do no evil if, while careful for intellectual culture, it holds the great instinctive affections as the highest in a woman's catalogue of duties; while enlarging the sphere of her activity, it maintains the righteousness of her doing first, thoroughly, that class of work called emphatically woman's work, before she invades the offices of men; while enriching her life by intellect, and ennobling her work by her own dignity, it still keeps to the pleasant prettiness, the personal charms, the lighter graces of her sex; while giving her freedom of action and the power of self-support, it does not take from her modesty, tenderness, or love; nor in making her the equal and companion of man, make her less than his lover—and his rival, not his mate. Without these provisos (the Modern Revolt will be the ruin of our womankind: with them, its most precious, its most royal gain and gift. And so may God and the good consciences of women grant.

NOTE

1 Only quite lately a farmer, Mrs. Millington, of Ash Grove Farm, near Bicester, took the prize for good farming over the heads of her male competitors; and there was, probably is still, a lady of rank, who owns a dairy at Notting Hill, who attends to the business herself, and drives her pair of bays to the door of those of her customers who have had any complaint to make, to see into their case herself.

Source: Reprinted from *Macmillan's Magazine* (December 1870).

"The Wild Women: as Politicians"

All women are not always lovely, and the wild women never are. As political firebrands and moral insurgents they are specially distasteful, warring as they do against the best traditions, the holiest functions, and the sweetest qualities of their sex. Like certain 'sports' which develop hybrid characteristics, these insurgent wild women are in a sense unnatural. They have not 'bred true'—not according to the general lines on which the normal woman is constructed. There is in them a curious inversion of sex, which does not necessarily appear in the body, but is evident enough in the mind. Quite as disagreeable as the bearded chin, the bass voice, flat chest, and lean hips of a woman who has physically failed in her rightful development, the unfeminine ways and works of the wild women of politics and morals are even worse for the world in which they live. Their disdain is for the duties and limitations imposed on them by nature, their desire as impossible as that of the moth for the star. Marriage, in its old-fashioned aspect as the union of two lives, they repudiate as a one-sided tyranny; and maternity, for which, after all, women primarily exist, they regard as degradation. Their idea of freedom is their own preponderance, so that they shall do all they wish to do without let or hindrance from outside regulations or the restraints of self-discipline; their idea of morality, that men shall do nothing they choose to disallow. Their grand aim is to directly influence imperial politics, while they, and those men who uphold them, desire to shake off their own peculiar responsibilities.

Such as they are, they attract more attention than perhaps they deserve, for we believe that the great bulk of Englishwomen are absolutely sound at heart, and in no wise tainted with this pernicious craze. Yet, as young people are apt to be caught by declamation, and as false principles know how to present themselves in specious paraphrases, it is not waste of time to treat the preposterous claims put forth by the wild women as if they were really serious—as if this little knot of noisy Maenads did really threaten the stability of society and the well-being of the race.

Be it pleasant or unpleasant, it is none the less an absolute truth—the *raison d'être* of a woman is maternity. For this and this alone nature has differentiated her from man, and built her up cell by cell and organ by organ. The continuance of the race in healthy reproduction, together with the fit nourishment and care of the young after birth, is the ultimate end of woman as such; and whatever tells against these functions, and reduces either her power or her perfectness, is an offence against nature and a wrong done to society. If she chooses to decline her natural office altogether, and to dedicate to other services a life which has no sympathy with the sex of humanity, that comes into her lawful list of preferences and discords. But neither then nor while she is one with the rest, a wife and mother like others, is she free to blaspheme her assigned functions; nor to teach the young to blaspheme them; nor yet to set afoot such undertakings as shall militate against the healthy performance of her first great natural duty and her first great social obligation.

The cradle lies across the door of the polling-booth and bars the way to the senate. We can conceive nothing more disastrous to a woman in any stage of maternity, expectant or accomplished, than the heated passions and turmoil of a political contest; for we may put out of court three fallacies—that the vote, if obtained at all, is to be confined to widows and spinsters only; that enfranchised women will content themselves with the vote and not seek after active office; and that they will bring into the world of politics the sweetness and light claimed for them by their adherents, and not, on the contrary, add their own shriller excitement to the men's deeper passions. Nor must we forget that the franchise for women would not simply allow a few well-conducted, well-educated, self-respecting gentlewomen to quietly record their predilection for Liberalism or Conservatism, but would let in the far wider flood of the uneducated, the unrestrained, the irrational and emotional—those who know nothing and imagine all—those whose presence and partisanship on all public questions madden already excited men. We have no right to suppose that human nature is to be changed for our benefit, and that the influence of sex is to become a dead letter because certain among us wish it so. What has been will be again. In the mirror of the prophet, which hangs behind him, the Parisian woman of the Revolution will be repeated wherever analogous conditions exist; and to admit women into active participation in politics will certainly be to increase disorder and add fuel to the fire of strife.

We live by our ideals. Individually they may fall into the dust of disappointment, and the flower of poetic fancy may wither away into the dry grass of disillusion. Nevertheless the race goes on cherishing its ideals, without which, indeed, life would become too hard and sordid for us all. And one of these ideals in all Western countries is the home. Home means peace. It means, too, love. Perhaps the two are synonymous. In the normal division of labour the man has the outside work to do, from governing the country to tilling the soil; the woman takes the inside, managing the family and regulating society. The more highly civilised a community is the more completely differentiated are these two functions. In the lower strata of society the women work in the fields with the men; but as yet we have not had handsome young lady cornets in the army, nor stalwart gentlemen occupied with the week's wash and Mary-maid's demands for Turk's heads and house-flannels.

Part of this ideal of home is the rest it gives the man when he returns to it after a hard day's work in the open—a hard day's struggle in the arena. Here his thoughts drift into a smoother channel, his affections have their full outlet, and to his wife and children he brings as much happiness as he receives. The darker passions which the contests of life arouse are shut out; the sweeter influences of the family, the calmer interests of the intellect, the pleasures of art and society remain. We are speaking of the ideal, to which we all in some sort aspire, and in which we believe—for others if not for ourselves. When we have come to think of it as mere moonshine we have achieved our own spiritual death; when we have acted and legislated as if it were moonshine we have decreed our national degradation.

But where will be the peace of home when women, like men, plunge into the troubled sea of active political life? Causes of disunion enough and to spare exist in modern marriage. We need not add to them. More especially we need not add to them by introducing a new and quite unnecessary wedge into brittle material of which highly strained nerves and highly developed tastes, with complexity of personal interests, have already destroyed the old cohesive quality. Imagine the home to which a weary man of business, and an ardent politician to boot, will return when his wife has promised her vote to the other side, and the house is divided against itself in very truth. Not all husbands and wives wear the same badge, and we all know miserable cases where the wife has gone directly and publicly counter to the husband. If these things are done in the green tree of restricted political action, what would happen in the dry of active political power? Women are both more extreme and more impressible than men, and the spirit which made weak girls into heroines and martyrs, honest women into the yelling *tricoteuses** of those blood-stained saturnalia of '92, still exists in the sex; and among ourselves as elsewhere.

The dissension that the exercise of this political right would bring into the home is as certain as to-morrow's sunrise. Those who refuse to see this are of the race of the wilfully blind, or of that smaller sect of enthusiasts who believe in a problematical better rather than an established good. It is also part and parcel of the temper, which desires looseness of family ties and extreme facility for divorce.

Of the wild women who make this disordering propaganda many are still Christians in some form or another—some believing that Christ was the actual living God Incarnate, others that He was a messenger from God, divinely inspired and directly appointed to teach men the way of holy living. And of His (the Master's) utterances none is more emphatic than this on marriage: 'He which made them at the beginning made them male and female, and said for this cause shall a man leave his father and mother and shall cleave to his wife, and they twain shall be one flesh.' Of His doctrine, nothing is more strenuously insisted on than the sweet and patient self-control which in non-essentials we call courtesy and in higher matters humility, patience, unselfishness, love. How do the women who still call themselves Christians reconcile the two positions? How can they in one breath exalt the character and the

---

* A reference to the French women who reputedly knitted at the bottom on the guillotines during the French Revolution [Editor's note].

mission of Christ, and in the next deride the essential meaning of His teaching? The frank agnostic may prefer to begin from the beginning, and to examine the whole structure of society as a simple matter of evolution and experience; but these wild women are not all frank agnostics; they are rather of that curious family which thinks to hold with the hare and hunt with the hounds, changing sides according to fancy and the exigencies of the moment. But the demand for these political rights, which would prove true dragons' teeth granted, is, of all modern things, the most anti-Christian that can be named—the most destructive of home peace and conjugal union, of family solidarity and personal love.

In this last word lies the core and kernel of the whole question. This clamour for political rights is woman's confession of sexual enmity. Gloss over it as we may, it comes to this in the end. No woman who loves her husband would wish to usurp his province. It is only those whose instincts are inverted, or whose anti-sexual vanity is insatiable, who would take the political reins from the strong hands which have always held them to give them to others—weaker, less capable, and wholly unaccustomed. To women who love, their 'desire is to their husbands'; and the feeling remains as an echo in the soul when even the master voice is silent. Amongst our most renowned women are some who say with their whole heart, 'I would rather have been the wife of a great man, or the mother of a hero, than what I am—famous in my own person.' A woman's own fame is barren. It begins and ends with herself. Reflected from her husband or her son, it has in it the glory of immortality—of continuance. Sex is in circumstance as well as in body and in mind. We date from our fathers; not our mothers; and the shield they won by valour counts to us still for honour. But the miserable little mannikin who creeps to obscurity, overshadowed by his wife's glory, is as pitiful in history as contemptible in fact. 'The husband of his wife' is no title to honour; and the best and dearest of our famous women take care that this shall not be said of them and theirs.The wild women, on the contrary, burke their husbands altogether; and even when they are not widows act as if they were.

The young who are wavering between the rampant individualism taught by the insurgent sect and the sweeter, dearer, tenderer emotions of the true woman would do well to ponder on this position. They cannot be on both sides at once. Politics or peace, the platform or the home, individualism or love, moral sterility or the rich and full and precious life of the nature we call womanly—married or single, still essentially womanly—they must take their choice which it shall be. They cannot have both. Nor can they have the ruder, rougher 'privileges' they desire in this identity of condition with man, and retain the chivalrous devotion, the admiration, and the respect of men. These are born of the very differences between the sexes. If men want the support of equality in friendship, they find that in each other; if they want the spiritual purification which goes with true and lofty love, they look for that in women. When women have become minor men they will have lost their own holding and not have gained that other.'

It may be said that certain men support this movement, of whom some may be poor creatures, but others are manly and chivalrous enough. But where was the movement yet that had not its apostles together with its camp followers? Among the small section of men who uphold this new heresy many have that large carelessness of good-nature, that indifference of self-confidence, which makes the giant submit to the dwarf. 'It pleases them and does not hurt us,' they say. 'If women want the suffrage give it to them in Heaven's name. We shall always be the stronger, whether or no.' Others go in for the unworkable theory of abstract justice, independent of general expediency; and the third lot consists of those effeminated worshippers who wrap themselves round in the trailing skirts of the idol and shout for her rights, because they are not virile enough to respect their own. These are specially the men who uphold the imposture of the New Morality, which may be translated into prurience for the one part, and jealousy for the other.

The one unanswerable objection to the direct political power of woman is that grim blood-tax which they cannot pay and men must. The State can call on any man to serve under arms if need be, and that need might easily be brought about by a war voted by those who are themselves exempt from its personal consequences. It is mere 'havers,' as the Scotch say, to hold that women would necessarily be on the side of peace. Some of the worst wars with which Europe has been afflicted have been brought about by women. Was Madame de Maintenon the advocate for peace? Had the Empress Eugénie no part in that delirious cry 'À Berlin!' which cost so much blood and treasure? Are there no Nihilists, preaching assassination and wholesale murder, to be found among young and beautiful Russian women? From the days of Judith onwards to our own has the world ever wanted for women with hearts of fire and wrists of steel burning to avenge and self-consecrated to strike? More hysterical and still more easily excited than the mob proper, a crowd of women can be stirred by passionate appeals as willow leaves are stirred by the wind. True *moutons de Panurge*, they will follow their leader, foreseeing no consequences, conscious of no danger; and peace would be no more assured under the monstrous regiment of women than it is now. The men, however, would have to do the work which the women had cut out, and the blood-tax would be voted by those who had naught to contribute. For we put aside the childish argument, 'We send our husbands and sons,' as unworthy of serious consideration. Nor is that other answer which is meant to be parallel, 'We run as much risk in childbed as you do in battle,' of more validity. It is not women only who have family ties and personal affections. The men who fall leave men as well as women to mourn them; and women need not, if they do not wish, bear children at all. Each individual man is obliged to fight if called on by the State; no individual woman need be a wife or mother if she does not like.

Such political women as the world has seen have not all been desirable. Some have earned the blue riband of renown; but these have been women who have influenced, not ruled. The charm and grandeur of Aspasia still illumine the historic past and vivify the dead pages; but *en revanche* the silly pretensions of those Athenian woman's rights women who, under Praxagora, were going to make a new law and a new human nature, are in a manner archetypal of all that has come after. In France, where women have always had supreme influence, so that the very blood and marrow of the nation are feminine—not effeminate—the political woman has been for the most part disastrous. Some bright exceptions shine out on the other side. Agnes Sorel, like Aspasia, was one of the rare instances in history where failure in chastity did not include moral degradation nor unpatriotic self-consideration; and Joan of Arc is still a symbol for all to reverence. But of the crowd of queens and mistresses and *grandes dames* who held the strings and made kings and statesmen dance as they listed, there is scarcely one whose work was beneficent. Even Madame Roland did more harm than good when she undertook the manipulation of forces too strong for her control, too vast for her comprehension. Had there been less of the feminine element in those cataclysmic days perhaps things would not have reached the extremes they did. Had Louis had Marie Antoinette's energy, and Marie Antoinette Louis's supineness, the whole story of the Reign of Terror, Marat, Charlotte Corday, and Napoleon might never have been written.

By the very nature of things, by the inherent qualities of their sex—its virtues, defects, necessities—women are at once tyrannical and individual. In America, when they get the upper hand, they wreck the grog-shops and forbid the sale of all liquor whatever. And these women who thus destroy a man's property and ruin his fortunes in their zeal for sobriety may saturate themselves with tea, ether, or chloral, to the destruction of their health and nerves. They may resort to all sorts of perilous experiments to prevent unwelcome results;—but these are their own affairs and the men have no right to interfere.

This tyrannous temper is part of the maternal instinct which women have inherited for such countless generations. No authority in the world is so absolute, so irresponsible, as that of a mother over her young children. She can make or mar them, physically and morally, as she will—as she thinks best. Even in the most highly civilised communities, where the laws are strictest and most vigilant, she can, if she so chooses, doom them to death by her bad management, or educate them on such false lines as lead to moral depravity. By the depth and strength of the maternal instinct is the race preserved, and by this alone; and the absolute authority of the mother is the child's safest shield.

But this very characteristic is fatal to political life, to generalized justice, to the suppression of sections for the good of the whole. The political woman repudiates all this as so much paltering with the Evil One. The general good is nowhere when compared with partial inconveniences. We have seen this notably exemplified in our own generation, when excited partisanship put its hand to the plough, rooting out wise legislation on the one hand and sowing poisonous immunities on the other. And so it will ever be with women while they retain their distinctive womanly qualities.

If we imagine for a moment what the woman's vote would give, and what it would do, we shall see the inherent absurdity of the proposal. To begin with, the confining of the vote to the husbandless is, as we have said, an impossibility. If it is a right conferred by citizenhood, property, and taxation, why should marriage carry with it the penalty of disfranchisement? The Married Woman's Property Act and the fact that a wife is the mistress of her own property, however acquired or conditioned, reduces this disfranchisement to an injustice as well as an absurdity. Nor, as was said, can the vote be confined to the capable and educated. All the little country shopkeepers and workwomen who know nothing beyond the curate, the church, the school feast, and the last new local baby; the laundress who cannot manage her unruly half-dozen hands; the rollicking landlady who would give her vote dead sure to the jolly candidate who drank his bottle like a man and paid for it like a prince; the widow with no more knowledge of men and life than to keep her boy like a little girl tied to her apron-string; the 'lodger,' with her doubtful antecedents and less than doubtful profession; all the good, weak, innocent women who know no more of politics than so many doves in a cage; all the wild, excited, unreasoning women who think that vice and virtue, misery and prosperity, a new human nature and a new political economy can be made by Act of Parliament—all these sending the majority to decide on taxes, wars, treaties, international questions of difficulty and delicacy!—all these directly influencing the imperial policy of our grand old country! And the men who stand by, tongue in cheek, laughing at the sorry farce they do not take the trouble to check, or who, woman-lovers to the point of self-absorption and sexual idolatry, believe, with the women themselves, that this preponderance will really be the beginning of a new era in national virtue! And all the while these wild women and their backers shut their eyes to the contempt with which other nations would regard us. Even France, for all her feminine qualities, has not done so mad a thing as this. Even France has not proposed to enfranchise her *lionnes* and *lorettes*—to admit into the Senate the direct personal power of the courtesan. It is reserved for England—the fad-ridden England of these later days—to hear in her Parliament this proposal to be hagridden; for that is simply what it would come to. The womanly women would retire or be pushed aside by the wild women, the small but noisy section which there is yet time to ignore or to suppress.

Doubtless there are few women of anything like energy or brain power who have not felt in their own souls the ardent longing for a freer hand in life. Men as a race are the stronger and the more capable, but every man is not every woman's superior; and women of character do not find their masters at all street corners. But if they have common sense and are able to judge of general questions, and not only of individuals, they know that to upset present political conditions for the admission of a few exceptions would be as disastrous to the well-being of society as to obliterate all other distinctions of sex.

This question of woman's political power is from beginning to end a question of sex, and all that depends on sex—its moral and intellectual limitations, its emotional excesses, its personal disabilities, its social conditions. It is a question of science, as purely as the best hygienic conditions or the accurate understanding of physiology. And science is dead against it. Science knows that to admit women—that is, mothers—into the heated arena of political life would be as destructive to the physical well-being of the future generation as it would be disastrous to the good conduct of affairs in the present. And social science echoes the same thing in all that regards wives and mistresses of honest families. As for the self-complacent argument that women would moralise politics, can anyone point out anywhere a race of women who are superior to their conditions? What is it that gives women their peculiar moral power over men but the greater purity born of their greater ignorance—their daintier refinement, because of their more restricted lives? Frankly, do young men respect most the young women who have read Juvenal and Petronius and those other classics of which their mothers, God bless them! did not know even the names, or those others whose innocent eyes have never yet been darkened or hardened by a knowledge of the shameful sins of life? When women have all in common with men will they retain aught of their distinctive beauty? Where do we find that they do? Are the women at the gin-shop bar better than the men at the gin-shop door—the field hands in sun-bonnets more satisfactory than those in brimless hats? If women are intruded into the political world with all its angry partisanship and eagerness for victory, how can they retain the ideal qualities which they have gained by a certain amount of sequestration from the madding crowd's ignoble strife? Are they alone, of all created things, uninfluenced by their environment, incapable of reversion to the lower original type? We may be sure that the world has done well for itself in the distinctions of habit that it has made in all ways between the sexes, and that those who would throw down the barriers are letting in the flood. But 'après nous le déluge!' The wild women who would scramble for the sceptre of political sovereignty have no great regard for the future or anything else but themselves. 'Let us enjoy, no matter who suffers; crucify the old ideal, and let our children run the risk.'

These words lead us back to the centre of the moral objections against the active political woman. It may be that the Christian ideal, the Christian doctrine, is a myth and a dream from start to finish. Be it so; but if so, let it be acknowledged. If indeed those sweet and lovely virtues of patience and unselfishness are follies, let the world confess it and make no more pretence to the contrary. If, however, they still have any significance, and are held by many as of divine authority, it seems rather self-contradictory that the half of the race which can best practise them refuses to do so, and would lay the burden on the shoulders of those for whom they are not always either righteous or possible. A fighter cannot be non-resisting; but we need not all be fighters, men and women indiscriminately. The gentle response of the Jewish women to the men's prouder boast of their material advantages has always seemed to us to carry in it the very soul of womanly sweetness. 'We thank Thee, O Lord God, that Thou hast made us according to Thy will.'

Well! whether it be according to the directly spoken will of God, or according to the mysterious law of evolution, working we know not whence, tending we know not whither—let it be by religion or by nature, society or science—there stands the fact four-square, the grand fundamental fact of humanity, difference of sex, and consequent difference of functions, virtues, qualities, and qualifications. As little as it is fitting for a man to look after the pap boat and the house linen, so is it for women to assume the political power of the State. Our men are not yet at such a low ebb in brains or morals as to need dispossession; nor, *pace* our platform orators, are the wild women, though undeniably smart, of such commanding intelligence as to create a new epoch and justify a new social ordering.

By the grace of good luck the question has been shelved for the present session, but the future is ahead. And as, unfortunately, certain of the Conservative party coquet with the woman's vote, believing that they shall thus tap a large Conservative reservoir, we are by no means clear of the danger. What we would wish to do is to convince the young and undetermined that political work is both unwomanly and unnatural; self-destructive and socially hurtful; the sure precursor to the loss of men's personal consideration and to the letting loose the waters of strife; and—what egotism will not regard—the sure precursor to a future régime of redoubled coercion and suppression.

For, after all, the strong right arm is the *ultima ratio*, and God will have it so; and when men found, as they would, that they were outnumbered, outvoted, and politically nullified, they would soon have recourse to that ultimate appeal—and the last state of women would be worse than their first.

Source: Reprinted from *Nineteenth Century* (July 1891).

"THE WILD WOMEN: AS SOCIAL INSURGENTS"

We must change our ideals. The Desdemonas and Dorotheas, the Enids and Imogens, are all wrong. Milton's Eve is an anachronism; so is the Lady; so is Una; so are Christabel and Genevieve. Such women as Panthea and Alcestis, Cornelia and Lucretia, are as much out of date as the chiton and the peplum, the bride's hair parted with a spear, or the worth of a woman reckoned by the flax she spun and the thread she wove, by the number of citizens she gave to the State, and the honour that reflected on her through the heroism of her sons. All this is past and done with—effete, rococo, dead. For the '*tacens et placens uxor*' of old-time dreams we must acknowledge now as our Lady of Desire the masterful *domina* of real life—that loud and dictatorial person, insurgent and something more, who suffers no-one's opinion to influence her mind, no venerable law hallowed by time, nor custom consecrated by experience, to control her actions. Mistress of herself, the Wild Woman as a social insurgent preaches the 'lesson of liberty' broadened into lawlessness and licence. Unconsciously she exemplifies how beauty can degenerate into ugliness, and shows how the once fragrant flower, run to seed, is good for neither food nor ornament.

Her ideal of life for herself is absolute personal independence coupled with supreme power over men. She repudiates the doctrine of individual conformity for the sake of the general good; holding the self-restraint involved as an act of slavishness of which no woman worth her salt would be guilty. She makes between the sexes no distinctions, moral or aesthetic, nor even personal; but holds that what is lawful to the one is permissible to the other. Why should the world have parcelled out qualities or habits into two different sections, leaving only a few common to both alike? Why, for instance, should men have the fee-simple of courage, and women that of modesty? to men be given the right of the initiative—to women only that of selection? to men the freer indulgence of the senses—to women the chaster discipline of self-denial? The Wild Woman of modern life asks why; and she answers the question in her own way.

'Rien n'est sacré pour un sapeur.' Nothing is forbidden to the Wild Woman as a social insurgent; for the one word that she cannot spell is, Fitness. Devoid of this sense of fitness, she does all manner of things which she thinks bestow on her the power, together with the privileges, of a man; not thinking that in obliterating the finer distinctions of sex she is obliterating the finer traits of civilisation, and that every step made towards identity of habits is a step downwards in refinement and delicacy—wherein lies the essential core of civilisation. She smokes after dinner with the men; in railway carriages; in public rooms—when she is allowed. She thinks she is thereby vindicating her independence and honouring her emancipated womanhood. Heaven bless her! Down in the North-country villages, and elsewhere, she will find her prototypes calmly smoking their black cutty-pipes, with no sense of shame about them. Why should they not? These ancient dames with 'whiskin' beards about their mou's,' withered and unsightly, worn out, and no longer women in desirableness or beauty—why should they not take to the habits of men? They do not disgust, because they no longer charm; but even in these places you do not find the younger women with cutty-pipes between their lips. Perhaps in the coal districts, where women work like men and with men, and are dressed as men, you will see pipes as well as hear blasphemies; but that is surely not an admirable state of things, and one can hardly say that the pit-brow women, excellent persons and good workers as they are in their own way, are exactly the glasses in which our fine ladies find their loveliest fashions—the moulds wherein they would do well to run their own forms. And when, after dinner, our young married women and husbandless girls, despising the old distinctions and trampling under foot the time-honoured conventions of former generations, 'light up' with the men, they are simply assimilating themselves to this old Sally and that ancient Betty down in the dales and mountain hamlets; or to the stalwart cohort of pit-brow women for whom sex has no aesthetic distinctions. We grant the difference of method. A superbly dressed young woman, bust, arms, and shoulders bare, and gleaming white and warm beneath the subdued light of a luxurious dinner-table—a beautiful young creature, painted, dyed, and powdered according to the mode—her lips red with wine and moist with liqueur—she is really different from mumping old Betty in unwomanly rags smoking at her black cutty-pipe by the cottage door on the bleak fell-side. In the one lies an appeal to the passions of men; in the other is the death of all emotion. Nevertheless, the acts are the same, the circumstances which accompany them alone being different.

Free-traders in all that relates to sex, the Wild Women allow men no monopoly in sports, in games, in responsibilities. Beginning by 'walking with the guns,' they end by shooting with them; and some have made the moor a good training-ground for the jungle. As life is constituted, it is necessary to have butchers and sportsmen. The hunter's instinct keeps down the wild beasts, and those who go after big game do as much good to the world as those who slaughter home-bred beasts for the market. But in neither instance do we care to see a woman's hand. It may be merely a sentiment, and ridiculous at that; still, sentiment has its influence, legitimate enough when not too widely extended; and we confess that the image of a 'butching' woman, nursing her infant child with hands red with the blood of an ox she has just poleaxed or of a lamb whose throat she has this instant cut, is one of unmitigated horror and moral incongruity. Precisely as horrible, as incongruous, is the image of a well-bred sportswoman whose bullet has crashed along the spine of a leopardess, who has knocked over a rabbit or brought down a partridge. The one may be a hard-fisted woman of the people, who had no inherent sensitiveness to overcome—a woman born and bred among the shambles and accustomed to the whole thing from childhood. The other may be a dainty-featured aristocrat, whose later development belies her early training; but the result is the same in both cases—the possession of an absolutely unwomanly instinct, an absolutely unwomanly indifference to death and suffering; which certain of the Wild Women of the present day cultivate as one of their protests against the limitations of sex. The viragoes of all times have always had this same instinct, this same indifference. For nothing of all this is new in substance. What is new is the translation into the cultured classes of certain qualities and practices hitherto confined to the uncultured and—savages.

This desire to assimilate their lives to those of men runs through the whole day's work of the Wild Women. Not content with croquet and lawn tennis, the one of which affords ample opportunities for flirting—for the Wild Women are not always above that little pastime—and the other for exercise even more violent than is good for the average women, they have taken to golf and cricket, where they are hindrances for the one part, and make themselves 'sights' for the other. Men are not graceful when jumping, running, stooping, swinging their arms, and all the rest of it. They are fine, and give a sense a power that is perhaps more attractive than mere beauty; but, as schoolboys are not taught gymnastics after the manner of the young Greeks, to the rhythmic cadence of music, so that every movement may be rendered automatically graceful, they are often awkward enough when at play; and the harder the work the less there is of artistic beauty in the manner of it. But if men, with their narrower hips and broader shoulders, are less than classically lovely when they are putting out their physical powers, what are the women, whose broad hips give a wider step and less steady carriage in running, and whose arms, because of their narrower shoulders, do not lend themselves to beautiful curves when they are making a swinging stroke at golf or batting and bowling at cricket? The prettiest woman in the world loses her beauty when at these violent exercises. Hot and damp, mopping her flushed and streaming face with her handkerchief, she has lost that sense of repose, that delicate self-restraint, which belongs to the ideal woman. She is no longer dainty. She has thrown off her grace and abandoned all that makes her lovely for the uncomely roughness of pastimes wherein she cannot excel, and of which it was never intended she should be a partaker.

We have not yet heard of women polo-players; but that will come. In the absurd endeavour to be like men, these modern *homasses* will leave nothing untried; and polo-playing, tent-pegging, and tilting at the quintain are all sure to come in time. When weeds once begin to grow, no limits can be put to their extent unless they are stubbed up betimes.

The Wild Women, in their character of social insurgents, are bound by none of the conventions which once regulated society. In them we see the odd social phenomenon of the voluntary descent of the higher to the lower forms of ways and works. 'Unladylike' is a term that has ceased to be significant. Where 'unwomanly' has died out we could scarcely expect this other to survive. The special must needs go with the generic; and we find it so with a vengeance! With other queer inversions the frantic desire of making money has invaded the whole class of Wild Woman; and it does not mitigate their desire that, as things are, they have enough for all reasonable wants. Women who, a few years ago, would not have shaken hands with a dressmaker, still less have sat down to table with her, now open shops and set up in business on their own account—not because they are poor, which would be an honourable and sufficing reason enough, but because they are restless, dissatisfied, insurgent, and like nothing so much as to shock established prejudices and make the folk stare. It is such a satire on their inheritance of class distinction, on their superior education—perhaps very superior, stretching out to academical proportions! It is just the kind of topsy-turvydom that pleases them. They, with their long descent, grand name, and right to a coat-of-arms which represents past ages of renown,—they to come down into the marketplace, shouldering out the meaner fry, who must work to live—taking from the legitimate traders the pick of their custom, and making their way by dint of social standing and personal influence—they to sell bonnets in place of buying them—to make money instead of spending it—what fun! What a grand idea it was to conceive, and grander still to execute! In this insurgent playing at shopkeeping by those who do not need to do so we see nothing grand nor beautiful, but much that is thoughtless and mean. Born of restlessness and idleness, these spasmodic make-believes after serious work are simply pastimes to the Wild Women who undertake them. There is nothing really solid in them, no more than there was of philanthropy in the fashionable craze for slumming which broke out like a fever a winter or two ago. Shop-keeping and slumming, and some other things too, are just the expression of that restlessness which makes of the modern Wild Woman a second Io, driving her afield in search of strange pleasures and novel occupations, and leading her to drink of the muddiest waters so long as they are in new channels cut off from the old fountains. Nothing daunts this modern Io. No barriers restrain, no obstacles prevent. She appears on the public stage and executes dances which one would not like one's daughter to see, still less perform. She herself knows no shame in showing her skill—and her legs. Why should she? What free and independent spirit, in these later days, is willing to be bound by those musty principles of modesty which did well enough for our stupid old great-grandmothers—but for us? Other times, other manners; and womanly reticence is not of these last!

There is no reason why perfectly good and modest women should not be actresses. Rightly taken, acting is an art as noble as any other. But here, as elsewhere, are gradations and sections; and just as a wide line is drawn between the cancan and the minuet, so is there between the things which a modest woman may do on the stage and those which she may not. Not long ago that line was notoriously overstepped, and certain of our Wild Women pranced gaily from the safe precincts of the permissible into those wider regions of the more than doubtful, where, it is to be supposed, they enjoyed their questionable triumph—at least for the hour.

The spirit of the day is both vagrant and self-advertising, both bold and restless, contemptuous of law and disregarding restraint. We do not suppose that women are intrinsically less virtuous than they were in the time of Hogarth's 'Last Stake;' but they are more dissatisfied, less occupied, and infinitely less modest. All those old similes about modest violets and chaste lilies, flowers blooming unseen, and roses that 'open their glowing bosoms' but to one love only—all these are as rococo as the Elizabethan ruff or Queen Anne's 'laced head.' Everyone who has a 'gift' must make that gift public; and, so far from wrapping up talents in a napkin, pence are put out to interest, and the world is called on to admire the milling. The enormous amount of inferior work which is thrown on the market in all directions is one of the marvels of the time. Everything is exhibited. If a young lady can draw so far correctly as to give her cow four legs and not five, she sends her sketches to some newspaper, or more boldly transfers them on to a plate or a pot, and exhibits them at some art refuge for the stage below mediocrity. It is heartbreaking when these inanities are sent by those poor young creatures who need the fortune they think they have in their 'gift.' It is contemptible when they are sent by the rich, distracted with vanity and idleness together. The love of art for its own sake, of intellectual work for the intellectual pleasure it brings, knows nothing of this insatiate vanity, this restless ambition to be classed among those who give to their work days where these others give hours. It is only the Wild Women who take these headers into artistic depths, where they flounder pitiably, neither dredging up unknown treasures, nor floating gaily in the sun on the crest of the wave. When we think of the length of time it has taken to create all masterpieces—and, indeed, all good work of any kind, not necessarily masterpieces—it is food for wonder to see the jaunty ease with which the scarce-educated in an art throw off their productions, which then they fling out to the public as one tosses crumbs to the sparrows. But the Wild Women are never thorough. As artists, as literati, as tradeswomen, as philanthropists, it is all a mere touch-and-go kind of thing with them. The roots, which are first in importance in all growths, no matter what, are the last things they care to master. They would not be wild if they did.

About these Wild Women is always an unpleasant suggestion of the adventuress. Whatever their natural place and lineage, they are of the same family as those hotel heroines who forget to lock the chamber door—those confiding innocents of ripe years, who contract imperfect marriages—those pretty country blossoms who begin life modestly and creditably, and go on to flaunting notoriety and disgrace. One feels that it is only the accident of birth which differences these from those, and determines a certain stability of class. It is John Bradshaw over again; but the 'grace' is queerly bestowed. As a rule, these women have no scruples about money. They are notorious for never having small change; they get into debt with a facility as amazing in its want of conscience as its want of foresight; and then they take to strange ways for redeeming their credit and saving themselves from public exposure. If the secret history of some account-books could be written startling revelations would be made. Every now and then, indeed, things come to light which it would have been better to keep hidden; for close association with shady 'promoters' and confessed blacklegs is not conducive to the honour of womanhood—at least as this honour was. Under the new *régime* blots do not count for so much. Every now and then, one, a trifle more shameless than her sisters, flourishes out openly before the world as an adept in a doubtful business—say, in the art of laying odds judiciously and hedging wisely. She is to be seen standing on her tub shouting with the best; and as little abashed by the unwomanliness of her 'environment' as are her more mischievous compeers on the political stump. She knows that money is to be made as well as lost in the ring, and she does not see why, because she is a woman, she may not pick out plums with the rest.

If she has money enough—she is sure to call it 'oof,' so as to be in line with the verbal as well as the practical blackguardism of the day—she has a stud of her own, and enters into all the details connected therewith with as much gusto as a village beldame enters into the life-events of her homely world. But while a foal is one of the most interesting things in life to one of these horsy Wild Women, a child is one of the least; and what young mother, with all the hopes and fears, the fervent love, the brilliant dreams, which lie about the cradle of her first-born, comes near in importance to that brood mare of racing renown, with her long-legged foal trotting by her side? The Wild Woman is never a delightful creature, take her how one will; but the horsy Wild Woman, full of stable slang and inverted instincts, can give points to the rest of her clan, and still be ahead of them all.

Sometimes our Wild Women break out as adventurous travellers; when they come home to write on what they have seen and done, books which have to be taken with salt by the spoonful, not only by the grain. Their bows are very large, and the string they draw preternaturally long. Experts contradict them, and the more experienced smile and shake their heads. But their own partisans uphold them; and that portion of the press where reason and manliness are suffocated by the sense of sex takes them as if they were so many problems of Euclid with Q.E.D. after 'the end.' How different these pseudo-heroines are from the quiet realities, such as Marianne North, to name no other, who did marvels of which they never boasted, contented with showing the unanswerable results! They 'covered down,' they did not paint in high lights and exaggerated colours the various perils through which they had passed. The Wild Woman of the immediate day reverses the system. Under her manipulation a steep ascent is a sheer precipice, a crack in the road is a crevasse, a practicable bit of crag-climbing is a service of peril where each step is planted in the shadow of death; and hardships are encountered which exist only on paper and in the fertile imagination of the fair tourist. If, however, these hardships are real and not imaginary, the poor, wild vagrant returns broken and overstrained, and finds, when perhaps too late, that lovely woman may stoop to other folly besides that of listening to a dear loo'ed lad; and that, in her attempt to imitate, to rival, perhaps to surpass, man on his rightful ground she is not only destroying her distinctive charm of womanhood, but is perhaps digging her own grave, to be filled too surely as well as prematurely.

We are becoming a little surfeited with these Wild Women as globe-trotters and travellers. Their adventures, which for the most part are fictions based on a very small substratum of fact, have ceased to impress, partly because we have ceased to believe, and certainly ceased to respect. *Que diable allait-il faire dans cette galère?* Who wanted them to run all these risks, supposing them to be true? What good have they done by their days of starvation and nights of sleeplessness? their perils by land and sea? their chances of being devoured by wild beasts or stuck up by bushrangers? taken by brigands or insulted by rowdies of all nations? They have contributed nothing to our stock of knowledge, as Marianne North has done. They have solved no ethnological problem; brought to light no new treasures of nature; discovered no new field for British spades to till, no new markets for British manufactures to supply. They have done nothing but lose their beauty, if they had any; for what went out fresh and comely comes back haggard and weather-beaten. It was quite unnecessary. They have lost, but the world has not gained; and that doctor's bill will make a hole in the publisher's cheque.

Ranged side by side with these vagrant Wild Women, globe-trotting for the sake of a subsequent book of travels, and the *kudos* with the pence accruing, are those who spread themselves abroad as missionaries, and those—a small minority, certainly—who do not see why the army and the navy should be sealed against the sex. Among these female missionaries are some who are good, devoted, pure-hearted, self-sacrificing—all that women should be, all that the best women are, and ever have been, and ever will be. But also among them are the Wild Women—creatures impatient of restraint, bound by no law, insurgent to their finger-tips, and desirous of making all other women as restless and discontented as themselves. Ignorant and unreasonable, they would carry into the sun-laden East the social conditions born of the icy winds of the North. They would introduce into the zenana the circumstances of a Yorkshire home. In a country where jealousy is as strong as death, and stronger than love, they would incite the women to revolt against the rule of seclusion, which has been the law of the land for centuries before we were a nation at all. That rule has worked well for the country, inasmuch as the chastity of Hindu women and the purity of family life are notoriously intact. But our Wild Women swarm over into India as zenana missionaries, trying to make the Hindus as discontented, as restless, as unruly as themselves. The zenana would not suit us. The meekest little mouse among us would revolt at a state of things which does not press too heavily on those who have known nothing else and inherited no other traditions. But it does suit the people who have framed and who live under these laws: and we hold it to be an ethnological blunder, as well as a political misdemeanour, to send out these surging apostles of disobedience and discontent to carry revolt and confusion among our Indian fellow-subjects. It is part of the terrible restlessness with which this age is afflicted, part of the contempt for law in all its forms which certain women have adopted from certain men, themselves too effeminate, too little manly to be able to submit to discipline. These are the men who hound on the Wild Women to ever fresh extravagances. Those pestilent papers which are conducted by these rebels against law and order are responsible for a large amount of the folly which all true lovers of womanly beauty and virtue deplore and fight against. It is they who hold up to public admiration acts and sentiments which ought to be either sternly repressed as public faults or laughed down as absurdities.

Unlike the female doctors, who, we believe, undertake no proselytising, and are content to merely heal the bodies while leaving alone the souls and lives of the 'purdah-women,' the zenana missionaries go out with the express purpose of teaching Christian theology and personal independence. We hold each to be an impertinence. Like the Jews, the Hindu men have ample means of judging of our Christianity, and what it has done for the world which professes it. They also have ample means of judging of the effects of our womanly independence, and what class of persons we turn out to roam about the world alone. If they prefer this to that, they have only to say so, and the reform will come from within, as it ought—as all reforms must, to be of value. If they do not, it is not for our Wild Women to carry the burden of their unrest into the quiet homes of the East; which homes, too, are further protected by the oath taken by the sovereign to respect the religion of these Eastern subjects. When we have taught the Hindu women to hunt and drive, play golf and cricket, dance the cancan on a public stage, make speeches in Parliament, cherish 'dear boys' at five-o'clock tea, and do all that our Wild Women do, shall we have advanced matters very far? Shall we have made the home happier, the family purer, the women themselves more modest, more chaste? Had we not better cease to pull at ropes which move machinery of which we know neither the force nor the possible action? Why all this interference with others? Why not let the various peoples of the earth manage their domestic matters as they think fit? Are our Wild Women the ideal of female perfection? Heaven forbid! But to this distorted likeness they and their backers are doing their best to reduce all others.

Aggressive, disturbing, officious, unquiet, rebellious to authority and tyrannous to those whom they can subdue, we say emphatically that they are about the most unlovely specimens the sex has yet produced, and between the 'purdah-woman' and the modern *homasses* we, for our own parts, prefer the former. At least the purdah-woman knows how to love. At least she has not forgotten the traditions of modesty as she has been taught them. But what about our half-naked girls and young wives, smoking and drinking with the men? our ramping platform orators? our unabashed self-advertisers? our betting women? our horse-breeders? our advocates of free love, and our contemners of maternal life and domestic duties?

The mind goes back over certain passages in history, and the imagination fastens on certain names which stand as types of womanly loveliness and love-worthiness. Side by side with them were the *homasses* of their day. Where there was a Countess of Salisbury, for whom not a man in the castle but would have died, cheerfully, gladly, rejoiced to carry his death as his tribute to her surpassing charm, there was also a Black Agnes, who did not disdain to insult her baffled foe, and who had none of the delightfulness which made the Countess of Salisbury so beloved—which made the even yet more distinctly heroic Jane de Montfort so prepotent over her followers. Here stands Lady Rachel Russell; there the arch-virago old Bess of Hardwick.. The one is our English version of Panthea, of Arria; the other is Xanthippe in a coif and peaked stomacher. On one canvas we have Lady Fanshaw; on the other, Lady Eldon— all the same as now we have certain sweet and lovely women who honour their womanhood and fulfil its noblest ideals, and these Wild Women of blare and bluster, who are neither man nor woman—wanting in the well-knit power of the first and in the fragrant sweetness of the last.

Excrescences of the times, products of peace and idleness, of prosperity and over-population—would things be better if a great national disaster pruned our superfluities and left us nearer to the essential core of facts? Who knows! Storms shake off the nobler fruit but do not always beat down the ramping weeds. Still, human nature has the trick of pulling itself right in times of stress and strain. Perhaps, if called upon, even our Wild Women would cast off their ugly travesty and become what modesty and virtue designed them to be; and perhaps their male adorers would go back to the ranks of masculine self-respect, and leave off this base subservience to folly which now disfigures and unmans them. *Chi lo sa?* It does no one harm to hope. This hope, then, let us cherish while we can and may.

Source: Reprinted from *Nineteenth Century* (October 1891).

BIOGRAPHICAL NOTE

Born in Keswick in 1822, Eliza Lynn Linton was the youngest of twelve children. Her father, the Rev. James Lynn, was a clergyman in Cumberland. Her mother died when she was six months old. In her day, Linton was well-received as a novelist of historical fiction. Her first novel, *Azeth the Egyptian* (1847), was favourably reviewed in the *Times*. Her second novel, *Amymone: A Romance of the Days of Pericles* (1848), was compared to Bulwer-Lytton's *Last Days of Pompeii*, and deemed part of England's "standard" literature. Today, she is remembered primarily as one of the first women to earn her living as a journalist, a job she commenced at the age of twenty-three in order to support herself while writing her first two novels. Chaperoned by the family solicitor, Linton came to London in 1845, and found work on the *Morning Chronicle*. Six years later, after quarrelling with the editor of the paper, she moved to Paris for several years, supporting herself by becoming a correspondent. After returning to England, she married William James Linton in 1858. He was an engraver, poet, journalist, republican, and widower with seven children. Their marriage was uncertain from the start, since Linton disliked his republicanism and his terrible ways with money. After nine years of marriage, William Linton moved to his house in the Lake District and eventually in 1867 to Connecticut in the United States. Eliza Linton headed back to London, relaunching her literary career with a series of anonymous articles on women for the *Saturday Review*. The series included "The Girl of the Period" reprinted here, and it caused a literary scandal for its immoderate views on women's emancipation and its outrageous stereotypes. Linton did not claim authorship of the series for sixteen years, during which time a *Girl of the Period* journal was started, and spin-off comedies and farces circulated along with rumours that the extremist author must be a man. When Linton finally did claim authorship, she did so with pride: "I neither soften nor retract a line of what I have said."

Though Linton was equally famous in her day for her fiction writing, short stories and travel writing, with such books as *The True History of Joshua Davidson, Christian and Communist* (1872), *Patricia Kemball* (1874), and *The Autobiography of Christopher Kirkland* (1885), it is her work during the same period as a journalist for the *Saturday Review*, *Macmillan's Magazine*, and the *Nineteenth Century* among others, that continues to be of importance today. Her controversial style, so admirably displayed in *The Girl of the Period*, continued to be a trademark in such later series, as her "Wild Women" pieces for the *Nineteenth Century*, part of which is reprinted here. Other essays, like "The Modern Revolt," show a rather more considered tone, but do not on the whole seem characteristic of her extravagantly vicious writing on women. In her own life, Linton supported equal but separate education for women, women's property rights, and women's rights to their children. But she was vehemently against women's claims for political rights. Having coined the term "the shrieking sisterhood" for her feminist opponents, Linton noted without surprise: "I have numbers of anonymous letters from women who wish to see my pen paralyzed and myself struck dead." She died of pneumonia on 14 July 1898 at the age of seventy-six.

SELECTED SECONDARY SOURCES

Anderson, Nancy Fix. "Eliza Lynn Linton: The Rebel of the Family (1880) and Other Novels." *The New Nineteenth Century: Feminist Readings of Underread Victorian Fiction.* Ed. Barbara Harman and Susan Meyer. New York: Garland, 1996. 117-33.

Colby, Vineta. *The Singular Anomaly: Women Novelists of the Nineteenth Century.* New York: New York UP, 1970.

Layard, George Somes. *Eliza Lynn Linton: Her Life, Letters, and Opinions.* London: Methuen, 1901.

Meem, Deborah T. "Eliza Lynn Linton and the Rise of Lesbian Consciousness." *Journal of the History of Sexuality* 7.4 (1997): 537-60.

MARGARET OLIPHANT
(1828-1897)

"THE CONDITION OF WOMEN"

Civilisation, like every other condition of humanity, has its dark as well as its bright side. Strangely enough, every material power which we invoke for our service, and to which the popular will, or more often the will of an individual, gives the first impetus, becomes, when once fairly errant and in progress, a kind of blind irresponsible independent agent, working by immutable laws of its own, beyond our reach either to quicken or arrest. The great dumb irrational slave comes into existence because we will it so—creeps upon his earlier way by our assistance—finally rules over us with an absolutism more arbitrary than any personal tyranny, and, irresistible and not to be controlled, goes on like a Fate towards the ruin and destruction involved in his being. Civilisation, beneficent, gentle, full of charities and courtesies, the great ameliorator of the world, is no less, as old experience has often proved, the Nemesis of the very race which has cherished him. It would have been easier to check at their fiercest the wild Gothic hordes, which carried a fresh force of barbarous life into the ancient capitals of the world, than to have arrested the noiseless tide of that silken degeneration which left these old empires helpless beneath the rude foot of the conqueror. These waves are not to be limited by a "Hitherto shalt thou come, and no further"—it is not in the power of either men or governments to curb the giant whom they have been able to bring into being; it is impossible to arrest him at the golden age, while luxury is still legitimate, art splendid, and the economy of national existence magnificent and noble. How to pause there, is the often tried problem of nations—it is one which none of the antique races ever solved. Those elegant, dissolute, nerveless, incapable communities, into the ranks of which, in an inglorious succession, sank the heroic republics of Greece, the Rome of the Caesars, and the empire of the Constantines, have been hitherto a kind of inevitable aftercome to every climax of national glory. To control the event by law or regulation, to attempt vain sumptuary enactments, or vainer moral remonstrances against the progress of luxury and enervation, has been tried by many a terrified government, blindly struggling against the blind natural force, inaccessible to reason, which obeyed the law of its own being, and knew no other: but the contest has always been a fatally unsuccessful one; and it would require no particular strain of argument, or rather of the facts on which arguments are founded, to prove that civilisation by itself was the most equivocal of

181

benefits—an influence which increased the comfort of one generation only to bring a greater destruction upon another—a force, in reality, not favourable, but inimical, to man.

It would almost seem, however, so far as we and the modern world are concerned, as if this fatal proclivity had in a great degree disappeared. True, it is not a hundred years yet since the French Revolution, which was a fiercer overthrow of all the artificial amenities of life than that which the barbarians of the North carried to the ancient empires of the world; and it is still a shorter time since all the Continental kingdoms trembled to the echoes of a conqueror's progress, and surrendered for a moment their very identity to make tributary crowns for his relations and dependents. But among ourselves, at least, there has been no such catastrophe—the evils of civilisation have counteracted themselves without any violent disturbance of the national life. We have gained our comforts, our security, our luxury, at a less price than that of our national vigour. The wealth of centuries has not bound us in silken chains of imbecility, or left us ready or probable victims to any invasion. On the contrary, though this is not our golden age—though there is no heroic glory in the firmament, no peculiar combinations of good fortune in our position— every circumstance in the history of the time proves that the race never was more vigorous, more irresistible, or less likely to be worsted. We talk of the evils of extreme civilisation, and we see them; but these evils, thank Heaven, are not symptoms of that fatal decadence which killed the civilised races of antiquity, and which has again and again left the hopes of the world in the hands of an army of savage and barbarous tribes, possessed of little more than that primitive force of *life* which was necessary for the revival of all the social conditions well-nigh extinguished by living too well.

It is not our business to enter into the causes of this almost unparalleled national exemption. Christianity is beyond question the surest controller of the doubtful powers of civilisation, and our faith has been blessed by Providence with a freedom and power of action denied to many of our neighbours. We have also had the one other, lesser, but most effectual safety-valve of extreme civilisation—a constantly remaining balance of savage possessions, open to the conquest and the enterprise and the ambition of all bold spirits— a margin of woods and plains and islands to be won out of the primitive grip of nature, and holding primitive wealth, the wholesome original of all other riches, in their bosom. With this balance of healthful savagery in our own possession, sanctified as its natural influence is by the aggressive, invasive, and irrestrainable activity of the Gospel, civilisation, however "extreme," loses its usual tendency. We are in no danger of making sumptuary laws, of regulating the burgesses wardrobe or the nobleman's plate-closet. Burgesses and noblemen alike send out young adventurers, as all the world knows—who would have been Rolands and Bayards in the days of chivalry—to every quarter of this prodigious empire which stands in need of such; and no man in the kingdom grudges to the mothers and sisters—nay, to the aunts, cousins, and sweet-hearts of these boys—flounces enough to set the island afloat if it pleases them. Luxury, present or prospective, affrights neither statesman nor philosopher in these realms; and it is not easy to make a British public believe that an American public can mean anything but a jest, when it throws the blame of its bankruptcy upon the extravagance of its womankind. It is possible that the course of years may reverse this picture, that civilisation may sink into effeminacy, and wealth run on to ruin with this kingdom, as with so many others; but at present, so far as human probabilities go, it seems our privilege to hold the balance, and solve to this extent at least every social problem of the world.

Let not so serious an introduction damp your courage, oh reader just and kind! We are not about to prefer an indictment of secret horrors, a muster-roll of the unacknowledged crimes of cities, against the civilised society of this realm and time. Sin, in all its varieties, belongs to no one condition of humanity, but lives where men live, in all places and in all ages. Civilisation may make crime more venomous and fiendish, as savage life makes it more brutal; but neither the one nor the other can be called the parent of this disease of the race. Our concern is with matters much less appalling. Civilisation among us stands at the bar to be judged by domestic juries, for offences against the social economy. In the present case, the complainants are women. Let us do their plea full justice: they are not the passionate women, making vehement appeal to public sympathy for personal wrongs too bitter to contain themselves within a private circle, to whose voices the world has not been unaccustomed hitherto. It is not any personal injury, but a general condition, which is the object of their statement, and they make their statement with reasonableness and gravity. It is, notwithstanding, somewhat too sweeping and extensive to be received without hesitation—being no less than a charge against civilisation of upsetting the commonest and most universal relation of life, and of leaving a large proportion of women, in all conditions, outside of the arrangements of the family, to provide for themselves, without at the same time leaving for them anything to do.

This is very hard, if it is true; and that it is true in many special instances, no one will deny. Special instances, however, do not make up a case so universal as we are called upon to believe this to be. It is not the common course of Providence which drops an individual now and then out of the current, but a circumstance so general as to change the current altogether. There were single ladies as there were single gentlemen as long as anybody can remember, yet it is only within a very short time that writers and critics have begun to call the attention of the public to the prevalence and multiplicity of the same. "What are we to do with our spinsters?" asks, with comic pathos, one of the many reviewers of the *Life of Charlotte Bronte*, and our enlightened contemporary, the *Athenaeum*, congratulates itself that even novels—those arbitrary matchmakers—begin to see the propriety of recognising the condition of old maid; and even though they ultimately marry their heroine, suffer her first to come to years of extreme discretion, and to settle upon her own mode of life. While, still more formal, one of the latest lady-accusers of civilisation not only prefaces her *Woman's Thoughts about Women* with the somewhat amazing limitation that "these thoughts do not concern married women," but adds in so many words, "this fact remains patent to any person of common sense and experience, that, in the present day, whether voluntarily or not, one-half of our women are *obliged* to take care of themselves—obliged to look solely to themselves for maintenance, position, occupation, amusement, reputation, life."

Now we cannot help thinking this a rather astounding statement. Is it really the condition of the feminine population of the three kingdoms? Persons of common sense and experience may well consider the question if it is so—and doubtless there is statistical information to be had on so important a subject. Judging by our own limited lights, we should have supposed that even our "unmarried daughters" still in the nursery, to whom a new doll is at present infinitely more attractive than the handsomest new Guardsman of the season, must have added their tiny quota to the tale, ere the "one-half" of single women had been fairly made out and numbered. One-half of the Englishwomen of the present time, not only unmarried, but voluntarily or otherwise unmarriageable—not only unmarried and unmarriageable, but without father, mother, brother, or family, sole units standing each upon her own responsibility before the world! Many an odd picture of this same world gets drawn by people in a corner, who find their own little horizon the limit of the scene; but never surely was there an odder or more remarkable misrepresentation than this—and it would be a curious inquiry to discover and settle those strange characteristics of the time which make so many people elect into a general rule the special conditions surrounding themselves, concluding upon their own argument as upon the most infallible demonstration, and perfectly clear on the fact that they are expounding a new order of things which had no existence in the ages that are past.

Here is, however, one of the chief accusations brought against our civilisation. Half the women in England are not married, and never will be; consequently a large proportion of Englishwomen have to seek their own maintenance and earn their own bread. But civilisation, while it makes this unnatural and anomalous arrangement, does not unmake the primitive arrangement by which labour out of doors, handicrafts, arts, and manual skill of all kinds, remain in the possession of men. There are consequently crowds of half-starved needlewomen, thousands of poor governesses, and a great many more feminine writers of novels than are supposed to be good for the health of the public; and so the tale is full. A woman who cannot be a governess or a novel-writer must fall back upon that poor little needle, the primitive and original handicraft of femininity. If she cannot do that, or even, doing it, if stifled among a crowd of others like herself, who have no other gift, she must starve by inches, and die over the shirt she makes. We are all perfectly acquainted with this picture, and there can be no doubt that, with countless individual aggravations, it is true enough; the only thing doubtful is, whether these unfortunate circumstances are peculiar to women, and whether it is mainly upon them that civilisation imposes this necessity and works this wrong.

Many a sermon has been preached already upon the singular life of Currer Bell. It would be late now to recur to a book which has already had its day of popularity, and waked its own particular circles of curiosity and wonder; yet there is one aspect of it which bears with no small force upon the present subject. In that remarkable but not very prepossessing family, there was one brother equally gifted we are told, and in extreme youth the most hopeful of any of them. Which seems to have had the best chance for life and success? The sisters were governesses all, and hated their disagreeable occupation: the brother was a tutor, and ruined himself disgracefully in his. Wherein stood the peculiar advantages of this young man, putting out of the question the vices by which he made an end of himself. Is a tutor in a private family of moderate rank better than a governess in the same? Is his position more secure, his prospects less discouraging, his pretensions more suitably acknowledged? Everybody knows that it is not so. Most people know also instinctively that the position of the poor gentlewoman who teaches the children of a rich family, is less humiliating than that of the poor gentleman employed in the same office, and that we could admire a hundred petty endurances in a woman which we should despise a man for tolerating. Why? We have no leisure to enter into the psychology of the question; simply, we do so by nature. A woman who endures worthily even the pettiest slights of meanness, has the privilege of suffering no diminution of dignity—whereas for the man in the same circumstances, the best we can wish is that he should throw his Horace at his patron's head, and 'list incontinently, or start for the diggings. He has no such privilege; and his patience must not go too far, under penalty of everybody's disdain.

The presence of the brother in this family of Brontes, which has been the subject of so many dissertations upon the condition of women, seems to us to change the *venue* entirely, and make the subject a much wider one. The women of the house did not like their occupation; what occupation would have contented these restless and self-devouring spirits? But the only one whose end was worse, and lower, and more debased than his beginning, was the brother. Civilisation, if that is the sinner, was far more bitterly in fault towards Branwell Bronte than towards Charlotte. It was the man for whose talents there was no outlet, for whose life there seemed no place in the world: it was not the woman, who did her duty, and in her season had her reward;

and so far as this example goes, the theory of undue limitation and unjust restraint in respect to women certainly does not hold. The limitation, the restraint, the bondage, the cruel laws and barriers of conventional life, may, notwithstanding, remain as cruel as ever, but their application is certainly not harder upon the daughters of the race than upon its sons.

For who does not know, who knows the world of modern society—and if no such case is near and present to ourselves, let us be thankful—how many young men are to be found throughout England, but especially in London, recently emerged from Oxford or Cambridge, educated after the highest standard of modern education, full of general ability, considerable enough to pass for genius with many of their friends, well-mannered, well-read, and neither idle nor vicious, who, notwithstanding, linger on that eminence of youthful training perhaps for years, feeling themselves able for anything, and doing nothing, till the chances are that, out of pure disgust, the more generous spirits among them throw their culture to the winds, and rush into something for which all their education had tended rather to disqualify than to train them? Perhaps parental intention—poor scapegoat of many a failure—has destined them for the Church; and but for the slight drawback of having no great faith in any particular doctrine, they are, in fact, better qualified to be incumbents of a tolerable living, than for anything else save the position of squire, which would suit them best of all. But the lads bear a conscience, and will not be ordained—not, at least, until the very latest shift. What are they to do? Sometimes, in spite of Mr. Thackeray, it happens that a man may be a very clever fellow, without being able even to write a newspaper article. So many as are able to do this feat "throw themselves into literature," as a matter of course, and something good comes of it in a few instances; but the majority swell the number of those unfortunates who do rueful comic stories, and live upon the humours of London cabmen and street-boys, sometimes advancing for a charmed moment to the beatitude of *Punch*. This is no fiction; we do not say "one-half" the young *alumni* of our universities are in this position, or represent it as a universal fate; but the class is large, numerous, full of capabilities, able to be of infinite service to its generation, if it but knew or saw what to do; and how, in the face of this, we should recognise a special injustice to woman, or groan over a conventional limitation of her powers of working, in presence of the very same restraint acting still more unfortunately upon the more natural and stronger workman, we cannot allow or perceive.

Yes, the rules of civilisation are hard, and conventional life is cruel; but the injury does not limit itself by any arbitrary law of sex, or imaginary line of demarcation between men and women. The burden lies upon all those educated classes, who, without fortune, have yet a position and habits which seem to make it needful that they should earn their bread by the toil of their brain, rather than by the labour of their hands—who must be banished to the antipodes before they can permit themselves to take up the original tools of nature, and who are in a much greater degree slaves of society and of their own social standing, than either the assured rich or the certain poor. In this vast London, which is the centre and focus of our extremity of civilisation, there are crowds of young men, trained to that pitch of bodily perfection and development which English public schools and universities, without doubt, keep up to a higher degree than any other educational institutions in the world—with a high average of intelligence, and all the advantages which are to be derived from that system of mental training which this country approves as the most complete—who, nevertheless, are as entirely at sea as to the best method of employing themselves and their faculties, as any woman with a feminine education equivalent to theirs could possibly find herself. Teaching, literature, art, which they have practised as amateurs to the admiration of their own families—or, last alternatives of all, Australia or a curacy, lie before them, which to choose. Even female novels, and the stories in minor magazines about "proud pale girls" who support themselves by the work of their own hands, are not less profitable or less noble than the stories in other minor magazines about freshmen and town adventures, to which civilisation drives scores who never learnt to dig, and can see no other way than this of helping themselves; and if it is hard to be a governess, let no one suppose it is much lighter or more delightful to be a tutor. The burden, the restraint, the limitation is true, but it is one of no partial or one-sided application; and this bondage of society, of conventional life, and of a false individual pride, bears with a more dismal and discouraging blight upon men; who are the natural labourers and bread-winners, than it can ever do upon women constrained by special circumstances to labour for their own bread.

As for needlewomen, few people who think on the subject will need to be told what a heavy equipoise of this evil all great towns carry within them. Poor penmen, lost far away down the miserable ranks of penny-a-liners—poor, poor, shabby unemployed clerks, as utterly incapable of using any implement of labour, save the sharp iron nibs of the pen, as ever woman was incapable of more than her needle—poor fluctuating vagabonds, who live by directing circulars for tradesmen, and to whom an election is a carnival. There is little comfort in contemplating this widened prospect of misery, nevertheless it is the real state of the case. The pen—not the pen of Savage or of Chatterton, or any other shipwrecked genius, but the mere mechanical instrument, which makes out cobblers' accounts, and keeps huxters' books, and directs circulars—counts its miserable craftsmen by thousands, down far below the ken of the criticising world, and sends sighs as pitiful out of cellars and garret's, as any that ever have breathed their melancholy inspiration into the "Song of the Shirt."*

---

* A poem by Thomas Hood, well-known in his day as a writer of comic verse and social commentary. "Song of the Shirt," a poem about the distress of the needlewomen or milliners, was first published in the Christmas number of *Punch* in 1843, and was immediately successful [Editor's note].

Let us not attempt to ignore this dark and sad other side to all the comfort and luxury of our modern life; but at the same time let no special complaint appropriate the greater share of the injury. It is a universal injury, an evil common to the time; it is not a one-sided and newly-discovered aggravation of the wrongs and disabilities of women.

There is, however, in almost all public discussions upon the social position of women, an odd peculiarity which betrays itself here with great distinctness: it is, that writers on the subject invariably treat this half of humankind as a distinct creation rather than as a portion of a general race—not as human creatures primarily, and women in the second place, but as women, and nothing but women—a distinct sphere of being, a separate globe of existence, to which different rules, different motives, an altogether distinct economy, belong. One would almost suppose, to take modern prelections upon this subject for our guide, that a different and more delicate gospel, a law of finer and more elaborate gradations, must be necessary for this second creation; and that the old morality which slumped the whole race in one, was a barbarous imposition upon the nature, not human, but feminine, which ought to have had more delicate handling. Yet in spite of all the new light which new experience throws, it still remains true that there is only one law and one Gospel, and that God has made provision for one moral nature, and not for two, even in those commandments which are exceeding broad. One fundamental and general ground of humanity is common to men and to women; one faith is propounded to both, without alteration of terms or change of inducements; one hope and one undiscriminated heaven shines on the ending of their days; they are born precisely after the same manner, and by the same event die;—they are, in fact—different, distinct, and individual as every detail of their responsible existence may be—one race; and without the slightest inclination to ignore or lessen the essential differences between them, we can see no true philosophy in any view of this subject which does not recognise the ground they hold in common, as well as the peculiar standing which they hold apart.

Let us not be misunderstood: we are not endeavouring to establish the "equality" of the two. Equality is the mightiest of humbugs—there is no such thing in existence; and the idea of opening the professions and occupations and governments of men to women, seems to us the vainest as well as the vulgarest of chimeras. God has ordained visibly, by all the arrangements of nature and of providence, one sphere and kind of work for a man and another for a woman. He has given them different constitutions, different organisations, a perfectly distinct and unmistakable identity. Yet above and beyond and beneath all their differences, he has made them primarily human creatures, answering, in the unity of an indivisible race, to His own government and laws; rebelling against them with a simultaneous impulse; moved by the same emotions; bound by the same obligations; under all diversities of detail, one creation. What folly could be greater than the supposition, that in this time of great public events, the public interest and opinion which follows breathlessly, with tears and with triumph, the course of affairs, for example, in India, should require two expressions instead of one, or two currents to flow in? The sympathy, the enthusiasm, the swell of answering heroic impulse, which the sight of heroes produces everywhere, is not communicated from man to man and from woman to woman, but from one human heart to another, in defiance of all limitations. The two creatures are as different as creatures made for different vocations, and different offices, can well be; yet in all the great fundamental principles of their mind and nature, the two are one.

At all events, most dear and impartial reader, whether you agree with us or not, we are bound to declare we think so—and, thinking so we cannot avoid thinking that there is a perfectly preposterous quantity of nonsense spoken about womankind by most of those people who profess to have studied the subject. To have studied the subject means, as we apprehend the words, to have formed certain theories upon it, cleverly propped up by certain facts, or, with a philosophy more sincere and single-minded, to have simply mistaken a little limited private circle for an epitome of society and the world: one or other of which blunders we cannot but think every one falls into, who represents Woman as a separate existence, suffering under the action of special principles which affect *her*, without affecting generally the whole race.

How then about our unmarried sisters, our unmarried daughters, that alarming independent army which a bold calculator affirms to amount to "one-half" of the women of these kingdoms? If there is really one-fourth of our population in these astounding circumstances, we fear the question is one beyond the power of the circulating libraries, and that even the remaining three-fourths, English, Scotch, and Irish, can scarcely solve so big a problem. On the whole, one would suppose that the best expedient for such an emergency was, after all, Australia, where there is no Act of Parliament to compel emigrant ladies to marry within three days of their landing, and where at least there is room and scope for the energy which over-civilisation cramps and keeps in bondage. If it is true that so large a proportion of women stand in circumstances of isolation so entire, and self-responsibility so complete, it is certainly very weak and very foolish of them to sacrifice, for a mere piece of womanish delicacy, that safety-valve which men in the same position avail themselves of so much—especially, we repeat, as it is certain there is no Act of Parliament coercing them to the necessity of marriage as soon as they have touched the wealthy shores of our great young colony; and the benevolence of leaving a little room among the crowd might well indemnify an emigrant sisterhood for the momentary joke of going out to be married, which every one among them had it quite in her own hands to prove untrue. If the evil has gone so far, or nearly so far—if the half of British women have to support themselves, and to do that by means of three, or at most four, limited occupations—to wit, teaching, needlework, domestic service, and novel-writing—we humbly submit that a little watchmaking, bookkeeping, or jewellery, additional thereto, would be a very inadequate remedy. To upset the ordinary social economy for any clamant grievance of a time, however just, would be the most shortsighted and ruinous policy imaginable. It is, besides, what is still more to the purpose, impossible. These great questions of the common weal are happily impervious to all philosophies, theories, and reasonings. They arrange themselves by laws of their own, which the warmest appeal of eloquence, and the most infallible array of argument, can neither reach nor influence. Nowhere in all the civilised world is the power of the Press so great as in this empire; but the *Times* itself, backed by every lesser brother of the art, cannot prop up a failing trade, or persuade the master-craftsman to employ a dearer or less profitable class of labour. Inevitable rules of necessity and self-interest sway the whole social economy. Obdurate as flint to all kinds of intellectual persuasions, it is perfectly elastic to every practical necessity, and answers to the changes of the time as a ship answers to its helm. If female work, which is always so much cheaper, is available in such a quantity as to enter into real competition with the work of men, we may safely trust the employers of Great Britain to know their own interests; if it is not, no sentiment is likely to have the slightest effect upon them. Trade, like civilisation, is an irrational and abstract influence, upon which individual hardships make no impression whatever. It has no particular regard for men, none for women, and very small concern for the general interests of the race. When it suits its own purposes to employ women, and even children, though at the cost of all health, loveliness, and domestic comfort, it does so without the slightest compunction; and if it had command of an equal amount of female material for other crafts as it has for cotton-mills and had for collieries, would doubtless employ them with the most sublime impartiality. No, let no one suppose it—there is no conspiracy of mankind to keep women excluded from the workshop or the manufactory. On the contrary, the work of women, if it abounded to only half the extent, could always undersell the work of men, and, consequently, would always retain a certain degree of unfair advantage. But if civilisation has unduly increased the class of poor gentlemen and poor gentlewomen—if the advance of education and refinement adds yearly to the number of those who will rather starve genteelly than "descend in the social scale"—let nobody run away from the real question with a false idea of special or peculiar injustice to women. The real drawback is, that while the rough work of nature always remains in one quarter or another, ready for those who will work at it, delicate labour for delicate hands is not capable of more than a certain degree of extension;

and that, under this burden of our social state, women, to whose hands Providence has not committed the establishment and support of families, are neither the only nor the primary sufferers.

Nevertheless, there can be no doubt that many people of sense, looking on while somebody else's clever son, finding nothing to do with himself, falls into disgust and uselessness, and that don't-care-for-anything superiority which mature minds find intolerable in youth, must have felt that the best thing they could wish for the lad was just one of those thoughtless, reckless, imprudent marriages, which are the bug-bears of all good boys and girls, and careful fathers and mothers; and his female contemporary is not less likely to be benefited by the same prescription; but imprudent marriages, philosophers tell us, are not in the ascendant, while prudence and regard for "social position" is. We are past the condition in which girls and boys, having nothing else to do, fall in love. Why should they not fall in love? The condition is natural, and so even is its attendant heartbreak, which does not kill the young people: but the matter changes when, instead of this love in idleness, the young men and the young women alike take to philosophy, and the latter concern themselves with questions about the relations of the sexes, which are by no means seemly subjects for their handling, and lead them into paths where they can scarcely fail to soil their feet. This volunteer occupation of women is a more disagreeable symptom of the time than the want of legitimate employments for them. False delicacies there may be in ordinary education, but nothing can well be more utterly false than that artificial courage which tempts many women, simply because they are women, to rush into subjects of which they can have little practical knowledge and no personal experience—to discuss the delicate laws of marriage, the subtle and intricate mutual rights and wrongs of the two great portions of humanity, and to make arbitrary and sweeping condemnations of those who may, in the real course and practice of life, have neither leisure nor inclination to defend themselves. Marriage is possibly an event of more absorbing importance in the life of a woman than in that of a man; but if it is, this mere fact is not enough to make her the natural critic and special pleader of the whole subject: rather the other way, for extreme personal interest is not supposed, in general cases, to clear the vision or steady the judgment. Yet we find it not only occupying a most prominent place in a considerable proportion of the feminine teachings of the day, but even earnestly recommended to the mind of young womankind as a subject on which they are bound to inform themselves. Do nothing of the sort, young ladies! Don't come to any conscientious convictions on the subject. Don't be persuaded to believe that you are more intimately and lastingly concerned in the matter than your lover is, or have any private course of casuistry to go through, in your professional position as a woman. If you have really and seriously come to the conclusion that to be married is the natural and best condition of existence, be married, for heaven's sake, and be done with it! Every human creature is bound to her duty (let us say it boldly), whether it has the solace of love to sweeten it or no. It may seem a frightful doctrine, yet it is the merest dictate of ordinary sense and wisdom. If a woman is certain that she is more fitted to be the mistress of a house, and the mother of a family, than anything else, and that this is her true vocation—spite of all natural human prejudices in favour of the natural preliminary of marriage, we are bound to declare that her first duty, as it seems to us, is to *be* married, even though it should be quite impossible for her to persuade herself that she is "in love" before. But if her sense of duty is not equal to this venture, the very worst thing she can do is to console herself by concluding most marriages to be unhappy, and the estate, in the greatest number of instances, an unholy state. And it is just this hankering after a condition of which she will neither accept the risk nor relinquish the thought, and of which, having no experience, she is quite unqualified to be a judge, which exposes unmarried women of philosophic tendencies—not young enough to be judged leniently as under the glamour of youth, and not old enough to have their arbitrary fancies subdued by the mellowing touch of age—to the disapproval of the sympathetic critic, and the derision of hastier judgments.

And it is also true, and a fact worth remembering, that the maiden lady is not an invention of these times. There were unmarried women long ago, before civilisation had made such fatal progress: while all the heroines in all the novels were still married at eighteen—before the life of Charlotte Bronte had even begun, or there was a woman in existence qualified to write it,—unmarried ladies existed in this world, where nothing is ever new. Judging by literature, indeed, Scotland herself, our respected mither, seems always to have had a very fair average of unmarried daughters; and for the instruction of womankind in general, and novel-writers in particular, we are bound to add that there were three such personages as Miss Austin, Miss Edgeworth, and Miss Ferrier, novelists of the old world, and representatives of the three respective kingdoms, whom none of their successors in the craft have yet been able to displace from the popular liking; so that we might suppose it was rather late in the day to begin *de novo* to teach unmarried women how, in spite of their unfortunate circumstances, it is still possible for them to keep themselves respected and respectable. Many hundred, nay, thousand years ago, there was even a certain characteristic and remarkable person called Miriam, who, wilful and womanlike, and unquestionably unmarried, was still so far from being disrespected or unimportant, that a whole nation waited for her, till she was able to join their journey. Our age, which likes so much to declare itself the origin of changes, is not the inventor of feminine celibacy. There were unmarried women before our time, and there will be unmarried women after it. Nay, not only so—but

Paul the apostle, eighteen hundred years ago, gave anything but an inferior place to the unwedded maidens of his time: "She that is unmarried careth for the things that belong to the Lord, how she may please the Lord," says the writer of the Epistles; and many an unmarried woman since his day has proved his statement, happily unwitting of all the philosophies which should prove to her how lonely and comfortless she ought to find herself, and what a hard case hers was, and how, notwithstanding, it behoved her to make some certain amount of sad and patient exertion to vindicate her womanly credit with the world.

Might it not be as well, in a general way, does any one think, to try Paul's version of the matter, and leave the statistics and the laws of marriage quietly alone?

We presume there must be something terribly wrong with that famous windmill, which has borne the assault of so many fiery knights, the thing called Female Education. Since the days of Hannah More—and how much further back beyond that virtuous era who will venture to say?—everybody has broken a spear upon this maiden fortress; yet, judging from the undiminished fervour with which it is still assaulted in the present day, we conclude that no one has succeeded in any measure of reformation. We do not profess to be very learned in the question—the mysteries of a female college have never been penetrated by our profane eyes, though we profess, like most other people, to have seen the product, and to be aware, in a limited way, what kind of persons our young countrywomen are, and in what manner they manage to fulfil the duties of the after-life, for which, in the first place, their education, in general, does not seem to unfit them. *That* is something in its favour to begin with—but we cannot help being rather doubtful about the value of the report as to the frivolity of female education, when we find the strange inaccuracies and blunders into which its critics fall regarding matters of social usage open to everybody's observation. There is that wise book, for instance, *Friends in Council,* which all proper people quote and admire. Wise books, we are ashamed to confess, inspire us with an instinctive aversion; yet, notwithstanding, we would quote honestly, if the volume were at our hand. There are sundry essays and conversations there touching upon this subject, in one of which the oracle informs us that it is no wonder to find women inaccessible to reason, considering all the homage and false worship with which they are surrounded in society during the first part of their lives, and which is all calculated to persuade them of their own superlative and angelical gifts, and elevation above ordinary fact and information. Is that so? Perhaps if every young girl who shone her little day in polite society, happened to be a great beauty, intoxicating everybody who approached her with that irresistible charm, it might be partially true; for that men, and women too, fall out of their wits at sight of a lovely face, and are beguiled into all manner of foolishness by its glamour, is indisputable; but even then we should decidedly claim it as a necessary condition, that the beauty herself had no young brothers to bring her down to common ground, and only a gracious sire of romance, never worried in the City, nor disturbed by factious opposition in the House. As for all ranks less than the highest, the thing is preposterous and out of the question; and even in the highest, every young girl is not a beauty, and society generously provides its little budget of mortifications for the moral advantage of neophytes. But for the daughter of the professional man, of the merchant, of all the throngs of middle life, to which, in reality, all great rules must primarily apply, if there is any truth in them,—what can possibly be more false, we had almost said more absurd? There are not days of euphuism or extravagant compliments. We do not permit the common acquaintances of common society to administer serious flattery to our womankind; and an average young lady of a moderate degree of intelligence, we apprehend, would—so far is the thing out of usage—be much more likely to consider herself affronted than honoured by the old hyperboles of admiration; and as for the home, good lack! what do *Friends in Council* know about it? Fathers who have bills to meet and clients to satisfy; mothers who are straining income and expenditure to a needful junction, and who have all the cares of the house upon their shoulders; brothers who vex the young lady's soul before her time with premature buttons,—are these the kind of surroundings to persuade a woman that she is angelical, and make her giddy with the incense of flattery and admiration? We appeal to everybody who knows anything of common life, and the existence of the family, which is true; and we humbly submit that one might object to take for gospel, without more effectual demonstration, anything else which the *Friends in Council* choose to advance upon female education, or any other of the vexed questions concerning womankind.

Again, another writer, whom we cannot place by the side of Mr. Helps, yet who ought probably, being a woman, to be better informed, writes thus of the same unfortunate girls, who are supposed by the previous authority to be dazzled out of their wits by the flattery of society.

"Tom, Dick, and Harry leave school and plunge into life; 'the girls' likewise finish their education, come home, and stay at home. That is enough. Nobody thinks it needful to waste a care upon them. Bless them, pretty dears, how sweet they are! papa's nosegay of beauty to adorn his drawing-room. He delights to give them all they can desire—clothes, amusements, society; he and mamma together take every domestic care off their hands.... From babyhood they are given to understand that helplessness is feminine and beautiful; helpfulness—except in certain received forms of manifestation—unwomanly and ugly. The boys may do a thousand things which are 'not proper for girls.'"

Where, oh where, are to be found those adorable papas who delight to give their daughters everything they can desire?—those mammas most dutiful, who take every domestic care off their hands? Are they in Bloomsbury? are they in Belgravia? might we have a chance of finding them in beautiful Edinburgh, or in rich Manchester? And where shall we be able to lay hands upon this ecstatic conception of the boys and brothers, who have learned self-dependence all their lives, are helpful and handy, and may do a thousand things which are not proper for the girls? We should very much like to know; and so, we do not doubt, would a very large number of young ladies still more immediately concerned. For, alas! we are obliged to confess that the greater number of the papas whom we have the personal honour of including in our acquaintance, are apt to hold unjustifiably strong opinions on the subject of milliners' bills—that the majority of the mammas are provokingly disposed to provide for the proper regulation of the future households of their daughters, by advancing these young ladies to an economical participation in domestic difficulties; and as for the boys, did anybody ever know a well-conditioned boy who was good for anything in this life but making mischief? In this holiday season one can speak feelingly—who is it that keeps the house in din and disorder from morning to night—who are the ogres who bring on mamma's headaches, who upset the girls' workboxes, who lose the books, who mislay the music, who play tricks upon the visitors, who run riot in the unmitigated luxury of total idleness, who are about as helpful as the kittens are, and whom the very littlest of little sisters patronise as incapables, who can do nothing for themselves? Oh happy people who have boys at home for the holidays! do you need to pause before answering the question?

"God bless all large families!" says a recent writer of sense and feeling, who knows something of the life of such, and who finds in them the best nurseries for mutual forbearance, good-temper, and kindness. Large families are common enough, let us be thankful, in our much-populated island; and nobody need fear that young women brought up in these will be educated in undue idleness, or with false ideas of their own angelic qualities. Among all those classes with whom economy is a needful virtue, every one who knows family life, knows very well that it is the girls who are in reality the helpful portion of the household—so much and so unquestionably so, that everybody congratulates the mother of many children who has one or two elder daughters at the head of them, on the fact that her first-born are girls not boys—natural coadjutors in her many duties; and those delightful urchins of Mr. Leech's, who make tents out of hoop-petticoats, and triumph with "the things Clara stuffs out her hair with," may safely be trusted to keep Clara from undue elation even under the intoxicating flatteries of the only person whom English society permits to flatter its daughter—her lover.

We might well add, what is a fact very patent to many people, that the chief secretaries and helpers of men largely engaged in public business, are in very many cases their daughters—oftener a great deal than their sons—and that from Milton and Sir Thomas More down to Fowell Buxton, those filial auxiliaries have attended the steps of great men in a singularly large proportion. To descend to a very much lower platform, it is his daughter who keeps the tradesman's books, and makes out his bills, almost universally; and every one who condescends to make personal visits to the baker's and the butcher's, and the fishmonger's, must have seen the little railed-in desk in the corner, where the grown-up daughter, if there is such a person, finds her invariable place. The amanuensis of the higher class, worked remorselessly by the great philanthropist, who finds his most devoted servant in his female child, and the accountant of the lower, whose bills are not always extremely legible, but who is kept at her post with an unvarying steadiness, ought to find some account made of them in books about women; and the almost entire omission of so large a class, proves better, perhaps, than anything we can say would do, how entirely it is a view out of a corner which is given to the public as the general aspect of womankind.

We do not speak abstractly, or in general terms; we say plainly and simply, that whatever theoretical faults there may be in English female education, it turns out women as little apt to fail in the duties of their life as any class of human creatures, male or female, under the sun. We say that it is a mere exploded piece of antique nonsense to assert that society flatters women into foolishness, or permits them to be flattered; and that those who find in the young girls of our families only helpless nosegays of ornament, unqualified to do service either to themselves or other people, are either totally unacquainted with household life, or have a determined "cast" in their vision, not to be remedied. All these things are patent and visible to every simple observer who has no theory to support; but truth often suffers herself to be obscured out of sheer unbelief in the power of misrepresentation; and we do not doubt that many a mother of a family, who knows a great deal better if she but took time to consider, receives the decision which comes to her in a book, with a show of authority, and an appearance of wisdom, supposing, though it does not tally with her own experience, that somehow or other it must be true. The next step is, that the wise book gets put into the hands of young people, to fill them at their outset with false ideas—not of themselves, for we have generally vanity enough, all of us, to keep us clear, in our own persons, of any share in the unjust condemnation—but, what is much worse, of their neighbours. We protest against the whole system loudly and earnestly. Why a young girl should have the disagreeable idea of sex dinned into her ears all day long—why she should be taught to make the most sweeping and wholesale condemnation of other classes round her—to believe that the servant-maidens who encompass her in almost every action of her life, and with whom she very likely holds a natural sympathy, are in a state of such universal depravity and degradation that the greater part of them are married, if at all, "just a week or two before maternity;" and that among the married people to whom she looks up, "a happy marriage is the most uncommon lot of all," and the condition most frequently "an unholy state,"—we confess we are totally at a loss to perceive. What is likely to be the natural product of such teaching? A woman perpetually self-conscious, no longer a spontaneous human creature, but a representative of her sex—conscious of purity in her own person, but doubting every other—fancying that she has found out a new condition, and a new development of feminity, yet holding fast by the hundred-year-old traditions of frivolous education and social flattery—"pretty dolls, the playthings of our lords and masters," and all the other humbug of ancient times—fancying, if she does not marry, that it is because her views are higher and her principles more elevated than those of the vulgar persons who do; and that, looking over their heads, she is able to perceive how unfit they are for the relations which she herself will not accept—a woman who sincerely pities other people's children, and other people's servants, and looks on with an observant scientific compassion at the world, which is going gradually to ruin, and out of which she is half afraid good-sense will die in her own person. Is it to this extent of wisdom and superiority that we desire to see our daughters grow?—is this the model after which we would willingly frame them? For our own part, we can only say, let us have back *Pamela*, and *Clarissa*, and the *Spectator*. If our young people are to be instructed in the social vices, by way of establishing their own morality, let Richardson once more be the support of virtue. It is better to tell the story of the much-tried milkmaid, which is visibly a fiction, than to preach philosophical suggestions of universal wickedness, which are supposed to be true.

It is very odd to remark how questionable many of those productions are, which are warranted by the newspapers to be suitable gift-books for young ladies. Chance threw in our way, some time ago, a little volume with a very innocent title, fresh from America, and the production of an elder sister of the world-famous Mrs. Stowe. With such a name on the title-page, who could entertain any doubts about *Letters to the People on Health and Happiness?* We did not certainly, though we were somewhat astounded to find the little book adorned with anatomical diagrams: but we cannot say that we were at all impressed with this symptom of the increased elevation and profundity of the age, when we found this volume to consist, not of an elderly lady's kindly counsels to her country-folk upon subjects within her own knowledge, but, in the first place, of surgical lectures upon the construction of the human frame; and, in the second, of an anatomy much more shocking, a sort of morbid dissection of the health and morals of the United States, full of hints and implications of the most unbelievable evil. Doing all justice to the entire lack of evil intention, or even of evil consciousness, on the part of the writer of this and of other such productions, we are obliged to add our sincere conviction that no French novel under rigorous *taboo*, bears more, or perhaps as much, mischief in it, as one of those didactic expositions of mysterious and secret vice, those public whispers of scandal, which do not indeed take away personal reputation, but which, so far as any one believes them, throw a blight upon the universal fair fame, and suggest to the inexperienced a horrible suspicion of everybody and of everything around them. Private scandal has no cloak to keep it from the contempt of every one whose opinion is worth caring for. Public scandal, which—strange shame to think of! is to be found in no hands more frequent than in those of women, puts on the robes of the preacher, and asserts for itself one of the highest of moral uses. Nothing in this country, which we have ever seen or heard of, dares go so far as the Letters of Miss Beecher. But why, of all classes in the world, our tender young girls, the margin of innocence, and, if you will, ignorance, which we are all heartily glad to believe in, fringing the garment of the sadder world, should be instructed in all the delicate social questions of an artificial life, and put up to every possible emergency of all the relationships between men and women, it seems to us impossible to conceive. Not to say that it is ridiculously unfair in the first instance, for people don't write books for the lads their compeers, instructing them how to arrange their love-affairs, and informing them what the young ladies think of their general conduct. The unfortunate boys have to collect their information on this subject at first hand, or to take the hints of their favourite novels; and we really think it might be a happy experiment to suspend all the talk for a generation, and leave their partners to follow their example.

We have left ourselves no great space to consider the circumstances of that inconsiderable and inferior portion of the feminine population of these kingdoms, the married women, for whose benefit—law itself has been moving, and Parliament talking itself hoarse. We say for whose benefit but we are glad to think that the new Act, whatever its action may be, so far from having been called for by any clamour of public necessity, is more a matter of theoretical justice, proved by individual cases, than of anything more broad and general. The progress of popular opinion had made it notable that there was one case in the jurisprudence of the country; in which a man of the richer classes could get himself relieved, and in which a man of the poorer could not; along with which, universal experience proved likewise, that, save under the unlikely circumstances of a sudden and extraordinary prostration of morals, divorce was by no means likely to be a favourite speculation in this empire. It is not very much with divorce, however, that women have to do. Save in cases horrible and extreme, *that* is not the woman's remedy. No law, no argument, no manner of thinking, can change the primitive order of nature; and in spite of all the risks of female inconsequence and vehemence, experience and reason alike prove that a woman must be frightfully put to it before she will cast from herself the name, if that were all, which is borne by her children, and which she herself has borne for years. This looks a small and superficial consideration, but there is more in it than meets the eye; it is one great demonstration, subtle and universal, of that different position of man and woman, which no law can alter. We can conceive no circumstances, for our own part, which could make the position of a woman, who had divorced her husband, tolerable to the ordinary feelings of the women of this country. So far as women are concerned, it must always remain the dreadful alternative of an evil which has such monstrous and unnatural aggravations as to be beyond all limits of possible endurance. We cannot comprehend it else; and with safe means of separation extended to them, very few even of the wives most bitterly insulted would desire, we should suppose, to adopt this last means of escape. For the power of lawful and formal separation placed within their reach, and for the possible security of their property and earnings, women unhappily compelled to bring their miseries into public vision may well be grateful; and we can suppose, that for women without children the new regulations must be all that could be desired. But who shall open the terrible complication of the rights of fathers and mothers? What Solomon shall venture to divide between the two that most precious and inalienable of all treasures, the unfortunate child whose very existence stands as a ceaseless protest of nature against their disjunction? From this most painful branch of the question the law retreats, not daring to put in its hand. The present state of affairs is not just—is cruel, frightful, almost intolerable—but national legislation, and all the wisdom of the wise, can find no arbitrary and universal law which could be juster. There is none, let us seek it where we will. Crime itself does not abrogate natural rights and quench natural love; and so long as there are divorced and separated parents, there must be in one way or other, on one side or another, a certain amount of painful and bitter injustice. Women, so far as the law goes, are at present the sufferers, and not the benefited parties; but if the arrangement were reversed, the principle would still be exactly the same. Partition can be made of worldly goods—security obtained for the wages of labour and the gifts of inheritance—but the great gift of God to married people remains undividable—a difficulty which the law shrinks from encountering, and which no human power can make plain. This is not a hardship of legislation, but one of nature. We are very slow to acknowledge the hardships of nature in these days, and still more reluctant to put up with them. All the progress which we have really made, and all the additional and fictitious progress which exists in our imagination, prompt us to the false idea that there is a remedy for everything, and that no pain is inevitable. But there *are* pains which are inevitable in spite of philosophy, and conflicting claims to which Solomon himself could do no justice. We are not complete syllogisms, to be kept in balance by intellectual regulations, we human creatures. We are of all things and creatures in the world the most incomplete; and there are conditions of our warfare, for the redress of which, in spite of all the expedients of social economy, every man and woman, thrown by whatever accident out of the course of nature, must be content to wait perhaps for years, perhaps for a life long, perhaps till the consummation of all things.

It is, however, an unfortunate feature in the special literature which professes to concern itself with women, that it is in great part limited to personal "cases" and individual details, and those incidents of domestic life which it is so easy, by the slightest shade of mistaken colouring, to change the real character of. The disputed questions and aggrieved feelings which rise between near relatives are, of all other human matters, the most difficult to settle; and arbitrary critics, who see this "case" and the other, from their own point of view—who are most probably informed only on one side, and have all their own theories and prejudices to sway their judgment—at all times make sad havoc with known facts and principles of human conduct, and often offer us a ludicrous travestie of the life which they profess to judge and set in order. All the greater questions of existence are common to men and women alike, and common to the higher literature which belongs equally to both. A kind of literature which is meant exclusively for one, must of necessity be an inferior species, and limits itself by its very profession of wisdom. Perhaps, if some pedagogic genius of "the male sect" were to address moral volumes to the husbands and brothers of England—to instruct them in the rights, privileges, and duties of their sex, and expound their true and wisest position towards the other, the eyes of female moralists might be opened to the true nature of their own prelections. No man, however, does so; the young men are supposed to be sufficiently instructed by the Gospel and the law, home and literature, life itself, and ordinary experience; the Gospel and the law of Heaven—the literature and the home of British purity—life in its truest sense, and experience of all those greatest incidents and events which guide it, belong to women as fully and as freely as they do to men. It is possible in these days to be well-read, well-informed—to have the loftiest poetry, the highest philosophy, the purest eloquence, open to one's mind, for one's own private delight and improvement, without knowing Latin or Greek; and Latin and Greek even are not impossible achievements, though they form the most remarkable difference, so far as we are aware, between the education of our sons and that of our daughters. But the supplementary literature of a sex—the private and particular address to one portion of humanity—is, however high its professions, nothing better than a confession of foolishness. It is as much as to say, over and over, with an undesirable repetition, that what is enough for the brother is not enough for the sister—that what the poets and philosophers, and even the apostles and prophets, have said and written, is primarily for *him*, and not for *her*; and that a secondary course of morals is the necessary food for the less noble capacity. If women in general adopt this theory, nobody of course has any right to thwart them;

but every honest critic, loving the benefit of the race, which is not a question of one but of both, ought to raise his voice against so petty and partial a policy. Everything which lowers the mind to a primary consideration of its own personal feelings, circumstances, and emotions, or which sets it speculating on the individual emotions, circumstances, and feelings of its neighbours, is in the end a process of debasement; and we should think it a very miserable prospect for the future, could we suppose, that while literature in general, and their Bible, is all we adopt for the moral guidance of our boys, our girls required the artificial bolstering of a quite additional support of virtue; and to protect them from becoming useless, vain, discontented, repining, and good-for-nothing, it was necessary to support a staff of volunteer lecturers, to communicate to them a certain *esprit du corps*, and make their womanhood, instead of a fact of nature, a kind of profession. If this is the case, is it not an odd mistake—not for the young people in love, who are privileged to say anything, but for our very philosophers themselves, who do all the supplementary feminine morality—to hold fast still by the old assertion that womanhood is purer by native right than manhood, and that women still are next to the angels? If they are, they ought to need rather less than more lecturing than falls to the share of the more obdurate rebel; either one thing or the other must be untrue.

Source: Reprinted from *Blackwood's Edinburgh Magazine* (February 1858).

"THE GRIEVANCES OF WOMEN"

A number of invitations have been sent out lately to ladies of all classes to attend a meeting of women in St. James's Hall (I think) in the beginning of this month. It is intended to press upon the notice of the new Government the claims of women to the suffrage. It will, no doubt, be largely attended, but not by the present writer or many others of her way of thinking, and that for the weakest of all possible reasons; but the occasion furnishes a not inappropriate opportunity of expressing some of the opinions of quiet and otherwise voiceless women, with as much dislike to platforms as their grandmothers would have had, upon the subject of feminine grievances, sentimental and otherwise.

Our reason for not going to this meeting or any like it is simple. We are so weak as to be offended deeply and wounded by the ridicule which has not yet ceased to be poured upon every such manifestation. We shrink from the laugh of rude friends, the smile of the gentler ones. The criticisms which are applied, not to one question or another, but to the general qualities of women, affect our temper unpleasantly. We would rather, for our parts, put up even with a personal wrong in silence more or less indignant than hear ourselves laughed at in all the tones of the gamut and held up to coarse ridicule. This is a confession of poverty of spirit and timidity of mind which I am entirely aware of, and somewhat ashamed to utter; but it belongs to my generation. In this way, I am sorry to say, a great many of the newspapers and public speakers of the coarser sort have us in their power, and are able to quash the honest opinion of a great many women whose views on the subject might be worth knowing perhaps, being the outcome of experience and average good sense, if no more. It is a disagreeable effort even to write on the subject for this very reason. Fair and honourable criticism is a thing which no accustomed writer will shrink from. Some of us have had a good deal of it in our day, and have not complained; even criticism which the subject of it may feel to be unfair, sometimes is not unbeneficial; but to be met with an insolent laugh, a storm of ridiculous epithets, and that coarse superiority of sex which a great many men think it not unbecoming to exhibit to women is a mode of treatment which affects our temper, and those nerves which the harshest critic is condescendingly willing to allow as a female property. I admit for my part the superiority of sex. It is not a pretty subject nor one for my handling. Yet it is a fact. As belonging to the physical part of our nature, which is universal—whereas the mental and moral part is not so—that superiority must always tell. It will keep women in subjection as long as the race endures. We may say and do what we will, but the fact will remain so, as it has always done. I do not believe that on any broad area culture or progress will largely affect it. But this is not an argument which it might be supposed fine minds would care to appeal to. It is the argument of the coalheaver, and unanswerable in his hands. As a matter of fact, however, it is not only the coalheaver who employs it, but a great many accomplished persons in other walks of life who might be supposed very capable of meeting and overcoming feminine reasoning without recourse to that great weapon. The one good result which has come of the many recent agitations on the subject is, I think, that the strong abuse poured upon those women who have not shrunk from exposing themselves to ridicule on these questions has a little turned the stomachs (it seems impossible to speak otherwise than coarsely upon such a subject) of the more generous order of men. This is a result, limited as it is, which never could have been attained had all women been as cowardly as I confess to being. The dash in our faces of such an epithet as that of the 'shrieking sisterhood,' for example, more effectual than any dead cat or rotten egg, would have driven us back, whatever our wrongs had been, into indignant and ashamed silence. But it is well that there are some bolder spirits who have encountered the storm, and made it apparent not only that rotten eggs are no arguments, but that the throwing of them is not a noble office. I am glad to forget the particulars of that famous speech of Mr. Smollett's some years ago which had so great an effect at the time, but it was very advantageous to the object against which it was directed. Notwithstanding this practical improvement, however men still laugh with loud triumphant derision, and women, cowards like myself, laugh, too, somewhat hysterically, lest they should be thought to entertain sentiments which evoke so much abusive mirth,—laugh on the wrong side of their mouths, to use a vulgar but graphic expression, and shrink from appearing to take any interest in a question which it is impossible to believe could fail to interest them but for this coercion. I am almost sure that we, women in general, would have preferred that the subject should never have been mooted at all, even when we felt it of the profoundest personal importance, rather than subject ourselves and our position, rights and wrongs and supposed weaknesses, and our character altogether, to discussion before our children and our dependants. It is not pleasant for a woman who has sons, for instance, to feel that they who owe her obedience and respect, are turned into a laughing tribunal before which her supposed pranks are to be exhibited and her fundamental imperfections set forth. But this has now been done for good or evil, and as it has produced, I believe, some good results, and is likely, I hope, to produce more, we can scarcely avoid being grateful, even if with very mixed feelings, to those who have received the first storm of nasty missiles, and borne all the opprobrious names, and have had all the vile motives imputed to them that experts can imagine. While these bold pioneers—let us hope, not without some enjoyment of the fight, such as conflict naturally brings with it—have been bearing the brunt of battle, we have looked on with a great deal of silent exasperation. That men should entertain those opinions of women which have been expressed so largely has been a painful revelation to many, and it has given a far keener point to the sense of injustice which exists more or less in every feminine bosom—injustice actual and practical, which may be eluded by all sorts of compromises and expedients, and injustice theoretical and sentimental, which it is more difficult to touch. When I say sentimental it is not in any ludicrous sense that I use the word. Any actual injury is trifling in comparison with an injurious sentiment, which pervades and runs through life. And I think the greatest grievances of women, those upon which all others depend and from which they spring, are of this kind. Most of us of a reasonable age prefer to keep our sense of injury, our consciousness of injustice, dormant, but it exists in all classes. It has been handed down to us from our mothers, it descends from us to our daughters. We know that we have a great many things to suffer, from which our partners in the work of life are exempt, and we know also that neither for these extra pangs do we receive sympathy, nor for our work do we receive the credit which is our due. But whenever such questions are brought under public discussion we are bewildered to find how little these inequalities in our lot are comprehended, and how doubly injurious is the estimate formed of us by our husbands, our brothers, and our sons. This has been all stirred up and made apparent by recent discussions, and for this generation at least it is no longer possible to hush it up and keep the feeling it produces to ourselves.

In what I have to say on this subject I do not wish to touch upon any actual wrong or cruelty to which women are by law subjected. As men seem to think that the laws which bear hardly on women are the bulwarks of their own existence, it is very unlikely that they will ever be entirely amended. It is curious that they should be so anxious to confine and limit the privileges of the companion who is avowedly the weaker vessel. The Liliputians bound down Gulliver by a million of little ligatures—but that was a proceeding full of sense and judgment, since he could have demolished a whole army of them. But if it had been a Liliputian hero who had been bound down by a larger race, it would have been absurd; and it is very inconceivable how it could be dangerous to men to liberate a smaller and weaker competitor, whom they coerce every day of their lives, and whose strength, weak as it is, is burdened by many drawbacks to which they are not subject. So it is, however, and so it is likely to be for a long time at least. But it is the general sentiment which affects my mind more than individual wrong. The wrongs of the law are righted in a great many—in perhaps most individual cases—by contracts and compromises, by affection, by the natural force of character, even by family pride, which does not desire its private affairs to be made the talk of the world. But sentiment is universal and tells upon all. I allow (as has been already said—though not without some contempt for those who stand upon it) the superiority of sex. I may also say that I decline to build any plea upon those citations of famous women, with which even Mr. Mill was so weak as to back up his argument. It does not seem to me of the slightest importance that there existed various feminine professors in Italy, in the Middle Ages, or even that Mrs. Somerville was a person of the highest scientific attainments. I allow, frankly, that there has been no woman Shakespeare (and very few men of that calibre: not another one in England, so that it is scarcely worth taking him into account in the averages of the human race). If such fanciful arguments were permitted, it might be as sound a plea to say that, with a few exceptions, Shakespeare embodied all that was noblest in his genius, not in men but in women, giving us a score of noble and beautiful human creatures, daughters of the gods, as against his one Hamlet. All this is however entirely beyond and beside the question. I do not want even to prove that women are equal to men, or to discuss the points in which they differ. I do not pretend to understand either Man or Woman, in capitals. I only know individuals, of no two of whom could I say that I think they are entirely equal. But there are two, visibly standing before the world (which is made up of them) to be judged according to their works, and upon these works I wish to ask the reader his and her opinion.

This is mine to start with—that when God put two creatures into the world (I hope that persons of advanced intelligence will forgive the old-fashioned phraseology, which perhaps is behind the age) it was not that one should be the servant to the other, but because there was for each a certain evident and sufficient work to do. It is needless to inquire which work was the highest. Judgement has been universally given in favour of the man's work, which is that of the protector and food-producer—though even here one cannot but feel that there is something to be said on the weaker side, and that it is possible that the rearing of children might seem in the eyes of the Maker, who is supposed to feel a special interest in the human race, as noble an occupation, in its way, as the other. To keep the world rolling on, as it has been doing for all these centuries, there have been needful two creatures, two types of creatures, the one an impossibility without the other. And it is a curious thought, when we come to consider it, that the man, who is such a fine fellow and thinks so much of himself, would after all be a complete nonentity without the woman whom he has hustled about and driven into a corner ever since she began to be. Now it seems to me that the first, and largest, and most fundamental of all the grievances of women, is this: that they never have, since the world began, got the credit of that share of the work of the world which has fallen naturally to them, and which they have, on the whole, faithfully performed through all vicissitudes. It will be seen that I am not referring to the professions, which are the trades of men, according to universal acknowledgment, but to that common and general women's work, which is, without any grudging, acknowledged to be their sphere.

And I think it is one of the most astonishing things in the world to see how entirely all the honour and credit of this, all the importance of it, all its real value, is taken from the doers of it. That her children may 'rise up and call her blessed' is allowed by Holy Writ, and there are vague and general permissions of praise given to those who take the woman's part in the conflict. It is allowed to be said that she is a ministering angel, a consoler, and encouragement to the exertions of the man, and a rewarder of his toil. She is given within due limitations a good deal of praise; but very rarely any justice. I scarcely remember any writer who has ever ventured to say that the half of the work of the world is actually accomplished by women; and very few husbands who would be otherwise than greatly startled and amazed, if not indignant, if not derisive, at the suggestion of such an idea as that the work of their wives was equal to their own. And yet for my part I think it is. So far as I can see, the working-man's wife who has to cook and clean, and wash and mend, and do all the primitive services of life for her family, has harder and more constant work than her husband has; and rising upward in the ranks of life, I think the same balance goes on, at least until that level of wealth and leisure is reached, at which the favourites of fortune, like the lilies, toil not neither do they spin. But I am not concerned with those heights. What dukes and duchesses do, and which of them work the hardest, will scarcely tell upon the argument; nor am I deeply versed in the natural history of millionaires. But so far as I am acquainted with the facts of existence, the woman's hands are everywhere as full of natural occupation as are those of the man. To talk of the great mass of working women, the wives of the poorer and labouring classes, in a pretty and poetical way as the inspirers of toil, the consolers of care, by whose smiles a man is stimulated to industry, and rewarded for his exertions, would be too ridiculous for the most rigid theorist. Whatever powers of this passive kind may be possessed by the wife of the bricklayer or carpenter will stand her in little stead if she does not put her shoulder to the wheel. 'A woman's work is never done,' is the much more genuine expression of sentiment on that level, which is by far the largest, of society. The man's work lasts a certain number of hours, after which he has his well-earned leisure, his evening to himself, his hours of recreation, or of lounging; but his wife has no such privileged amount of exemption from toil. Her work is 'never done.' She has the evening meal, whatever it may be, to prepare, and to clear away, and the children to get to bed, and the mending to do, in the hours when he is altogether free, and considers himself with justice to have a right to his freedom. In very few cases does it occur to the woman to grumble at this, or to wonder why her lot should be harder than his. It is natural; it is her share. The whole compact of their married life is based upon this, that she should do her work while he does his; and hers is the share which is 'never done.' I do not say a word against this law of Nature; but I object that while this is the case, the poor woman who works so hard is considered as a passive object of her husband's bounty, indebted to him for her living, and with no standing-ground or position of her own. She is so considered in the eye of the law; and though the foolishness of the sentiment is too manifest in her individual case to be insisted upon, yet she is implied in the general sweeping assertion which includes all married women. 'Men must work and women must weep,' says the ballad. I would like to know what the fisher-women of our sea-coasts say to this lugubrious sentiment, or how much time they find to indulge in that luxury.

It is scarcely necessary to follow domestic history up through all its lines for the purpose of proving that everywhere this rule is the same. A poor woman with a house full of children has everywhere and in all circumstances her work cut out for her; and when the element of gentility comes in, and there are appearances to be kept up, that labour is indefinitely enlarged. Which of the two does the reader suppose has most to do: the merchant's clerk, for instance, who earns his salary by six or eight hours' work in his office, or his

wife who has to pinch and scrape, and shape and sew, and sit late at nights
and rise early in the mornings, in order to keep a neat and cheerful house
and turn out the children in such a guise as to do no discredit to their father's
black coat? If I had to choose between the two, I should choose the husband's
share and not the wife's. The man is more exposed to outside risks and dis-
comforts; but the moment he enters his home he is privileged to rest and be
waited on as much as if he were a Sultan. The same rule exists everywhere.
Among shop-keepers of all but the highest class, the wife, in addition to her
natural work, takes her share in the business, and such is the case in a great
many other occupations. She keeps the books; she makes out the bills; in one
way or another she overflows from her own share of the work into his. The
poor clergyman's wife (I know one such with such hands of toil, scarred and
honourable!—hands that have washed and scrubbed, and cooked and sewed,
till all their lady softness is gone) is his curate as well. Where is there any class
of life in which this is not the case? When we come to the higher levels of society the circumstances are changed a little. Usually wealth means a cessation
more or less of labour. But a great lawyer, or a great doctor for instance, may
have reached the very height of success without having his actual toil diminished; and his wife in that case may be carried high upon the tide of his success to a position of ease and luxury which bears little proportion to the
labour with which he must still go on, keeping up the reputation and the
career which he has made. Even in that case she will have a great establishment to manage, servants to rule, and social duties to perform, and always,
the first and most sacred duty of all, the children to care for, which makes her
life anything but an unoccupied one. But the wife of a professional man who
is struggling into work and celebrity has as tough a task as her humbler neighbour. In the present constitution of society, people upon a certain level of
position are supposed to live pretty much alike whether their income is
counted by hundreds or by thousands. A smaller and less costly house, a par-
lourmaid instead of a butler, are the only concessions which custom makes;
but things must be as 'nice' in the small house as in the great, and neither in
their table nor in their apparel can the poorer pair afford to show any greatly perceptible difference between themselves and their wealthier friends.
They must 'go out' in much the same way. They must even entertain now and
then in much the same way; they must take as much pains with the education
of their children, and they must not even be very much behind in the decoration of their house. How is all this to be done upon an income so much
inferior—upon the probably precarious earnings which this year are a little
more and next year may be a great deal less? This dreadful problem, which
can never be lost sight of day by day, if any satisfactory solution is to be given
to it, is almost entirely the wife's share of the business. She it is who must take
it in hand, to secure as much as can be had of comfort and modest luxury and
beauty, out of the poor blank sum of money, which in itself is barren of all

grace. She must watch over all the minutiae of household living; she must keep a careful eye upon weekly bills, and invent daily dinners, and keep servants in order, and guide the whole complicated machinery so that nothing shall jar or creak, and no part of it get out of gear. Housekeeping is a fine science, and there are some women who show a real genius in it; but genius that makes everything easy is rare; and in general it is a hard struggle to carry on that smooth and seemingly easy routine of existence which seen outside appears to go of itself. Try to let it go by itself for ever so short a time and you will find the difference. This is the woman's share of the work, in addition to that perennial occupation, the nurture of her children, to whom she very likely gives their earliest lessons, as well as the foundation of moral training, which tells most upon their after lives. Her day is full of a multiplicity of tasks, some greater, some smaller, but all indispensable; since without that guidance, and supervision, and regulation, life would be but a chaos of accidents, and society could not exist at all. I say nothing of those frequently recurring trials of maternity, common to all classes, interrupting yet intensifying that round of common toil, in which young married women are perpetually exposed to dangers as great as those of an army in active service; nor of all the heavy burdens, the illnesses and languors that accompany it. When it is necessary to find a word which shall express the last extreme of human exertion, we all know where old writers find it—in those throes of the whole being, that crisis of body and soul, which women alone have to go through.

Thus a woman has not only certain unparalleled labours in her life to which the man can produce no balance on his side, but she has her work cut out for her in all the varieties of existence. She is the drudge of humanity in its uncivilised state, and in the very highest artificial condition she carries with her natural burdens which no one else can bear.

But for this she gets absolutely no credit at all. I am not complaining of actual hardship. There are bad husbands in the world, as there are bad wives; but the number of these domestic tyrants is small, and for every man who breaks his wife's heart and makes her life wretched, there are perhaps hundreds, between whom and their wedded companions there exist the most perfect understanding and sympathy. I believe nothing can be more certain than the large predominance of happiness over unhappiness in married life. I am not speaking of tyrannical men, or women crushed under their sway, but of a great and general misconception, a sentimental grievance. Practically it may do no harm at all—theoretically it does the greatest harm. The position assigned to women is thus almost entirely a fictitious one. A man's wife is considered to be his dependent, fed and clothed by him of his free will and bounty, and all the work that she does in fulfilment of the natural conditions of their marriage is considered as of no account whatever in the matter. He works, but she does not; he toils to maintain her, while she sits at home in ease and leisure, and enjoys the fruits of his labour, and gives him an ornamental compensation in smiles and pleasantness. This is the representation of married life which is universally accepted. Servants have a right to their wages, and to have it understood that their work is honest and thorough—when it is so; but wives must allow it to be taken for granted that they do nothing; that their work is the merest trifle not worth reckoning in the tale of human exertions. The cajoleries by which they extract bonnets and millinery in general out of their husband's purse, who owes nothing to them, while they owe everything to him, is the commonest of jokes – a joke tolerated and even repeated by many men who know better. I repeat I am not making a complaint of actual hardship. Bonnets, except in the pages of 'Punch,' are seldom such accidental circumstances, and still more seldom obtained by cajoleries. When the income is large enough to be divided the wife has generally her settled allowance, and the husband has as little to do immediately with the bonnets as with the legs of mutton on the table; and in cases where the income is too small for such an arrangement, the spending of it is generally in the wife's hands. But these compromises of fact which alone would make life liveable do not lessen the injury of the assumption which continues to exist in spite of them.

A very trifling incident directed my thoughts to this not very long ago. It was of no importance whatever, and yet it contained the whole question in it. I was making an insignificant journey in company with a married pair, between whom there was the most perfect understanding and good intelligence. The lady wore a pair of very shabby gloves, to which, by some accident or other, attention was called. The husband was shocked and ashamed. 'One would think,' he said, 'that I could not afford to buy you gloves.' Now here were the facts of this case. Both had a little money, the wife's share being, I think, about equal to her husband's. He had been a University Don, and was then a 'Coach,' taking pupils. Some six or eight young men were living in his house, and of course his wife had her cares of housekeeping so much enlarged as to make them an engrossing and constant occupation. She had besides a large family of small children. If she did not work as hard for her living as he did, then the words have no meaning; but so little did this good man suppose her exertions to be worth, so little share had she, according to his ideas, in the actual business of life, that he spoke of his want of gloves as a reflection upon him, as he might have spoken of the neglected appearance of a child. He had no wish to be illiberal—he was fond of his wife and proud of her, and very willing to keep her in gloves and anything else she wanted, but he had no feeling of right in the matter; no sense that her position ought to be anything else than that of absolute dependency. Had it been necessary to bring in a stranger to do the wife's work, that stranger would have been highly paid and a very independent person indeed. But the work of the wife represented nothing to her husband, and gave her, save by his grace and bounty, no right to anything, not even to her gloves and bonnets, her share of the living which she so largely helped to earn.

In this respect, however, the most liberal and the most generous men are often as much at fault as the coarsest. They will not allow the importance of the second part in the universal duet. They will give liberally, and praise freely, but they will not acknowledge 'My wife has as much to do as I have. Without her work mine would not have half its value; we are partners in the toil of living, and she has earned the recompense of that toil as well as I.' No one will say this, nor will the world acknowledge it. What the world does say when a woman outside of the bonds of marriage claims to be allowed to work for her bread as she best can is, that she ought to go back to her proper sphere, which is home. But in that proper sphere, and at her own individual work, all credit is taken from her, her exertions are denied, her labour is undervalued. The only chance for her to get her work acknowledged is to do it very badly, when there will be an outcry. But when it is well done it is ignored, it is taken as a matter of course, it is never thought upon at all.

Let this be contrasted with the reverse case—a case by no means unfrequent, though left out of account in all popular calculations. When it happens that the woman is the richest of the two partners in life, when the living comes from her side, or when she earns it, she is considered bound to assert no consciousness of the fact. It is a horror and shame to all spectators when she makes any stand upon her moneyed superiority. That she should let it be seen that she is the supporter of the household, or remind her husband that he is in any way indebted to her, is a piece of bad taste and bad feeling for which no blame is too severe. And the woman herself is the first to feel it so. But that which seems the depth of meanness and ungenerosity in a woman is the natural and everyday attitude of the man. It is a point of honour on her part to ignore to the length of falsehood her husband's inferiority to herself in this respect; whereas the fact of her dependence upon him is kept continually before her eyes, and insisted upon, both seriously and jocularly, at every point of her career.

In all this there has been no question of the comparative mental capacity of women and men. It is a question on which I can throw little light, and which I have no space to discuss. But with the injurious sentiment which I have tried to set forth the question of intellectual inferiority has nothing to do. Granting that the natural work of women is inferior to that of men, it is no less a distinct, complete, and personal work. When the question of professional labour comes in, and the claims of those women who desire to share the trades of men and compete with them have to be considered, the point becomes open to discussion. It may be said that a woman should not be permitted to be a doctor or a lawyer, because her abilities are inferior to those of men; but as in every discussion of this kind she is bidden to go back to her natural trade, it is clear that upon the ground of domestic life and its occupations she is *dans son droit,* and entitled to have her claims allowed.

As to the other question of throwing open some professions, it is a much more difficult one. I think that here, too, there is a great deal of ungenerous sentiment on the part of men, so much as to be astonishing and incomprehensible *vu* the strong sense of superiority which exists in the male bosom from the age of two upwards. It cannot be fear of a new competitor, and yet it looks like it. The doctors, a most liberal and highly cultivated profession, have shown themselves in this particular not more enlightened than the watch-makers, who have also resisted the entrance of women into their trade with violence; though nobody can know better than medical men how heavily weighted a woman is, how much more energy she must require to carry her to actual success in a profession, and how certain it is accordingly that only a few exceptionally endowed individuals can ever enter into those lists which are so fiercely guarded. But why not let convenience and general utility be the rule here as in all other matters? Every new piece of machinery in the manufacturing districts has been mobbed and wrecked at its first introduction, just as the female students would have been on one occasion had the gentlemen of the profession had their way; but the machine, if it is a good one, always triumphs in the end. My own opinion is that the advantage to women of having a woman-doctor to refer to is incalculable. To discuss the peculiar ailments of their mysterious frames with a man is always a trial and pain to the young. Necessity hardens them as they go on in life, and prejudice, and the idea that women cannot be properly educated, or that by expressing a preference for a female doctor they are exposing themselves to be ridiculed as supporters of women's rights, keep many a woman silent on the subject; but Nature herself surely may be allowed to bear testimony on such a point. I cannot imagine it to be desirable in any way that women should get over their sense of personal delicacy even with the doctor. But at all events the question whether women should be doctors or not is one, it might be supposed, to be argued quite dispassionately. They could not invade the profession all at once in such numbers as to swamp it, and as their opponents have always indignantly maintained their want of capacity for its exercise, there could not surely be a doubt in their minds as to the failure of the experiment and their own eventual triumph. But here once more the sentiment involved is a greater injury than the fact. Not only were the gates of knowledge barred, but the vilest insinuations, utterly beyond possibility of proof, were launched against the few blameless women who did nothing worse than ask for the privilege of studying for an enlightened profession. One or more writers, supposedly English gentlemen, in a very well known and influential English paper, asserted boldly that the women-students in Edinburgh and elsewhere desired to study medicine from prurient curiosity and the foulest of motives. This was said in English print in full daylight of the nineteenth century, and nobody, so far as I can remember, objected to it. The journalist was not denounced by his brethren, and public opinion took it quite coolly, as a thing it was no shame to say.

I ask the reader, who will probably have heard similar insinuations made in society, what is his opinion on the subject? Such a shameful accusation could be susceptible of no kind of proof; the only thing that could be proved about it would be that it came out of a bad imagination. The women assailed could not come forward at whatever cost and establish their innocence. When a man utters a slander as to an actual fact, his accusation can be brought to the test, and its falsehood proved and himself punished; but the imputation of an odious motive is a far more dangerous offence, for no one can descend into the heart of the accused to bring forth proofs of its purity. Any vile fancy can in this way asperse its neighbours with impunity, and it is not an uncommon exercise. But the fact that nobody cared, that there was no protest, no objection, and that this was thought quite a permissible thing to say and publish of some half-dozen inoffensive women, is the extraordinary point in the matter. It is an injury by far more deadly and serious than a more definite offence.

I have no room to touch upon education, or other important points, but something must be said on the question of the Parliamentary franchise for women. My opinion on this point resolves itself into the very simple one, that I think it is highly absurd that I should not have a vote, if I want one—a point upon which I am much more uncertain. To live for half a century, and not to have an opinion upon politics, as well as upon most other subjects, is next to an impossibility. In former days, when the franchise was a privilege supposed to be possessed only by persons of singular and superior qualifications, such as the freemen of a borough, for instance, or the aldermen of a corporation, women, being altogether out of the question for these dignities, might bear their deprivation sweetly, as an effect of nature. Even the ten-pound franchise represented something—a solidity, a respectability—perhaps above the level of female attainment. But now that the floodgates have been opened, and all who contribute their mites to the taxation have a right to a voice, the question is different. When every house is represented, why not my house as well as the others? and indeed, I may ask, on what ground is my house, paying higher rates than a great many others, to be left out? Now that all the powers of education, judgment, knowledge, as well as property and place, are left out of the considerations, and this is the only qualification required, the stigma upon us that we are, in intelligence and trustworthiness, below the very lowest of the low, would be unbearable if it were not absurd. When even the franchise was a new thing in course of development the stigma was not so great, but now that there remains only one further step to take, and the suffrage is about to become the right of every male individual with a thatch over his head, it is difficult to understand the grounds on which women householders are shut out. I do not comprehend the difficulty of separating, in this respect, the independent and self-supporting woman from the much larger number of those who are married. In every other case the law makes no difficulty whatever about such a separation, and in this I think it is very easy. If house-holding and ratepaying are the conditions of possessing the franchise, a man and his wife hold but one house and pay one set of rates. She has merged her public existense in his—for the convenience of the world it is quite necessary and desirable that there should be but one representative of the household. The two of them together support the State and its expenditure only as much as the female householder does who lives next door; they do not pay double taxes, nor undertake a double responsibility; and the married woman is by no means left out of the economy of the State. She is represented by her hus-band. She votes in her husband; her household has its due dignity and impor-tance in the commonwealth. The persons who are altogether left out are those who have no husband to represent them, who pay their contributions to the funds of the country out of their own property or earnings, and have to transact for themselves all their business, whatever it may be. Some of them have never had husbands; in which case it is sometimes asked, with the grace-ful courtesy which characterises the whole discussion, why such a privilege should be bestowed upon these rejected of all men, who have never been able to please or to attract what is called 'the other sex.' But this is illogical, I sub-mit, with diffidence, since if these poor ladies have thus missed the way of sal-vation, their non-success should call forth the pity rather than the scorn of men who feel their own notice to be heaven for a woman, and who ought to be anxiously desirous to tender any such trifling compensation as a vote as some poor salve to the mortification of the unmarried. Some of us, on the other hand, have been put down from the eminence of married life sum-marily, and by no fault of ours. We have been obliged to bear all the burdens of a citizen upon our shoulders, to bring up children for the State, and make shift to perform alone almost all the duties which our married neighbours share between them. And to reward us for this unusual strain of exertion we are left out altogether in every calculation. We are the only individuals in the country (or will soon be) entirely unrepresented, left without any means of expressing our opinions on those measures which will shape, probably, the fate of our children. This seems to me ridiculous—not so much a wrong as an absurdity. I do not stand upon my reasoning or power of argument. Probably it is quite feeble, and capable of swift demolition. I can but come back to my original sense of the complete absurdity and falseness of the position.

Upon this homely ground, however, of tax-paying, a possibility occurs. I think that for my part I should not be unwilling to compound for the politi-cal privileges which are denied to me. The ladies at St. James's Hall will think it a terrible dereliction from principle; yet I feel it is a practical way out of the difficulty—out of the absurdity. It would be a great relief to many of us, and it would deliver us from the sting of inferiority to our neighbour next door.

We should be able to feel, when the tax-gatherer came round, that for that moment at least we had the best of it. Let there be a measure brought in to exempt us from the payment of those rates which qualify every gaping clown to exercise the franchise. It will not be a dignified way of getting out of it, but it will be a way of getting out of it, and one which will be logical and convey some solace to our wounded pride. I for one am willing to compound.

In all these inequalities and injustices, however, the chief grievance to women is the perpetual contempt, the slur upon them in all respects, the injurious accusation, so entirely beyond all possibility of proof that denial means nothing. How it can have been that men have continued for all these ages to find their closest companions and friends among those whose every function they undervalue and despise, is one of the greatest problems of human nature. We are so wound and bound together, scarcely one man in the world who does not love some woman better than he loves any other man, or one woman who does not love some man before all other mortal creatures, that the wonder grows as we look at it. For the sentiment of men towards women is thoroughly ungenerous from beginning to end, from the highest to the lowest. I have thought in my day that this was an old-fashioned notion belonging to earlier conditions of society, and that the hereditary consciousness of it which descended to me, as to all women, was to be disproved by experience. But experience does not disprove it. There are, of course, many individual exceptions, yet the general current of sentiment flows full in this way. Whatever women do, in the general, is undervalued by men in the general, because it is done by women. How this impairs the comfort of women, how it shakes the authority of mothers, injures the self-respect of wives, and gives a general soreness of feeling everywhere, I will not attempt to tell. It is too large a subject to be touched by any kind of legislation; but without this the occasional wrongs of legislation, the disabilities at which we grumble, would be but pin-pricks, and would lose all their force. They are mere evidences of a sentiment which is more inexplicable than any other by which the human race has been actuated, a sentiment against which the most of us, at one period or other of our lives, have to struggle blindly, not knowing whence it originates, or how it is to be overcome.

Source: Reprinted from *Fraser's Magazine* (May 1880).

BIOGRAPHICAL NOTE

Margaret Oliphant, daughter of Francis Wilson and Margaret Oliphant, was born in 1828 in Musselburgh, Scotland. At the age of twenty-one, she published *Passages in the Life of Mrs. Margaret Maitland* (1849), the first of over one hundred book-length publications she was to produce.

In 1853 Oliphant married her cousin, Francis Wilson Oliphant, an artist, and began to write for *Blackwood's Magazine*. During the next four years, she wrote four novels and had two children. By 1859 Francis's poor health compelled the family to move, at great expense, to Italy, where he died. Margaret was left pregnant, and heavily in debt with only her energy and writing talents to support her. *Blackwood's* proved to be indispensable in giving her work. Between 1862 and 1865 four of her novels in the "Chronicles of Carlingford" series were published in the magazine. They proved to be the writings for which she is most remembered, *Salem Chapel* (1863) being a particular success. In 1864, her beloved daughter died in Rome; that same year, she accepted financial responsibility for the three children of her recently-widowed brother. With five children to support, two of them her own sons, for whom she had great educational plans, Oliphant worked indefatigably as a novelist, biographer, historian, and reviewer of the literature of the day for *Blackwood's Magazine*.

The essays reprinted here, "The Condition of Women" (1858) and "The Grievances of Women" (1880) are representative samples of the quality of her work. They also suggest that Oliphant's reputation and self-assessment as a work-a-day reviewer falls somewhat short of the mark. Though driven by financial need, her writing is persuasively and thoughtfully heterodox. A committed conservative in political and social matters, she was nonetheless well able to admire a good argument or a good story when she saw one, on whatever side of the political spectrum it might locate itself and however compelled to reject it she might ultimately be. "The Condition of Women," rejects the notion that society shapes women into empty-headed fools, arguing strenuously and with great brio for women's capabilities. The later essay, "The Grievances of Women," indicates that Oliphant has done considerable rethinking on the subject; here she argues that women's greatest problem lies in the great contempt in which they are held by men, not by a lack of education, political rights or abilities.

In the last decade of her life, Oliphant continued to write at an extraordinary pace, producing important work including a history of the publishing house that had been her financial mainstay, *Annals of a Publishing House; William Blackwood and His Son, Their Magazine and Friends* (1897). She died at her home in Windsor, a novelist whose fiction had gone out of fashion, but a writer whose work is nonetheless a powerful commentary on her age.

Selected Secondary Sources

Cohen, Monica. "Maximising Oliphant: Begging the Question and the Politics of Satire." *Victorian Women Writers and the Woman Question*. Ed. Nicola Diane Thompson. Cambridge: Cambridge UP, 1999. 99-115.

Colby, V.R. *The Equivocal Virtue.* New York: Archon, 1966.

D'Albertis, Deirdre. "The Domestic Drone: Margaret Oliphant and a Political History of the Novel." *Studies in English Literature* 37.4 (1997): 805-830.

Helsinger, Elizabeth K., Robin Lauterback Sheets, and William Veeder. *The Woman Question: Society and Literature in Britain and America, 1837-1883.* Vol. 3. Chicago: U of Chicago P, 1983.

Jay, Elisabeth. *Mrs. Oliphant, "A Fiction to herself": A Literary Life.* Oxford: Clarendon Press, 1995.

Onslow, Barbara. "'Humble Comments for the Ignorant': Margaret Oliphant's Criticism of Art and Society." *Victorian Periodicals Review* 31.1 (1998): 55-74.

Shattock, Joanne. "Margaret Oliphant: Journalist." *Victorian Journalism: Exotic and Domestic.* Ed. Barbara Garlick and Margaret Harris. Queensland: U of Queensland P, 1998. 95-107.

Trela, D.J., ed. *Margaret Oliphant: Critical Essays on a Gentle Subversive.* London: Associated UP, 1995.

Helen Taylor
(1831-1907)

"Women and Criticism"

Few things are more interesting to an observer of mankind than the endless variety and absolutely contradictory nature of the objections raised, in society and contemporary literature, to every possible proposal for altering anything. It seems to be in the nature of the human mind to hold that no reason can be necessary for doing nothing; this is so natural a thing to do, apparently, that the inducements and the justification for it are, at all times, self-evident to all the world. But, when any one proposes to break in upon any established order whatever, by any plan which is actually intended to be carried into practical operation, then there arises a multitudinous host of objections, not from one side only but from every side, a tumult of clashing arguments, of opposing difficulties, a cross-fire which sometimes reminds us of Falconbridge—

"From north to south
Austria and France shoot in each other's mouth,"

when those who fancy themselves allies unintentionally destroy one another's position, by blows aimed at an intermediate enemy.

It is this variety and inconsistency in the objections raised to all reforms which is one of the chief elements in the priceless value, for human progress, of free discussion. If the truth had to do battle alone against all its adversaries the task would be a much harder one than it is at present, and the result, if not more uncertain, would certainly be much longer deferred. But, where discussion is free, the *mêlée* is generally so confused that whoever will consent to fight at all can hardly help dealing some blows at error. He who strikes at random may fight against truth too, but, if there is one distinguishing mark of truth as opposed to error, it is its vital power, its strength to endure, the ineradicable energy with which it revives from apparent annihilation. A much weaker blow will kill falsehood, and, as a general rule, the same weakness of mind which makes people hold an opinion on insufficient grounds makes them find very insufficient arguments strong enough to overthrow it. Thus, while it is true that error is manifold, yet its opponents are manifold also. A consistent reasoner will often be surprised at the weapons with which a victory may be gained for his own side; yet a logical intellect is not so hard and dry a thing but that some of the most humorous scenes of the comedy of human life may receive their keenest relish from the sense of incongruity between cause and effect.

But, of all the battle-fields of confused and diverse opinion, none is more strangely and chaotically intermingled than the perennial dispute, which all the world loves to join in, as to the comparative merits, duties, faults, and virtues of men and women. Feelings, passions, fancies, sentiments, resentments, hopes, dreams, fears, come pouring in, all eager to do their part in settling the matter, so that, in this particular contest, prejudice and ignorance seem calm and rational in comparison with the rest of the combatants. Nor is this abundance of personal feeling astonishing when we come to consider the subject, since every one is personally concerned in it; no one can help being a man or a woman at some time if he lives long enough. The cattle plague may be discussed among sailors, or fine art with Quakers, in which case it might be possible to secure judges who possess the qualification, so essential in the eyes of many critics, for fitness to judge—that, however little they know of the subject, they care less. But, however little a woman may know of physiology, or psychology, or history, or politics, or social science, or mental science, or difficult subjects of that sort, she is not likely to doubt that she knows woman's nature, which, after all, is only a form of that which all these sciences put together are intended to investigate. What gentle, timid, home-keeping lady will hesitate to pronounce (firm in the consciousness of her own incapacity) what nature destined for all time to be the lot of one half the human race? Is she not a woman herself, and, being so, must she not understand women? Do we not all know ourselves? And, knowing ourselves, as we all do, so well, does it not of necessity follow that we know all who resemble us in any important respect? And, knowing ourselves, is it not evident that we must know what is good for us? And, knowing these things by nature, it cannot be going out of a woman's sphere, nor need any strength of mind, to pronounce what ought to be the relative position of men, women, and children, in politics, arts, sciences, and domestic life. It is, indeed, so difficult to find a woman unprejudiced about women, that those who think least of their own capacities are more confident as to the absence of capacity in women, than those ladies (if any there are) who lay claim to strength of mind can be as to the presence of it. For the women who profess to be in some degree competent to consider the subject, generally only hazard the suggestion that women might possibly prove equal to men if they were placed in the same circumstances, and they propose only that the law shall make no distinctions, and so leave things to adjust themselves. But those who think they know woman's proper place from their own internal consciousness, want laws to keep her there. Not content to remain in that vague state of mind which only suits scientific accuracy, and requires experiment and test before considering any fact as certain; content still less with that impartiality which may do well enough for the lawgiver or statesman, but which does not become an ignorant woman; they demand a positive recognition by law and institutions of the difference between two things, of which difference these ladies are perfectly sure, because they know one of the two quite well.

When all women, strong or weak-minded, have given in their contribution to this universally-interesting subject, it is far from being exhausted. If women naturally have an opinion upon it because they are women, men have one because they are not. Even those who think the only suitable relations between the two are those of superiority and subordination cannot deny this. The question of where the lamb was entitled to drink from, was not less interesting to the wolf than to the lamb. It would be taking a very narrow view of the matter to deny that the wolf had, at least, a right to be heard, in support of claims on which so much of his comfort in life depended. The fact is, that the nearer we could come to a complete equality between men and women in the laws and institutions under which they live, the better chance would there be of getting at something like impartial opinion on the subject. The nearer it could be brought to being nobody's interest to think one way or another about it, the nearer we should be to arriving at some cool and unbiased judgment. No observer can help seeing at present that the interests at stake are too important to permit much impartiality. People are either, consciously or unconsciously, blinded by their personal wishes and experience, or else, making a strenuous effort to be magnanimous, they endeavour to secure themselves against being selfish by an entire renunciation of all personal claims. The common opinion that women are more enthusiastic and less reasoning than men, and that men are more deliberate, and know better what they mean when they say a thing, than women, may perhaps explain why, on the whole, most women decide against, and most men in favour of themselves. But, if women were really entitled in justice to any rights and privileges which most of them disclaim, it may be doubted whether the fact of their renouncing such rights from pure although mistaken motives of duty would be any evidence of unfitness for their exercise.

Yet, among the many answers commonly given when the question is asked, Why women should not have all occupations and privileges open to them, and be free to adopt or renounce masculine, as men are feminine, pursuits? none reappears more frequently than the assertion that women themselves do not wish for any such freedom. With many persons it is a received axiom that women do not like liberty. There is nothing, it would seem, that a woman more dislikes than being permitted to do what she likes. Husbands and fathers know by experience that women never wish to have their own way. One reason for this appears to be that women are endowed by nature with so strong and peculiar an idiosyncrasy that they must necessarily run counter to it if they are let alone. The laws of nature are so powerful in women that it is essential to make human laws in aid of them. The instincts of their sex so imperiously demand of women to do what is feminine, that it is necessary for men to forbid them to do anything masculine. Therefore it stands to reason that women who wish to be guided by womanly instinct must place themselves under the guidance of men. Possessed by an innate sense of feminine propriety, women feel that if the law did not protect them against themselves they would be inclined to do many unsuitable things. With men it is different; no laws are needed to define what men may or may not do, for men, with their less acute moral perceptions, are not likely to do what is unsuited to them. But legislative enactments can alone keep women from leaving their firesides to plunge into the fierce contentions and angry passions of the political world; were they free to choose for themselves it is to be feared they would desert their infants in order to command armies; their love of beauty and their physical weakness would induce them to apply themselves to the most repulsive and laborious occupations, such as no man would like to see a woman employed in, and from which they would naturally, but perhaps very unfairly, drive out their more robust masculine competitors. Then, too, being gentle, docile, and retiring, naturally fitted to obey, is it not likely that if left to their own guidance, they would show themselves quarrelsome, self-willed, and altogether unmanageable?

Leaving those who will to unravel these very curious series of logical sequences, or perhaps leaving these contradictory propositions to neutralize one another, it may be worth while to go on a few steps further, and consider the question on the ground of general principles, which cover a much larger space than the mere distinction between men and women: for, the moment we step beyond the charmed circle which shuts in women in most people's imagination, we find ourselves on ground where it is comparatively usual to appeal to reason, and to expect that reasons shall have some sort of consistency in them. On no other subject is it commonly held that so small an amount of experimental evidence is sufficient to build up such a wide induction as on this. It is the commonest thing in the world to hear even educated people, who, on other topics, pride themselves on having some foundation for what they say, confound together in one group millions of women, of different races and different religions, brought up in different climates, and under different institutions, and predict, with quiet security, how all these would act under utterly untried conditions—such as perfect political and social freedom of which the history of the world has never yet furnished even a single instance whereon to ground a sober judgment. How utterly this whole way of treating such a subject is opposed to all the scientific tendencies of our time, it is hardly worthwhile to stop to point out.

The growing habit of studying history from a philosophical point of view, and drawing generalizations from its teaching in a scientific spirit, will, no doubt, do much to induce men (and women too) to consider the destinies, the duties, and the rights of women in a serious and logical manner, and to lay aside the jokes and the sentimental preferences which at present encumber and entangle all discussion on the subject. It may even be presumed, that, fortified with such studies, some women may no longer shrink from being called "strong-minded," as from an abusive epithet, and that men may only hesitate to apply it to them, as being more complimentary than they are often likely to deserve.

But, when rational habits of thought, and a comparatively widely extended acquaintance with scientific methods of observation and experiment, have done much good work on the public mind, still we cannot expect a thorough cure in the fanciful method of treating women's rights, until legislation, by loosening a little the tightness of its bonds, opens the door to observation, and permits a few, however timid, experiments to be made. At present it is hard to complain of those who appeal to their own imagination as warrant for their highly imaginative assertions of what would happen if any changes were introduced into the condition of women, for to what else can they appeal? The truth is, as we take it, that the law is a great deal too minute in its legislation on this subject; for, if we come to consider it, we find that it is marked in the highest degree by the characteristic of early and antiquated legislation: it protects the interests of both men and women a great deal too much, and, by taking too much care of them, will not allow them to take care of themselves. It is this same meddlesome spirit which in former times produced sumptuary laws, and fixed the rate of interest and of wages; which forbade the exportation of gold and other valuable commodities from the realm, and gave rise to the whole system of commercial protection.

But the striking and brilliant success of free trade principles has happily had a powerful effect in opening the eyes of every civilized people to the mischievous effects of over-legislation. The benefit of the promulgation of such principles ought not to stop even at this result, great as it is. For the philosophical principles, and the whole train of reasoning which lead to free trade, not merely indicate that over-legislation is a check upon individual energy and enterprise, but point to the direction which all the legislation should take, viz.—to development, and not to the repression, of the faculties of those who have to obey it. That the law is made for man, not man for the law, is the spirit of modern legislation, and we recognise the working of this spirit where we see the law removing hindrances to human energy, not where we see it imposing them. The hindrances that we are willing to see imposed by the law are only those that prevent people from hindering one another, not such as are imagined to be beneficial to themselves. We are willing to see a man hindered from stealing another man's goods, but we murmur if he is not allowed to sell his own at as low a price as he pleases. The application of any such principle will show at once how very defective is our present legislation as regards women, and how antiquated is the train of reasoning by which such legislation is defended. Indeed, the only logical defence of our present legislation would be that it considers only the interests of men, and looks upon women as a subject, and even as an antagonistic class, whose hands are to be bound for the benefit of those whom the law really intends to protect. It is not impossible that some such point of view was that which really actuated those who originated our present system, many parts of which have come down to us from times when men had not, even in thought, got beyond the idea that—

"Those should take who have the power,
And those should keep who can."

But the most violent assertor of the sacred rights of sex would shrink now from making such a notion the ground either of his own claims or her own abnegation. Agreeing, therefore, as most disputants would probably do, that no one wants to oppress and enslave women for other people's benefit, we are thrown back upon the theory, that, solely for their own good, they are excluded from all the professions, from all political rights, from a share in the great national institutions for education, and from every other privilege possessed only by men. The energy and the enterprise women might show in any of all these departments is checked by the law, only in order to protect them, just as our traders and manufacturers used to be protected against foreign competition. The development of their faculties is forbidden to take place in these directions, only in order that they may be turned into more healthy and natural channels, just as particular industries used to be encouraged by law because it used to be thought that our island possessed peculiar facilities for those, and just as particular methods of manufacture used to be enjoined because it was supposed that our people would employ wrong methods if the law did not restrict them to right ones. Now, on the supposition (which lies at the root of the Protective system) that our lawgivers know the true interest of every individual of the nation better than he can know it for himself, there can be no objection to all this as a whole, and, if we think we see reason to object to the working of any particular portion of the system, we must set ourselves to show what are its specially inconvenient results, and what good might be expected to come from the relaxation of particular restraints. Just as, under a system of commercial protection, it would be necessary to show that some particular trade is an exceptional one in order to get it freed from the general rule, so, on such a supposition, we must show that some particular profession or occupation is (unlike the majority of others) suited for women, before we can get it opened to them.

It is precisely this necessity, arising, as we have endeavoured to show, from ignoring the fundamental principles of modern government, that opens the door to the flood of peculiarly contradictory and imaginative discussion which characterises every attempt at carrying out some little modification of the highly "protected" condition of women. For how can discussion on this subject be otherwise than imaginative? By the nature of the case those who are urging change are asking to be allowed to try experiments. Until experiments have been tried, we can only imagine what would be their practical results. When we are reduced to imagination one man's imagination is as good as another's, and the Irishman in the story would perhaps have said that a conservative's imagination is "better too." The reformer imagines great benefits, the conservative imagines dire disaster, to be the consequences of most change. What can decide between the two, except that invincible "logic of facts" to which protective law sternly forbids a hearing? Deprived of this impartial umpire, people disport themselves in all the wide regions of fanciful conjecture; analogy is put forward for sober argument; figurative phrases as logical proof; a single example as conclusive evidence; personal taste as the law of nature; accidental circumstances as the immutable condition of the universe. And it is the natural consequence of such discussion's being fanciful that it should also be contradictory. For no two men's imagination depicts a thing exactly in the same light. No two reformers desire, and no two conservatives dread, a change for precisely the same reasons. One man wishes a thing because it does what another man deprecates it for not doing. Thus many persons at the present moment shrink from opening the medical profession to women, because they think it might make them less delicate; others fear that such a movement, by enabling women always to consult physicians of their own sex might foster a morbid degree of delicacy. Thus two different descriptions of imagination may figure the results of the same change as making women too delicate and not delicate enough. In this particular instance, as in many others of the same sort, it is not difficult to detect that the fancy of the objectors has seized hold of different parts of the same subject, and exaggerated a part into the whole. One class persists in regarding exclusively the probable effect upon the physicians, the other that on the patients; and both are apt to forget that, in so very extensive a portion of humanity as the whole female sex, there may easily be room for such varieties of character as would be healthily affected by both sets of influences.

From all these workings of the imagination there is no final appeal but to facts. Experiments must be tried before we can hope to arrive at trustworthy conclusions. They can be tried cautiously if we fancy, as many people do fancy, that, in dealing with women, we are dealing with very explosive materials. But, until we are willing to try them in some way we cannot deny that those who are willing to appeal to facts are more candid, and those who desire to have recourse to experiment are more practical, than those who are content to defend the present state of things by vague predictions of possible evil, while they refuse to put their own predictions to even the most gentle test.

Just such predictions of national ruin were made arguments against free trade, and against such arguments no reply could be so effectual as the national prosperity which free trade has produced. But, until free trade had actually been tried, this argument was not available for its supporters. Having been tried, and having succeeded, free trade, however, remains an example of how human energy can find the best and easiest channels for itself when relieved from all restrictive legislation; an example likely in time to modify old opinions on many topics, and perhaps on none more than on the freedom that can safely be allowed to women.

Source: Reprinted from *Macmillan's Magazine* (September 1866).

BIOGRAPHICAL NOTE

Helen Taylor was the daughter of Harriet Taylor Mill and John Taylor, a partner in a firm of druggists, and the stepdaughter of John Stuart Mill. Upon the death of her mother in 1858, Taylor took her place as John Stuart Mill's constant companion. A strong feminist, like her mother, she encouraged Mill's interest in the Victorian women's movement; apparently, she was instrumental in supporting Mill's decision to publish his famous *The Subjection of Women* in 1869. She also edited his autobiography for publication in 1873.

Taylor shared Mill's classic liberal view on the primacy of attaining political and legal rights for women. As Barbara Caine's discussion of John Stuart Mill's value to Victorian feminism suggests, Taylor supported the separation of campaigns for women's full citizenship from those that, like the campaign for the repeal of the Contagious Diseases Act, focussed on women's sexual status in Victorian society (Caine, 226). The essay reprinted here from *Macmillan's Magazine*, "Women and Criticism," argues the classic liberal case for women's full citizenship by appealing for "free trade" in legislation regarding women.

SELECTED SECONDARY SOURCES

Caine, Barbara. *Victorian Feminists.* Oxford: Oxford UP, 1992.

MILLICENT GARRETT FAWCETT
(1847-1929)

"THE EMANCIPATION OF WOMEN"

Mr. Frederic Harrison's interesting paper, entitled "The Emancipation of Women," in last month's *Fortnightly*, invites a few words of comment and criticism from those who are not able to share the conclusions at which he seems to arrive. There is very much, however, in his paper with which the advocates of the emancipation of women will find themselves in sympathy, and to these points I propose in the first instance to draw attention.

Mr. F. Harrison's position as to the claim of women to the highest kind of education and training, his exalted estimate of the value to the world of the work in it that can only be done by woman, his claim for women, not only of equality but of supremacy, in the home, with all the changes this would imply in domestic life, differentiate his position completely from the position as regards the relation of women to men, of which Milton is the worthiest and ablest exponent, namely, that women are essentially inferior and subordinate to men, that man is the final cause of God's creation, and that woman was made to minister to him and serve him. Mr. Harrison's tone throughout is as far as possible from this: he, indeed, expressly repudiates it; he speaks in his eloquent way of "the brutal egoism of past ages and of too many present men of the world which classes women as the inferiors of men"; he calls this view "the cheap sophistry of the vicious and overbearing," and maintains that "such a view is the refuge of coarse natures and stunted brains." He refers to the "base apathy which is satisfied with the actual condition of woman as it is."

In the matter of education, speaking, it must be assumed, on behalf of the Positivists who meet in Fetter Lane, if not for the whole body, he says that Positivism "calls aloud" for radical improvement. Mr. Harrison, in claiming that Positivism "calls aloud" for scientific education for women, does not refer to the fact that there are people, such as Professor and Mrs. Sidgwick, Miss Clough, Miss Davies, Mrs. William Grey, and Miss Shirreff, who have done better than "call aloud," and have quietly done the work of providing improved education for girls and women. Positivism ought to be grateful to them, though they are for that emancipation of women which Positivism denounces. To call aloud for a good thing is good, as far as it goes; but to provide it is better. So far from being contented with the present or past position of women, Mr. Harrison scorns "the brutal oppression" with which women have been treated in the past, and says that in the present, even among the advanced populations of the West, the practice in regard to women's education is on a par with that of the Mohammedan and Hindoo peoples. He advocates "an education for women on the same lines as that of men, to be given by the same teachers and covering the same ground, though not necessarily to be worked out in common, or in the same form and with the same practical detail. It must be an education, essentially in scientific basis, the same as that of men, conducted by the same, and those the best attainable, instructors —an education certainly not inferior, rather superior, to that of men." In the next paragraph, in order still more thoroughly to emphasise his repudiation of the old view of women's sphere, he says: "We look forward to the good feeling of the future to relieve women from the agonizing wear and tear of families too large to be reared by one mother," and also anticipates that this good feeling of the future "will set women free" from factory labour.

The foregoing brief survey is enough to show how little Mr. F. Harrison is in sympathy with the ordinary view of those who oppose the emancipation of women; indeed, his essay, although in form it is a protest against women's emancipation, is in great part a product of the movement of this century for their emancipation.

But while those who are frankly in sympathy with the evolution of the independence of women find much to agree with in Mr. Harrison's premises, they will find little or nothing to agree with in the conclusions he draws from them; and I think they can fairly charge him with misrepresentation (doubtless unconscious) of their views and objects, and also of their methods of working for them. They will also charge him with a remarkable and almost ludicrous degree of unpracticality, both with regard to his hopes for the future and his knowledge of the present; and, lastly, with this: that with all his repudiation of the old theory that woman is essentially the inferior of man, and only of importance in proportion as she ministers to his comfort and enjoyment, and his fine phrases about "the chivalrous and saintly ideal of woman as man's guardian angel and queen of the home," he really wishes to give women no freedom for the development of individual powers and gifts: he wishes to tie them down to one career and one only—that of housewives.

I will deal with these points one by one. First, I charge Mr. Harrison with misrepresentation: and here I say again that I know he is not guilty of intentional misrepresentation; he never misrepresents except when he does not know, or when his rhetorical high horse runs away with him. But with this reservation I maintain that he does misrepresent in the article I am criticising, and that rather badly. By implication, if not by direct assertion, he seeks to identify the movement of anarchy and revolution with the movement for developing the social and political independence of women. No misrepresentation can be more unfounded. There are people who are in rebellion against all order in society; who think marriages should be dissolvable at will; that parents ought to have no control over their children; that no harm would be done if women wore men's clothes, and men women's; that all laws against theft and other offences against property ought to be abolished; that all distinctions of nationality ought to be swept away; that any quack or imposter who chooses to put a brass plate on his door calling himself a physician, a lawyer, or what not, should occupy exactly the same position as those who have entered the various professions after complying with the constituted educational tests of fitness. Everybody who reads the newspapers, and keeps his ears and eyes open, knows that people of this kind exist: whatever they may call themselves, they are in effect anarchists, against all order and against all authority. But they are not the people who have had anything whatever to do with the movement for the emancipation of women. Many of them are actively hostile to it. I ask Mr. Harrison to produce one bit of work done by these people that has helped in any way to procure better education for women, to open employments to them, or to obtain a recognition of their claim to civil rights and just laws. To identify, or, rather, attempt to identify, them with the workers for women's emancipation as My Harrison does, will only mislead those who are entirely ignorant of the matter in hand. None of the leaders of the women's rights movement in England have ever countenanced for a moment anarchic methods or anarchic aims. Many of them, on the contrary, recognising women's instinctive leanings towards morality and order, look upon their more active participation in public affairs, and especially their admission to the Parliamentary suffrage, as a valuable reinforcement of the party of order against the attacks of the anarchists whom Mr. Harrison so justly denounces. A lady long resident among members of the Greek Orthodox Church told me that she had received a letter from one of them in which the phrase "the Pope and all other Protestants" occurred. Mr. Harrison gives an example of similar depth of ignorance, but with less excuse for it, when he identifies the movement for social anarchy with the movement for the emancipation of women.

But this misrepresentation does not stand alone. We come now to a second. Mr. Harrison speaks of the "brutal egoism" of past ages in their estimate of women; he himself shows another kind of egoism; it is not at all brutal, it is amusing. He cannot free himself from the masculine egoism that, because many of us wish women to have greater freedom in the matter of education, employments, and civil and political rights, we therefore wish them to be like men. Those who are still in bondage to this idea have not shaken off the superstition of the innate inferiority of women. To acknowledge superiority is to acknowledge a desire, latent or open, to resemble the superior being. We recognise the difference between men and women, and maintain just as strongly as Mr. Harrison does, that this difference is not one of inferiority or superiority, but one that influences character, conduct, methods of looking at things, and modes of action in innumerable and infinitely complex ways. Make a woman queen of the greatest empire in the world, place on her shoulders political responsibilities from early girlhood to old age of the weightiest kind, she remains a woman "for a' that." Make her a doctor, put her through the mental discipline and the physical toil of the profession; charge her, as doctors so often are charged, with the health of mind and body of scores of patients, she remains womanly to her finger-tips, and a good doctor in proportion as the truly womanly qualities in her are strongly developed. Poor women are very quick to find this out as patients. Not only from the immediate neighbourhood of the New Hospital for women, where all the staff are women doctors, but also from the far east of London, do they come, because "the ladies," as they call them, are ladies, and show their poor patients womanly sympathy, gentleness and patience, womanly insight and thoughtfulness in little things, and consideration for their home troubles and necessities. It is not too much to say that a woman can never hope to be a good doctor unless she is truly and really a womanly woman. And much the same thing may be said with regard to fields of activity not yet open to women. Take one where Mr. Harrison has ranged himself with our opponents—the share of women in political activity. We do not advocate the representation of women because there is no difference between men and women; but rather because of the difference between them. We want women's special experience as women, their special knowledge of the home and home wants, of child life and the conditions conducive to the formation of character to be brought to bear on legislation. By giving women greater freedom we believe that the truly womanly qualities in them will grow in strength and power, and we hold this belief, not merely as a pious opinion, but as a fact that is proved by a comparison of the various civilisations of various countries. Where women are practically the slaves of men, they have the defects of slaves: they "speak with men's voices," they flatter men's vices, and thereby often manage by cajolery to achieve their own little objects; they neglect the truly womanly qualities, the protecting motherly instincts, the mercy, fidelity, purity, and love of a truly womanly nature. The emancipation of women has probably gone further in England and America at the present time than in any other countries. We are not afraid to compare the womanliness of the women of these countries, as practically shown in the care of children, in endeavours to save and prevent human wreckage, with the womanliness of the women, say of Spain, Egypt or Dahomey. Give a rose good soil and a sunny aspect; let its branches shoot out so that it makes plenty of young wood; do not try to bend and twist it into a too rigorous formality of shape, and you will get the best out of your tree that it is capable of; by giving it a good chance, do not be afraid that you will turn it into an oak or a fuchsia.

There is no wish whatever on the part of the women's rights party to "annihilate," as Mr. Harrison says, "the difference of sex." But this silly cry of doing the impossible thing of annihilating the difference of sex is set up regularly, step by step, whenever women wish to avail themselves of any of the things which men have tried and found good. In the time of Mrs. Hannah Moore, it was unwomanly to learn Latin; Sidney Smith tried to reassure the readers of the *Edinburgh* eighty years ago that the womanly qualities in a woman did not really depend on her ignorance of Greek and Latin, and that a woman might even learn mathematics without "forsaking her infant for a quadratic equation." Later it was unwomanly to write a book, and within my own memory it was unwomanly to skate or ride in a hansom cab. More lately still, when the Albemarle Club was about to be started, the most gloomy forebodings as to its effect "on the foundations of society" and the womanliness of women were indulged in. A highly cultivated lady, a member of the Positivist Society, said to me à *propos* of the Club: "But do you wish *every* distinction between men and women to be abolished?" She joined the club soon after its formation, and has certainly not neglected her opportunities of frequenting it; but I have not heard either from herself or her friends that she has been "unsexed" thereby.

One more misrepresentation is the charge, implied rather than distinctly formulated, that those who favour the emancipation of women have a low estimate of the value and importance of women's domestic work. Mr. Harrison speaks of "debasing the moral currency," and "desecrating the noblest duties of woman"; and it can only be supposed from the context that this means that those who favour the emancipation of women take a low view of women's work in the home as mother of families. Again no assumption can be more entirely unfounded. From Mary Wollstonecraft and Miss Martineau, the spokeswomen for women's freedom have always held in the highest esteem the value and importance of women's work in the home. The fact that to the mother in nearly all classes is consigned the training of children in their most impressionable years, in itself is one of the strongest claims that has ever been put forward for raising the education and social status of women. The woman who brings up a family well does work of inestimable value to the State. She is contributing to the greatness of her country in its highest sense if she provides it, not only with so many head of human beings, whose worth may be reckoned like that of cattle, but with men and women "true in word and deed, brave, sober, temperate, chaste." To argue that because this work is so invaluable and requires so many fine qualities of heart and brain, therefore all women shall be given the Hobson's choice of marriage or nothing else in the way of a satisfactory career, appears to me an error rather similar to that which so long maintained religious tests at the universities. Reverence was supposed to be shown to religious teaching as embodied in the tenets of the Church of England, by making every aspirant for a university degree or a college fellowship declare his allegiance to the thirty-nine articles. In some colleges no one was admitted to a fellowship who had not previously partaken of the Holy Communion. Men of deeply religious mind who were either troubled by doubt, or were members of other church bodies, were thereby excluded from university life; but Gallios of all types took the tests gaily, and even joined in the sacrament, scoffing in their hearts and with a jest on their lips. This is now universally recognised as a poor way of honouring religion; and it appears to those who favour the emancipation of women, but a poor way of honouring marriage to give girls practically no choice between marriage and a life of perpetual childhood.

Many of the shipwrecks of domestic happiness which most people can call to mind, have been caused either by the wife having no real vocation for the duties and responsibilities of marriage, or from her having married without deep affection for her husband, simply because she felt it was a chance she ought not to miss of what is euphemistically called "settling herself in life." Such a marriage is as much a sale as the grosser institutions of the East can provide. It is a desecration of holy things; a wrong to the man, and a wrong to the children who may be born of the marriage. A girl I know was saved the other day from one of these wretched marriages that do so much to cause the names of the victims to them to reappear in the newspapers under the heading of "Probate and Divorce." She was in a position in society in which it would require abnormal force of character for a young woman to take up any professional pursuit or absorbing occupation. A man of wealth and position had paid her great attention, and every one supposed they were on the point of an engagement, when she heard that he was engaged to some one else. Her pride was wounded, but not her heart. She said to her mother, "I am sorry in a way; I should have accepted him if he had asked me, for I don't think anything better was likely to offer; but I don't care for him in the least, and I don't think I ever should," I mention this incident because most people will recognise it as a type; a type which George Eliot portrayed in literature when she described the marriage of Rosamond and Lydgate. Of course it is possible that the heroine of my tale was not speaking the truth; but supposing that she was, what she contemplated doing was on a par with what goes on between twelve and two every morning in the Haymarket and Piccadilly Circus. It is to sell what should never be sold: sensual and materialising, it is this and things like it, which really "debase the moral currency," and "desecrate the noblest duties of woman," not factory or any other honest labour, nor any claim on the part of women for a fuller recognition of their citizenship.

I come now to what I conceive to be the unpractical character of Mr. Harrison's paper. In two or three lines he says that he looks "to the future to set women free from the crushing factory labour, which is the real slave trade of the Nineteenth Century"; In other passages he appears to be averse to women engaging in any remunerative work, professional or industrial, and has a little sneer (that, I take it, of a rich man who has never had to work for a living) at the professional woman contemplating her banker's pass-book with satisfaction. In reply to all this we would ask him how he proposes to provide for the millions of women who earn their own living in various forms of industry? The new census returns are not yet obtainable in full detail; but the census of 1881 showed that three and a half millions of women in Great Britain and Ireland were earning weekly wages. Mr. Harrison proposes to "set them free from factory labour"; but he must know that in innumerable cases this would be setting them free to starve. One of the nail and chain-making women, when threatened last summer with legislative interference with her labour, was asked if her hard work did not hurt her. She replied, "My work didn't hurt me: if I hadn't done it, what my mouth missed would have hurt me." Mr. Harrison makes no attempt to grapple with the practical problem of women's work, and makes no suggestion as to how best to help to make the hours and wages of their work more conducive to a satisfactory life for the workers as human beings. Here, as elsewhere, in his paper, rhetoric and fancy take the place of solid practical good sense. He, no doubt, feels that each woman ought to be provided for in superintending and beautifying the home of some man, presumably as his wife and the mother of his children. His lamentations that this is impossible, because there are more women than men in this country, furnish one of the most curious passages that I have read for a long time, even on this most discussed subject of the whole duty of women. To him the unmarried woman is a blighted being, and his feeling heart bleeds for her, and he "calls aloud" to proclaim his distress and sympathy. "We know," he says, "that in a disorganized condition of society there are *terrible accumulations of exceptional and distressing personal hardship. Of course, millions of women have, and can have, no husbands!*" It would, perhaps, be hypercritical to remark that the rhetorical "millions" ought to be changed for "nearly a million." But what is far more striking is, that when Mr. Harrison speaks of "terrible accumulations of exceptional and distressing personal hardship," the first image that rises in his sympathizing mind is that of "women who have, and can have, no husbands." He must surely dwell in a kingdom of fancy and imagination, or the first sentence would have been followed by a second much more closely in touch with the tragedies of common life. It is not the women who have no husbands, but the women who have bad husbands, who are most deserving of compassion—women, whose stories appear week by week in the newspapers, who are driven to suicide by the nameless and hideous brutalities to which they have been subjected; women who are driven on the streets that their husbands may loaf in idleness on their earnings; women who live in daily and hourly terror of their lives from their husband's personal violence; and cases worse even than any of these that recall and exceed the worst horrors of the story of the Cenci. Mr. Harrison must live in a world where he never hears or knows these things, or surely he would not be so lachrymose over the supposed woes of women "who have, and can have, no husbands"; it is true that in the next part of the same sentence he extends his compassion to women who are not well provided with other relatives, "women who have no parents, no brother, no true family." If I am not misinformed, the Positivist theory is that every woman should be maintained in the home, without herself earning money, by the exertions of either father, husband, son, brother, or some other male relative. People who have never been, since childhood, in absolute pecuniary dependence on others, can with difficulty measure the bitterness of the position, otherwise they would not need so often to be reminded—[...]

But whatever the value of the theory that every woman ought to be dependent upon some man for food, clothing, books, amusements, and all the other necessaries and amenities of life, it is becoming year by year less in correspondence with the facts of our national life. Speaking roughly, all working-class women and many middle-class women work for wages up to the time of their marriage, and many of them work after their marriage. Miss Clara Collett, in her chapter on women's industries in Mr. Charles Booth's book, *Life and Labour of the People,* says that in London young women working as tailoresses prefer to work for strangers rather than for their fathers, even when their fathers are in the same trade and able to employ them. The reason is very simple: in the first case they get wages, in the second they do not. It is hardly too much to say that it is not till women have had an opportunity of working for wages outside the home that the value of their work in the home has received the recognition it deserves. Economic independence has paved the way for that wider emancipation which Mr. Harrison is opposing. That the movement for women's emancipation has an economic foundation, based on the changes in methods of production utilising the labour of women, affords strong ground for believing in its durability; it also suggests an explanation of the fact that the movement is furthest advanced in England and America, the countries where this industrial change is more developed than elsewhere; and lastly, why symptoms of this movement towards freedom on the part of women are observable in every country in the world which has shared in the industrial changes of modern times. Mr. Harrison, and many others, often attribute the women's rights movement to the fact that there are more women than men in England, and therefore the supply of men is not sufficient to provide every woman with a husband; but his simple explanation ceases to be applicable when we look at the women's rights movement in America; for there men are in a majority, almost exactly equal to the majority of women in England. In New Zealand and the Australian colonies generally men largely outnumber the women, but there, in many respects, the emancipation of women has gone further than elsewhere.

There are signs in Mr. Harrison's paper that he has hardly kept himself acquainted with the industrial change that has taken place in the position of women. He runs into one sentence his belief that there is nothing but the trifles of "law and convention" to prevent women being members of Parliament, professors of Hebrew and anatomy, "*surgeons, nay, tailors,* joiners, cab-drivers, or soldiers, if they gave their minds to it." The words I have italicised show how little he knows of the actual world of women's work: a few women are surgeons; that, perhaps, he could not be expected to know; but thousands of women are tailors—the clothes of the British army are made by women. To quote Miss Clara Collett again, her article on "Women's Work in Leeds"[1] shows that the number of women employed in tailoring is rapidly increasing—

CENSUS RETURNS OF THE TAILORING AND MACHINING IN LEEDS.

	Women	Men	Total
1861	131	1,323	1,454
1881	2,740	2,148	4,888

Miss Collett is unable, like the rest of us, to give the figures for 1891, but she estimates the number of women and girls now employed in this trade in Leeds at 10,000. Thus, while Mr. Harrison was exclaiming that there was nothing but law and convention to prevent women engaging in the masculine pursuit of making clothes, he must have been unaware that law and convention had nothing to say in the matter, and that probably more than half the men in England are wearing clothes made by women.

But while Mr. Harrison is unpractical in his ignorance of what is actually taking place under his very eyes, he is equally unpractical where he most assumes the wisdom of the practical man. How can he suppose that the work of working women gets itself done if it were true, as he asserts, that every mother was "for months a simple invalid?" The robust way in which the working woman, as a rule, goes through the child-bearing period of her life, tempts one to hope that some women who enjoy ill health on these occasions would be more robust if they were less idle. A nail and chain-making woman, who joined the deputation to Mr. Matthews in June, was asked by him to describe the nature of her work. She answered in a way that was more to the point than might at first sight appear: "I ha' had fourteen children, sir, and I never was better in my life." Her well-developed frame, bright complexion, and hearty voice, corroborated her words; and yet here is Mr. Harrison saying that women are physically unfitted by the law of nature for hard work, and that if they undertake it either the work will be done by "an unsexed minority of women, or it means a diminution and speedy end to the human race." The array of facts is all against Mr. Harrison. The present century is the time, speaking roughly, in which women have entered the field of industry otherwise than in domestic work. It took between four hundred and five hundred years for the population to double itself between 1448 (before the black death) and 1800; but in the ninety years since 1801, it has been multiplied by four-and-a-half, that is, from less than nine millions to nearly forty millions. Of all arguments against women's emancipation, that based on the "end of the human race" theory has, in the presence of the census cables, the least power to alarm us. Mr. Harrison does not confine what he has to say in this so-called biological objection to women's work to women as mothers. He says that "all women," with very few exceptions, are "subject to functional interruption absolutely incompatible with the highest forms of continuous pressure." This assertion I venture most emphatically to deny. The actual period of child-birth apart, the ordinarily healthy woman is as fit for work every day of her life as the ordinarily healthy man. Fresh air, exercise, suitable clothing, and nourishing food, added to the habitual temperance of women in eating and drinking, have brought about a marvellously good result in improving their average health. Mr. Harrison indulges his readers with the well-worn old joke about an army composed of women, a certain percentage of whom will always be unable to take the field from being in childbed. It might be retorted that a percentage of the actual army is invalided from a less reputable cause; but it is undesirable to vie with Mr. Harrison in irrelevant observations. No one wishes women to serve in the army, or to be dock-labourers or butchers, because they are physically unfit for the work involved; but they are not physically or mentally unfit to vote, or to engage in a large number of industrial, scientific, and professional pursuits, and these privileges and occupations therefore we wish to see opened to them.

Mr. Harrison appears to me to be misled by a desire too much to map out the whole of human life with tape measure and ruler, and to carry the idea of division of labour into fields where it has no true application. To woman he assigns the affections; to man, activity. He is tempted sometimes into speaking as if he believed men were incapable of affection, and as if it were only abnormal men who have the strong clinging affection for their children that most women have. This is not true of human nature as I have observed it. At least, I have never considered those men abnormal or "unsexed" in whom family affection was strongly developed. The side where women are strongest, says Mr. Harrison, is affection. The side where men are strongest is activity. Intelligence, he is good enough to add, is common to both, as if activity and affection were not also common to both. A man incapable of affection, a woman incapable of practical activity, would be monstrosities, fit only for the gaol or the asylum. How beside the mark all this mapping out of qualities according to fixed rules appears to those who approach the subject from the practical side, and find themselves in contact with the infinite complexities of the actual characters of men and women or boys and girls in the nursery!

Let us try by another practical test the value of Mr. Harrison's efforts to contribute to the solution of difficulties and problems as they arise in real life. Take the case of a family consisting of half-a-dozen daughters. There is sufficient work perhaps at home for one of them; if they have neither beauty nor wealth they are very likely not to marry. What are they to do? Mr. Harrison's reply is that their "function is to educate, not children only, but men"; and also to "keep the family true, refined, affectionate, and faithful." This is all very well; but my six healthy young women would retort, "What men? Whose family? Papa wouldn't like it at all if we tried to educate him, and we think our family is fairly refined and affectionate, and would not be less so if there were rather fewer of us in it." Again, take another practical case. A girl comes and says, some years ago her father lost his health, then his business went to pieces; her brother tried to carry it on, and he, too, failed, and has now gone to try his fortunes in Australia. What would I advise her to do? She is not well educated enough to teach; her friends are kind, but not rich, and she has been staying with them a long time, and then follows a free rendering into English of "come sa di sale," &c. The answer is hard enough any way; but as the emancipation of women goes on, and more occupations and pursuits are open, it becomes easier. If Mr. Harrison had his way it would be impossible to give any answer at all, except to tell the girl that she was one of the "unsexed minority," or was a specimen of "exceptional and distressing personal hardship." For I imagine that no one, in reply to such an applicant, would have the impertinence to tell her that her "function was to educate men" and to keep the family refined and affectionate, that this task must absorb "her whole energies, her entire life," and that it would be degrading, therefore, for her to mix this "sacred duty with the coarse occupations" of earning a living.

My last charge against Mr. Harrison is, that while in words he repudiates the subordination of women to men, and the notion that the woman is of value only in so far as she ministers to the comfort and enjoyment of the man, he cannot really divest himself of it. It comes round to this: the emancipation of women, the giving to women a full choice of a large number of useful and honourable occupations other than marriage would, in Mr. Harrison's view, be "worse than a return to slavery and polytheism. If only a small minority of women," he says, "availed themselves of their freedom, the beauty of womanliness would be darkened in every home." To translate this from the general to the particular, it might run thus: "If only a small minority of women smoked and rode astride, the sentiment of many men and women as to what was fitting would be wounded." This is absolutely undeniable, but it is surely overdoing it to say it would be worse than a return to polytheism and slavery. J.K.S., author of *Lapsus Calami*, has put his thoughts on this subject in a verse which I think embodies a good deal of the true inwardness of Mr. Harrison's reasoning:—

TO ONE THAT SMOKES.

"Spare us the hint of slightest desecration,
    Spotless preserve us an untainted shrine;
Not for thy sake, oh goddess of creation,
    Not for thy sake, oh woman, but for mine."

A great deal of Mr. Harrison's wish to confine women practically to domesticities, to prevent them from having the opportunities of earning a living, to force them into marriage whether they have a real vocation for it or not, is explained when we remember that it is "not for thy sake, oh woman, but for mine." The theory that the woman is not so much the friend and comrade of the man as a goddess to be set in a shrine and worshipped, receives a shock when brought in contact with the realities of life. Hence, also, Mr. Harrison's weeping and wailing over this "materialistic age," where men "despise what is pure, lofty, and tender, and exalt what is coarse, vulgar, and vainglorious," "an age of nihilism," of "disorganization," of "scepticism, mammon worship, and false glory." This railing against the evolution of society which is taking place before us, is probably to be accounted for by the fact that it does not closely correspond to Positivist ideals, and in fact seems going further and further from them. Therefore, in Mr. Harrison's view, the times are out of joint, and he really believes that it rests with the Positivist Society to set them right. He says, "We," *i.e.* the Positivists, "are defending the principle of the womanliness of women." There has been nothing showing such a want of the sense of proportion since the Bishops of Winchester and Gloucester rose in convocation "to defend the honour of their Lord's Godhead." The womanliness of women is one of those great facts of nature which do not require the exertions of the Positivist Society to buttress it: but this is what Mr. Harrison cannot bring himself to believe. The saying, "The sun will rise to-morrow—subject to the constitution of the United States," finds a parallel in several passages of this remarkable paper. To give another example: "Is it," Mr. Harrison exclaims, "to be left to the religion of humanity to defend the primaeval institution of society?" To this absurd question there can be but one answer—when the supply of negatives provided by the English language appears inadequate to their demands, schoolboys substitute the word "scarcely;" we are tempted to employ the same word on this occasion. Whatever may be the special perils and difficulties of the present time, our case is not as desperate as that. Positivism claims to be a religion of faith in human nature; but its professors exhibit a pitiable want of faith, a practical infidelity, when they talk as if the womanliness of women existed only in virtue of their exertions, and appear to think that if thirty or forty people meeting in Fetter Lane relaxed their endeavours "the primaeval institutions of society" would collapse.

NOTE

1   *Economic Journal*, September, 1891.

Source: Reprinted from *Fortnightly Review* (November 1891).

BIOGRAPHICAL NOTE

Leader of the Victorian suffrage movement, political economist and social campaigner, Millicent Garrett Fawcett was the daughter of Newson Garrett, wealthy corn and coal merchant, and Louise Dunnell of Aldeburgh, Suffolk. Her sister, Elizabeth Garrett Anderson, was reknowned for her fight to become a doctor. Like her sisters, Fawcett was educated at home by a governess, with some local schooling. Once this formal schooling was complete at fourteen, she continued her education at home.

Fawcett's feminism was strongly influenced by John Stuart Mill's Liberalism, with its stress on free-trade, self-reliance and individualism. Attending one of Mill's electoral speeches in 1865, she was inspired to develop her belief in women's suffrage. Shortly after, she met Henry Fawcett, Radical MP and professor of Political Economy at Cambridge. They were married in 1867, despite some fierce opposition from her family, particularly from Elizabeth who had earlier rejected a proposal from him.

The Fawcett's marriage was an extremely happy one, since both partners shared the same views on women's suffrage. Henry Fawcett's position as MP aided his wife's activism. He also encouraged her to write; her first article on lectures for women in Cambridge appeared in *Macmillan's Magazine* in 1868. Her next work, *Political Economy for Beginners* (1870), dismissed by later critics as a compendium of her husband's work, was extremely well-received, going through ten editions and used as a school book. Later publications include *Essays and Lectures on Political Subjects* (1872) with her husband, and an unsuccessful novel, *Janet Doncaster* (1875).

Through the course of the 1880s, Fawcett gradually emerged as one of the leaders of the suffrage movement. Henry's early death in 1884 left her with extra time that she chose to devote to suffrage. She assumed the leadership of the National Union of Women's Suffrage Societies (NUWSS) in 1890 upon the sudden death of Lydia Becker and retained that position until 1919 in spite of the occasional battle for leadership as the character of the feminist movement changed over the turn of the century.

Throughout her time with the NUWSS, Fawcett maintained her focus on suffrage, though she was also deeply committed to women's education and was involved in the plan to establish lectures for women at Cambridge, a plan that eventually led to the founding of Newnham College. Her belief that suffrage must be the main focus of the women's movement led her to distance herself from the campaign to repeal the Contagious Diseases Acts begun in 1870. Though she did not accept the Acts, as did her sister Dr. Elizabeth Garrett Anderson, she nonetheless feared the effect of the highly controversial repeal campaign on the suffrage movement. In the 1880s however, Fawcett's views on the necessary separation of moral issues from the fight for suffrage underwent significant change. Strongly moved by W.T. Stead's series of articles on "white slavery," the traffic in young girls in London, she rethought the necessity for this separation, writing letters to the editor in Stead's support and arguing for the need for women's participation in control of the law. She also met Josephine Butler during this time, and was deeply impressed. Her biography of Butler, written in association with E.M. Turner, was published in 1927.

With the turn of the century, and accelerating change in the character of the feminist movement, Fawcett found herself again revising her stand on a number of issues. A. Liberal who had rejected free education in 1870 in the belief that it lessened parental responsibility, and a feminist who campaigned for equal grounds for divorce but worried about sexual freedom, Fawcett agreed to the NUWSS's 1912 decision to support Labour candidates. She protested, however, against the protective legislation for working women advocated by her Labour companions. She was also ambivalent about the increasing militancy of groups like the Women's Social and Political Union (WSPU). Though admiring the militants' courage, she was nonetheless uneasy, firmly believing in the power of reason and persuasion for the suffrage cause. Her 1891 essay, "The Emancipation of Women," reprinted here, conveys some of this uneasiness, as she rejects Frederic Harrison's association of anarchy and revolution with the suffrage movement. "There are people who are in rebellion against all order in society; who think marriages should be dissolvable at will ... But they are not the people who had anything whatever to do with the movement for the emancipation of women."

Ultimately Fawcett resigned her membership after the First World War over the issue of family allowances, which she believed would destroy family life. In 1919, she retired from political work, though continuing to work for the cause. She travelled widely, and continued to write. Her 1912 *History of a Great Movement* was followed by *The Women's Victory—and After* (1920), *What I Remember* (1924), and *Josephine Butler* (1927). She died in 1929.

SELECTED SECONDARY SOURCES

Caine, Barbara. *Victorian Feminists*. Oxford: Oxford UP, 1992.

Oakley, Ann. "Millicent Garrett Fawcett: Duty and Determination," *Feminist Theorists: Three Centuries of Women's Intellectual Traditions*. Ed. Dale Spender. London: Pandora, 1983.

Strachey, Ray. *Millicent Garrett Fawcett*. London: Pandora, 1931.

Mona Caird
(1854-1932)

"Marriage"

It is not difficult to find people mild and easy-going about religion, and even politics may be regarded with wide-minded tolerance; but broach social subjects, and English men and women at once become alarmed and talk about the foundations of society and the sacredness of the home! Yet the particular form of social life, or of marriage, to which they are so deeply attached, has by no means existed from time immemorial; in fact, modern marriage, with its satellite ideas, only dates as far back as the age of Luther. Of course the institution existed long before, but our particular mode of regarding it can be traced to the era of the Reformation, when commerce, competition, the great *bourgeois* class, and that remarkable thing called "Respectability," also began to arise.

Before entering upon the history of marriage, it is necessary to clear the ground for thought upon this subject by a protest against the careless use of the words "human nature," and especially "woman's nature." History will show us, if anything will, that human nature has an apparently limitless adaptability, and that therefore no conclusion can be built upon special manifestations which may at any time be developed. Such development must be referred to certain conditions, and not be mistaken for the eternal law of being. With regard to "woman's nature," concerning which innumerable contradictory dogmas are held, there is so little really known about it, and its power of development, that all social philosophies are more or less falsified by this universal though sublimely unconscious ignorance.

The difficulties of friendly intercourse between men and women are so great, and the false sentiments induced by our present system so many and so subtle, that it is the hardest thing in the world for either sex to learn the truth concerning the real thoughts and feelings of the other. If they find out what they mutually think about the weather it is as much as can be expected—consistently, that is, with genuine submission to present ordinances. Thinkers, therefore, perforce take no count of the many half-known and less understood ideas and emotions of women, even as these actually exist at the moment, and they make still smaller allowance for potential developments which at the present crisis are almost incalculable. Current phrases of the most shallow kind are taken as if they expressed the whole that is knowable on the subject.

There is in fact no social philosophy, however logical and far-seeing on other points, which does not lapse into incoherence as soon as it touches the subject of women. The thinker abandons the thought-laws which he has obeyed until that fatal moment; he forgets every principle of science previously present to his mind, and he suddenly goes back centuries in knowledge and in the consciousness of possibilities, making schoolboy statements, and "babbling of green fields" in a manner that takes away the breath of those who have listened to his former reasoning, and admired his previous delicacies of thought-distinction. Has he been overtaken by some afflicting mental disease? Or does he merely allow himself to hold one subject apart from the circulating currents of his brain, judging it on different principles from those on which he judges every other subject?

Whatever be the fact, the results appear to be identical. A sudden loss of intellectual power would have exactly this effect upon the opinions which the sufferer might hold on any question afterwards presented to him. Suddenly fallen from his high mental estate, our philosopher takes the same view of women as certain Indian theologians took of the staple food of their country.[1] "The Great Spirit," they said, "made all things, except the wild rice, but the wild rice came by chance." The Muse of History, guided by that of Science, eloquently protests against treating any part of the universe as "wild rice"' she protests against the exclusion of the ideas of evolution, of natural selection, of the well-known influence upon organs and aptitudes of continued use or disuse, influence which every one has exemplified in his own life, which every profession proves, and which is freely acknowledged in the discussion of all questions except those in which woman forms an important element. "As she was in the beginning, is now, and ever shall be—!"

There is a strange irony in this binding of women to the evil results in their own natures of the restrictions and injustice which they have suffered for generations. We chain up a dog to keep watch over our home; we deny him freedom, and in some cases, alas! even sufficient exercise to keep his limbs supple and his body in health. He becomes dull and spiritless, he is miserable and ill-looking, and if by any chance he is let loose, he gets into mischief and runs away. He has not been used to liberty or happiness, and he cannot stand it.

Humane people ask his master: "Why do you keep that dog always chained up?"

"Oh! he is accustomed to it; he is suited for the chain; when we let him loose he runs wild."

So the dog is punished by chaining for the misfortune of having been chained, till death releases him. In the same way we have subjected women for centuries to a restricted life, which called forth one or two forms of domestic activity; we have rigorously excluded (even punished) every other development of power; and we have then insisted that the consequent adaptations of structure, and the violent instincts created by this distorting process, are, by a sort of compound interest, to go on adding to the distortions themselves, and at the same time to go on forming a more and more solid ground for upholding the established system of restriction, and the ideas that accompany it. We chain, because we *have chained*. The dog must not be released, because his nature has adapted itself to the misfortune of captivity.

He has no revenge in his power; he must live and die, and no one knows his wretchedness. But the woman takes her unconscious vengeance, for she enters into the inmost life of society. *She* can pay back the injury with interest. And so she does, item by item. Through her, in a great measure, marriage becomes what Milton calls "a drooping and disconsolate household captivity," and through her influence over children she is able to keep going much physical weakness and disease which might, with a little knowledge, be readily stamped out; she is able to oppose new ideas by the early implanting of prejudice; and, in short, she can hold back the wheels of progress, and send into the world human beings likely to wreck every attempt at social reorganization that may be made, whether it be made by men or by gods.[2]

Seeing, then, that the nature of women is the result of their circumstances, and that they are not a sort of human "wild rice," come by chance or special creation, no protest can be too strong against the unthinking use of the term "woman's nature." An unmanageable host of begged questions, crude assertions, and unsound habits of thought are packed into those two hackneyed words.

Having made this protest, we propose to take a brief glance at the history of marriage, then to consider marriage at the present day, and finally to discuss the marriage of the future. We begin with a time when there was no such thing as monogamy, but it is not necessary for our purpose to dwell upon that age. The first era that bears closely upon our subject is the matriarchal age, to which myths and folk-lore, in almost all countries, definitely point. The mother was the head of the family, priestess, and instructress in the arts of husbandry. She was the first agriculturist, the first herbalist, the initiator (says Karl Pierson) of all civilization. Of this age many discoveries have lately been made in Germany. The cave in which the mother took shelter and brought up her family was the germ of our "home." The family knew only one parent: the mother; her name was transmitted, and property—when that began to exist—was inherited through her, and her only. A woman's indefeasible right to her own child of course remained unquestioned, and it was not until many centuries later that men resorted to all kinds of curious devices with a view of claiming authority over children, which was finally established by force, entirely irrespective of moral right.

The idea of right always attaches itself in course of time to an established custom which is well backed up by force; and at the present day even persons of high moral feeling see no absurdity in the legal power of a man to dispose of his children contrary to the will of their mother. Not only does the man now claim a right to interfere, but he actually claims sole authority in cases of dispute. This would be incredible were it not a fact.

During the mother-age, some men of the tribe became wandering hunters, while others remained at home to till the soil. The hunters, being unable to procure wives in the woods and solitudes, used to make raids upon the settlements and carry off some of the women. This was the origin of our modern idea of *possession* in marriage. The woman became the property of the man, his own by right of conquest. Now the wife is his own by right of law.

It is John Stuart Mill, we believe, who says that woman was the first being who was enslaved. A captured wife probably lost her liberty even before animals were pressed into man's service. In Germany, in early times, women were in the habit of dragging the plough. This and many similar facts, we may remark in passing, show that there is no inherent difference in physical strength between the two sexes, and that the present great difference is probably induced by difference of occupation extending backward over many generations.

The transition period from the mother-age to the father-age was long and painful. It took centuries to deprive the woman of her powerful position as head of the family, and of all the superstitious reverence which her knowledge of primitive arts and of certain properties of herbs, besides her influence as priestess, secured her. Of this long struggle we find many traces in old legends, in folklore, and in the survival of customs older than history. Much later, in the witch-persecutions of the Middle Ages, we come upon the remnants of belief in the woman's superior power and knowledge, and the determination of man to extinguish it.[3] The awe remained in the form of superstition, but the old reverence was changed to antagonism. We can note in early literature the feeling that women were evil creatures eager to obtain power, and that the man was nothing less than a coward who permitted this low and contemptible influence to make way against him.

During the transition period, capture-marriages, of course, met with strenuous opposition from the mother of the bride, not only as regarded the high-handed act itself, but also in respect to the changes relating to property which the establishment of father-rule brought about. Thus we find a hereditary basis for the (no doubt) divinely instilled and profoundly natural repugnance of a man for his mother-in-law! This sentiment can claim the authority of centuries and almost equal rank as a primitive and sacred impulse of our nature with the maternal instinct itself. Almost might we speak of it tenderly and mellifluously as "beautiful."

On the spread of Christianity and the ascetic doctrines of its later teachers, feminine influence received another check. "Woman!" exclaims Tertullian with startling frankness, "thou art the gate of hell!" This is the keynote of the monastic age. Woman was an ally of Satan, seeking to lead men away from the paths of righteousness. She appears to have succeeded very brilliantly! We have a century of almost universal corruption, ushering in the period of the Minne-singers and troubadours, or what is called the age of chivalry. In spite of a licentious society, this age has given us the precious germ of a new idea with regard to sex-relationship, for art and poetry now began to soften, and beautify the cruder passion, and we have the first hint of a distinction which can be quite clearly felt between love as represented by classical authors and what may be called modern, or romantic, love—as a recent writer named it. This nobler sentiment when developed and still further inwoven with ideas of modern growth, forms the basis of the ideal marriage, which is founded upon a full attraction and expression of the whole nature.

But this development was checked, though the idea was not destroyed, by the Reformation. It is to Luther and his followers that we can immediately trace nearly all the notions that now govern the world with regard to marriage. Luther was essentially coarse and irreverent towards the oppressed sex; he placed marriage on the lowest possible platform, and, as one need scarcely add, he did not take women into counsel in a matter so deeply concerning them. In the age of chivalry the marriage-tie was not at all strict, and our present ideas of "virtue" and "honour" were practically non-existent. Society was in what is called a chaotic state; there was extreme licence on all sides, and although the standard of morality was far severer for the woman than for the man, still she had more or less liberty to give herself as passion dictated, and society tacitly accorded her a right of choice in matters of love. But Luther ignored all the claims of passion in a woman; in fact, she had no recognized claims whatever; she was not permitted to object to any part in life that might be assigned her; the notion of resistance to his decision never occurred to him—her *rôle* was one of duty and of service; she figured as the legal property of a man, the safeguard against sin, and the victim of that vampire "Respectability" which thenceforth was to fasten upon, and suck the life-blood of all womanhood.

The change from the open licence of the age of chivalry to the decorum of the Philistine *régime*, was merely a change in the *mode* of licentiousness, not a move from evil to good. Hypocrisy became a household god; true passion was dethroned, and with it poetry and romance; the commercial spirit, staid and open-eyed, entered upon its long career, and began to regulate the relations of the sexes. We find a peculiar medley of sensuality and decorum: the mercenary spirit entering into the idea of marriage, women were bought and sold as if they were cattle, and were educated, at the same time, to strict ideas of "purity" and duty, to Griselda-like patience under the severest provocation. Carried off by the highest bidder, they were gravely exhorted to be moral, to be chaste, and faithful and God-fearing, serving their lords in life and in death. To drive a hard bargain, and to sermonize one's victims at the same time, is a feat distinctly of the Philistine order. With the growth of the commercial system, of the rich burgher class, and of all the ideas that thrive under the influence of wealth when divorced from mental cultivation, the status of women gradually established itself upon this degrading basis, and became fixed more and more firmly as the *bourgeois* increased in power and prosperity.

Bebel speaks of Luther as the interpreter of the "healthy sensualism" of the Middle Ages.[4] Any "healthy sensualism," however, which did not make itself legitimate by appeal to the Church and the law was rigorously punished under his system. Women offenders were subject to hideous and awful forms of punishment. Thus we may say that Luther established, in the interests of sensuality and respectability, a strict marriage system. He also preached the devastating doctrine which makes it a duty to have an unlimited number of children. Of course he did not for a moment consider the woman in this matter; why should a thick-skinned, coarse-fibred monk of the sixteenth century consider sufferings which are overlooked by tender-hearted divines of the nineteenth century? The gentle Melanchthon on this subject says as follows: "If a woman becomes weary of bearing children, that matters not; let her only die from bearing, she is there to do it." This doctrine is not obsolete at the present day. It is the rule of life among the mass of our most highly respectable classes, those who hold the scales of public morality in their hands, and whose prerogative appears to be to judge in order that they be not judged.

As an instance of the way in which an exceptionally good man can regard this subject—his goodness notwithstanding—we may turn to the Introduction, by Charles Kingsley, to Brook's *Fool of Quality*, which Kingsley edited. A short account is given of the life of Brook, who flourished (in a very literal sense) in the time of the Restoration, and who was saved, as his biographer points out in joy and thankfulness, from the vices of that corrupt age, by an early marriage. Kingsley goes on to describe the home where all that is commendable and domestic reigned and prospered.

He dwells lovingly on that peasant picture of simple joys and happy cares, upon the swarms of beautiful children who cluster round their father's knee and rescue him from the dangers of a licentious age. Kingsley mentions, just in passing, that the young wife watches the happy scene from a sofa, having become a confirmed invalid from the number of children she has borne during the few years of her married life. But what of that? What of the anguish and weariness, what of the thousand painful disabilities which that young woman has suffered before her nature yielded to the strain—disabilities which she will have to bear to her life's end? Has not the valuable Brook been saved from an immoral life? (Of course Brook could not be expected to save himself!—we are not unreasonable.) Have not Propriety and Respectability been propitiated? And the price of all this? Merely the suffering and life-long injury of one young woman in a thoroughly established and "natural" manner; nothing more. Kingsley feels that it is cheap at the price. *Brook is saved!* Hallelujah!

It is difficult to think without acrimony of the great reformer, conscious though we may be of the untold benefits which he has bestowed upon mankind. It is because of Luther that women are martyred daily in the interests of virtue and propriety! It is to Luther that we owe half the inconsistencies and cruelties of our social laws, to Luther that we owe the extreme importance of the marriage-rite, which is to make the whole difference between terrible sin and absolute duty.

> "The Catholic Church had before Luther taught that marriage was a sacrament. We should be the last to defend the truth of such a conception, but we must call attention to the fact that it emphasized something beyond the physical in the conjugal relation, it endowed it with a *spiritual* side. The conception of marriage as a spiritual as well as physical relation seems to us the essential condition of all permanent happiness between man and wife. The intellectual union superposed on the physical is precisely what raises human above brute intercourse.... We believe that the spiritual side must be kept constantly in view if the sanctity of marriage is to be preserved. Here it is that Luther, rejecting the conception of marriage as a sacrament, rushes, with his usual impetuosity, into the opposite and more dangerous extreme."[5]

Luther in destroying the religious sanctity of marriage destroyed also the idea of spiritual union which the religious conception implied; he did his utmost to deprive it of the elements of real affection and sympathy, and to bring it to the very lowest form which it is capable of assuming. It was to be regarded merely as a means of avoiding general social chaos; as a "safeguard against sin;" and the wife's position—unless human laws have some supernatural power of sanctification—was the most completely abject and degraded position which it is possible for a human being to hold.

That Luther did not observe the insult to womanhood of such a creed is not to be wondered at, since the nineteenth century has scarcely yet discovered it. Of course from such ideas spring rigid ideas of wifehood. Woman's chastity becomes the watch-dog of man's possession. She has taken the sermon given to her at the time of her purchase deeply to heart, and chastity becomes her chief virtue. If we desire to face the matter honestly, we must not blink the fact that this virtue has originally no connection with the woman's own nature; it does *not* arise from the feelings which protect individual dignity. The quality, whatever be its intrinsic merits, has attained its present mysterious authority and rank through man's monopolizing jealousy, through the fact that he desired to "have and to hold" one woman as his exclusive property, and that he regarded any other man who would dispute his monopoly as the unforgivable enemy. From this starting-point the idea of a man's "honour" grew up, creating the remarkable paradox of a moral possession or attribute, which could be injured by the action of some other person than the possessor. Thus also arose woman's "honour," which was lost if she did not keep herself solely for her lord, present or to come. Again, we see that *her* honour has reference to someone other than herself, though in course of time the idea was carried further, and has now acquired a relation with the woman's own moral nature, and a still firmer hold upon the conscience. However valuable the quality, it certainly did not take its rise from a sense of self-respect in woman but from the fact of her subjection to man.

While considering the development of this burgher age, one must not forget to note the concurrence of strict marriage and systematic or legalized prostitution. The social chaos of the age of chivalry was exchanged for comparative order, and there now arose a hard-and-fast line (far more absolute than had existed before in Germany) between two classes of women: those who submitted to the yoke of marriage on Luther's terms, and those who remained on the other side of the great social gulf, subject also to stringent laws, and treated also as the property of men (though not of *one* man). We now see completed our own way of settling the relations of the sexes. The factors of our system are: respectability, prostitution, strict marriage, commercialism, unequal moral standard for the two sexes, and the subjection of women.

In this brief sketch we have not dwelt upon the terrible suffering of the subject sex through all the changes of their estate; to do so in a manner to produce realization would lead us too far afield and would involve too many details. Suffice it to say that the cruelties, indignities, and insults to which women were exposed are (as every student of history knows) hideous beyond description. In Mongolia there are large cages in the marketplace wherein condemned prisoners are kept and starved to death. The people collect in front of these cages to taunt and insult the victims as they die slowly day by day before their eyes. In reading the history of the past, and even the literature of our own day, it is difficult to avoid seeing in that Mongolian marketplace a symbol of our own society, with its iron cage, wherein women are held in bondage, suffering moral starvation, while the thoughtless gather round to taunt and to insult their lingering misery. Let any one who thinks this exaggerated and unjust, note the manner in which our own novelists, for instance, past and present, treat all subjects connected with women, marriage, and motherhood, and then ask himself if he does not recognize at once its ludicrous inconsistency and its cruel insults to womanhood, open and implied. The very respect, so called, of man for woman, being granted solely on condition of her observing certain restrictions of thought and action dictated by him, conceals a subtle sort of insolence. It is really the pleased approval of a lawgiver at the sight of obedient subjects. The pitiful cry of Elsie in *The Golden Legend* has had many a repetition in the hearts of women age after age—

"Why should I live? Do I not know
The life of woman is full of woe!
Toiling on, and on, and on,

With breaking heart, and tearful eyes,
And silent lips, and in the soul
The secret longings that arise
Which this world never satisfies!"

So much for the past and its relation to the present. Now we come to the problem of to-day. This is extremely complex. We have a society ruled by Luther's views on marriage; we have girls brought up to regard it as their destiny; and we have, at the same time, such a large majority of women that they cannot all marry, even (as I think Miss Clapperton puts it)[6] if they had the 'fascinations of Helen of Troy and Cleopatra rolled into one.' We find, therefore, a number of women thrown on the world to earn their own living in the face of every sort of discouragement. Competition runs high for all, and even were there no prejudice to encounter, the struggle would be a hard one; as it is, life for poor and single women becomes a mere treadmill. It is folly to inveigh against mercenary marriages, however degrading they may be, for a glance at the position of affairs shows that there is no reasonable alternative. We cannot ask every woman to be a heroine and choose a hard and thorny path when a comparatively smooth one, (as it seems), offers itself, and when the pressure of public opinion urges strongly in that direction. A few higher natures will resist and swell the crowds of worn-out, underpaid workers, but the majority will take the voice of society for the voice of God, or at any rate of wisdom, and our common respectable marriage—upon which the safety of all social existence is supposed to rest—will remain, as it is now, the worst, because the most hypocritical, form of woman-purchase. Thus we have on the one side a more or less degrading marriage, and on the other side a number of women who cannot command an entry into that profession, but who must give up health and enjoyment of life in a losing battle with the world.

Bebel is very eloquent upon the sufferings of unmarried women, which must be keen indeed for those who have been prepared for marriage and for nothing else, whose emotions have been stimulated and whose ideas have been coloured by the imagination of domestic cares and happiness. Society, having forbidden or discouraged other ambitions for women, flings them scornfully aside as failures when through its own organization they are unable to secure a fireside and a proper "sphere" in which to practise the womanly virtues. Insult and injury to women is literally the key-note and the foundation of society.

Mrs. Augusta Webster amusingly points out the inconsistencies of popular notions on this subject. She says:—"People think women who do not want to marry unfeminine; people think women who do want to marry immodest; people combine both opinions by regarding it as unfeminine; people think women who do want to marry immodest; people combine both opinions by regarding it as unfeminine for women not to look forward longingly to wifehood as the hope and purpose of their lives, and ridiculing and contemning any individual woman of their acquaintance whom they suspect of entertaining such a longing. They must wish and not wish; they must by no means give, and they must certainly not withhold, encouragement—and so it goes on, each precept cancelling the last, and most of, them negative." There are, doubtless, equally absurd social prejudices which hamper a man's freedom, by teaching girls and their friends to look for proposals, instead of regarding signs of interest and liking in a more wholesome spirit. We shall never have a world really worth living in until men and women can show interest in one another, without being driven either to marry or to forego altogether the pleasure and profit of frequent meeting. Nor will the world be really a pleasant world while it continues to make friendship between persons of opposite sexes well-nigh impossible by insisting that they *are* so, and thereby in a thousand direct and indirect ways bringing about the fulfilment of its own prophecy. All this false sentiment and shallow shrewdness, with the restrictions they imply, make the ideal marriage—that is, a union prompted by love, by affinity or attraction of nature and by friendship—almost beyond the reach of this generation. While we are on this part of the subject it may be worth while to quote a typical example of some letters written to Max O'Rell on the publication of *The Daughters of John Bull*. One lady of direct language exclaims fiercely, "Man is a beast!" and she goes on to explain in gleeful strains that, having been left a small fortune by a relative, she is able to dispense with the society of "the odious creature." Of course Max O'Rell warmly congratulates the "odious creature." "At last," another lady bursts forth, "we have some one among us with wit to perceive that the life which a woman leads with the ordinary sherry-drinking, cigar-smoking husband is no better than that of an Eastern slave. Take my own case, which is that of thousands of others in our land. I belong to my lord and master, body and soul; the duties of a housekeeper, upper nurse, and governess are required of me; I am expected to be always at home, at my husband's beck and call. It is true that he feeds me, and that for his own glorification he gives me handsome clothing. It is also true that he does not beat me. For this I ought, of course, to be duly grateful; but I often think of what you say on the wife and servant question, and wonder how many of us would like to have the cook's privilege of being able to give warning to leave."

If the wife feels thus we may be sure the husband thinks he has his grievances also, and when we place this not exaggerated description side by side with that of the unhappy plight of bored husbands commiserated by Mrs. Lynn Linton, there is no escaping the impression that there is something very "rotten in the state of Denmark." Amongst other absurdities, we have well-meaning husbands and wives harassing one another to death for no reason in the world but the desire of conforming to current notions regarding the proper conduct of married people. These victims are expected to go about perpetually together, as if they were a pair of carriage-horses; to be for ever holding claims over one another, exacting or making useless sacrifices, and generally getting in one another's way. The man who marries finds that his liberty has gone, and the woman exchanges one set of restrictions for another. She thinks herself neglected if the husband does not always return to her in the evenings, and the husband and society think her undutiful, frivolous, and so forth if she does not stay at home alone, trying to sigh him back again. The luckless man finds his wife so *very* dutiful and domesticated, and so *very* much confined to her "proper sphere," that she is, perchance, more exemplary than entertaining. Still, she may look injured and resigned, but she must not seek society and occupation on her own account, adding to the common mental store, bringing new interest and knowledge into the joint existence, and becoming thus a contented, cultivated, and agreeable being. No wonder that while all this is forbidden we have so many unhappy wives and bored husbands. The more admirable the wives the more profoundly bored the husbands!

Of course there are bright exceptions to this picture of married life, but we are not dealing with exceptions. In most cases, the chain of marriage chafes the flesh, if it does not make a serious wound; and where there is happiness the happiness is dearly bought and is not on a very high plane. For husband and wife are then apt to forget everything in the absorbing but narrow interests of their home, to depend entirely upon one another, to steep themselves in the same ideas, till they become mere echoes, half creatures, useless to the world, because they have run into a groove and have let individuality die. There are few things more stolidly irritating than a very "united" couple. The likeness that may often be remarked between married people is a melancholy index of this united degeneration.

We come then to the conclusion that the present form of marriage—exactly in proportion to its conformity with orthodox ideas—is a vexatious failure. If certain people have made it a success by ignoring those orthodox ideas, such instances afford no argument in favour of the institution as it stands. We are also led to conclude that modern "Respectability," draws its life-blood from the degradation of womanhood in marriage and prostitution. But what is to be done to remedy these manifold evils? How is marriage to be rescued from a mercenary society, torn from the arms of "Respectability" and established on a footing which will make it no longer an insult to human dignity?

First of all we must set up an ideal, undismayed by what will seem its Utopian impossibility. Every good thing that we enjoy to-day was once the dream of a "crazy enthusiast" mad enough to believe in the power of ideas and in the power of man to have things as he wills. The ideal marriage then, despite all dangers and difficulties, should be *free*. So long as love and trust and friendship remain, no bonds are necessary to bind two people together; life apart will be empty and colourless; but whenever these cease the tie becomes false and iniquitous, and no one ought to have power to enforce it. The matter is one in which any interposition, whether of law or of society, is an impertinence. Even the idea of "duty" ought to be excluded from the most perfect marriage, because the intense attraction of one being for another, the intense desire for one another's happiness, would make interchanges of whatever kind the outcome of a feeling far more passionate than that of duty. It need scarcely be said that there must be a full understanding and acknowledgment of the obvious right of the woman to *possess herself* body and soul, to give or withhold herself body and soul exactly as she wills. The moral right here is so palpable, and its denial implies ideas so low and offensive to human dignity, that no fear of consequences ought to deter us from making this liberty an element of our ideal, in fact its fundamental principle. Without it, no ideal could hold up its head. Moreover, "consequences" in the long run are never beneficent, where obvious moral rights are disregarded. The idea of a perfectly free marriage would imply the possibility of any form of contract being entered into between the two persons, the State and society standing aside, and recognizing the entirely private character of the transaction.

The economical independence of woman is the first condition of free marriage. She ought not to be tempted to marry, or to remain married, for the sake of bread and butter. But the condition is a very hard one to secure. Our present competitive system, with the daily increasing ferocity of the struggle for existence, is fast reducing itself to an absurdity, woman's labour helping to make the struggle only the fiercer. The problem now offered to the mind and conscience of humanity is to readjust its industrial organization in such a mway as to gradually reduce this absurd and useless competition within reasonable limits, and to bring about in its place some form of cooperation, in which no man's interest will depend on the misfortune of his neighbour, but rather on his neighbour's happiness and welfare. It is idle to say that this cannot be done; the state of society shows quite clearly that it *must* be done sooner or later; otherwise some violent catastrophe will put an end to a condition of things which is hurrying towards impossibility. Under improved economical conditions the difficult problem of securing the real independence of women, and thence of the readjustment of their position in relation to men and to society would find easy solution.

When girls and boys are educated together, when the unwholesome atmosphere of social life becomes fresher and nobler, when the pressure of existence slackens (as it will and *must* do), and when the whole nature has thus a chance to expand, such additions to the scope and interest of life will cease to be thought marvellous or "unnatural." "Human nature" has more variety of powers and is more responsive to conditions than we imagine. It is hard to believe in things for which we feel no capacity in ourselves, but fortunately such things exist in spite of our placid unconsciousness. Give room for the development of individuality, and individuality develops, to the amazement of spectators! Give freedom in marriage, and each pair will enter upon their union after their own particular fashion, creating a refreshing diversity in modes of life, and consequently of character. Infinitely preferable will this be to our own gloomy uniformity, the offspring of our passion to be in all things exactly like our neighbours.

The proposed freedom in marriage would of course have to go hand-in-hand with the co-education of the sexes. It is our present absurd interference with the natural civilizing influences of one sex upon the other, that creates half the dangers and difficulties of our social life, and gives colour to the fears of those who would hedge round marriage with a thousand restraints or so-called safeguards, ruinous to happiness, and certainly not productive of a satisfactory social condition. Already the good results of this method of co-education have been proved by experiment in America, but we ought to go farther in this direction than our go-ahead cousins have yet gone. Meeting freely in their working-hours as well as at times of recreation, men and women would have opportunity for forming reasonable judgments of character, for making friendships irrespective of sex, and for giving and receiving that inspiring influence which apparently can only be given by one sex to the other.[7] There would also be a chance of forming genuine attachments founded on friendship; marriage would cease to be the haphazard thing it is now; girls would no longer fancy themselves in love with a man because they had met none other on terms equally intimate, and they would not be tempted to marry for the sake of freedom and a place in life, for existence would be free and full from the beginning.

The general rise in health, physical and moral, following the improvement in birth, surroundings, and training would rapidly tell upon the whole state of society. Any one who has observed carefully knows how grateful a response the human organism gives to improved conditions, if only these remain constant. We should have to deal with healthier, better equipped, more reasonable men and women, possessing well-developed minds, and hearts kindly disposed towards their fellow-creatures. Are such people more likely to enter into a union frivolously and ignorantly than are the average men and women of to-day? Surely not. If the number of divorces did not actually decrease there would be the certainty that no couple remained united against their will, and that no lives were sacrificed to a mere convention. With the social changes which would go hand in hand with changes in the status of marriage, would come inevitably many fresh forms of human power, and thus all sorts of new and stimulating influences would be brought to bear upon society. No man has a right to consider himself educated until he has been under the influence of cultivated women, and the same may be said of women as regards men.[8] Development involves an increase of complexity. It is so in all forms of existence, vegetable and animal; it is so in human life. It will be found that men and women as they increase in complexity can enter into a numberless variety of relationships, abandoning no good gift that they now possess, but adding to their powers indefinitely, and thence to their emotions and experiences. The action of the man's nature upon the woman's and of the woman's upon the man's, is now only known in a few instances; there is a whole world yet to explore in this direction, and it is more than probable that the future holds a discovery in the domain of spirit as great as that of Columbus in the domain of matter.

With regard to the dangers attending these readjustments, there is no doubt much to be said. The evils that hedge around marriage are linked with other evils, so that movement is difficult and perilous indeed. Nevertheless, we have to remember that we now live in the midst of dangers, and that human happiness is cruelly murdered by our systems of legalized injustice. By sitting still circumspectly and treating our social system as if it were a card-house which would tumble down at a breath, we merely wait to see it fall from its own internal rottenness, and *then* we shall have dangers to encounter indeed! The time has come, not for violent overturning of established institutions before people admit that they are evil, but for a gradual alteration of opinion which will rebuild them from the very foundation. The method of the most enlightened reformer is to crowd out old evil by new good, and to seek to sow the seed of the nobler future where alone it can take root and grow to its full height: in the souls of men and women. Far-seeing we ought to be, but we know in our hearts right well that fear will never lead us to the height of our ever-growing possibility. Evolution has ceased to be a power driving us like dead leaves on a gale; thanks to science, we are no longer entirely blind, and we aspire to direct that mighty force for the good of humanity. We see a limitless field of possibility opening out before us; the adventurous spirit in us might leap up at the wonderful romance of life! We recognize that no power, however trivial, fails to count in the general sum of things which moves this way or that—towards heaven or hell, according to the preponderating motives of individual units. We shall begin, slowly but surely, to see the folly of permitting the forces of one sex to pull against and neutralize the workings of the other, to the confusion of our efforts and the checking of our progress. We shall see, in the relations of men and women to one another, the source of all good or of all evil, precisely as those relations are true and noble and equal, or false and low and unjust. With this belief we shall seek to move opinion in all the directions that may bring us to this "consummation devoutly to be wished," and we look forward steadily, hoping and working for the day when men and women shall be comrades and fellow-workers as well as lovers and husbands and wives, when the rich and many-sided happiness which they have the power to bestow one on another shall no longer be enjoyed in tantalizing snatches, but shall gladden and give new life to all humanity. That will be the day prophesied by Lewis Morris in *The New Order*—

"When man and woman in an equal union
Shall merge, and marriage be a true communion."

NOTES

1 See Tyler's *Primitive Culture.*

2 With regard to the evil effects of ignorance in the management of young children, probably few people realize how much avoidable pain is endured, and how much weakness in after-life is traceable to the absurd traditional modes of treating infants and children.

   The current ideas are incredibly stupid; one ignorant nurse hands them on to another, and the whole race is brought up in a manner that offends, not merely scientific acumen, but the simplest common-sense.

3 *Sex-Relations in Germany.* By Karl Pierson.

4 Bebel on *Woman.*

5 *Martin Luther; his Influence on the Material and Intellectual Welfare of Germany—The* Westminster Review. New Series, No. CXXIX, January, 1884, pp. 38-9. VOL. 130.-NO. 2.

6 *Scientific Meliorism.* By Jane Hume Clapperton.

7 Mr. Henry Stanton, in his work on *The Woman Question in Europe,* speaks of the main idea conveyed in Legouvé's *Histoire des Femmes* as follows:—"Equality in difference is its key-note. The question is not to make woman a man but to complete man by woman."

8 Mrs. Cady Stanton* believes that there is a sex in mind, and that men can only be inspired to their highest achievements by women, while women are stimulated to their utmost only by men.

Source: Reprinted from *Westminster Review* (August 1888).

"A DEFENCE OF THE SO-CALLED 'WILD WOMEN'"

The first impulse of women whom Mrs. Lynn Linton calls 'wild' is probably to contradict the charges that she makes against them in the course of three ruthless articles, but reflection shows the futility as well as the inconsequence of such a proceeding. After all, those who have lost faith in the old doctrines are not so much concerned to prove themselves, as individuals, wise and estimable, as to lead thinking men and women to consider the nature of popular sentiments with regard to the relation of the sexes, and to ask themselves whether the social fiat which for centuries has forced every woman, whatever

---

* Elizabeth Cady Stanton, American feminist abolitionist [Editor's note].

be her natural inclinations or powers, into one avocation be really wise or just; whether, in truth, it be in the interests of the race to deprive one half of it of liberty of choice, to select for them their mode of existence, and to prescribe for them their very sentiments.

To the task of opposing the conclusions of Mrs. Lynn Linton her adversaries must bring considerable force and patience, and for this singular reason, that she gives them nothing to answer. One cannot easily reply to strings of accusations against the personal qualities of women who venture to hold views at variance with those at which the world arrived at some happy and infallible epoch in its history. The unbeliever finds himself thrown back upon the simple school-room form of discussion, consisting in flat contradiction, persistently repeated until the energies give out. As this method appears undignified and futile, it seems better to let most of the charges pass in silence, commenting only on one or two here and there in passing. It is of no real moment whether Mrs. Lynn Linton's unfavourable impression of the women who differ from her in this matter be just or unjust, the question is simply: are their views nearer or farther from the truth than the doctrines from which they dissent? As regards their personal qualities, it must in fairness be remembered that the position of the advocate of an unpopular cause is a very trying one; the apostles of a new faith are generally driven, by the perpetual fret of opposition and contempt, to some rancour or extravagance; but such conduct merely partakes of the frailty of human nature, and ought not to prejudice a really impartial mind against the views themselves.

Such a mind will consider principles and not persons; and although the absurdities of its champions may tell against the spread of a new doctrine among the mass, it certainly ought not to retard it among thinkers and students of history, who must be well aware that the noblest causes have not been able to command infallible advocates, nor to protect themselves from perilous friends.

It would be interesting to make a collection from the writings of Mrs. Lynn Linton of all the terrific charges that she has brought against her sex, adding them up in two columns, and placing side by side the numerous couples that contradict each other. At the end of this sad list one might place the simple sentence of defence, 'No, we aren't!' and although this would certainly lack the eloquence and literary quality of Mrs. Lynn Linton's arguments, I deny that it would yield to them in cogency.

There is nothing that is mean, paltry, ungenerous, tasteless, or ridiculous of which the woman who repudiates the ancient doctrines is not capable, according to this lady, unless, indeed, they are such abject fools that they have not the energy to be knaves. The logic is stern: either a woman is a 'modest violet, blooming unseen,' unquestioning, uncomplaining, a patient producer of children regardless of all cost to herself; suffering 'everyone's opinion to influence her mind' and 'all venerable laws hallowed by time ... to control her actions'—either this, or a rude masculine creature, stamping over moors with a gun that she may ape the less noble propensities of man; an adventuress who exposes herself to the dangers of travel simply that she may advertise herself in a book on her return.; a virago who desires nothing better than to destroy in others the liberty that she so loudly demands for herself. There is, according to Mrs. Lynn Linton, no medium between Griselda and a sublimated Frankenstein's monster, which we have all so often heard of and seldom seen. Mrs. Lynn Linton's experience in this respect appears to have been ghastly. This is greatly to be regretted, for it has induced her to divide women roughly into two great classes: the good, beautiful, submissive, charming, noble, and wise on the one hand, and on the other, the bad, ugly, rebellious, ill-mannered, ungenerous, and foolish. The 'wild women' are like the plain and wicked sisters in a fairy tale, baleful creatures who go about the world doing bad deeds and oppressing innocence as it sits rocking the cradle by the fireside. It seems hard for the poor elder sisters to be told off to play this dreadful role, amid the hisses of the gallery, and they deserve some sympathy after all, for truly the world offers temptations to evil courses, and innocence at the cradle can be desperately exasperating at times! It has a meek, placid, sneaky, virtuous way of getting what it wants, and making it hot and uncomfortable for unpopular elder sisters. After all, in spite of Mrs. Lynn Linton, there is no more finished tyrant in the world than the meek sweet creature who cares nothing for her 'rights,' because she knows she can get all she wants by artifice; who makes a weapon of her womanhood, a sword of strength of her weakness, and does not disdain to tyrannise over men to her heart's content by an ungenerous appeal to their chivalry. She is a woman—poor, weak, helpless, and her husband may not call his soul his own! Tears are a stock-in-trade, and nerves a rock of defence. She claims no rights—she can't understand what all this absurd talk is about—she is quite satisfied with things as they are. Personal dignity she has none; it would sadly interfere with her successful methods of insinuating herself through life, in serpentine fashion; she gets what she can as best she may, living by her wits; a mere adventuress, after all, in spite of her unblemished character; appealing to men's passions, frailties, chivalry; often differing from a class of women whose very name she would scarcely mention, in the nature of her surroundings and her supreme sense of respectability, rather than in the essential nature of her position.

But far be it from me to affirm, in simple opposition to Mrs. Lynn Linton, that all women of the old school are of this kind. My object is not merely to bring a counter-charge, but to point to the type which power on the one side and subordination on the other tend to produce. There are thousands, however, of the time-honoured school who never dream of attempting this unconscious retaliation. Many of them neither demand rights nor win their way by artifice. They accept their lot, just as it is, in a literal spirit, being just enough developed to see the meanness of trading upon the chivalry of men, and not enough so to resent being placed in a position which makes them dependent, utterly and hopelessly, upon their favour. These women—the most pathetic class of all—have been so well drilled to accept their position without question, that they launch their complaints only at Fate and Nature, if ever they are moved to complain at all. Their conscience and their generosity forbid them to make use of the usual weapons of a dependent race, artifice and flattery; so that they are denied even this redress, which less sensitive women enjoy without stint. These half-developed women respond loyally to the stern demands made upon them by public sentiment; they are martyrs to 'duty' in its narrowest sense; they turn a meek ear to society when it addresses homilies to them, inculcating the highest principles, and showering upon them the heaviest responsibilities, without dreaming of bestowing corresponding rights.

In short, the women of the old order and the women of the new have faults and virtues each after their own kind, and it is idle to make general affirmations about either class.

It is well, therefore, to check the inherent instinct to contradict when Mrs. Lynn Linton says that women of the new faith are evil and ugly; one must say rather that this is a mere matter of opinion, formed from the impression each person gathers from individual experience, and from the bias with which that experience is met. Let, however, the impression be as unfavourable to the 'wild women' as it may, it is neither fair nor philosophic to refuse to consider their claims. The liberal-minded will remember that the claims of a class hitherto subordinate always seem preposterous, and that the more complete has been their exclusion, the more ridiculous will appear their aspiration. Yet this inclination to treat with derision any new demand for liberty stands on a level with the instinct of the street-urchin to jeer at anything to which he is unaccustomed, as, for example, any person in foreign garments, though he excel a thousand times in dignity and comeliness the natives of the country.

It is not very surprising if some of the apostles of the new faith, irritated by the most powerful hindrances of law, sentiment, tradition—baffling, subtle, unceasing as these are—have made the mistake, as I think, of seeking to emphasise their demand for the liberty that men enjoy by imitating men's habits and manners, and by seizing every occasion to take part in the fierce battle for existence, as if that were a desirable thing in itself, instead of an unhappy necessity. They are not alone in their error, however; they are not singular when they fail to see that the life that men now lead, in the effort to 'earn a living and to succeed,' is crazy and perilous to themselves and to the race. To add to that great body of struggling men another body of struggling women would evidently not mend matters, and it is clear that the hopes which we may hold for the future of the race through the emancipation of women cannot rest on the prospect of their entering the tumultuous arena of competition, and spending their strength in that fruitless fashion. Undeniably it would be wiser if women would use their influence to render the conflict less fierce, to slacken the greed for money, success, display, and to turn the ambitions of men to more rational and fruitful ways.

But, however true all this may be, it is unluckily also true that women have to live, and that even those who have a father or a husband have, at most, food and shelter, they have not independence. The wife among the less prosperous of the middle classes, who takes upon her shoulders at least half the burden of the household—to put it very mildly—may toil all her life and grow worn with anxiety and worry, but she will still be as dependent upon her husband's will or caprice as if she were an idler living upon his unearned bounty. Women are beginning to feel this more or less distinctly, and to desire to earn a little money for themselves, so that they may possess some means of subsistence that is really their own, small though it may be. This is surely natural enough, however evil may be the consequences of an inrush of women workers into the labour market. Since the work of women in their homes is not of a kind to give them independence, they are beginning to seek for employment of a sort that is recognised as deserving of reward, knowing that their pecuniary position eternally stands in the way of any improvement as regards their legal and social status, and that it often obliges them to submit to a thousand wrongs and indignities which could not otherwise be placed upon them.

A certain number of rebels are bending all their energies to the removal of this invincible hindrance, and to attain this end they are forced to join more or less in the struggle for a livelihood. It will be a happy day for humanity when a woman can stay in her own home without sacrificing her freedom. Shortsighted is the policy which would keep the wife and mother helpless in the hands of the man whose home she sustains and holds together, which would give her but a meagre share of right to the children which have cost her so much to bear and tend, while burdening her with the fullest responsibility regarding them. To this point I would especially call the attention of that large portion of the community who are convinced of the importance of the fireside and the home, who believe that in every other locality the woman is out of her sphere. Would they not use their influence most wisely, from their own point of view, in seeking to remove some of the heavy penalties that are attached to the enjoyment of home and fireside, and to make them deserve a little better all the sentiment that has been lavished upon them?

It is easy indeed to see the frightful peril to the well-being of the race that lies in the labour of women outside the home; that peril can scarcely be exaggerated; but if women demand the natural human right to take their share of the opportunities, such as they are, which the world has to offer—if they desire the privilege of independence (a privilege denied them, work as they will, within the home), by what right does society refuse their demand? Men are living lives and committing actions day by day which imperil and destroy the well-being of the race; on what principle are women only to be restrained? Why this one-sided sacrifice, this artificial selection of victims for the good of society? The old legends of maidens who were chosen every year and chained to a rock by the shore to propitiate gods or sea-monsters seem not in the least out of date. Sacrifices were performed more frankly in those days, and nobody tried to persuade the victims that it was enjoyable and blessed to be devoured; they did not talk about 'woman's sphere' to a maiden chained to the rock within sight of the monster, nor did they tell her that the 'true woman' desired no other destiny. They were brutal, but they did not add sickly sentiment to their crime against the individual; they carried out the hideous old doctrine of vicarious sacrifice, which is haunting us like an evil spirit to this day, in all good faith and frankness, and there was no attempt to represent the monster as an engaging beast when you got to know him.

Society has no right to exact these sacrifices; every member of it must stand equal in its sight, if it would claim the name of a free state. On the soil of such a state there must be no arbitrary selection of victims for the general good made from a certain class, or, still worse, from a certain sex. One can imagine the heaven-assaulting howl that would go up were it proposed to deal in this way with a certain body of men; if it were decreed that they should be restricted from seeking their fortunes as might seem good to them, restrained only by the laws that all the rest of the community were called upon to obey. No argument about the welfare of the race would reconcile a nation of free-born men to such a proposal. Yet this is the argument that free-born men do not hesitate to use regarding women.

The attempt to force upon these any sacrifice on the sole ground of their sex, to demand of them a special act of renunciation on that account, gives us an exact analogue of the old tribute to its gods of a nation which chose its victims not by fair hazard from the entire population, but from a class set apart for the cruel purpose. Such actions are subversive of all social life, for the existence of a community depends finally upon its respect for individual right. Upon these rights society is built; without them, nothing is possible but an aggregation of tyrants and slaves, which does not deserve the name of a society, since it is bound together by force, and the union between its members is accidental, not organic. On what rests finally my safety and freedom as a citizen, but on the understanding that if I leave your rights intact you will also respect mine?

But, further, the argument which takes its stand upon the danger to society of the freedom of women, besides being unfair (since it would select a whole sex for the propitiatory victims), is, on its own ground, unsound. True, indeed, is it that if all women were to rush into the labour market and begin to compete with men and with one another, the result would be evil; but it is *not* true that if they were to be placed on an equality with men in the eye of the law, if in marriage they were free from legal or pecuniary disadvantage, if in society they had no special prejudices to contend with—it is not true in that case that the consequence of this change in their position would be detrimental to the real interests of society. On the contrary, its influence would be for good, and for more good than perhaps any one now dares to believe. And among the many causes of this beneficent result we may number this, that women would be able to choose the work for which they were best suited. We should have fewer governesses who loathed teaching, fewer wives who could do most things better than look after a house, and fewer mothers to whom the training of children was an impossible task. Moreover, society would rejoice in more of that healthy variety among her members which constitutes one of the elements of vitality. There is room for all kinds of women, did we but realise it, and there is certainly no reason why the present movement should sweep away all those of the ancient type in whom Mrs. Lynn Linton takes delight. They have their charm, but it must be acknowledged that, for all their meekness, nothing would please them better than tyrannically to dictate their own mode of life to their sisters. By what charter or authority does the domestic woman (like the person in the train who wants the window up) attempt to restrict within her own limits women who entirely disagree with her in opinion and in temperament?

Granted for a moment that Mrs. Lynn Linton and her followers are justified of Heaven in their views, and that it always was and always will be necessary for women to dedicate themselves wholly to the production of the race, still this truth—if such it be—must be left to demonstrate itself without any tyranny, direct or indirect, from those who realise it, otherwise they violate the condition of social liberty. The history of all persecutions, religious and otherwise, ought to warn us against the danger of allowing the promulgation of the true faith by forcible means, and I include among forcible means all forms of prejudice and sentiment, for often these are far more powerful than legal enactments. Let us not forget the glorious privilege of the citizen of a free state to be in the wrong, and to act upon his error until the torch-bearers of truth shall be able to throw light upon his pathway. That once accomplished, his adherence will be worth having.

The demand that all women shall conform to a certain model of excellence, that they shall be debarred from following the promptings of their powers and instincts, whatsoever be the pretext for the restriction, is the outcome of an illiberal spirit, and ought to be resisted as all attacks on liberty ought to be resisted. The fact that the attack is made upon liberties which, as yet, are only candidates for existence, is the sole reason why Englishmen do not resent the aggression as they would resent any other interference with personal freedom.

Let it be remembered, for the consolation of those who fear the results of this new movement, that if modern women are lapsing from the true faith, if they are really insurgents against evolutionary human nature, and not the indications of a new social development, then their fatal error will assuredly prove itself. Should some harm be suffered in the proving, that is merely the risk that has to be taken in all free states for the possibility of progress.

These, then, are the principles upon which women of the new faith claim tolerance for their views, be they right or wrong. Having claimed these initial rights, they then proceed to give their reasons for holding such views, and for the rebellion which they preach against the old order.

To the time-honoured argument that nature intended man to be anything and everything that his strength of muscle and of mind permitted, while she meant woman to be a mother, and nothing else, the rebels reply, that if a woman has been made by nature to be a mother, so has a cow or a sheep; and if this maternal capacity be really an infallible indication of function, there is nothing to prevent this reasoning from running downhill to its conclusion, namely, that the nearer a woman can become to a cow or a sheep the better.

If popular feeling objects to this conclusion, and yet still desires all women to make maternity their chief duty, it must find another reason for its faith, leaving nature's sign-posts out of the question. On these sign-posts man himself is privileged to write and rewrite the legends, though of this power he seems at present to be unconscious, persistently denying it even while his restless fingers are busy at their work.

This dear and cherished appeal to nature, however, will never be abandoned by the advocates of the old order while breath remains to them. But if they use the argument they ought not to shrink from its consequences, nor, indeed, *would* they, but that it happens that women, as a matter of fact, have risen above the stage of simple motherhood, accustoming their critics to attributes distinctively human; and these having by this time become familiar, no longer seem alarming or 'unnatural.' In our present stage of development we demand of woman that she shall be first of all a mother, and then that she develop those human qualities which best harmonise with her position as such. 'Be it pleasant or unpleasant,' Mrs. Lynn Linton says, 'it is none the less an absolute truth—the *raison d'être* of a woman is maternity.... The cradle lies across the door of the polling-booth and bars the way to the Senate.'

We are brought, then, to this conclusion: that if there be any force in what is commonly urged respecting nature's 'intentions' with regard to woman, her development as a thinking and emotional being beyond the point where human qualities are superficially useful to her children is 'unnatural' and false, a conclusion which leads us straight away to Oriental customs and to Oriental ethics. Moreover, another consideration confronts us: nature, besides designing women to be mothers, designed men to be fathers; why, then, should not the man give up his life to his family in the same wholesale way? 'The cases are so different,' it will be said. Yes, and the difference lies in the great suffering and risk which fall solely to the share of the mother. Is this a good reason for holding her for her whole life to this painful task, for demanding that she shall allow her tastes and talents to lie idle and to die a slow and painful death, while the father, to whom parenthood is also indicated by 'nature,' is allowed the privilege of choosing his own avocations without interference? Further, if women's functions are to be determined solely by a reference to what is called nature, how, from this point of view, are we to deal with the fact that she possesses a thousand emotional and intellectual attributes that are wholly superfluous to her merely maternal activities? What does Mrs. Lynn Linton consider that 'nature intends' by all this: In the present order of society, speaking roughly, a woman, to whom maternity seems unsatisfying or distasteful, has either to bring herself to undertake the task for which she is unfitted, or to deny her affections altogether. To man, the gods give both sides of the apple of life; a woman is offered the choice of the halves—either, but not both.

Yet every new development of society, every overthrow of ancient landmarks, tends to prove more and more conclusively that this fetish 'nature,' who is always claimed as the patroness of the old order, just when she is busy planning and preparing the new, has *not* separated the human race into two distinct sections, with qualities entirely and eternally different. If this were so—if women were, in fact, the only beings under heaven not modifiable by education and surroundings, then we should be forced to reconstruct from the foundation our notions of natural law, and to rescind the comparatively modern theory that it is unwise to expect effects without causes, and causes without effects, even in the mysterious domain of human nature. We would live once more in a world of haphazard and of miracle, in which only one fact could be counted upon from age to age, viz., the immutable and stereotyped 'nature' of women.

Unless we are prepared for this antique and variegated creed, we cannot consistently pronounce, as Mrs. Lynn Linton cheerfully pronounces, what the sphere and *raison d'être* of either sex are, and must be, for evermore. It seems, indeed, safe to predict that women will continue to bear children, but it is far from safe to prophesy to what extent that function will in the future absorb their energies and determine the horizon of their life. We know that although men have been fathers from the beginning of human history, they have not made fatherhood the keynote of their existence; on the contrary, it has been an entirely secondary consideration. They have been busy in influencing and fashioning a world which their children are to inherit—a world that would be sorrier than it is if men had made the fact of parenthood the central point of their career. Women have been forced, partly by their physical constitution, but more by the tyranny of society, to expend their whole energies in maternal cares, and this has been the origin of a thousand evils: it has destroyed the healthy balance of their nature, thrown work on to unfit shoulders, formed a sort of press-gang of the most terrible kind, inasmuch as unwilling motherhood is worse than unwilling military service; and it has deprived the very children on whose behalf this insane cruelty has been wrought, of the benefit of possessing mothers and teachers whose character is developed all round, whose faculties are sound and healthy, whose minds are fresh, buoyant, and elastic, and stored with such knowledge of nature and life as would make them efficient guides and guardians to those helpless ones who are at the outset of their career. It may seem paradoxical, but is none the less true, that we shall never have really good mothers until women cease to make their motherhood the central idea of their existence. The woman who has no interest larger than the affairs of her children is not a fit person to train them.

For the sake of men, women, and children, it is to be hoped that women will come to regard motherhood with new eyes; that the force of their artificially fostered impulses will become less violent; and that there may be an increase in them of the distinctly *human* qualities and emotions in relation to those merely instinctive or maternal. It is this *change of proportion* in the force of human qualities that virtually creates a new being, and makes progress possible. In the light of this truth, how false are all the inferences of phrases such as 'Nature intends,' 'Nature desires;' she intends and desires nothing—she is an abject slave. *Man* intends, *Man* desires, and 'Nature,' in the course of centuries, learns to obey.

This worship of 'nature' is a strange survival in a scientific age of the old image-worship of our ancestors. She is our Vishnu or Siva, our Odin and Thor, a personal will who designs and plans. This is a subtle form of superstition which has cunningly nestled among the folds of the garment of Science, and there it will lurk safe and undetected for many years, to discourage all change, to cast discredit on all new thought, to hold man to his errors, and to blind him to his own enormous power of development.

It is this insidious superstition that prevents even intelligent people from recognising the effect upon women of their circumstances. Professions are known to leave their mark on men, although the influence of a man's profession is not so incessant and overwhelming as are the conditions of women's lives, from which there is no escape from the cradle to the grave; yet it is always grudgingly and doubtfully admitted, if at all, that this fact offers an explanation for any bad quality in the feminine character, any weakness or excess of which women may be guilty. No one seems to realise how age after age they have been, one and all, engaged in the same occupations, subjected to the same kind of stimulus and training; how each individual of infinitely varying multitudes has been condemned to one function for the best years of life, and that function an extremely painful and exhausting one. No one seems to understand that these causes must produce effects, and that they have produced the effect of creating in women certain tyrannous and overwrought instincts which we say, reverentially and obstinately, 'Nature has implanted in woman.' We might more accurately say 'Suffering, moral and mental starvation, physical pain, disease induced by the over-excitement of one set of functions, one-sided development—these have implanted impulses which we have the assurance to call sacred.'

At the present time, some very interesting researches are being carried on, which tend to show, so far as they have gone, that the physical nature of women has been literally destroyed by the over-excitement and ill-usage, often unwitting, which public sentiment has forced them to submit to, while their absolute dependence on men has induced them often to endure it as if it were the will of Heaven.

These researches show that through these centuries of overstrain, one set of faculties being in perpetual activity while the others lay dormant, women have fallen the victims of chronic disease, and this condition of disease has become also a condition of a woman's existence. Have we not gone far enough along this path of destruction, or must we still make motherhood our chief duty, accept the old sentiment about our subservience to man, and drive yet farther into the system the cruel diseases that have punished the insanities of the past, taking vengeance upon the victims of ill-usage for their submission, and pursuing their children from generation to generation with relentless footsteps? Such is the counsel of Mrs. Lynn Linton and her school. Upon the effects of all this past ill-treatment is founded the pretext for women's disabilities in the present. They are physically weak, nervous, easily unstrung, and for this reason, it is urged, they must continue to pursue the mode of life which has induced these evils. This is strange reasoning.

The suffering of women to-day is built upon their suffering of yesterday and its consequences. It is surely a rather serious matter to cut off a human being from whatever the world has to offer him in this one short life! From this point of view what force or meaning have Mrs. Lynn Linton's taunts and accusations against her sex, even though they were all perfectly just? It is possible that women, in virtue of their susceptible physical constitution and nervous system (a quality, by the way, which distinguishes the man of genius from the ordinary being), are more responsive than men are to their surroundings, and all that Mrs. Lynn Linton says, if true, about the wildness of ignorant women in times of excitement—she cites for an example the *tricoteuses* of the French Revolution—might perhaps be explained on this ground. A quick response to stimulus is *not* the mark of a being low in the scale of existence, though it may lead to extravagant deeds when untutored. But Mrs. Lynn Linton will not look at this question philosophically; she hurls accusations at her sex as if it pleased her to add another insult to those which the literature of centuries with that exquisite chivalry which we are so often warned our freedom would destroy—has never tired of flinging at the defenceless sex. It does not strike Mrs. Lynn Linton to inquire into the real causes that underlie all these problems of a growing human nature; she prefers the simple finger of scorn, the taunt, the inexpensive sneer.

Why does she so harshly condemn the results of the system of things which she so ardently approves? To make her position more difficult to understand, Mrs. Lynn Linton dwells with some insistence on the effects upon her sex of their training. She speaks of 'ideal qualities which women have gained by a certain amount of sequestration from the madding crowd's ignoble strife.... Are the women at the gin-shop bar,' she demands, 'better than the men at the gin-shop door; the field hands in sunbonnets more satisfactory than those in brimless hats?' This is to prove that women have no real moral superiority. Elsewhere is asked: 'Can anyone point out anywhere a race of women who are superior to their conditions?' All this is strange reasoning from one who takes her stand in the fiats of 'nature' as distinguished from the influences of sur-roundings.

One might ask: 'Can anyone point out anywhere a race of men who are superior to their conditions?' But this possible question never seems to strike Mrs. Lynn Linton, for she exposes herself all through the article to the same form of demand, and she nowhere attempts to meet it. Her mode of warfare is indeed bewildering, for she attacks from both sides, makes double and antagonistic use of the same facts, and she does not at all object to assertions clearly contradictory, provided they are separated in time and space by the interval of a paragraph or two.

Her arguments, when formidable, mutually and relentlessly devour each other, like so many plus and minus quantities which, added together, become cancelled and leave a clean zero between them.

Unconscious, however, of this cannibalism among her legions, the authoress finds herself at the close of her article with a gigantic and robust opinion which nothing—not even her own arguments—can disturb.

As an instance of this strange suicidal tendency of her reasoning we may compare the already quoted paragraphs setting forth the effects of environ-ment upon the woman's temperament with the even more determined asser-tion of its eternal, unalterable, and God-ordained nature. Confront these two statements, and what remains? Mrs. Lynn Linton seems to half surren-der her position when she says that '... there are few women of anything like energy or brainpower who have not felt in their own souls the ardent long-ing for a freer hand in life;' but the following sentence seems to play still more into the hands of the enemy: 'Had Louis the Sixteenth had Marie Antoinette's energy and Marie Antoinette Louis's supineness, the whole story of the Reign of Terror, Marat, Charlotte Cordé, and Napoleon might never have been written.' What doctrine of Mrs. Lynn Linton's does it even seem to support?

In unblushing contradiction of this sentiment Mrs. Lynn Linton asserts that political women have always been 'disastrous,' and that even Mme. Roland 'did more harm than good when she undertook the manipulation of forces that were too strong for her control, too vast for her comprehension.'

Were the forces of the French Revolution within the grasp of any one person?

'Women are both more extreme and more impressionable than men,' Mrs. Lynn Linton says; 'and the spirit which made weak girls into heroines and martyrs, honest women into the yelling *tricoteuses* of the blood-stained saturnalia of '92, still exists in the sex, and among ourselves as elsewhere.'

In short, when a 'weak' girl espouses martyrdom she is prompted thereto by a sort of hysteria, male heroism alone being heroic.

While admitting, nay, emphasising, on the one hand the fact of the remodelling force of circumstances, Mrs. Lynn Linton denies that feminine character and intelligence can ever be altered by one hair's breadth, except—and here comes the third and crowning contradiction—except for the worse.

Among the many other minor points which Mrs. Lynn Linton has touched upon are several which call for special comment from the point of view opposed to hers. For example, we are asked to believe that the peace of the home practically depends on the political disabilities of woman; or, in other words, that a man is unable to endure in his wife opinions differing from his own. I do not believe that men are quite so childish and petty as this; but if they are, it is indeed high time that they should learn the lesson of common courtesy and tolerance.

The device of keeping peace between two persons by the disarmament of one of them is ingenious and simple, but there is a temptation to think that such peace as that, if peace it can be called, would be well exchanged for strife. Does peace, indeed, mean the stagnation that arises from the relationship between the free and the fettered, or does it mean the generous mutual recognition of the right of private judgment? Identity of opinion between two people, even when not produced artificially, is not always inspiriting to either of them. The denial of political power to women, if it ever does prevent dissension, achieves at best, on the part of the wife, unreasoning acquiescence and not rational agreement.

Mrs. Lynn Linton says that 'amongst our most renowned women are some who say with their whole heart, "I would rather have been the wife of a great man, or the mother of a hero, than what I am—famous in my own person."' That is a matter of taste, but it seems strange that those famous women should not have acted upon their predilections. Against the following sentence I cannot refrain from expressing a sense of revolt; but the revolt is on behalf of men rather than of women. 'But the miserable little mannikin who creeps to obscurity, overshadowed by his wife's glory, is as pitiful in history as contemptible in fact. The husband of the wife is no title to honour; and the best and dearest of our famous women take care that this shall not be said of them and theirs.'

Are men, then, to be treated as if they were a set of jealous schoolboys, or superannuated invalids whom the discreet person allows to win at chess, because they have a childish dislike to being beaten?

It is consoling to remember that the ideas on which such feelings rest are giving way slowly but surely in all directions. It is only when the rebellion is extended over evidently new ground that Mrs. Lynn Linton and her followers begin to sound the tocsin,* assuring the rebellious woman that she shows 'a curious inversion of sex, disdaining the duties and limitations imposed on her by nature.' As a final taunt, Mrs. Lynn Linton says: 'All women are not always lovely, and the wild women never are.' This reminds one of the exasperated retort of an angry child who has come to the end of his invention— a galling if somewhat inconsequent attack upon the personal appearance, which is the last resort of outraged juvenile nature.

Nothing perhaps can better show the real attitude of this lady and her followers on this question than her irritation against those who are trying to bring a ray of sunlight into the harems and zenanas of the East:—

> Ignorant and unreasonable (she says), they would carry into the sun-laden East the social conditions born of the icy winds of the North.... In a country where jealousy is as strong as death, and stronger than love, they would incite women to revolt against the rule of seclusion, which has been the law of the land for centuries before we were a nation at all. That rule has worked well for the country, inasmuch as the chastity of Hindu women and the purity of the family life are notoriously intact.

If Mrs. Lynn Linton approves of the relation of the sexes in the East, and looks upon it with an eye of fondness because it dates back into ages whose savagery clings to us, and breaks out in the blood of civilised men to this day, then she may well set herself in opposition to the rebellion among modern women against the infinitely less intolerable injustice which they suffer in the West. Did we happen to be living in harems in South Kensington or Mayfair, with the sentiment of the country in favour of that modest and womanly state of seclusion, it is easy to imagine with what eloquence Mrs. Lynn Linton would declaim against the first hint of insurrection—although in that case, by the way, the strictly unfeminine occupation of writing articles would be denied her.

The really grave question raised in these essays is that of the effect of the political and social freedom of women upon the physical well-being of the race; for while past conditions have been evil, future ones may conceivably be equally so, though they could with difficulty be worse. This is indeed a serious problem which will require all the intelligence of this generation to solve. But first I would suggest what appears to be a new idea (strange as this may seem), namely, that the rights of the existing race are at least as great as those of the coming one. There is something pathetically absurd in the sacrifice to their

---

* Alarm or signal [Editor's note].

children of generation after generation of grown people. Who were the gainers by the incessant sacrifice? Of what avail was all that renunciation on behalf of those potential men and women, if on their attainment of that degree they, too, have to abandon the fruits of so much pain and so many lost possibilities, and begin all over again to weave *ad infinitum* this singular Penelope's web? The affairs of the present are carried on by the adult population, not by the children; and if the generations of adults are going to renounce, age after age, their own chances of development—resigning, as so many mothers do, opportunities of intellectual progress and spiritual enlightenment for the sake of their children—how in the name of common sense will they benefit humanity? For those children also, when their minds are ripe for progress, must, in accordance with this noble sentiment, immediately begin in *their* turn to renounce, and resign, and deny themselves, in order to start another luckless generation upon the same ridiculous circle of futility! I fear that it is not unnecessary to add that I do not here inculcate neglect of children, but merely claim some regard for the parent whom it cost previous parents so much to bear, and rear, and train. I protest against this insane waste of human energy, this perpetual renunciation for a race that never comes. When and where will be born that last happy generation who are to reap all the fruit of these ages of sacrifice? Will they wallow in the lost joys of sad women who have resigned ambitions, and allowed talents to dull and die in this thankless service? Will they taste all the experience that their mothers consented to forego? Are all these things stored up for them, like treasure that a miser will not spend, though he perish in his garret for lack of warmth and nourishment? Not so, but rather for every loss suffered by the fathers the children will be held debtors.

As regards the fears that are entertained on all sides at the prospect of women taking part in political life, or in any occupation which custom has not hitherto recognised as feminine, the advocates of freedom might ask why nobody has hitherto felt the least alarm about the awful nervous strain which the ideal submissive woman has had to undergo from time immemorial in the bearing and rearing of vast families, and the incessant cares of a household, under conditions, perhaps, of straitened means. Is there anything in the world that causes more nervous exhaustion than such a combination of duties? Doctors are, for once, agreed that worry is the most resistless of all taxes upon the constitution. Monotony of life has the same tendency, and a lack of variety in interests and thought undeniably conduces to the lowering of the vitality. Yet nobody has taken fright at the fatal combination of all these nerve-destroying conditions which belongs essentially to the lot of woman under the old *régime.*[1]

The one sort of strain which seems to be feared for the feminine constitution is the strain of brain-work, although, as a matter of fact, mental effort, if not prolonged and severe, enhances and does not exhaust the vitality.

It is true it cannot be carried on simultaneously with severe physical exertion of any kind. To go on having children year after year, superintending them and the home while doing other work outside, would indeed have disastrous consequences for women and for the race, but who would wish to see them do anything so insane? Such a domestic treadmill is stupid and brutal enough without the addition of the mental toil. It is the treadmill that must be modified.

If the new movement had no other effect than to rouse women to rebellion against the madness of large families, it would confer a priceless benefit on humanity. Let any reasonable woman expend the force that under the old order would have been given to the production of, say, the third, fourth, or fifth child upon work of another kind, and let her also take the rest and enjoyment, whatever her work, that every human being needs. It is certain that the one or two children which such a woman might elect to bear would have cause to be thankful that their mother threw over 'the holiest traditions of her sex,' and left insane ideas of woman's duties and functions to her grandmothers.

But there are many modern women who in their own way are quite as foolish as those grandmothers, for they are guilty of the madness of trying to live the old domestic life, without modification, while entering upon a larger field of interests, working simultaneously body and brain under conditions of excitement and worry. This insanity, which one might indeed call by a harsher name, will be punished as all overstrain is punished. But the cure for these things is not to immerse women more completely in the cares of domestic life, but to simplify its methods by the aid of a little intelligence and by means which there is no space to discuss here. The present waste of energy in our homes is simply appalling.

Surely the imprisonment and distortion of the faculties of one sex would be a ruinous price to pay for the physical safety of the race, even if it secured it, which it does not, but, on the contrary, places it in peril. If it were really necessary to sacrifice women for this end, then progress would be impossible, for society would nourish within itself the germ of its own destruction. Woman, whose soul had been (by supposition) sacrificed for the sake of her body, must constitute an element of reaction and decay which no unaided efforts of man could counteract. The influence, hereditary and personal, which women possess secures to them this terrible revenge.

But there is another consideration in connection with this which Mrs. Lynn Linton overlooks. If the woman is to be asked to surrender so much because she has to produce the succeeding generation, why is the father left altogether out of count? Does *his* life leave no mark upon his offspring? Or does Mrs. Lynn Linton, perhaps think that if the mother takes precautions for their welfare to the extent of surrendering her whole existence, the father may be safely left to take no precautions at all?

'The clamour for political rights,' this lady says, 'is woman's confession of sexual enmity. Gloss it over as we may it comes to this in the end. No woman who loves her husband would usurp his province.' Might one not retort: No man who loves his wife would seek to hamper her freedom or oppose her desires? But in fact nothing could be more false than the assertion that the new ideals imply sexual enmity. On the contrary, they contemplate a relationship between the sexes, which is more close and sympathetic than the world has ever seen.

Friendship between husband and wife on the old terms was almost impossible. Where there is power on the one hand and subordination on the other, whatever the relationship that may arise, it is not likely to be that of friendship. Separate interests and ambitions, minds moving on different planes—all this tended to make strangers of those who had to pass their lives together, hampered eternally by the false sentiment which made it the right of one to command and the duty of the other to obey. But now, for the first time in history, we have come within measurable distance of a union between man and woman as distinguished from a common bondage. Among the latest words that have been said by science on this subject are the following from the *Evolution of Sex*, by Professors Geddes and Thompson:—

> Admitting the theory of evolution, we are not only compelled to hope, but logically compelled to assume, that those rare fruits of an apparently more than earthly paradise of love, which only the forerunners of the race have been privileged to gather, or, it may be, to see from distant heights, are yet the realities of a daily life to which we and ours may journey.

As for Mrs. Lynn Linton's accusations against the wild women as regards their lack of principle and even of common honesty, they are surely themselves a little 'wild.'

The rest of her charges are equally severe, and they induce one to wonder through what unhappy experiences the lady has gone, since she appears never to have encountered a good and generous woman outside the ranks of her own followers—unless it was a born idiot here and there! Even the men who disagree with her are either knaves or fools!

I would exhort the 'wild women' to be more tolerant, and to admit the truth that they number many wise opponents, as well as many wise and generous supporters, among men. The matter is too serious to be wrangled about. The adversaries of the 'wild woman' have hit upon not a few truths in their time, and have done much service in forcing the opposite party to think their position out in all its bearings. From the 'wild' point of view, of course, their conclusions seem false, because they deal with facts, when they find them, without sufficiently comparing and balancing them with other facts, perhaps rather less obvious, and, above all, without taking into account the one very significant fact that human nature is as sensitive as a weather-glass to its conditions and susceptible of infinite modification.

Mrs. Lynn Linton expresses herself with indignation against the mothers who allow their daughters to have a certain amount of freedom; 'they know,' she says, 'the dangers of life, and from what girls ought to be protected.' If they disregard the wisdom of experience, on whose soul lies the sin? Is the wolf to blame who passes through the open fence into the fold? Yes, certainly he is; the negligence of the shepherd does not turn the wolf into a lamb. But, as a matter of fact, the illustration is not a true one. The social 'wolf' attacks the lambs only if the lambs exceed the limits of what society expects from them as regards liberty. A girl walking alone in London meets with no trouble, whereas in Paris or Vienna she might run the risk of annoyance. It is clearly in the interests of every one that those limits should be as much as possible extended. The greater number of girls who are allowed this independence the less the risk, and the less the hindrances and difficulties for all concerned. The burden on mothers of an army of daughters who cannot stir from their home without a bodyguard is very severe. Mrs. Lynn Linton does her best to check this tendency, to give more self-reliance to girls, and would throw society back upon its path towards its abandoned errors.

The quarrel, in fact, between Mrs. Lynn Linton and her opponents is simply the time-honoured quarrel between yesterday and to-day, between reaction and progress, between decaying institutions and the stirrings of a new social faith.

There was a time when Mrs. Lynn Linton had sympathies with the struggle of a soul towards a new faith, but that is all over; and she has no sympathy left for any belief which is not 'hallowed by time,' for any attitude of mind (at least in her own sex) that is not unquestioning and submissive.

The world will occupy itself in fighting out the question for a long time to come; and the question will entangle itself inevitably with the whole matter of the relation of the sexes being involved in these.

The emancipation of woman and the emancipation of the manual worker will go hand in hand. If this generation is wise and sane, it will conduct these two movements in a fashion new to history. Taking warning by the experience of the past, it will avoid the weak old argument of violence (even in language) as a strong and intelligent teacher avoids the cowardly and senseless device of corporal punishment. It will conduct its revolution by means of the only weapon that has ever given a victory worth winning: Intelligence.

Mankind has tried blood and thunder long enough; they have not answered. The counter-stroke is as strong as the original impetus, and we expiate our error in the wearisome decades of a reaction. No revolution can be achieved to any purpose that is not organic; it must rest upon a real change in the sentiment and constitution of humanity. We are not governed by armies and police, we are governed by ideas; and this power that lies in human opinion is becoming strengthened with every advance that we make in civilisation, and in the rapidity with which ideas are communicated from man to man, and from nation to nation. The whole course of civilisation tends towards the dethronement of brute force in favour of the force of thought and of sentiment. It behooves women, above all, to conduct their movement in a quiet, steady, philosophic, and genial spirit; regarding the opposition that they receive, as much as possible, from the point of view of the student rather than of the partisan; realising that in this greatest of all social revolutions they must expect the fiercest resistance; that men in opposing them are neither better nor worse than all human beings of either sex have shown themselves to be as soon as they became possessors of power over their fellows. The noblest cannot stand the test, and of average men and women it makes bullies and tyrants. If this general fact be borne in mind throughout the struggle, it will be easier to avoid the feelings of bitterness and rancour which the sense of injustice creates; it will remind those engaged in the encounter to regard it with calmer eyes, as one would regard the history of past events; it will teach them to be prepared for defeat while hoping for success, and not to be too much dismayed if the change for which they have striven so hard must be delayed until long after they are dead, and all those who would have rejoiced in it are no longer there to see the sun rise over the promised land. It will teach them, too, to realise more strongly than most of us are inclined to do, that men and women are brothers and sisters, bound to stand or fall together; that in trying to raise the position and condition of women, they are serving at least as much the men who are to be their husbands or sons; that, in short—to quote the saying of Hegel—'The master does not become really free till he has liberated his slave.'

NOTE

1   'The idea of the pilgrimage [to the hill-top] was to get away from the endless
    and nameless circumstances of everyday existence, which by degrees build a
    wall about the mind, so that it travels in a constantly narrowing circle.... *This is
    all—there is nothing more;* this is the reiterated preaching of house-life ... the con-
    stant routine of house-life, the same work, the same thought in the work, the lit-
    tle circumstances daily recurring will dull the keenest edge of work?'—*The Story
    of My Heart,* by Jefferies.

Source: Reprinted from *Nineteenth Century* (May 1892).

BIOGRAPHICAL NOTE

There is little biographical or critical material available on Mona Caird. Born in 1854 at Ryde in the Isle of Wight, she was the only daughter of John Alison, a Victorian inventor of some small repute. Her first publications, *Whom*

Nature Leadeth and One That Wins (both 1887), like her later works, The Wing of Azrael (1889), A Romance of the Moors (1891), The Daughters of Danaus (1894), and A Sentimental View of Vivisection (1896), received little critical commentary. She was best known, according to a contemporary assessment, for her peculiar views on marriage and the extraordinary splash caused by her 1888 article, "Marriage," first published in the Westminster Review and reprinted here. As Karl Beckson reports, Caird's article was taken up by the popular press and, in a classic device of the new journalism, the Daily Telegraph asked its readers, "Is Marriage a Failure?" Two months and twenty-seven thousand responses later, the Daily Telegraph was obliged to refuse any further correspondence on a topic that clearly caught the late-Victorian public interest. A selection of these letters to the editor was published later in the same year by Harry Quilter, a well-known barrister, critic and editor of the Universal Review under the title Is Marriage a Failure? (Beckson, 134). Caird's article also elicited a response from Eliza Lynn Linton, the celebrated opponent of the women's movement, whose come-back article, titled "The Wild Women," was printed in the Nineteenth Century. Caird's own "Defence of the So-called Wild Women," a retort to Linton's piece and also published in Nineteenth Century, is reprinted here.

SELECTED SECONDARY SOURCES

Beckson, Karl. London in the 1890s: A Cultural History. New York: Norton, 1992.

Boos, Florence S. "A History of Their Own: Mona Caird, Frances Swiney, and Fin de Siecle Feminist Family History." Contesting the Master Narrative: Essays in Social History. Ed. Jeffrey Cox and Shelton Stromquist. Iowa City: U of Iowa P, 1998. 69-92.

Heilmann, Ann. "Mona Caird (1854-1932): Wild Woman, New Woman, and Early Feminist Critic of Marriage and Motherhood." Women's History Review 5.1 (1996): 67-95.

Pratt, A.T.C. People of the Period. Vol. II. London, 1897.

Pykett, Lyn. "The Cause of Women and the Course of Fiction: The Case of Mona Caird." Gender Roles And Sexuality in Victorian Literature. Ed. Christopher Parker. Brookfield, VT: Ashgate, 1995.